OXFORD MONOGRAPHS IN
INTERNATIONAL LAW

General Editor: Professor Ian Brownlie CBE, QC, FBA
*Chichele Professor of Public International Law in the
University of Oxford and Fellow of All Souls College, Oxford.*

THE UNITED NATIONS AND THE
DEVELOPMENT OF COLLECTIVE SECURITY

OXFORD MONOGRAPHS IN
INTERNATIONAL LAW

The aim of this series of monographs is to publish important and original pieces of research on all aspects of public international law. Topics which are given particular prominence are those which, while of interest to the academic lawyer, also have important bearing on issues which touch the actual conduct of international relations. None the less the series is wide in scope and includes monographs on the history and philosophical foundations of international law.

RECENT TITLES IN THIS SERIES

The Concept of Internaitonal Obligations
Erga Omnes
M. RAGAZZI

The Termination and Revision of Treaties
in the Light of New Customary International Law
N. KONTOU

Land and Maritime Zones of Peace
in International Law
S. P. SUBEDI

International Management of Hazardous Wastes:
The Basel Convention and Related Legal Rules
K. KUMMER

Human Rights in the Private Sphere
A. CLAPMAN

Self-Determination and National Minorities
T. D. MUSGRAVE

Regime of Straits in International Law
B. B. JIA

Naval Weapons Systems and the
Contemporary Law of War
J. J. BUSUTILL

THE UNITED NATIONS AND THE DEVELOPMENT OF COLLECTIVE SECURITY

The Delegation by the UN Security Council of its Chapter VII Powers

DANESH SAROOSHI

OXFORD
UNIVERSITY PRESS

OXFORD
UNIVERSITY PRESS

Great Clarendon Street, Oxford OX2 6DP

Oxford University Press is a department of the University of Oxford.
It furthers the University's objective of excellence in research, scholarship,
and education by publishing worldwide in

Oxford New York

Athens Auckland Bangkok Bogotá Buenos Aires Calcutta
Cape Town Chennai Dar es Salaam Delhi Florence Hong Kong Istanbul
Karachi Kuala Lumpur Madrid Melbourne Mexico City Mumbai
Nairobi Paris Sao Paulo Singapore Taipei Tokyo Toronto Warsaw
with associated companies in Berlin Ibadan

Oxford is registered trade mark of Oxford University Press
in the UK and in certain other countries

Published in the United States
by Oxford University Press Inc., New York

British Library Cataloguing in Publication Data

Data available

Library of Congress Cataloging-in-Publication Data
Sarooshi, Danesh.
The United Nations and the development of collective security:
the delegation by the UN Security Council of its chapter VII powers/
Danesh Sarooshi.
p. cm.
Includes bibliographical references.
1. United Nations—Armed Forces. 2. United Nations.
Security Council. 3. Security International. I. Title.
KZ6376.S27 1998 341.23′23—dc21 98–42947

ISBN 0–19–826863–7
ISBN 0–19–829934–6 (Pbk)

Printed in Great Britain
on acid-free paper by
Biddles Ltd, www.biddles.co.uk

To my wife, Mary, and my family—the Sarooshis and the Huddlestons—for their continual love, friendship, generous support, and encouragement.

General Editor's Preface

Dr. Sarooshi's important work is an edited version of a thesis prepared at the London School of Economics under the supervision of Judge Rosalyn Higgins, D.B.E., Q.C., F.B.A. It is historically fitting that the study should emerge from the University of London which has had a major role in teaching the law of International Organizations at the graduate level.

The subject of the monograph is one of the most central to international affairs and combines issues of legal logic with the deep waters of power politics and the delicate question of the use of United Nations organs to provide some level of legitimacy to sometimes problematical enterprises. The result can be commended not only to lawyers but to specialists in international relations.

IAN BROWNLIE

Oxford
8th October 1998

Acknowledgements

This study is a revised version of a thesis submitted in 1997 for the degree of Doctor of Philosophy in the London School of Economics and Political Science, University of London. It would not have been produced without the constant guidance, assistance, inspiration, and personal friendship of my doctoral supervisor Judge Rosalyn Higgins DBE, QC. The suggestion of the subject was made by Judge Higgins and her guidance in seeing this work through to its finish was essential. Judge Higgins gave much more than was required from a doctoral supervisor as evidenced, for example, by her obtaining special dispensation after being elected to the International Court of Justice to continue supervision of my thesis.

I wish also to single out and acknowledge the very important contribution that has been made by Professors Ian Brownlie CBE, QC, FBA, and Maurice Mendelson QC. This work has benefited greatly from their valuable comments, encouragement, and suggestions.

I would like to thank the following people who assisted me greatly during interviews conducted in New York and New Haven by discussing, often at great length, the subject of this book: Anastasia Caryanides, Sir Marrack Goulding, Cameron Hume, Dr Roy Lee, Robert Rosenstock, Paul Szasz, Dr Shashi Tharoor, Sir Brian Urquhart, Elizabeth Wilmshurst, and Dr Ralph Zacklin; and Professors Michael Reisman and Bruce Russett of Yale University.

Thanks are also due to Dapo Akande, Dr Amazu Asouzu, Anthony Aust CMG, Daniel Bethlehem, Professor Christine Chinkin, Professor Hugh Collins, Professor James Crawford SC, Professor Eileen Denza CMG, Professor Peter Duffy QC, Richard Gardiner, Professor Christopher Greenwood, David Hutchinson, Professor Jeffrey Jowell QC, Dr Peter Khan, Kofi Kufuor, Dr Dominic McGoldrick, Professor Peter Muchlinski, Professor Rein Mullerson, Judge Dolliver Nelson, Professor Dawn Oliver, Professor David O'Keeffe, Professor Alain Pellet, Professor Bruno Simma, Professor Detlev Vagts, Professor Colin Warbrick, and Michael Wood CMG, who, by providing valuable assistance during different stages of writing, have each made their unique contribution to this work.

Finally, I would like to thank the Delegates and Staff of Oxford University Press for the care they have bestowed on the preparation of the book.

D.S.
London
June 1998

Foreword

The collective use of force as a military sanction does not operate in the way originally intended by the United Nations Charter. Article 43 of the Charter contains provisions for all members to undertake to make available to the Security Council, on its call and in accordance with a special agreement or agreements, forces and facilities necessary for the maintenance of international peace and security. This has not been done. The Cold War made the conclusion of such agreements impossible. And since the end of the Cold War there has not been the political will to return to the original intentions of the Charter.

In the absence of the intended agreements the United Nations has built up instead a peacekeeping capacity, where UN forces enter a territory with the permission of the State concerned and where UN nations volunteer to participate. But sometimes the use of military sanctions has been unavoidable. In 1950 the United Nations authorized action in collective self-defence, under unified command, against North Korea. In resolution 678 (1991) the Security Council authorized 'all necessary measures' against Iraq if it did not withdraw from Kuwait by the date specified. This was understood by all concerned to be an authorization of military sanctions to be carried out on the UN's behalf by a coalition of volunteering States.

Before long, under new policies enunciated by Secretary-General Boutros Ghali in *Agenda for Peace*, NATO was given military tasks in relation to the support of UNPROFOR in Bosnia and then in support of UNCRO in Croatia. It was active in support of the designated safe areas.

At the time of writing, further action has been taken by NATO relating to possible military action in Kosovo, on the basis of a Security Council resolution even less precise in its terms than that authorizing military action by the coalition forces in Iraq.

The constant development of United Nations practice in response to the changing demands of the international situation leads necessarily to the question: what are the limits to institutional creativity? What deviations from what was intended in the Charter are to be regarded as lawful, imaginative adaptations to contemporary needs? And what are to be regarded as going that step too far to be consistent with legality, and as *ultra vires*?

One cannot begin to answer these important questions without an intellectual framework for ascertaining the permitted parameters of delegation of powers by the Security Council. It is this framework that Dr Sarooshi offers.

The work is not only important but it is pioneering. Never before has the entire corpus of delegated powers within the United Nations been subjected to scrutiny and a coherent analysis offered. Dr Sarooshi avoids mere recitation of what is by now a vast and complex practice. He early in the volume offers a detailed and powerful analysis of the legal nature of delegation and of the limits under Chapter VII of the Charter to that process. This original perspective is then used as an operational guide to all the particular aspects of the problem which comprise this study.

Dr Sarooshi has been able to discern, from the huge corpus of UN practice, patterns and groupings which make for the coherent study of a fascinating and important problem. Only rarely are delegations of powers articulated as such. But the author is able to show that certain events in fact constitute a delegation of powers by the Security Council to the Secretary General; others constitute a delegation of powers to UN subsidiary organs; yet others are a delegation to member States; while others are a delegation of powers to regional arrangements. What has seemed until now, even to the attentive student of United Nations practice, a vast amorphous array of events, has in this book been brought into coherent and logical groupings.

There are already established legal guideposts for analysing some of these—for example, the Charter itself prescribes the powers both of the Security Council and of the Secretary General. The same is true, to an extent, of the relationship between the Security Council and regional arrangements. But in other areas Dr Sarooshi has to go back to first principles and bring his theory of legitimate delegation to bear. This is true, for example, of the Chapters on delegation to member States and to subsidiary organs.

The subject matter is profoundly and thoroughly researched and the legal ideas are both original and significant. Those who seek to grapple with Charter issues of legality relating to UN action in such diverse cases as in Southern Rhodesia, Somalia, Haiti, Bosnia, now have, for the first time, a fully articulated legal frame of reference. Dr Sarooshi has thus provided a service to international civil servants and to foreign offices, as well as to academics.

His book makes an important contribution to our understanding of the development of collective security within the United Nations and provides relevant yardsticks for assessing legality.

Judge Rosalyn Higgins
International Court of Justice,
Peace Palace, The Hague

Contents

Summary

Contents
Outline

Table of Cases

Introduction

Be united, O concourse of the sovereigns of the world, for thereby will the tempest of discord be stilled amongst you, and your peoples find rest. Should any one among you take up arms against another, rise ye all against him, for this is naught but manifest justice.

Bahá'u'lláh, in a Tablet to Queen Victoria, 1867

This book provides a legal analysis of the institutional mechanisms and processes which the United Nations employs to use force to maintain or restore international peace. In so doing it focuses both on the law pertaining to the use of force by the United Nations and on the development of the emerging institutional processes which the United Nations uses to maintain international peace.

The UN Charter constitutes a collective security system which gives the Security Council the primary role to maintain and restore peace and, under Chapter VII, broad powers to achieve these objectives. In the past the veto-power of the Permanent Members of the Council made the exercise of these powers difficult. Therefore there were occasional attempts made, during the Cold War, to achieve these objectives through various techniques such as assignment to another organ,[1] delegation of Chapter VII powers to a single State,[2] or a delegation of Chapter VII powers to Member States while attempting to retain a modicum of control.[3] Since the end of the Cold War the problem presents itself differently. The demands are so great, and the availability of its own military and financial resources so limited, that once again the Security Council is looking for ways to address the problem. The Council has done this by delegating its Chapter VII powers to some States (for example the coalition against Iraq) and by invocation of the regional possibility (a delegation of power to regional arrangements). These delegations of power have been coupled in many cases with a delegation of a power of command and control over such forces to either the UN Secretary-General or a UN subsidiary organ.

The delegation of powers by an organ of an international organization is not new; however, the delineation of the contours of a legal framework that governs such a process is. In the case of a delegation of Chapter VII powers, such a delineation raises a plethora of legal issues. The questions of whether

---

[1] For example, the Uniting for Peace resolution (GA Res. 377 (V), 3 Nov. 1950) sought to confer on the General Assembly certain powers in the area of international peace and security.

[2] See the case of Southern Rhodesia: *infra* Section II(1) in Chapter 5.

[3] See, for example, the case of Korea: *infra* Section II(2)(b) in Chapter 3 and Section I(1) in Chapter 5.

the Security Council can delegate, to whom, under what conditions, and what limitations exist on the delegate in the exercise of Chapter VII powers, raise further questions of where the margins of legality lie, of what is creative interpretation of the Charter, and what *is ultra vires*. To understand this, we need both to have a firm grasp of the theory of delegation; and to understand in precise detail the relevant practice. By examining these issues, guidance may also be obtained as to the likely future developments in the legal framework governing collective action to maintain peace under the auspices of the United Nations.

1

The General Legal Framework Governing the Process of a Delegation by the UN Security Council of its Chapter VII Powers

With the creation of the UN in 1945 it was envisaged that the UN Security Council would play a central role in the maintenance or restoration of international peace and security. To this end, UN Member States agreed in Article 24 of the Charter to confer on the Council primary responsibility for the maintenance of international peace and security.[1] The specific powers which the Charter gives the Council to achieve this objective are contained in Chapter VII.[2] Chapter VII gives the Council certain prerogatives:[3] the sole authority to determine when a threat to, or breach of, the peace has occurred;[4] the authority to order provisional measures;[5] and the authority to order enforcement measures to be taken against a State,[6] that is to impose economic and military sanctions against a State or entities within a State.[7] It

---

[1] See further on Article 24 the following commentaries on the Charter: *La Charte des Nations Unies*, (Cot, J-P., and Pellet, A., eds.) (1991), p. 447; and *The Charter of the United Nations: A Commentary* (Simma, B., ed.) (1994), p. 397.

[2] Article 24(2) of the UN Charter.

[3] The enforcement powers of the Council are based on broad discretionary findings. In fact at the San Francisco Conference it was deliberately left to the Security Council to decide on a case-by-case basis when to use its enforcement powers: see Doc. 881, III/3/46, 12 *UNCIO Docs*. 502, 505 (1945).

[4] This exclusive authority is contained in Article 39 of the Charter. The *travaux préparatoires* of Article 39 validates this interpretation: see the statement by the rapporteur of Committee III/3 that dealt with Article 39, *United Nations Conference on International Organization*, 12 (1945), p. 505. See also Judge Weeramantry in his opinion (dissenting on other points) in the *Lockerbie* case, *Provisional Measures Phase, ICJ Reports* (1992), p. 66 at p. 176; Cot and Pellet, *supra* note 1, p. 645; and Simma, *supra* note 1, p. 608.

[5] This authority is contained in Article 40 of the Charter. With respect to Article 40 see the following: Cot and Pellet, *supra* note 1, p. 667; and Simma, *supra* note 1, p. 617.

[6] The word enforcement as used here has a meaning different from the way in which it is often used in domestic legal systems: it does not necessarily mean action designed to ensure compliance with law. See also Cassesse, A., *International Law in a Divided World* (1994), p. 215.

[7] The authority to impose economic sanctions is contained in Article 41, and for military sanctions is contained in Article 42. See further on Article 41 the following: Cot and Pellet, *supra* note 1, p. 691; Simma, *supra* note 1, p. 621; and Reisman, M., and Stevick, D., 'The Applicability of International Law Standards to United Nations Economic Sanctions Programmes', *European Journal of International Law*, 9 (1998), p. 86. See further on Article 42 the following: Cot and Pellet, *supra* note 1, p. 705; and Simma, *supra* note 1, p. 628. On the taking of enforcement action against entities within a State, see *infra* notes 3–5 and corresponding text in Chapter 5.

seems clear that the Security Council has under Chapter VII the sole prerogative to decide when it can order enforcement measures to be taken and the discretion as to what type of measures should be taken.[8] Both these determinations are essentially political in character.[9]

The Charter does not, however, expressly state which entities the Council can use in its efforts to ensure the maintenance or restoration of international peace and security. In the vast majority of cases where the Council has imposed economic or military sanctions against a State or non-State entity, the Council has attempted to ensure the implementation of these sanctions by delegating its Chapter VII powers to UN principal organs,[10] UN subsidiary organs, UN Member States, and regional arrangements or agencies ('regional arrangements'). The reason for such delegations of power is a practical one. The Security Council has had to delegate its Chapter VII powers to entities that have an enforcement capacity which the Council at present lacks: in particular, it lacks a military force which it can use directly to carry out military enforcement action.[11] In the following Chapters an analysis is made of the legal considerations relating to these delegations of power.[12] It is, however, the process of delegation by the Council of its Chapter VII powers which is the subject of this Chapter. The concern of this Chapter is to construct the general legal framework which governs this process by examining the following issues: the nature of the process of a delegation of Chapter VII powers; the competence of the UN Security Council to delegate its Chapter VII powers; the limitations which exist on this competence; and the International Court of Justice and the justiciability of a delegation of Chapter VII powers.

I. THE NATURE OF THE PROCESS OF A DELEGATION OF CHAPTER VII POWERS

A delegation of powers in the law of international institutions can be defined as taking place whenever an organ of an international organization which possesses an express or implied power under its constituent instru-

---

[8] Kirk, for example, has observed: '[the] Freedom [of the Security Council] to decide when to apply coercive measures is matched by an equal discretion as to what measures may be taken'. (Kirk, G., 'The Enforcement of Security', *Yale LJ*, 55 (1946), p. 1081 at p. 1089.) See also Dinstein, Y., *War, Aggression and Self-Defence* (1994), pp. 281–2.

[9] See Kelsen, H., *The Law of the United Nations* (1951), pp. 732–7; and Dinstein, *ibidem*, p. 282.

[10] In particular, the Council has delegated its Chapter VII powers to the UN Secretary-General: see Chapter 2, below.

[11] Cf. the original system intended by the Framers of the Charter: see *infra* notes 1–3 in Chapter 4.

[12] For the delegation of powers to UN principal organs, UN subsidiary organs, UN Member States, and regional arrangements, see the following respective Chapters: 2, 3, 4, 5, and 6.

ment conveys the exercize of this power to some other entity. In many cases this will involve a delegation of competence which enables the delegate to carry out acts which would otherwise be unlawful. However, a characteristic of power, the implicit coercive or forceful element that demands compliance with a decision, cannot always be delegated. The main reason for this being that the nature or institutional structure of the body that possesses the power may be so different from the delegate that transfer of this element of power is not possible. However, in this respect the case of a delegation of Chapter VII powers by the Council to UN Member States is unique. The nature of the power being transferred is in essence coercive, and when this is combined with the capability of Member States to exercize this coercive element it can truly be said that there is a delegation of power and not just authority or competence.

Of particular importance in the context of a delegation of Chapter VII powers is that there is a conferral on the delegate of a degree of legitimacy of action. The source of this legitimacy is that the Security Council has, through the Charter, been given by UN Member States the primary responsibility for the maintenance of international peace and security.[13] This issue of legitimacy deserves further attention since it is important in terms of the collective security function of the Security Council:[14] an important part of which now is the delegation of Chapter VII powers.

The UN Charter constitutes a collective security system with the Security Council as its focus. A collective security system can be defined in broad terms as a system where a collective measure is taken against a member of a community that has violated certain community defined values.[15] An important feature of collective security is the maintenance of the status quo of the system.[16] This relies, however, on the perception by States that their individual interest is best served by ensuring that the interests of the

---

[13] This represents an application of Franck's more general point that 'The United Nations is the creature of a treaty and, as such, it exercizes authority legitimately only in so far as it deploys powers which the treaty-parties have assigned to it.' (Franck, T., 'Fairness in the International Legal and Institutional System', *Hague Recueil des Cours*, 240 (1993-III), p. 9 at p. 190.)

[14] See generally on the legitimacy of Security Council action: Caron, D., 'The Legitimacy of the Collective Authority of the Security Council', *AJIL*, 87 (1993), p. 552; and Murphy, S., 'The Security Council, Legitimacy, and the Concept of Collective Security After the Cold War', *Columbia Journal of Transnational Law*, 32 (1994), p. 201.

[15] Cf. Herndl who states that the use of collective force against an 'aggressor' is the core of a system of collective security. (Herndl, K., 'Reflections on the Role, Functions and Procedures of the Security Council', *Hague Recueil des Cours*, 206 (1987-VI), p. 297.)

[16] In this way collective security and legitimacy are closely linked: as Inis Claude has stated more generally in respect of the concept of legitimacy: 'The history of political theory offers ample evidence of the perennial interest of philosophers in the problem of legitimacy, an interest which more often than not has been intimately linked with the highly practical concerns of rulers or rebels, intent upon maintaining or challenging the political status quo.' (Claude, I., 'Collective Legitimization as a Political Function of the United Nations', *International Organization*, 20 (Summer 1966), p. 367.

community of States—in Charter terms, international peace and security—is preserved.[17] In the case of the Charter, it is the Security Council which has been given the authority to determine the content of the community value or interest in a particular case and consequently that its violation necessitates a collective security response.[18] There is underlying this a general assumption that the community values which the system aims to preserve are the result of a process of consensus or are in any case acceptable to the members of the community.[19] In the case of the UN, this process culminated with the conclusion and adoption of the Charter: this is the source of legitimacy of action by the Council when using its Chapter VII powers.[20]

The way in which the delegate exercizes delegated Chapter VII powers is important for the Council's legitimacy.[21] If there is a perception by the generality of UN Member States that the purpose of a particular delegation of powers by the Council is to act as a cloak for the actions of one or a select few States then the legitimacy of the Council decision is compromised. This may be further compromised in practice if States act to undermine the legitimacy of the actions by the States exercizing the delegated powers. In order to prevent such erosions of legitimacy, the legal elements of the process of a delegation of powers assume importance. In particular, the procedural and substantive limitations the Charter places on the competence of the Council to delegate its Chapter VII powers. This is an application of Franck's point that 'the legitimacy of the exercize of power by the Security Council depends upon the public perception that it is being exercized in accordance with the Charter's applicable defining rules

---

[17] As Simma has stated in more general terms: 'the element which distinguishes a "community" from its components is a "higher unity", as it were, the representation and prioritization of common interests as against the egoistic interests of individuals'. (Simma, B., 'From Bilateralism to Community Interest in International Law', *Hague Recueil des Cours*, 250 (1994-VI), p. 9 at p. 245.)

[18] As Chinkin states: 'A step has been taken away from the traditional third party option of neutrality based upon a State's perception of its own self-interest, towards some collective obligations in the face of a breach of international peace and security based upon the collective view of the Security Council as to the interests of the international community.' (Chinkin, *Third Parties in International Law* (1993), p. 313.)

[19] On the concept of community, see Franck, T., 'Community Based on Autonomy', *Columbia Journal of Transnational Law*, 36 (1997), p. 41; Simma, B., 'From Bilateralism to Community Interest in International Law', *Hague Recueil des Cours*, 250 (1994-VI), p. 217 at pp. 243–8; and Arangio-Ruiz, G., 'The "Federal Analogy" and UN Charter Interpretation: A Crucial Issue', *EJIL*, 8 (1997), p. 1 at pp. 12–18.

[20] Cf. the view that because the United Nations is not responsible to individuals but only States, that it has no legitimacy to use force. In other words, there is no constituency from which the UN could draw such a mandate or authority.

[21] See also Quigley, J., 'The Privatization of Security Council Enforcement Action: A Threat to Multilateralism', *Michigan Journal of International Law*, 17 (1996), p. 249 at p. 276.

and standards'.[22] In this way, the law contributes to the maintenance of legitimacy in the process of a delegation by the Council of its Chapter VII powers.[23]

A delegation of powers does not involve the transfer of a power *in toto*. Accordingly, the organ of an international organization which delegates a power does not prima facie denude itself of the right to exercize the power.[24] This has two consequences. First, the delegation of power can always be revoked by the delegating organ.[25] Second, when an organ delegates a power then it retains the right to exercize that power.[26] Thus it is possible for a delegating authority to exercize its power concurrently with the delegate while the delegation exists. In cases where this occurs, any decisions taken by the principal organ in the exercize of the power in question prevails over any decisions taken by the delegate in the exercize of the delegated power. This flows from the authority and control which a UN principal organ possesses over the exercize of its delegated powers.[27] Accordingly, practice in this area has seen the General Assembly change the way a power which it delegated to the Secretary-General is being exercized: either by deciding certain questions itself[28] or by subsequently assigning the exercize of decision to some other body, such as the International Civil

[22] Franck, T., 'The Security Council and "Threats to the Peace": Some Remarks on Remarkable Recent Developments', in *Peace-Keeping and Peace-Building: The Development of the Role of the Security Council*, (Dupuy, R-J., ed.) (1993), at p. 85.

[23] However, just as importantly, a change in perception of what is legitimate can lead to changes in the law. A change in perception of what is legitimate will eventually be reflected in a change in law assuming there is participation by States in the general process of law creation.

[24] In respect of, for example, English law cases which support this view, see de Smith, S., Woolf, H., & Jowell, J., *Judicial Review of Administrative Action* (1995), at p. 362.

[25] See also Conforti, B., *The Law and Practice of the United Nations* (1996), p. 219.

[26] In respect of English and Australian cases and authority that support this approach see Dixon, M., 'Delegation, Agency and the Alter Ego Rule', *Sydney Law Review*, 11 (1987), p. 326 at p. 332 and cases cited therein; and Malcolm, D., 'The Limitations, if Any, on the Powers of Parliament to Delegate the Power to Legislate', *Australian Law Journal*, 66 (1992), p. 247 at p. 253 and cases cited therein.

Judge Bustamente adopts an interesting variant on this position when finding in the *Expenses* case that the General Assembly had acted lawfully when exercising powers in the area of peace and security. He found that, faced with not being able to exercise its powers, 'what the Council did, in my opinion, was not to delegate . . . but to return to the Organization the mandate which the latter had conferred upon it under Article 24 of the Charter. The principal reassumes the exercize of his powers when the agent renounces his mandate or is prevented from exercising it. Thus, as a body representative of all the Member States, the Assembly would be reassuming the exercize of the competence and the responsibility conferred by them on the Security Council under Article 24.' (*Expenses* case, *ICJ Reports* (1962), p. 151 at pp. 292–3.) On the delegation of powers to the Security Council by Member States, see *infra* notes 103–19 and corresponding text.

[27] For the existence of this requirement, see *infra* notes 145–55 & 159 and corresponding text.

[28] See, for example, General Assembly resolution 34/165, Section II, para. 3, relating to the repatriation grant to UN staff.

Service Commission.[29] Thus the delegation of power by a principal organ does not preclude that organ from later exercizing its power in a manner which is contrary to how the delegate has exercized the power. In fact this authority and control which the delegator exercizes over the decisions of its delegate is, as explained below in the context of the Security Council, an essential requirement for the delegation of extensive discretionary powers to be lawful.[30]

There are, however, two exceptions to this general rule. First, where the delegating organ stipulates that it will be bound by decisions of the delegate exercising the delegated power. The competence of a UN principal organ to prescribe such a limitation upon itself has been acknowledged in the context of UN subsidiary organs by the International Court of Justice in the *Administrative Tribunal* case. In this case the Court found that the UN General Assembly could establish an Administrative Tribunal competent to render judgments binding on the Assembly.[31] The second exception is where a principal organ establishes a subsidiary organ to perform functions it cannot itself exercize in which case the principal does not have any substantive powers of review over the decisions of its delegate. This follows from the fact that the principal organ has not delegated any of its substantive powers to the subsidiary but only the competence to perform certain functions in the particular area.[32] In conformity with this approach it has been the practice of UN principal organs in some cases to limit in express terms their powers of review over the performance of such functions by its subsidiary organ.[33]

There is great variety in the form which a delegation of powers takes under the law of international institutions. It is, however, important that the delegator expressly state its intention to delegate its powers: a delegation of powers can never be implied by the delegate. This requirement, which is part of the wider law of international institutions,[34] was applied by the

---

[29] The UN Legal Counsel has stated in respect of the constitutionality of this action: 'Whether these steps were undertaken because of some perceived dissatisfaction by the Assembly with the way in which the Secretary-General has been executing a part of his mandate or, more frequently, because of the desire to make possible coherent inter-organizational decisions in furtherance of the "common system", no legal (as distinct from policy or practical) objection can be raised against the diminution of a voluntary delegation of powers by the General Assembly. The same would be true if the Assembly were to adopt a decision specifying General Service salary scales at a given point, in spite of its general delegation to the Secretary-General of the power to set such scales, (Staff Regulations of the United Nations, Annex 1, para. 7) except to the extent such a decision might diminish any contractual or acquired rights of the staff concerned.' (*UNJYB* (1982), p. 193.)

[30] See *infra* note 159 and corresponding text.

[31] *Administrative Tribunal* case, *ICJ Reports (1954)*, pp. 56–7. See also on this issue and the decision of the Court: *infra* notes 68–75 and corresponding text in Chapter 3.

[32] See *infra* notes 31–4 and corresponding text in Chapter 3.

[33] See, for example, the case of the UN War Crimes Tribunals: *infra* notes 78–84 in Chapter 3.

[34] See also Schermers, H., and Blokker, N., *International Institutional Law* (1995), p. 153.

European Court of Justice in the case of *Meroni* v. *High Authority*.[35] The Court in dealing with the lawfulness of a delegation of powers by one of the organs of the European Community stated the following: '. . . [a] delegation of powers cannot be presumed and even when empowered to delegate its powers the delegating authority must take an express decision transferring them'.[36] Accordingly, in the case of a delegation of Chapter VII powers by the UN Security Council, the only appropriate form for such a delegation is by means of a resolution. This approach is, moreover, reflected in the practice of the Council.[37] This position is given added cogency when it is recalled that the particular decision-making processes of the Council require the potential use of the veto in respect of substantive issues—in other words the passage of a resolution which is subject to the veto—for a decision to be considered a decision of the Council.[38] The decision by the Security Council to delegate a substantive power is a non-procedural matter for the purposes of Article 27(3) of the Charter.[39] It would not be sound for decisions of the Council to exercize its Chapter VII powers to be made subject to the veto, which they very clearly are, but for decisions by the Council to delegate the exercize of these powers not to be subject to this requirement. Accordingly, the decision by the Council to delegate its Chapter VII powers is a non-procedural matter and thus subject to the requirement of the veto.[40] The Security Council cannot circumvent its stipulated decision-making processes under the Charter by means of delegation.

Moreover, in the context of Chapter VII powers, the Council must make an Article 39 determination before it can delegate these powers. An Article 39 determination is a prerequisite for any action under Chapter

---

[35] Case 9156, [1958] *ECR* 133.

[36] *Ibidem*, p. 151. Similarly, and still in the context of European institutions, the report of the UK Government on renegotiation of its Membership of the EC when explaining the role of the EC Commission states: '[t]he Commission can issue legislative instruments in the fields in which such a power has been expressly delegated to it, either by the Treaties or by legislative acts of the Council'. (*Membership of the European Community: Report on Renegotiation*, Presented to Parliament by the Prime Minister by Command of Her Majesty, March 1975, Cmnd. 6003, p. 37.) Of considerable importance to the UK Government in this regard was that '[t]here can be no extension of the areas in which the Commission is competent to act, except by express decision of the Council'. (*Ibidem*.)

[37] For example, in the case of UN Member States and regional arrangements a delegation of Chapter VII powers takes place by means of a Council resolution. (See, for examples, Chapters 5 & 6.) See also, in the case of UN subsidiary organs: *infra* note 176 in Chapter 3.

[38] On the power of the veto as part of the Security Council's decision-making processes, see *infra* notes 148 *et sequentia* and corresponding text. This does not of course detract from the utility and flexibility of the other working methods and procedures which the Security Council may use to carry out its work: see Wood, M., 'Security Council Working Methods and Procedure: Recent Developments', *ICLQ*, 45 (1996), p. 150.

[39] In respect of Article 27(3), see further: *infra* note 148 and corresponding text.

[40] See also, in the case of subsidiary organs for example, the text following *infra* note 180 in Chapter 3.

VII.[41] Just because the Council is purporting to delegate its Chapter VII powers does not mean that it can disregard the Charter requirements which it must itself observe if it were to exercize these powers.[42] As such, the Council must make either an express or implied Article 39 determination in a resolution before it can delegate its Chapter VII powers.[43]

In order to understand further the nature and contours of the process of delegation of Chapter VII powers by the Council there are four distinctions which need to be made.

First, a specific delegation of powers or functions is to be distinguished from a general delegation of powers or functions. A specific delegation of powers or functions by the Security Council involves the entrusting of a particular power or function to a specific entity. For example, a Council resolution will either expressly or impliedly refer to a specific UN organ, State, or regional arrangement when delegating powers. A general delegation of powers is not, however, so specific in its terms. As such, a general delegation of powers does not apply in the case of UN organs, since an effective transfer of power in these cases requires a degree of specificity. The Council makes a general delegation of power in those cases where it purports to transfer to all UN Member States the competence to exercize a particular power acting either individually or through a regional arrangement as opposed to specifying States or a regional arrangement. The main advantage of a specific delegation of powers to UN Member States as opposed to a general delegation is that the former provides, in the context of military enforcement action, a basis for an effective command and control process.[44]

The second distinction is that between the delegation of a power and the delegation of a function. A function as it is being used here refers to a mere power of implementation as opposed to a 'power' which is a discretionary power of decision making. Accordingly, the difference between these two situations lies in the degree to which real power—in other words effective decision-making power—has been transferred. This is ascertained by examination of whether the delegating organ can be said to be directing its own mind to the particular decision. If so, then there is in law no 'delegation of power'.[45] This distinction is of practical importance, since in the context of the United Nations a principal organ may be given, for example, an express competence under the Charter to entrust the performance of its

---

[41] See Judge Weeramantry in the *Lockerbie* case, *ICJ Reports (1992)*, p. 66 at p. 176. See also Cot and Pellet, *supra* note 1, p. 645; and Simma, *supra* note 1, p. 608.

[42] See *infra* Section III(2)(b)(iii).

[43] For the distinction between, and examples of, express and implied Article 39 determinations, see Cot and Pellet, *supra* note 1, p. 645 *et seq.*

[44] See, for example, the case of Korea: *infra* Section II(2)(b)(i) in Chapter 3.

[45] See also Willis, J., 'Delegatus Non Potest Delegare', *The Canadian Bar Review*, 21 (1943), p. 257 at p. 258.

functions to another organ, but this does not provide *per se* a legal basis for the principal to be able to delegate its powers to that other organ.[46]

The importance of this distinction was also highlighted by the European Court of Justice case of *Meroni* v. *High Authority*.[47] The High Authority had purported to delegate the power to collect a levy to two subsidiary organs which had been specifically created to administer a scheme designed to control the price of iron ore on the international market, the Scrap Equalization Fund.[48] In *Meroni*, the lawfulness of this purported delegation of power was the primary issue under consideration. One of the preliminary questions the Court had to address was whether the principal organ had in fact delegated certain of its powers, or whether it had only granted to its subsidiary organs the competence to make resolutions the application of which belonged to the High Authority.[49] The Court found that the High Authority had in fact delegated powers to the subsidiary organs since the High Authority did not 'take over as its own the deliberations' of the subsidiary organs which led to the fixing of the equalization rate such that those deliberations did not in reality constitute a decision of the High Authority itself.[50] Accordingly, a primary indicator of whether effective decision-making powers have been transferred to a delegate is the degree to which the delegator is involved in the decision-making processes of its delegate. If the degree of control is virtually total then there has not been an effective delegation of power.[51] The application of this to the context of the Council means that an effective delegation of powers has not occurred where, for example, the Council has already decided on the way in which a particular action is to be carried out and only the implementation of the decision is delegated.[52] This case involves a delegation of function not power.

The third distinction is that between a delegation of powers to an entity as opposed to an authorization of an entity to carry out a specified

---

[46] See, for example, the case of the Security Council and Article 98 of the UN Charter: *infra* notes 8–10 in Chapter 2.

[47] Case 9156, [1958] *ECR* 133.

[48] The subsidiary organs were the Office Commun des Consommateurs de Ferrailles and the Caisse de Perequation des Ferrailles Importees.

[49] Case 9156, [1958] *ECR* 133 at 147.

[50] *Ibidem*, p. 149.

[51] Similarly, Hartley contends, in the context of European Community law, that if the purported delegation of powers requires the delegate to exercize its powers subject to rules laid down by the delegating authority which are so restrictive that the delegate's role is merely executive then there is no effective delegation of power. In such a case the purported 'delegation' is of no practical significance, since the way in which the power is exercized will not be affected. (Hartley, T., *The Foundations of European Community Law* (1994), p. 119.)

[52] In the context of UN subsidiary organs, an interesting consequence of this distinction is that a subsidiary organ may not always be exercising expressly delegated powers, but only those powers which are necessary for the implementation of a designated function. See for example *infra* notes 34–8 and corresponding text in Chapter 3.

objective. An authorization is more limited than a delegation of powers: both in terms of the specification of the objectives to be achieved and the qualitative nature of the powers transferred to achieve the designated objective. An example of such a distinction is provided by the *Application for Review* case.[53] In this case the Court had to decide whether the UN Committee on Applications for Review of Administrative Tribunal Judgments (hereinafter the 'Committee')—a UN subsidiary organ established by the General Assembly to review decisions of the UN Administrative Tribunal—had the competence to request advisory opinions of the International Court of Justice. The Court found that the Commitee did possess this competence. In determining the specific source of the Committee's competence, the Court had a choice of two provisions of the UN Charter: Article 96(1) or Article 96(2). Article 96(1) confers on the General Assembly the authority to request advisory opinions of the Court; while Article 96(2) gives the General Assembly the competence to authorize other UN organs to request advisory opinions of the Court on legal activities arising within the scope of their activities. The Court found that since the General Assembly could not perform the same function as the Committee—the review of decisions of the Administrative Tribunal—the source of the Committee's power to request an advisory opinion was not as a result of a delegation of the Assembly's own power under Article 96(1). The Court held:

This is not a delegation by the General Assembly of its own power to request an advisory opinion; it is the creation of a subsidiary organ having a particular task and invested with the power to request advisory opinions in the performance of that task.[54]

Thus the Court found that the Committee was 'duly authorized under Article 96, paragraph 2, of the Charter to request advisory opinions of the Court for the purpose of Article 11 of the Statute of the United Nations Administrative Tribunal'.[55] The Court found, moreover, that the General Assembly's power under Article 96(1) is much broader than the authorization given to the Committee to request advisory opinions of the International Court. Article 96(1) gives the General Assembly the power to request an advisory opinion of the International Court on any legal question while the Committee's competence to request an advisory opinion is restricted to those 'legal questions arising within the scope of [its] activities'.[56] To summarize, the Court, illustrating the distinction between an

[53] *Application for Review of Judgment No. 158 of the United Nations Administrative Tribunal,* Advisory Opinion, *ICJ Reports (1973),* p. 166 at p. 174.
[54] *Ibidem.*
[55] *Ibidem,* p. 175.
[56] Article 11 of the Statute of the Administrative Tribunal, as quoted in the *Application for Review* case, *ibidem,* p. 173. This limitation was of considerable importance to the decision of the International Court in finding that the World Health Organization did not have the

authorization and a delegation, found that the Committee had both a much narrower designated objective and more limited powers that it could use in order to achieve that objective, as opposed to the General Assembly. This approach of the Court confirms that there is in some cases a distinction between a principal organ authorizing an entity to perform certain tasks and a principal organ delegating its own powers to an entity to carry out similar or the same tasks. An authorization in many cases will be more limited than a delegation of powers.

An authorization, thus, may represent the conferring on an entity of a very limited right to exercize a power, or part thereof; or the conferring on an entity of the right to exercize a power it already possesses, but the exercize of which is conditional on an authorization that triggers the competence of the entity to use the power. While the case of a delegation will usually represent an unencumbered right to exercize the same power as the delegator: in many cases a power of broad discretion. It is this single characteristic of a delegation of power—the transfer of a power of discretionary decision making—that allows it to be distinguished in general terms from an authorization.

This distinction is of importance to our enquiry, since it will determine whether a particular transfer of power is subject to the legal framework governing a delegation of Chapter VII powers which is set out below and in the five Chapters which follow. However, a formal distinction between an authorization and a delegation of power does not always exist. In the case of an authorization by the Council of States to use force, the Council is not, in legal terms, simply making an authorization, but upon closer examination is in fact delegating to Member States its Chapter VII powers.[57] The Council may be using the term 'authorization', but what it is doing in substance is delegating its Chapter VII powers to Member States. In the case where the Council 'authorizes' States or a regional arrangement to use force to achieve, for example, certain humanitarian objectives and in so doing transfers certain of its own discretionary powers under Chapter VII in order to do so, then this is, applying our earlier discussion, a delegation of power from the Council since it involves a transfer of the Council's own powers of discretionary decision making, and as such is subject to the legal framework governing a delegation of Chapter VII powers.[58]

Even the case of what may at first seem to be an authorization by the Security Council of UN Member States to exercize their inherent right of

competence to make a request for an advisory opinion on the legality of the use of nuclear weapons since the Court found that this was not within the 'scope of their [*in casu*, the World Health Organization's] activities'. (*Legality of the Threat or Use of Nuclear Weapons, ICJ Advisory Opinion ICJ Reports* (1996), p. 66 at para. 31.) Cf. the application of this requirement in the *Application for Review* case, *ICJ Reports* (1982), p. 325 at pp. 333–4.

[57] See, for examples, *infra* Chapter 5.   [58] See, for examples, *infra* Chapters 5 and 6.

individual or collective self-defence as provided for by Article 51 of the Charter will usually involve a delegation of power.[59] Once there is an authorization by the Security Council of military action, it is unlikely that the Council is simply authorising individual or collective self-defence measures. Those cases where such a use of force would be justified by reference to authorized self-defence would not be many, since in most cases where the Council becomes involved the stated objectives of the military action are much broader than those which would be justified under the right of self-defence of States, whether under Article 51 of the Charter or under customary international law.[60] In this case, States may act in a way—in terms of *jus ad bellum*—which is not otherwise allowed under the law of self-defence.[61] For example, in the case of the Security Council's authorization of Member States to use force in response to Iraq's invasion of Kuwait, the Council in resolution 678 authorized States not only to repel Iraq's armed attack but also to 'restore international peace and security in the area'.[62] Accordingly, States were empowered to take action which went beyond what is allowed by the concept of self-defence in international law. In this way, what initially may have been the exercize by States of their right to individual or collective self-defence changed with the involvement of the Council. With the passage of resolution 678 the Council had moved past a simple authorization of collective self-defence into a delegation of its own discretionary powers to UN Member States.[63] This provides an example then of the more general point that it is rare for there to be collective self-defence authorized by the Security Council unless it is patent from the face of the resolution that this is all the Council is authorizing and that there is no mention of States taking action to maintain or restore international peace and security.[64] The involvement of the Council will, in most cases, necessarily confer a collective security nature on an

---

[59] It seems well accepted that the Council can authorize measures taken by States in self-defence. See, for example, Higgins, R., 'International Law and the Avoidance, Containment and Resolution of Disputes', *Hague Recueil des Cours*, 230 (1991-V), p. 9 at p. 334; and Rostow, N., 'The International Use of Force after the Cold War', *Harvard International Law Journal*, 32 (1991), p. 411 at p. 420.

[60] See Brownlie, I., *International Law and the Use of Force by States* (1963), p. 335; and Dinstein, *supra* note 8, pp. 175–277.

[61] With respect to *jus in bello*, however, see *infra* notes 64–5 and corresponding text in Chapter 4.

[62] The case of Iraq is considered in detail: *infra* Section I(2)(a) in Chapter 5.

[63] See further: *infra* Section I(2)(a) in Chapter 5.

[64] If, however, the Security Council were to pass a resolution which was only reaffirming, in express terms, the right of States to continue to use force as an exercize of their inherent right to self-defence in a particular situation, then this would represent an authorization by the Council and not a delegation since the Council is not as such transferring to States any of its own Chapter VII powers of discretionary decision-making but is rather authorizing States to exercize a power they already possess, but the continual use of which is, however, dependent on a Council authorization under Article 51 of the Charter.

operation.[65] There is, accordingly, a presumption that where the Council authorizes the use of force by States then this represents a delegation by the Council of its Chapter VII powers and not just a reaffirmation of States' right to use force in self-defence. To conclude on this point, the only case in which a Council resolution that authorizes military action would be authorizing self-defence measures is where the resolution expressly refers to this right and does not authorize measures which could possibly exceed the scope of this right as it exists under international law.

The fourth, and final, distinction to be made is that between an immediate delegation and a contingent delegation of powers. For example, in the case of a contingent delegation the actual transfer of power by a Council resolution only has effect when a stipulated set of facts comes into existence.[66] The existence of such a contingent delegation continues until the Council expressly terminates the effect of the resolution.

Having made these observations about the nature of the process of a delegation of Chapter VII powers it is now appropriate to discuss the scope of the general competence of the Council to delegate its Chapter VII powers. There are two general concerns that are relevant to such a question.

First, the issue of the *vires* of the organ being able to delegate its powers: that is, does the organ of an international organization have the legal competence to make such a delegation of power. In general terms, to resolve this issue consideration must be had first, of course, to the constituent treaty of the organization, and second to any inherent competence that such an organ may derive from the law of international institutions and which it thus possesses by virtue of its status as an organ of an international organization.

Second, the issue of institutional competence. By institutional competence I mean the peculiar nature and decision-making processes of an organ which may make it unique and which may have been the reason in the first

---

[65] Moreover, Kaikobad states: '[T]o suggest that the Council has the power to authorize measures in self-defence appears to be a contradiction in terms, for if an authorization in the sense of a mandate is given by the Council, the measures cease by definition to be a species of collective self-defence *stricto sensu* and constitute *ipso facto* operations carried out pursuant to the authorization.' (Kaikobad, K., 'Self-Defence, Enforcement and the Gulf Wars, 1980–88 and 1990–91', *BYIL*, 63 (1992), p. 300 at p. 355.)

[66] A possible example of such contingent resolutions were those proposed by the UK Delegation to the UN Security Council in 1973. Higgins has described the proposed resolutions, which are in substance contingent resolutions, in the following terms: 'What was particularly new about the United Kingdom paper was the listing of another cluster of questions which would operate "by veto or by challenge". In other words, a certain class of decisions would initially take the form of resolutions which would go into effect simply upon the recommendation of the Secretary-General. And they would go into effect if no Member of the Security Council chose to challenge them within a specified period.' (Higgins, R., 'A General Assessment of United Nations Peace-Keeping', in *United Nations Peace-Keeping* (Cassese, A., ed.), p. 1 at pp. 8–9.)

place for States to confer on the organ the very power which that organ itself now seeks to delegate to another. This concern is encapsulated in the latin maxim *delegatus non potest delegare*: a delegate cannot delegate. Application of this maxim to the Security Council, discussed below,[67] leads, as we shall see, to limitations being placed on the competence of the Council to delegate its powers. Inextricably linked to this issue is the concept of accountability: that the initial conferment of powers on an entity carries with it the responsibility for the way in which those powers are being exercized. Thus with a subsequent delegation of these powers the lines of accountability may become unclear. In the context of the Security Council, the question then becomes: which entity is accountable for the exercize of delegated Chapter VII powers, the Council or its delegate? This issue, as explained below, will not necessarily prohibit a delegation of powers, but it does impose some limitations on the way in which the Council may delegate its powers.

II. THE GENERAL COMPETENCE OF THE SECURITY COUNCIL TO DELEGATE ITS CHAPTER VII POWERS

It is one thing for a UN principal organ to possess a particular power, but it is another for that organ to be able to delegate that power. To be able to delegate its powers a principal organ of an international organization must possess either the express or implied competence to do so.[68] Both the possession by a principal organ of either an implied or express power and the competence to delegate this power are necessary preconditions for a lawful delegation of power to occur.

The Security Council possesses a general competence to delegate its powers to certain entities. This is not provided for in express terms by the Charter, but derives its existence from two main sources.

The first is that it exists as a general principle of law for the purposes of Article 38(1)(c) of the Statute of the International Court of Justice and as such is applicable to the United Nations. The existence of such a general competence constituting a 'general principle of law' is indicated by the fact that constitutions of a large number of States, both from common and civil law systems, allow their organs of government to delegate powers.[69]

---

[67] See *infra* Section III(2)(a).

[68] As Kelsen states: 'No organ can legally delegate power to another organ without being authorised by the constitution to do so.' (Kelsen, *supra* note 9, p. 142.)

[69] See, for example, express and implied provisions of the constitutions of the following States: Australia (*International Encyclopedia of Comparative Law, National Reports* (Knapp, V., ed.), vol. 1 (A), p. A-52); Belgium (*The Legal Systems of the World Their Comparison and Unification, Sources of Law* (David, R., ed.), vol. 2, Chapter 3 (1984), p. 52); Canada (see, for

Accordingly, the Security Council, as a UN principal organ, may be said to possess such a general competence to delegate by virtue of Article 38(1)(c) of the ICJ Statute which is, according to Article 92 of the Charter, an integral part of the Charter. Moreover, the Council possessing a general competence to delegate its Chapter VII powers is in accord with the object and purpose of Chapter VII: the object and purpose being that the Council should be able to take such action as it deems necessary to maintain or restore international peace and security.[70]

The second source of the Security Council possessing a general competence to delegate its powers is the law of international institutions. It is contended that it is a general principle under the law of international institutions that a principal organ of an international organization possesses a general competence to delegate certain of its powers to other entities. The existence of such a general competence as part of the corpus of the law of international institutions was affirmed in the case of *Meroni* v. *High Authority*,[71] where the European Court of Justice found that the High Authority could delegate certain of its powers under the Treaty of Rome even where the Treaty did not expressly provide for such a delegation.[72]

The general competence of the Council to delegate its powers is not,

example, the Canadian Supreme Court case of *Gavin et al.* v. *The Queen* (1956) *ILR*, pp. 154–7); France (see Article 38 of the 1958 French Constitution, contained in Finer, S., Bogdanor, V., and Rudden, B., *Comparing Constitutions* (1995), p. 213 at pp. 224–5; see also *International Encyclopedia of Comparative Law, National Reports* (Knapp, V., ed.), vol. 1 (E/F), pp. F-51, F-53, and Rudden, B., *A Source-Book on French Law: Public Law: Constitutional and Administrative Law, Private Law: Structure, Contract* (1991), p. 24); Germany (see Articles 80 and 129 of the German Basic Law, contained in Finer, S., Bogdanor, V., and Rudden, B., *Comparing Constitutions* (1995), p. 127 at pp. 164, 198–9; see also Kischel, U., 'Delegation of Legislative Power to Agencies: A Comparative Analysis of United States and German Law', *Administrative Law Review*, 46 (1994), p. 213); Greece (*International Encyclopedia of Comparative Law, National Reports, ibidem*, vol. 1 (G/H), p. G-50); Iceland (*ibidem*, vol. 1 (I), p. I-2); India (*ibidem*, vol. 1 (I), p. I-9); Ireland (*ibidem*, vol. 1 (I), pp. I-64, I-65); Italy (*ibidem*, vol. 1 (I), p. I-94; see also La Pergola, A., and Del Duca, P., 'Community Law, International Law and the Italian Constitution', *AJIL*, 79 (1985), p. 598 at p. 604); Japan (*International Encyclopedia of Comparative Law, ibidem*, vol. 1 (J/K), p. J-7); and the United States of America (see, for example, Kischel, *ibidem*; and Davis, K., *Administrative Law Treatise* (2nd edn. 1978), at pp. 149–50).

[70] This is an expression of the more general point made earlier by Grayson Kirk who in 1946 stated: 'The general principle . . . which runs consistently throughout the Charter, was that the Council should have the greatest possible flexibility in handling a situation which menaced the peace of the world.' (Kirk, *supra* note 8, p. 1088.)

[71] Case 9156, [1958] *ECR* 133.

[72] The Court found: '. . . the possibility of entrusting to bodies established under private law, having a distinct legal personality and possessing powers of their own, the task of putting into effect certain "financial arrangements common to several undertakings" . . . cannot be excluded'. *(Ibidem*, p. 151.) See also the Opinion of the Advocate-General in this case who acknowledges the existence of such a general competence in the context of a treaty which establishes an international organization: *Opinion of Mr Advocate-General Romer in Meroni* v. *High Authority* [1958] *ECR* 177 at 190.

however, unlimited. The possession by a principal organ of a general competence to delegate its powers does not mean that every particular exercize of this competence will be lawful. The lawfulness of a particular delegation of powers will depend on whether the organ purporting to delegate its powers has exceeded the limitations which exist on its general competence to delegate.[73]

This general competence of an international organization to be able to delegate its powers is, moreover, limited to a delegation of powers within the Organization.[74] That is, it does not include a competence to be able to delegate powers of discretion to an entity that is external to the Organization. In the case under discussion, this means that the Security Council can use its general competence to delegate its Chapter VII powers, subject to certain limitations,[75] to other UN principal and subsidiary organs without any further Charter authority being required. The case of a delegation of

[73] These are examined in detail *infra* Section III.

[74] In the case of the EC, this was established by, for example, the case of *Romano* v. *INAMI* [1981] *ECR* 1241 (Case 98/80). There is, however, a delegation of functions, as distinct from powers, that occurs in some cases from the European Community institutions to Member States or an international body in whose establishment and operation it participates with one or more third States as a means of guaranteeing the effectiveness of an internal policy by extending it to independent external aspects in agreement with the third States concerned: see also Lenaerts, K., 'Regulating the regulatory process: "delegation of powers" in the European Community', *European Law Review*, 18 (1993), p. 23 at pp. 27–40. For the distinction between a delegation of powers and functions, see *supra* note 45 and corresponding text.

This general principle also operates in some domestic contexts where courts have been willing to recognize the legality of a delegation of governmental power to an official governmental body but not the delegation of the same type of power to a private individual or organization: see, for example, Lanham, D., 'Delegation of Governmental Power to Private Parties', *Otago Law Review*, 6 (1985), p. 50; but cf. the US position as explained by, *inter alia*, Krent, H., 'Fragmenting the Unitary Executive: Congressional Delegations of Administrative Authority Outside the Federal Government', *Northwestern University Law Review*, 85 (1990), p. 62, and Lawrence, D., 'Private Exercise of Governmental Power', *Indiana Law Journal*, 61 (1986), p. 647. The reason, in part, for judicial distaste for such delegations is that the nature of a private-law institution is such that it will in many cases be inappropriate—due primarily to its institutional and decision-making processes—for the exercize of a public power in an impartial manner. It is the nature of the power and the different nature of the delegate which is thus, in many cases, the source of the objection. This is to be distinguished, however, from the case of a delegation of Chapter VII powers to States or regional arrangements, since in these cases the intended delegate is a public law entity and does, albeit in other spheres, exercize other public law powers. This does not mean that such delegations of power are lawful, but rather that they are not prima facie unlawful. The competence of the Council to make such delegations of power must still be established, and this is dealt with in Chapters 4 and 6.

[75] These limitations are twofold. First, limitations which pertain to a delegation of Chapter VII powers in general: these limitations are dealt with *infra* Section III. Second, those limitations which attach to the exercize of Chapter VII power by the particular entity: these limitations are discussed in the context of the delegation of powers to the UN Secretary-General and UN subsidiary organs in Chapters 2 and 3, correspondingly.

Chapter VII powers to UN Member States and regional arrangements is, however, different. The general competence to delegate does not extend to these entities since they are, clearly, entities external to the Organization. This approach is buttressed when it is realized that all UN organs are under a legal obligation to act in the interests of the Organization,[76] but that entities external to the Organization are not under such an obligation.[77] Accordingly, a specific competence must be found in either express or implied terms for the Council to be able to delegate its Chapter VII powers to such entities. This does not mean, however, that such specific competencies do not exist in the case of UN Member States and regional arrangements: the basis for such competencies are in fact the subject of discussion in Chapters 4 and 6.

Although the competence of the Security Council to delegate its Chapter VII powers to an entity is thus dependent on the nature of the particular entity to which powers are being delegated, there is an important common issue. The issue of limitations. The limitations which exist on the general competence of the Council to delegate its Chapter VII powers, which are explained below, also apply, *mutatis mutandis*, to the exercize by the Council of a specific competence to delegate these powers to an entity external to the Organization since they represent fundamental limitations on the competence of the Council to delegate its Chapter VII powers. There are, however, additional limitations that pertain to the exercize of delegated Chapter VII powers which depend on the nature of the particular delegate. Since these can only be determined by consideration of the particular entity which is exercizing the delegated powers, these are examined in the context of the delegation of powers to the UN Secretary-General, subsidiary organs, Member States, and regional arrangements, in the Chapters which follow.

The nature of the relationship between the general and specific competencies and their respective limitations is such that if there is a conflict between the specific competence and the general competence then the specific competence prevails: *expressio unius est exclusio alterius*. Put differently, the general competence of the Council to delegate its powers cannot be used to delegate a power in a situation which is prohibited by the limitations on the Council's specific competence.

---

[76] See, for example, in the case of the UN Secretary-General: *infra* note 28 in Chapter 2 and corresponding text.

[77] This is distinct from the more general obligation of Member States under Article 2(5) of the Charter to 'give the United Nations every assistance in any action it takes in accordance with the present Charter, and [that all Members] shall refrain from giving assistance to any State against which the United Nations is taking preventive or enforcement action'.

III. LIMITATIONS ON THE GENERAL
COMPETENCE OF THE SECURITY COUNCIL
TO DELEGATE ITS CHAPTER VII POWERS

The delegation of powers is a necessary part of any system of governance.[78] However, it is also generally recognized that restrictions on such delegations are just as necessary. In the case of the limitations on the general competence of UN principal organs to delegate their powers these are twofold. First, the principal organ must possess the power which it is purporting to delegate. Second, there are those limitations which result from application of—the reasons for which are explained below—[79] the *delegatus non potest delegare* maxim to the UN Charter: *in casu*, these limitations are that the Council is prohibited from delegating certain of its Chapter VII powers; that the Council can only delegate broad powers of discretion subject to certain constraints; when powers are being delegated the limitations on the exercize of the power must be imposed on the delegate; and that the terms of a Council resolution which delegates Chapter VII powers are to be interpreted narrowly.

1. A principal organ must possess the power it is purporting to delegate

A fundamental precondition for a lawful delegation of powers by an organ of an international organization is that the powers purportedly being delegated can only be those which the organ itself either expressly or impliedly possesses under its constituent treaty.[80] An organ cannot delegate powers which it does not itself possess.[81] This derives from the general principle of law: *nemo dat quod non habet*: one cannot give what one does not possess.[82]

2. The limitations which derive from application of the delegatus non potest delegare *doctrine*

In order to determine the effect of the *delegatus non potest delegare* maxim on the delegation by the Council of its Chapter VII powers it is, first,

---

[78] See *supra* note 69. On the more general issue of the United Nations as a form of government, see Brownlie, I., 'The United Nations As a Form of Government', *Harvard International Law Journal*, 13 (1972), p. 421.

[79] See *infra* Section III(2)(a).

[80] See also Schermers and Blokker, *supra* note 34, p. 153.

[81] As Kelsen has observed: 'It stands to reason that an organ can delegate only the power conferred upon it by the constitution.' (Kelsen, *supra* note 9, p. 142.)

[82] For application of this principle to another area of international law, the acquisition of title to territory, see, for example, the *Island of Palmas* case, *ILR*, 4, p. 103 at p. 104.

necessary to examine the content of the maxim and to explain why it is applicable to the Council, and, secondly, to determine which limitations on the general competence of the Council to delegate its Chapter VII powers the maxim prescribes as necessary.

The *delegatus non potest delegare* maxim, or what is otherwise known as the non-delegation doctrine, deals with the extent to which the exercize of a power entrusted to an authority may be delegated to another entity.[83] De Smith, Woolf, and Jowell in their work *Judicial Review of Administrative Action* state the following:

A discretionary authority must, in general, be exercized only by the authority to which it has been committed. It is a well-known principle of law that when a power has been confided to a person in circumstances indicating that trust is being placed in his individual judgment and discretion, he must exercize that power personally unless he has been expressly empowered to delegate it to another.... It applies to the delegation of all classes of powers ...[84]

In domestic constitutional and administrative law the maxim has been used, for example, as a basis for invalidating delegations of governmental power;[85] and as an element of statutory interpretation, leading, with other reasoning, to narrower constructions of statutory authority than might otherwise be derived.[86] It is, however, beyond the scope of our present enquiry to undertake a detailed examination of the way in which the maxim is applied in various domestic systems of law. For our purposes, the issue is

---

[83] See also Willis, *supra* note 45, p. 257.

[84] De Smith, Woolf, & Jowell, *supra* note 24, pp. 357–8. The nature of the power being delegated—executive, legislative, or judicial—does not in general terms affect the applicability of the non-delegation doctrine, except that domestic courts may require much stricter application of the doctrine in the context of judicial powers: see, for example, de Smith, Woolf, & Jowell, *supra* note 24, p. 359; and Wade, W., and Forsyth, C., *Administrative Law* (1994), at pp. 353–4. The question of the extent to which the non-delegation doctrine applies to judicial powers is not, however, within the scope of our present enquiry, since the Security Council does not possess under the Charter a judicial function in respect of disputes between States: see Sarooshi, D., 'The Legal Framework Governing United Nations Subsidiary Organs', *BYIL*, 67 (1996), p. 413 at pp. 462–73.

The nature of the power that was being delegated has been used by the US Supreme Court to render a delegation of power *ultra vires*. In the case of *Bowsher* v. *Synar* the Court held that certain budget-cutting responsibilities that were delegated under the 'Gramm–Rudman Act' (the Balanced Budget and Emergency Deficit Control Act of 1985) were unconstitutional, for the reason that the Act delegated 'executive' functions to a 'legislative' officer. (*Bowsher* v. *Synar*, 478 US 714 at 733–4.)

[85] See, for example, the following US cases: *Immigration and Naturalization Service* v. *Chadha*, 462 US 919, see further on this case *infra* notes 92–4 and corresponding text; *Bowsher* v. *Synar*, 478 US 714 at 733–4, see further on this case *supra* note 84; *A.L.A. Schechter Poultry Corp.* v. *United States*, 295 US 495 at 551; and *Panama Ref. Co.* v. *Ryan*, 293 US 388. For example, in *Schechter Poultry Corporation* v. *United States*, Chief Justice Charles Evans stated: 'The Congress is not permitted to abdicate or transfer to others the essential legislative functions with which it is thus vested.' *(Ibidem*, 529–30.) Cf. Davis, K., *Administrative Law Treatise* (2d edn. 1978), at pp. 149–50.

[86] See *infra* note 171 and corresponding text.

application of the maxim to the delegation by the Security Council of its Chapter VII powers and the consequences of this application.

(a) Application of the non-delegation doctrine to the Security Council

The non-delegation doctrine is applicable to the UN Security Council for three reasons. First, the doctrine is applicable since it is a general principle of law for the purposes of Article 38(1)(c) of the Statute of the International Court of Justice and as such is applicable to the United Nations and thus the Security Council. The doctrine is applied in some form to delegations of governmental power in a variety of States which represent both common and civil law systems.[87] Second, the fundamental object and purpose of the maxim is applicable to the Security Council. Finally, accountability for the exercize of certain powers—which is also an important reason for the existence of the maxim—is applicable to the Council.

The object and purpose of the *delegatus non potest delegare* maxim is to ensure that powers are to be exercized by the entity to which those powers have been initially delegated in the way that has been provided.[88] The

---

[87] Uwe Kischel when comparing the delegation of legislative power to agencies in US and German law finds five general points of agreement. (Kischel, *supra* note 69, p. 239.) First, the legislature cannot delegate as it pleases. Second, the legislature must provide the administration with guidance on how to carry out their authorization to make rules. Third, the existence of such guidance will be the standard by which to determine the legality of the delegation. Fourth, the standard is not immutable but may depend on the field of law to which the authorization pertains as well as on the possible impact of the regulations. Fifth, certain core legislative functions, especially those mentioned in the respective constitutions, cannot be delegated at all. (*Ibidem.*) In examining the way that a delegation of power has been treated in domestic legal systems it is contended that the US approach is more useful in the context of international law than the German approach. The reason for this is that the German constitution (*Grundgesetz*) contains express provision for the delegation of governmental powers; while the US constitution, like the UN Charter, contains no such express provision. For the situation in the US and Germany, see also David, *supra* note 69, p. 68. For examples of English law cases where the non-delegation doctrine was used to hold actions to be *ultra vires* because the effective decision was taken by a person or body to whom the power did not properly belong, see Wade and Forsyth, *supra* note 84, pp. 349–50. See also in the context of English law: Freedland, M., 'The rule against delegation and the *Carltona* doctrine in an agency context', *Public Law* (1996), p. 19; and Lanham, D., 'Delegation and the Alter Ego Principle', *Law Quarterly Review*, 100 (1984), p. 587. For discussion of the application of the doctrine in Australia see Lanham, *ibidem*, Malcolm, D., 'The Limitations, if Any, on the Powers of Parliament to Delegate the Power to Legislate', *Australian Law Journal*, 66 (1992), p. 247, and Dixon, M., 'Delegation, Agency and the Alter Ego Rule', *Sydney Law Review*, 11 (1987), p. 326; and in Canada, see Keyes, J., 'From *Delegatus* to the Duty to Make Law', *McGill Law Journal*, 33 (1987), p. 49. In the case of France, see, for example, the decision of the French Conseil Constitutionnel: *Cons. Const. 25–6.6.1986*, [1986] *RDCC* 61, paras. 13–14; in the case of Brazil, see Knapp, *supra* note 69, vol. 1 (B), pp. B-43, B-44; and in the case of Italy, see Knapp, *supra* note 69, vol. 1 (I), p. I-94.

[88] Thus, Wade and Forsyth, in the context of English administrative law, state the following: '[a]n element which is essential to the lawful exercize of power is that it should be exercized by the authority upon whom it is conferred, and by no one else'. (Wade and Forsyth, *supra* note 84, p. 347.)

reason for this is that where a power has been given to an entity there is also a concomitant responsibility, a legal responsibility,[89] on the delegate to exercize the power for the purpose—or even possibly in the way—stipulated by the delegator.[90] Accordingly, the naming of a person to exercize power by the entity that initially delegates power may involve an implicit assumption that the person was chosen due to particular institutional or other characteristics.[91] In the US domestic context, this type of approach was used by the US Supreme Court in the case of *Immigration and Naturalization Service* v. *Chadha* to strike down a 'legislative veto' exercized by the US House of Representatives (a one-House legislative veto) over an act of

[89] Crawford states, albeit in more general terms, that where there is power there should be legal responsibility: Crawford, J., *Democracy in International Law* (1994), p. 22. In the context of a delegation of governmental powers in the United States, see Schoenbrod, D., *Power Without Responsibility: How Congress Abuses the People through Delegation* (1993). This is important since even in those cases where a delegation of powers is lawful, the responsibility for the exercize of powers cannot in general terms also be transferred as this rests with the person to whom powers have been initially given. For application of this principle in the context of a delegation of Chapter VII powers to Member States, see *infra* Section III in Chapter 4. In the context of both the UK and New Zealand, Oliver and Drewry have observed: '. . . delegation cannot affect or prevent the exercize of the function or power by the appropriate minister, and delegation does not affect the responsibility of the minister for the actions of a person acting under delegation'. (Oliver, D., and Drewry, G., *Public Service Reforms: Issues of Accountability and Public Law* (1996), pp. 129–30.)

[90] As such the application of the non-delegation doctrine does not depend on there being a separation of powers between the organs of governance. The point is that it is the designated institutional decision-making processes and nature of the entity exercizing the powers which are the relevant factors in determining application of the doctrine. See, however, on the delimitation of powers between principal organs as specified by the Charter and the effect of this limitation on the powers of the Council to establish and delegate powers to subsidiary organs: *infra* Section III (3) in Chapter 3.

[91] An interesting application of this object and purpose of the maxim has arisen in respect of one of the interfaces between domestic US law and the law of the Charter: the command and control of US troops which are part of a UN force. Article 2, Section 2, of the US Constitution states that the US President is Commander-in-Chief of all US military forces. The problem which arises in the context of the UN is whether the President can delegate his Commander-in-Chief powers to the UN. The problem—which at this point in time is purely academic—arises when US forces have been committed under Article 43 to use by the Council for enforcement action. As Glennon and Wayward have stated: 'Ending an enforcement action requires a substantive Security Council decision that can be vetoed by any one of the five permanent Members. Because an Article 43 force serves under Security Council command once called into service, the President could not, under the terms of the Charter, make an independent decision to withdraw American troops. At this point, American forces would no longer be under presidential control, creating constitutional difficulties.' (Glennon, M., and Hayward, A., 'Collective Security and the Constitution: Can the Commander in Chief Power Be Delegated to the United Nations?', *The Georgetown Law Journal*, 82 (1994), p. 1573 at p. 1594.) Thus by committing US troops to a UN force which is under UN control in a particular enforcement action, the President has in effect delegated his power as Commander-in-Chief to the UN.

For discussion of the analogous constitutional considerations relating to German participation in UN military actions, see Zöckler, M., 'Germany in Collective Security Systems—Anything Goes?', *EJIL*, 6 (1995), p. 274.

the Executive.[92] The Supreme Court found that the exercize of 'legislative veto' in the case of Mr Chadha (who was seeking to remain in the United States) was 'essentially legislative in purpose and effect'.[93] Having characterized the legislative veto as an exercize of legislative power, the Supreme Court struck it down since it could, as the exercize of a legislative power, only be exercized in the manner stipulated by the Constitution—by a law passed by both Houses of Congress and submitted to the President for his signature or veto—and not, as took place *in casu*, by action by a purported one-House legislative veto.[94] This represents an application of Freedman's contention that if a court were to conclude,

that the Framers regarded the proper exercize of a specific legislative power as closely dependent upon the unique institutional competence of Congress, the non-delegation doctrine would prohibit Congress from delegating that power to another. In these circumstances, the act of delegation would so alter the manner of the power's exercize that the resulting arrangement would no longer be compatible with the Framers' reasons for vesting the power in an institution whose character and nature are defined in the special ways—of political responsiveness and broad based diversity—that those of Congress are. The informing principle of institutional competence as a guide to the constitutionality of the delegation of legislative power thus focuses on the tension between the nature of the particular power delegated and the character of the particular institution chosen to exercize it.[95]

Application of this object and purpose of the maxim to the law of international institutions is validated by an understanding of the process of establishment of an international organization. An international organization is established by the negotiation, conclusion, and adoption of a constituent treaty. Thus the conferment of any power on an organ of an international organization is after careful consideration by the States which negotiated the constituent treaty.[96] In many cases the conferment of a power on a

---

[92] 462 US 919. On the way in which a legislative veto over Executive action would take place, see McMahon, E., '*Chadha* and the Nondelegation Doctrine: Defining a Restricted Legislative Veto', *Yale Law Journal*, 94 (1985), p. 1493 at pp. 1494–5. See also on the *Chadha* case: Franck, T., and Bob, C., 'The Return of Humpty-Dumpty: Foreign Relations Law After the Chadha Case', *AJIL*, 79 (1985), p. 912.

[93] 462 US 919 at 952. The US Supreme Court cited as evidence of the veto's legislative character its alteration of the legal rights of persons outside the legislative branch and its determination of policy. (*Ibidem*, 952, 954.)

[94] 462 US 919 at 955–8.

[95] Freedman, J., 'Delegation of Power and Institutional Competence', *University of Chicago Law Review*, 43 (1976), p. 307 at p. 336. This approach reflects more generally the scholarly concept of 'structural due process' or 'due process of lawmaking'. With regard to the application of this concept to delegation in the US and German Law contexts, see: Kischel, *supra* note 69, pp. 248–9. On the issue of due process see also: Linde, H., 'Due Process of Lawmaking', *Nebraska Law Review*, 55 (1976), p. 197; Tribe, L., 'Structural Due Process', *Harv. CR-CLL Rev.*, 10 (1975), p. 269; and Farber, D., and Frickey, P., *Law and Public Choice* (1991), pp. 118–31.

[96] This idea was expressed in a different form by President Winiarski in the *Expenses* case when he stated: '[T]he fact that an organ of the United Nations is seeking to achieve one of the

particular organ is due to its peculiar institutional characteristics. Thus the argument runs that when States initially delegate powers to an international organization, an implicit part of this initial delegation of power is the assumption that powers are to be exercized only by the organ which was specified as having the competence to do so by the constituent treaty. Accordingly, to reiterate, the presumption is that the exercize of these powers should not be delegated to another entity. This is of particular importance to the Security Council due to the peculiar institutional characteristics of its decision-making process, especially the existence of the veto—the price of agreement on Chapter VII.[97] Suffice to note here, however, that these characteristics do not in general prevent the Council from delegating Chapter VII powers, but rather operate, as explained below, as a limitation on the Council's competence to delegate its Chapter VII powers.[98]

The final reason why the *delegatus non potest delegare* maxim is relevant to the delegation of powers by the Council is the notion of accountability which is also applicable to the work of the Council. An important reason for the non-delegation doctrine is to ensure that the authority to which power has initially been delegated remains accountable for the way in which the power is being exercized.[99] The fact that the Security Council when taking measures to maintain or restore international peace and security is required by Article 24(2) of the Charter to 'act in accordance with the Purposes and Principles of the United Nations' means implicitly that the Council is accountable to a degree for its actions. As the UN War Crimes Tribunal for the former Yugoslavia stated in its decision on the defence motion on jurisdiction in the *Tadic* case: 'Support for the view that the Security Council cannot act arbitrarily or for an ulterior purpose is found in the nature of the Charter as a treaty delegating certain powers to the United Nations. In fact, such a limitation is almost a corollary of the principle that the organs of the United Nations must act in accordance with the powers delegated to them. It is a matter of logic that if the Security Council acted arbitrarily or for an ulterior purpose it would be acting outside the purview of the powers delegated to it in the Charter.'[100] Thus it is that Franck states: '[t]he legality

---

UN's purposes does not suffice to render its action lawful. The Charter, a multilateral treaty which was the result of prolonged and laborious negotiations, carefully created organs and determined their competence and means of action.' (*Expenses* case, *ICJ Reports (1962)*, at p. 230.)

[97] See further on the veto: *infra* note 148 and corresponding text.

[98] See *infra* Section III(2)(b).

[99] See the statement by Justice Harlan in the US Supreme Court case of *Arizona* v. *California:* 373 US 546 at 626 (Harlan J., dissenting in part).

[100] *Prosecutor* v. *Tadic (Jurisdiction)*, 105 *ILR*, p. 420 at p. 432 (para. 15 of the judgment). See also Paenson who states that international organizations 'derive their powers essentially from a delegation by the States [which created the organization]'. (Paenson, I., *Manual of the*

of actions by any UN organ must be judged by reference to the Charter as a "constitution" of *delegated* powers'.[101]

The important question that arises is to whom is the Council accountable for the exercize of its Chapter VII powers? In the context of the *delegatus non potest delegare* maxim, accountability is to the entity which has delegated powers in the first place. Thus in the UN context it is necessary to determine whether the Chapter VII powers of the Security Council are as a result of a delegation of powers, and, if so, to determine which entity delegated these powers. The entity which has delegated powers to the Council is the entity to which the Council is responsible, that is, accountable in law, when exercising these powers.[102]

It has been argued by Degni-Segui in Cot and Pellet's *La Charte des Nations Unies* that it was UN Member States who delegated powers through Article 24 of the Charter to the Security Council. He states:

L'objet de la délégation ne semble pas *a priori* poser problème. A s'en tenir à la lettre du texte, c'est la fonction primordiale du maintien de la paix qui est transférée de la sphère de compétence de chacun des Etats membres à celle du

Terminology of Public International Law (Law of Peace) and International Organizations (1983), p. 362.)

However, viewing the Charter as a delegation of powers cannot be the sole reference to judge the legality of actions of UN organs. The reasons for this are twofold. First, it is well accepted that UN organs can exercize implied powers in the performance of their functions. Moreover, it is similarly well accepted that a source of constitutional authority for the exercize of certain powers by a UN organ is the subsequent practice of an organ. (See, for example, the *Namibia* case, *ICJ Reports (1971)*, at p. 22.) Both these cases represent a situation where the powers being exercized by a UN organ were not those which had been initially delegated in express terms by UN Member States, and, moreover, their exercize may not have even been envisaged by UN Member States when creating the Charter in 1945. Second, not all of the powers given to UN organs were 'delegated powers' or even if they were the content of the powers under the Charter in many cases is much broader than the powers originally possessed by UN Members. This is an illustration of the law-making effect of the constituent instrument of an international organization.

[101] Franck, T., 'The "Powers of Appreciation": Who is the Ultimate Guardian of UN Legality?' (Editorial Comment), *AJIL*, 86 (1992), p. 519 at p. 521. This general approach has support from an early decision of the US Supreme Court, *McCulloch* v. *Maryland*, where Chief Justice Marshall speaks of the US Constitution as a constitution of 'limited' 'enumerated powers' which have been delegated to the Government by all the people of the United States. (*McCulloch* v. *Maryland*, 17 US (4 Wheat.) 316 (1819), as reproduced in Franck, T., *Comparative Constitutional Process: Cases and Materials* (1968), p. 134 *et sequentia*.)

Throughout this book reference is made to the UN Charter as a constitution. For a more detailed justification for such a characterization, see the analysis in Crawford, J., 'The Charter of the United Nations as a Constitution', in *The Changing Constitution of the United Nations* (Fox, H., ed.) (1997), p. 3; Simma, B., 'From Bilateralism to Community Interest in International Law', *Hague Recueil des Cours*, 250 (1994-VI), p. 209 at pp. 258–62; and Herdegen, M., 'The "Constitutionalization" of the UN Security System', *Vanderbilt Journal of Transnational Law*, 27 (1994), p. 135 at p. 150. But cf. Arangio-Ruiz, G., "The Federal Analogy" and UN Charter Interpretation: A Crucial Issue', *EJIL*, 8 (1997), p. 1.

[102] This is different, however, from the issue of who is responsible in legal terms for the exercize of delegated Chapter VII powers: the Security Council or its delegate: see *supra* note 89.

Conseil de sécurité. Cette fonction est transmise avec les pouvoirs y afférents. Cela revient à dire qu'il s'agit en fait d'une délégation de pouvoirs. Mais en poussant l'analyse plus loin l'on n'aura aucune peine à découvrir que la délégation porte en définitive sur la souveraineté. La fonction du maintien de la paix constitue, en effet, une prérogative de puissance publique, qui participe de la souveraineté de l'Etat. La délégation intervenant dans un tel domaine, on peut s'accorder avec le professeur VIRALLY pour soutenir qu'elle 'ne peut s'analyser qu'en une délégation de souveraineté.'[103]

However, Delbruck, in Simma's *Charter of the United Nations*, contends that such an interpretation of Article 24 is problematic and that the source of the Council's enforcement powers is not in fact a delegation of powers by UN Members.[104] Delbruck observes that the Council is an organ of the UN and therefore derives its powers from the UN Charter itself.[105] His argument is that it is not possible for 'Member States' to delegate powers to the Council since technically it is the Charter which confers these powers on the Council and not Member States. Delbruck contends that if one were to speak, as does Degni-Segui, of a delegation of sovereign rights by Member States then this would only refer to the founding of the Organization: that is, the conclusion of the founding treaty and its acceptance and ratification by the Members. Thus Delbruck argues that the interpretation of Article 24(1) according to which the Member States 'agree that in carrying out its duties under this responsibility the Security Council acts on their behalf' is legally erroneous and superfluous.[106] What Delbruck is in effect saying is that the Charter, as the constituent instrument of an international organization, has itself created certain enforcement powers and conferred these on the Council.

This approach is overly formalistic. It is true that the Member States cannot themselves delegate powers to the Council since in formal terms it is through the Charter that Member States gave powers to the Council. This does not mean, however, that the Charter, as a treaty, cannot act as a mechanism by which States, or, as explained below, the international community, can delegate specific powers to an organ of an international organization. Thus it is the Charter which confers the powers, but the original source of that power—which is transferred via the Charter—is UN Member States acting collectively. Moreover, to prescribe such a meaning to Article 24(1) is to give effect to the clear terms of the Article when it states that the Member States 'agree that in carrying out its duties under this responsibility, the Security Council *acts on their behalf*.'[107] Accordingly, it is contended

---

[103] Cot and Pellet, *supra* note 1, p. 450.
[104] Simma, *supra* note 1, p. 404.
[105] *Ibidem.*   [106] *Ibidem.*
[107] Emphasis added. This has also been affirmed by State representatives in both express and implied terms in statements in the Security Council which are too numerous to recount here: see, for examples, statements by State representatives in respect of decisions taken to

that UN Member States have delegated Chapter VII powers to the Security Council through the mechanism of the Charter.

Thus the analysis of Degni-Segui and Virally is accurate when they state that Members have delegated powers to the Council through Article 24(1). However, where one may differ from their analysis is in the nature of the power which was delegated: that it was not sovereignty *per se* but an international police power of States. It is contended that the pre-Charter power of States to maintain international peace was a recognized right of States under customary international law.[108] States possessed, prior to the Charter, a competence which is analogous to that given to the Security Council: the competence to use force to maintain or restore international peace. It is beyond the scope of this present work to examine the *opinio juris* and practice of States in respect of this international police power. It suffices, however, to note in this case the views of several eminent authorities who support the position that the right existed as part of custom. Fawcett, for example, argued that States possessed, prior to the Charter, an international police power, or what he alternatively refers to as a right to hegemonial intervention. He states:

It [an international police power] has often been exercized in the past century and a half by the great powers, acting either alone or in concert, to correct misrule, localise civil strife or neutralise alien intervention, where those conditions have appeared seriously to threaten their interests or security.[109]

The existence of the right to exercize such an international police power as part of customary international law was also recognized by Sir Hersch Lauterpacht in the seventh edition of *Oppenheim's International Law*. Sir

---

delegate Chapter VII powers to the UN Secretary-General, UN subsidiary organs, UN Member States, and regional arrangements: *infra* Chapters 2–6.

[108] The qualitative nature of the power of States to take action to maintain international peace prior to the Charter is not exactly the same as the analogous competence of the Security Council under the Charter. Prior to the Charter, collective or individual action to maintain or restore 'international peace and security' did not as such exist. The term 'international peace and security' was first introduced by the UN Charter. Under the League of Nations Covenant, the condition for the application of enforcement powers was not the rather broad formulation 'threat to the peace' as used in Article 39 of the Charter, but the much narrower formulation of an illegal resort to war found in Article 16 of the Covenant. Thus the cases where States— even after the formation of the League of Nations—could individually resort to the use of force to protect the common good was fundamentally different from those cases where the Security Council is authorized to do so. As Stone has observed: 'On its face, this [Article 39] confers an international authority over the wills and action of the sovereign Members far exceeding that of the League. . . . It created, indeed, collective power of judgment over the international peace-breaker quite lacking in the Covenant.' (Stone, J., *Legal Controls of International Conflict* (1959), p. 192.) However, it is contended that although the terms which justified the use of force under the Charter differed from that under the Covenant, States did possess a power analogous to that of the Council to use force in order to maintain peace.

[109] Fawcett, J., 'Intervention in International Law', *Hague Recueil des Cours*, 103 (1961-II), p. 351. See also Cassesse, *supra* note 6, p. 218.

Hersch notes in the treatise that '[i]f a State in time of peace or war violates such rules of the Law of Nations as are universally recognised by custom or are laid down in law-making treaties, other States have a right to intervene and to make the delinquent submit to the rules concerned'.[110] Thus there is authority for the view that, prior to the Charter, States had the right to wage war in order to maintain or restore a notion of international peace and security which they could unilaterally determine: an international police power. As Fawcett has argued: 'the collective intervention which the Security Council may undertake under the Charter is derived historically from hegemonial intervention or the international police power, as it was practised in the three centuries before the drafting of the United Nations Charter'.[111] It is precisely this international police action which Brownlie argues is today the function of the competent organ or organs of the United Nations.[112]

However, even if it is accepted that Member States did not, prior to the Charter, possess a policing power, this does not mean that Article 24(1) is without legal effect. In this case it is argued that Article 24(1) represents a delegation of a policing power from the international community—that is, the vast majority of States at any particular period in time—to the Security Council.[113] Thus in this case it is not individual States which have delegated the power to take action to maintain international peace and security to the Security Council, but the international community.[114] The validity of this contention relies on the proposition that the powers which can be exercized by the collective totality of sovereign States is greater than the sum of the individual powers of these States. This proposition finds a parallel in domestic law-making procedures. Members of the US Congress, for example, cannot make law individually. However, when all the Members are constituted as Congress they can make, subject of course to constitutional

---

[110] Oppenheim, L., *International Law: A Treatise* (7th edn., 1948) (Lauterpacht, H., ed.), p. 276. Moreover, Stowell in his 1921 work on *Intervention in International Law* argued that the concept did exist and that its most frequent application was intervention to prevent an unnecessary war or to bring a conflict to an end by imposing a settlement. (Stowell, E., *Intervention in International Law* (1921), p. 286.)

[111] Fawcett, *supra* note 109, p. 369.

[112] Brownlie, I., *International Law and the Use of Force by States* (1963), p. 345. Brownlie does, however, state that 'Even in the nineteenth century its operation [the international police power] was haphazard and its content nebulous.' (Brownlie, *ibidem.*) Cf. Hall who questioned the legality of this historic notion of an international police power: Hall, W., *International Law* (1909), p. 348.

[113] The ability of States to act in the area of maintaining international peace and security is a right and not an obligation. Thus the Security Council has clearly inherited a discretionary right to act to restore international peace and security, but not an obligation to act: see *supra* notes 3–9 and corresponding text.

[114] Note the use of the term 'States' and not 'Members'. Strictly speaking the 'Members' of the UN did not exist before the entry into force of the Charter: States only became 'Members' through the Charter, that is once the Charter had entered into force.

limitations, law. Similarly, it is contended that when the international community acts then it can confer powers on an international organization which sovereign States acting individually could not. This idea was implicitly recognized by the International Court of Justice when discussing the international legal personality of the United Nations in the *Reparations* case. The Court opined:

> ... fifty States, representing the vast majority of the Members of the international community, had the power, in conformity with international law, to bring into being an entity possessing objective international personality, and not merely personality recognised by them alone ...[115]

It seems very doubtful that a State acting individually or in concert with a few other States could confer such 'objective international personality' on an entity,[116] but, as the Court noted, the 'vast majority of the Members of the international community' do possess this competence.[117] Thus where the international community has delegated the exercize of enforcement powers to the Council, the Council is responsible to the international community for the way in which these powers are exercized.[118] However, it is the view of this writer that States did possess an international police power prior to

[115] *Reparations for Injuries suffered in the Service of the United Nations, ICJ* Reports (1949), p. 174 at p. 185.

[116] The Special Rapporteur of the Institut de Droit International, Rosalyn Higgins, in the 'Final Report of the Legal Consequences for Member States of the Non-Fulfilment by International Organizations of their Obligations Towards Third Parties' stated the following: 'While the unique situation of the United Nations, with its near universal Membership, may invest it with objective legal personality, this should not be presumed to apply to all international organisations. Treaties establishing such organisations may provide them with legal personality so far as the states parties to the constitutive treaty are concerned ... But nothing in the *Reparation for Injuries* case provides for objective legal personality for each and every international organisation.' (Higgins, R., 'Final Report of the Legal Consequences for Member States of the Non-Fulfilment by International Organizations of their Obligations Towards Third Parties', *Report of the Institut de droit International*, 66-I *AIDI* (1995), p. 251 at p. 16 of Report.

[117] The limitation which exists on this law-making power of the international community is *jus cogens*. This is reflected in Article 53 of the Vienna Convention on the Law of Treaties which states that a treaty is void if, at the time of its conclusion, it conflicts with a peremptory norm of general international law (*jus cogens*). Moreover, Article 53 defines a peremptory norm of general international law as 'a norm accepted and recognized by the international community of States *as a whole* as a norm from which no derogation is permitted and which can be modified only by a subsequent norm of general international law having the same character'.

[118] The converse of this argument is that where States have not delegated a particular power to an international organization when establishing the organization, then the Member States cannot be liable for the acts of the organization in the exercize of the power in question. As Seyersted has observed: 'It is not possible ... to hold the Member states responsible for acts of the organisation which involve no delegation of powers from these states.' (Seyersted, F., *Objective International Personality of Intergovernmental Organisations* (1963), p. 70.) See also Crawford, J., 'The Charter of the United Nations as a Constitution', in *The Changing Constitution of the United Nations* (Fox, H., ed.) (1997), p. 3 at p. 12.

the UN Charter and thus that Article 24(1) represents a delegation of this type of power by States to the Council.[119] Accordingly, in the exercize of its Chapter VII powers the Security Council is responsible to UN Member States.[120]

There are two aspects of this accountability worth noting. First, it does not mean that the Security Council is responsible for the exercize of these powers only to those States which created the UN Charter in 1945: the Negotiating States.[121] The Council is responsible to all UN Member States.[122] This of course includes States which joined as Parties after 1945.[123]

The second point to note about this accountability of the Council is that it cannot be to individual Member States. The nature of the delegation of powers in Article 24(1), as explained above, is that States acting collectively have decided through the Charter to confer enforcement powers upon the Council. Thus as States become a Party to the Charter they decide to join other Members in delegating their power to the Security Council. Accordingly, accountability for the way in which Chapter VII powers are exercized by the Council can only be to the collective of Member States. This causes difficulties when deciding in practice to which entity is the Council accountable in the exercize of its Chapter VII powers. Even though the General Assembly contains the totality of UN Member States, it is clear that under the Charter the Security Council is not responsible to the Assembly for the way in which Chapter VII powers are exercized.[124] However, the General Assembly does provide a forum where

[119] Suy also contends that UN Member States have 'delegated their powers to the Council in the field of maintenance of international peace and security'. (Suy, E., 'The Role of the United Nations General Assembly', in *The Changing Constitution of the United Nations* (Fox, H., ed.) (1997), p. 55 at p. 64.) See also Franck, T., 'The United Nations as Guarantor of International Peace and Security', in *The United Nations at Age Fifty: A Legal Perspective* (1995), p. 25 at p. 37; and Judge Bustamente in the *Expenses* case, *ICJ Reports* (1962), p. 151 at pp. 292–3.

[120] See also Gill, T., 'Legal and Some Political Limitations on the Power of the UN Security Council to Exercise its Enforcement Powers under Chapter VII of the Charter', *Netherlands Yearbook of International Law*, 26 (1995), p. 33 at p. 125.

[121] A Negotiating State is defined in Article 2(1)(e) of the 1969 Vienna Convention on the Law of Treaties as 'a State which took part in the drawing up and adoption of the text of the treaty'.

[122] The position of a responsibility of the Security Council owed to non-Members is, however, not so clear. On the issue of third parties in international law generally, see Chinkin, C., *Third Parties in International Law* (1993).

[123] A State Party is defined in Article 2(1)(g) of the 1969 Vienna Convention on the Law of Treaties as 'a State which has consented to be bound by the treaty and for which the treaty is in force'.

[124] Cf. Koskenniemi, M., 'The Place of Law in Collective Security', *Michigan Journal of International Law*, 17 (1996), p. 455 at p. 486; and Gill, T., 'Legal and Some Political Limitations on the Power of the UN Security Council to Exercise its Enforcement Powers under Chapter VII of the Charter', *Netherlands Yearbook of International Law*, 26 (1995), p. 33 at pp. 125–6.

the expression of a particular opinion by the majority of UN Member States may be made.[125] This opinion is, however, to be ascertained by the statements of State representatives and not by the adoption of a formal General Assembly resolution, although the latter may of course provide evidence of the intention of Member States. The main effect of this process of accountability is that the legitimacy of Security Council action may be compromised.[126] However, it is the International Court of Justice which is the entity in the UN system that is best placed to determine the *vires* of a particular delegation of powers by the Security Council. Further discussion of the scope of the competence of the International Court to carry out such a review in this area is undertaken below in the section on the justiciability of the delegation by the Council of its Chapter VII powers.[127]

To return to our more general point and to conclude on this section, the *delegatus non potest delegare* maxim applies to the work of the Council. It is now appropriate to examine the restrictive effect of the maxim on the Council's competence to delegate its Chapter VII powers.

(b) The restrictive effect of the non-delegation doctrine on the Security Council

There are four restrictions which the non-delegation doctrine imposes on the Council's competence to delegate its Chapter VII powers. First, the Council is prohibited from delegating certain of its Chapter VII powers. Second, the Council can only delegate broad powers of discretionary decision making subject to certain conditions. Third, when powers are being delegated the limitations on the exercize of the power must be imposed on the delegate. Finally, the terms of a Council resolution which delegates Chapter VII powers are to be construed narrowly.

(i) *The Council is prohibited from delegating certain of its Chapter VII powers*

The Council is proscribed from delegating two types of Chapter VII discretionary powers.[128] First, the determination that a threat to, or breach of, the

---

[125] Cf. Suy who contends that the General Assembly can exercize supervision over the way in which the Council exercizes its Chapter VII powers primarily by means of consideration of the annual and special reports of the Security Council which the Assembly has, under Article 15 of the Charter, the express competence to consider: Suy, E., 'The Role of the United Nations General Assembly', in *The Changing Constitution of the United Nations* (Fox, H., ed.) (1997), p. 55 at p. 64. Another possibility in this respect is the sole power of the General Assembly over the budget of the Organization. It has been suggested by other writers that this should be used by the Assembly as a way of controlling the exercize of Chapter VII powers by the Security Council: see on this issue *infra* note 235 in Chapter 3.

[126] See on this issue of legitimacy: *supra* notes 21–3 and corresponding text.

[127] See *infra* Section IV.

[128] Cf. the view by Bothe that the non-delegation doctrine prohibits the delegation by the Council of any of its Chapter VII powers: Bothe, M., 'Les limites des pouvoirs du Conseil de sécurité', in *Peace-Keeping and Peace-Building: The Development of the Role of the Security*

peace has come into existence or has ceased to exist. Second, the delegation of an unrestricted power of command and control over a military enforcement force.

The decision that a threat to, or breach of, international peace and security has occurred and then has ceased to exist is the very *raison d'être* of Chapter VII: an Article 39 determination is the gateway to action under Chapter VII.[129] States delegated to the Council the competence to decide that a threat to, or breach of, the peace had occurred or that such a situation had ceased to exist on the condition that it would be the Council which is the only entity exercising this power.[130] Accordingly, application of the *delegatus potest non delegare* doctrine means the Council cannot delegate this power to any other entity. Moreover, the institutional safeguard of the veto that attaches to the Council's decision-making processes is an additional reason why the Council cannot delegate its Article 39 power of determination. It was always intended that the five Permanent Members should be able to veto a decision that a particular situation constituted a threat to, or breach of, the peace or that such a situation had ended. The provision of the veto power of the five Permanent Members in respect of an Article 39 determination may not necessarily be guaranteed if the Council were able to delegate this power of determination to, for example, UN Member States. This approach is supported when an examination is made of Chapter VIII of the Charter. There is provision in Article 53 for regional arrangements to carry out military enforcement action in order to maintain international peace and security. The provision continues to state, however, that such action cannot be carried out 'without the authorization of the Security Council'. Thus it is not even for a regional arrangement to decide when a matter constitutes a threat to international peace and security and, moreover, to decide whether it could take enforcement action on this

Council (Dupuy, R-J., ed.) (1993), p. 67 at p. 73. Similarly, Wembou argues that the non-delegation doctrine prohibits a delegation by the Council of its powers to the UN Secretary-General or to UN Member States: Djiena-Wembou, M-C., 'Réflexions sur la validité et la portée de la résolution 678 du Conseil de Sécurité', *African Journal of International & Comparative Law*, 5 (1993), p. 34 at pp. 45–6, and Djiena Wembou, M-C., 'Validité et portée de la résolution 794 (1992) du Conseil de Sécurité', *African Journal of International & Comparative Law* 5 (1993), p. 340 at pp. 348–50.

[129] See *supra* note 41 and corresponding text.

[130] See Goodrich, L., and Simons, A-P., *The United Nations and the Maintenance of International Peace and Security* (1955), p. 490. Similarly, Kelsen states that '[t]he Charter authorizes the Security Council, and only the Security Council, not the individual members or any other central organ of the United Nations, to ascertain the existence of the conditions under which the use of force within the system of collective security may take place'. (Kelsen, H., 'Collective Security and Collective Self-Defence under the Charter of the United Nations', *AJIL*, 42 (1948), p. 783 at p. 786.) Moreover, Goodrich and Simons argue that if the Council should decide to use measures under Articles 41 and 42 of the Charter it would subsequently have to decide under what conditions the enforcement measures should be terminated. (*Ibidem*.)

basis.[131] This is a matter reserved solely for the Council. Only once the Council has itself decided that a matter is a threat to, or breach of, international peace and security can it then decide to empower the regional arrangement to carry out military enforcement action. It would not be accurate to argue that the Council is allowed to delegate its Article 39 power of determination to individual Member States but not to regional arrangements, since a regional arrangement is, after all, only a collection of UN Member States.[132] Thus to conclude on this point, the Security Council cannot delegate to Member States the competence to make either an Article 39 determination or a determination that such a situation has ceased to exist.

The second substantive limitation is that the Council cannot delegate to Member States an unrestricted power of command and control over a force carrying out authorized military enforcement action. There are two reasons for this. First, the Council itself does not possess such a power. Second, the Council must at all times retain overall authority and control over the exercize of delegated Chapter VII powers.

The Security Council is given overall authority to exercize command and control over a UN force carrying out military enforcement action by virtue of Articles 46 and 47 of the Charter.[133] However, the Council does not possess a total power of command and control over a force carrying out military enforcement action due to Article 44 of the Charter. This provision concerns the specific case under Chapter VII in which the Security Council is to use forces from Member States to undertake military enforcement action. In such a case the Security Council must, before calling upon a Member State to provide contingents under the Article 43 special agreements, invite this State to participate in the Council's decision to send into combat the contingents it has undertaken to provide. Due to the non-conclusion of Article 43 agreements, it is clear that Article 44 does not apply directly to the case of a force carrying out UN authorized military enforcement action. However, the reference in Article 44 to Article 43

---

[131] See *infra* note 4 and corresponding text in Chapter 6.

[132] See *infra* note 9 and corresponding text in Chapter 6.

[133] Article 46 of the Charter states that any plans for the application of armed force are to be made by the Security Council with the assistance of the Military Staff Committee. On Article 46, see Cot and Pellet, *supra* note 1, p. 732; and Simma, *supra* note 1, p. 643. Note, however, that as early as 1948, the Military Staff Committee pointed out in its report to the Security Council that unanimity could not be achieved on either the question of the overall strength and composition of the armed forces or on the Committee's future work. (*GAOR*, Fourth Session (1948), Supplement No. 2, at p. 95.)

The Military Staff Committee was given two roles under Article 47: to advise and to direct. The advisory role is provided for in a broad manner in Article 47(1). The Committee is to give advice on all questions relating to the Security Council's military requirements for the maintenance of international peace and security. Article 47(3) of the Charter states that the Committee 'shall be responsible under the Council for the strategic direction of any armed forces placed at the disposal of the Security Council'.

agreements only exists since this was the mechanism by which the Security Council was to be provided troops to carry out military enforcement action. In the case where troops are voluntarily provided, the guarantee which Article 44 provides to these troop-contributing States must still apply since the object and purpose of the provision remains applicable.[134] This object and purpose may best be summed up by quoting the phrase coined by the Delegate of The Netherlands at the San Francisco Conference: 'no military action without representation'.[135] Accordingly, the Council when delegating the power of command and control to another entity[136] must ensure that States who contribute troops to that force are given the right to be consulted on the way in which their troops are to be used to carry out enforcement action. If the Security Council were to purport to delegate Chapter VII powers without this requirement then it would be purporting to delegate a power wider than it itself possesses, since States which contribute troops to a force that is to carry out military enforcement action have the right to be consulted and participate in the decision on the way in which their troops are to be used.

The second reason why the Council cannot delegate to Member States an unrestricted power of command and control is that the Council must at all times retain overall authority and control over the exercize of its delegated Chapter VII powers. As explained below in some detail, an implied condition of a delegation of Chapter VII powers is that the Council retains at all times the competence to change the way that the delegated powers are being exercized.[137] The importance of this overall authority and control by the Council is reiterated when one recalls that the exercize of delegated Chapter VII powers is part of a collective security effort and therefore the Council should exercize overall authority and control over the use of its delegated Chapter VII powers to ensure that this is in accord with the interests of the UN.[138]

---

[134] Cf. the view that whatever rights States that are required to contribute troops may have under Article 44 need not necessarily extend to those that provide troops voluntarily. The latter if they do not agree with the decisions of the Security Council could arguably decide to remove their troops; while the former *ex hypothesi* could not. Cf., however, *infra* notes 38–40 in Chapter 4.

[135] See Goodrich, L., and Hambro, E., *The Charter of the United Nations* (1946), p. 168. It is suggested that in order for States to ensure their participation in decisions pertaining to enforcement action in which their peacekeeping troops are involved, they could make their contribution of troops conditional on both their consent to such action and the right to participate in decisions relating to the way this action is to be undertaken. Such a condition, which would be specified in an agreement between a troop-contributing state and the United Nations, is in accord with the above-mentioned object and purpose of Article 44.

[136] The Council has at different times delegated the power of command and control over a force carrying out military enforcement action to the UN Secretary-General, a UN subsidiary organ, UN Member States, and a regional arrangement: see Chapters 2–6.

[137] See *infra* notes 145–59 and corresponding text.

[138] See *supra* note 76 and corresponding text. The representative of the UK made the point

(ii) The Council can only delegate broad powers of discretion subject to certain constraints

The non-delegation doctrine requires that, in general, broad powers of discretion should not be delegated.[139] It is contended that this operates as a general rule of the law of international institutions which governs a delegation of powers. The general rule was confirmed by the European Court of Justice in the *Meroni* case. The Court in *Meroni* v. *High Authority* found that the consequences resulting from a delegation of powers are very different depending on whether it involves clearly defined executive powers the exercize of which can, therefore, be subject to strict review in the light of objective criteria determined by the delegating authority, or whether it involves a discretionary power, implying a wide margin of discretion.[140] The Court held the following:

A delegation of the first kind cannot appreciably alter the consequences involved in the exercize of the powers concerned, whereas a delegation of the second kind, since it replaces the choices of the delegator by the choices of the delegate, brings about an actual transfer of responsibility.[141]

In casu, the Court went on to find that the only lawful delegation of powers as authorized by Article 3 of the ECSC Treaty is that which relates to clearly defined executive powers, the use of which must be entirely subject to the supervision of the High Authority.[142] The Court found that a purported delegation by the High Authority of its discretionary powers to bodies, other than those established by the Treaty of Rome, is unlawful

in the Council debates preceding the adoption of the resolution which authorized the use of the UN flag for the forces fighting in Korea: '[The adoption of the resolution was important to emphasize] the unity of all those nations that are now banded together for a common purpose, and to indicate that they are acting in accordance with a higher law than one which is dictated merely by narrow national interests.' (*UNSCOR*, Fifth Year, No. 18, 476th meeting, p. 4.) See also the statement by the representative of Zimbabwe in the Security Council: S/PV. 3063, pp. 54–5.

[139] Thus, for example, de Smith, Woolf, & Jowell state that under English law it is improper for an authority to delegate wide discretionary powers to another authority over which it is incapable of exercising direct control, unless it is expressly empowered so to delegate, and that even in this case the degree of control maintained by the delegating authority over the acts of the delegate may be a material factor in determining the lawfulness of the delegation. (de Smith, Woolf, & Jowell, *supra* note 24, p. 365.)

[140] *In casu*, the Court found that there no objective criteria by which the subsidiary organs could take decisions and accordingly that they had to exercize a wide margin of discretion in carrying out the tasks entrusted to them by the High Authority. (*Meroni* case, Case 9156, [1958] *ECR* 133 at p. 154.) However, the European Court of Justice is prepared to give a very wide interpretation to the concept of implementation. For example, in *Chemiefarma* v. *Commission* the European Court found that the concept of 'implementation' includes the adoption of regulations whose provisions are of a legislative character. (*Chemiefarma* v. *Commission*, Case 41/69, [1970] *ECR* 661.) See also the cases of *Rey Soda* v. *Cassa Congluaglio Zuccherio* Case, 23/75, [1975] *ECR* 1279; and *Commission* v. *Council*, Case 16/88, [1989] ECR 3457, para. 10.

[141] Meroni case, *ibidem*, p. 152.   [142] *Ibidem*.

under the Treaty of Rome.[143] In reaching this decision the Court in effect applied the non-delegation doctrine. The Court found:

To delegate a discretionary power, by entrusting it to bodies other than those which the Treaty has established to effect and supervise the exercize of such power each within the limits of its own authority, would render that guarantee ineffective.[144]

Thus the actual transfer of responsibility was not in itself the reason why the Court found the purported delegation of powers to be unlawful. The problem was that the High Authority could not under the terms of establishment of the subsidiary organs exercize direct authority and control over them in terms of being able to change their decisions.[145] From the tenor of the Court's judgment it seems clear that if the High Authority had retained the right to change the decisions of its subsidiary organs then the delegation would have been lawful.[146] The rationale for this is that the institutional

[143] The Court found as follows: '. . . the delegation of powers granted to the Brussels agencies by Decision No 14/55 gives those agencies a degree of latitude which implies a wide margin of discretion and cannot be considered as compatible with the requirements of the Treaty. The decision . . . is unlawful from the point of view of the Treaty and it must . . . be annulled.' (*Meroni* case, *ibidem*, p. 154.) The case of *Meroni* has important consequences for the delegation of power by the Security Council since Article 53 of the Treaty of Rome authorizes the High Authority to delegate powers to a subsidiary organ for the same reason as that in Article 29 of the Charter: 'for the performance of its functions'. Article 53 of the Treaty of Rome authorizes a delegation of those powers 'necessary for the performance of the tasks set out in Article 3'. See further: Chapter 3 which deals with the delegation by the Council of its Chapter VII powers to UN subsidiary organs.

[144] *Meroni* case, *ibidem*, p. 152. As Hartley points out when discussing this aspect of the *Meroni* decision: 'This distinction between discretionary and non-discretionary (ministerial) powers is, of course, known to English administrative law and its adoption here may be justified on the ground that the authors of the Treaties were prepared to grant executive discretionary powers to the Commission because they had confidence in it; they might not have been prepared to see these same powers exercized by an outside body not subject to the safeguards applicable to the Commission itself.' (Hartley, *supra* note 51, p. 124.)

[145] As the Advocate-General in his earlier report in this case had noted in more general terms: 'Let it suffice for me to extract two points which, in a modern State founded on the rule of law, seem to me to be generally accepted as conditions governing the delegation of the administrative powers of public authorities to private associations: the delegation must be governed by a law which specifies the content of the delegation precisely and which must guarantee not only sufficient control by the State, but also complete legal protection against the measures adopted by these associations. . . . In my opinion, these two points are also of necessity fundamental for our Community law, because the Treaty does not expressly lay down rules concerning this question.' (*Opinion of Mr Advocate-General Romer in Meroni v. High Authority* [1958] *ECR* 177 at 190.)

[146] The Court states: 'In reserving to itself the power to refuse its approval, the High Authority has not retained sufficient powers for the delegation resulting from Decision No 14/ 55 to be contained in the limits defined above.' (*Meroni* case, *ibidem*, p. 154.) Moreover, under UK law an otherwise invalid delegation of power to a private party may be saved if the delegator reserves a power to review a decision: see de Smith, Woolf, & Jowell, *supra* note 24, p. 365; and *R v. Greater London Council; Ex parte Blackburn* [1976] 1 WLR 550. The Court of Appeal held in *Blackburn* that the power of review may be vested in someone other than the delegator provided that the body given the review power is one to whom the power could lawfully be delegated. (This latter part of the Court's judgment has already been applied in the UN context. In the *Application for Review* case the International Court of Justice engaged in

safeguards inherent in the decision-making processes of the High Authority would be effectively guaranteed if the Authority could at any time change the decision of its delegate.

This point about the institutional decision-making processes of the delegator being brought to bear, or for our purposes having the potential to do so, on a decision is of fundamental importance.[147]

The main institutional characteristic of the Security Council's decision-making process is the power of the veto. The provision of the veto in respect of any decisions taken by the Council under Chapter VII seems to have been an important reason why States conferred on the Council the primary responsibility for the maintenance or restoration of peace and the competence to exercize Chapter VII powers.[148] The importance of the veto power being given to the five Permanent Members in respect of, *inter alia*, pro-

the inquiry, and found, that the General Assembly had the implied power to create a Committee which was established to review decisions of the Administrative Tribunal. (*Application for Review* case, *ICJ Reports (1973)*, p. 166.)) Moreover, within the law of the European Communities there is a more general obligation on a principal organ to conduct 'adequate supervision' over the performance of its functions by a subsidiary organ. In the *Fives Lille Cail Cases*, the ECJ held that the High Authority had committed a wrongful act by exercising insufficient supervision over the Joint Office of Scrap Consumers. The Court considered that the lack of supervision was inexcusable (*First Fives Lille Cail Case* (19/60, 2 and 3/61), 15 Dec. 1961, [1961] *ECR* 297), and subsequently granted damages (*Second Fives Lille Cail Case* (*Laminoirs Case*) [1965] *ECR* 934–41). In the context of mechanisms of supervision by the European Council over the exercize of powers it has delegated to the European Commission, see Bradley, K. St C., 'Comitology and the Law: Through a Glass, Darkly', *Common Market Law Review*, 29 (1992), p. 693 *et seq*. Similarly, in the US domestic context the presence of administrative safeguards for the exercize of a delegated discretionary power was held to be important. In the case of *Amalgamated Meat Cutters* v. *Connally*, the District Court for the District of Columbia decided to uphold the constitutionality of the Economic Stabilization Act of 1970 on the basis of the substantial and procedural safeguards the Act contained which were designed to prevent the administrative abuse of power. (337 Fed. Supp. (DDC 1971) 737, at 764.) Judge Leventhal especially emphasized judicial review, congressional oversight, the procedural requirements of the Administrative Procedure Act, and previous and expectable future administrative experience in administering price controls that would lead to the development of more precise standards. (*Ibidem*, 746–63.)

[147] The importance of the decision-making processes of an organ of an international organization being part of its institutional characteristics was stated earlier by the International Court of Justice in the *Voting Procedure* case. The Court found: 'The voting system . . . forms one of the characteristics of the organs. Taking decisions by a two-thirds majority vote or by a simple majority vote is one of the distinguishing features of the General Assembly, while the unanimity rule was one of the distinguishing features of the Council of the League of Nations. These two systems are characteristic of different organs, and one system cannot be substituted for the other without constitutional amendment.' (*ICJ Reports (1955)*, at p. 75.) See also Judge Bustamente, *ibidem*, p. 82; Judge Lauterpacht, *ibidem*, pp. 108–13; and Judge Fitzmaurice in the *Namibia* case, *ICJ Reports (1971)*, pp. 285–6.

[148] The general requirement provided for by Article 27(3) is that any Security Council decision on a non-procedural issue is subject to the veto of any of the five Permanent Members. See on the veto power: Cot and Pellet, *supra* note 1, p. 495; Simma, *supra* note 1, p. 430; Blum, Y., *Eroding the United Nations Charter* (1993), Chapter 9; Kelsen, *supra* note 9, pp. 245–58; McDougal, M., and Gardner, R., 'The Veto and the Charter: An Interpretation for Survival', *Yale Law Journal*, 60 (1951), p. 209; Bailey, S., *Voting in the Security Council* (1969), pp. 26–41, and *Procedure of the Security Council* (1997); and Caron, *supra* note 14, pp. 566–88.

posed enforcement measures was emphasized in the San Francisco Declaration of 7 June 1945, where the USA, former USSR, China, and the UK stated:

In view of the primary responsibilities of the permanent Members, they could not be expected, in the present condition of the world, to assume the obligation to act in so serious a matter as the maintenance of international peace and security in consequence of a decision in which they had not concurred. Therefore, if a majority voting in the Security Council is to be made possible, the only practicable method is to provide, in respect of non-procedural decisions, for unanimity of the permanent Members plus the concurring votes of at least two of the non-permanent Members. . . . For all these reasons, the four sponsoring Governments agreed on the Yalta formula and have presented it to this Conference as essential if an international organization is to be created through which all peace-loving nations can effectively discharge their common responsibilities for the maintenance of international peace and security.[149]

Moreover, the veto was and still is perceived as an important institutional limitation on the use of Chapter VII enforcement powers by the Council. As Herdegen has observed:

Under the Charter, the primary safeguard against an unbalanced dynamism does not lie with judicial control, but rather with a political check—the veto. . . . Thus the primary restraint and check against excessive interventionism by the Security Council lies with an inherent element of the decision-making process within this body itself. This element, and not dynamic intervention by the ICJ, is the main guardian of the Security Council's abstention from irrationality and abuse of powers.[150]

The question which arises is does the existence of the veto as a particular institutional requirement of the Council's decision-making processes mean that the Council cannot delegate its Chapter VII powers using its general or specific competence to delegate? Strict application of the non-delegation doctrine may well prohibit the Council from delegating certain of its Chapter VII powers.[151] In this regard, the importance of the veto has been

---

[149] 'Statement by the Delegations of the Four Sponsoring Governments on Voting Procedure in the Security Council', Annex to the Commentary to Article 27 in Simma, *supra* note 1, p. 467 at p. 469. Moreover, as Degni-Segui states in respect of the choice of the Security Council as having the primary responsibility for the maintenance of peace and security: '. . . le choix du Conseil de sécurité s'explique par le nombre et la qualité de ses membres, animés du souci des Etats membres "d'assurer l'action rapide et efficace de l'Organisation". Le Conseil de sécurité offre, en effet, par rapport à l'Assemblée générale, l'avantage d'être un organe restreint au sein duquel les cinq grandes puissances ont un siège permanent et disposent en outre d'un droit de veto. Au-delà du Conseil de sécurité c'est, en définitive, à elles qu'est dévolu le rôle principal du maintien de la paix. Celle-ci ne peut être maintenue sans leur appui financier et militaire. Le droit de veto, dont l'exercice relève d'un pouvoir discrétionnaire, vient davantage renforcer leur poids politique et juridique, si bien qu'aucune décision ne peut être prise par le Conseil sans le consentement de l'un quelconque du "club des cinq" et *a fortiori* contre eux.' (Cot and Pellet, *supra* note 1, pp. 450–1.)

[150] Herdegen, *supra* note 101, p. 154.

[151] See, for example, *supra* Section III(2)(b)(i).

explained by Degni-Segui in Cot and Pellet's *La Charte des Nations Unies* in the following terms:

On peut difficilement soutenir, en effet, qu'un organe qui a reçu délégation de pouvoir puisse à son tour en déléguer l'exercice à un autre organe. De plus, l'article 24, paragraphe 1, comme il a été indiqué plus haut, met à la charge du Conseil l'obligation de s'acquitter de sa mission. Comme plusieurs délégations l'ont souligné au sein du Conseil, celui-ci doit lui-même assumer ses responsabilités et non 's'esquiver' lorsqu'il se trouve devant un cas difficile et . . . les passer à un autre organe des Nations Unies. Il a été curieusement soutenu qu'en 'renvoyant la question à l'Assemblée générale (. . .) celui-ci (le Conseil) s'acquitte de sa responsabilité en la matière'. Cette thèse méconnaît l'esprit de la Charte qui, précisément, par l'emploi discrétionnaire du veto, interdit qu'aucune 'action' en matière du maintien de la paix puisse intervenir sans l'accord d'un seul Membre permanent, *a fortiori* de tout le Conseil. C'est dans ce sens que le professeur VIRALLY observe qu'aux yeux des fondateurs de l'Organisation, il est préférable que le système de sécurité collective ne fonctionne pas, que l'Organisation par conséquent, demeure sans agir face à un conflit déterminé, plutôt que de prendre des mesures qui risqueraient d'entraîner une crise entre les grandes puissances.[152]

It is not just the existence of the veto as an institutional requirement of the decision-making processes of the Council which may prohibit a delegation of powers. The additional institutional decision-making process which has been provided by the Charter as a fundamental guarantee when the Council is exercising Chapter VII powers is that the ten non-permanent Members can also veto in effect a resolution by voting against a particular resolution. This is the case since Article 27(3) requires an 'affirmative vote of nine members' for the adoption of a resolution.[153]

However, in general terms it is contended that there should not be strict application of the non-delegation doctrine because of the veto such that the Council cannot delegate its discretionary powers.[154] It has been explained above that if a delegating organ exercises a sufficient degree of authority

---

[152] Cot and Pellet, *supra* note 1, p. 457.

[153] Thus, assuming a strict application of the non-delegation doctrine, in order for the Council—when delegating its powers to, for example, a subsidiary organ—to respect the institutional decision-making processes which it is required to comply with under the Charter—it would have to establish a subsidiary organ with composition identical to that of the Council. Identical composition is necessary in order to guarantee the veto power of both the Permanent and non-permanent Members. Moreover, it is contended that the UN Member States which are non-permanent Members of the Council at the time would have to be part of the composition of any such subsidiary organ since to change the Members would violate Article 23(2) of the Charter which provides for the election of the non-permanent Members for a period of two years. In the case of a strict application of the non-delegation doctrine, the establishment of a subsidiary organ cannot be used by the Council, in the case where the non-permanent Members are using their veto to oppose the involvement of the Council in a particular Chapter VII operation, to seek to change the composition of the non-permanent Members of the Council by establishing a subsidiary organ composed of the Permanent Members but several different non-permanent Members.

[154] Cf. *supra* Section III(2)(b)(i).

and control over the exercize of its delegated power this may provide sufficient guarantee that the delegator's decision-making processes are brought to bear on the exercize of the power.[155] As long as the Council exercizes effective overall authority and control over the use of its delegated Chapter VII powers, the role of the five Permanent Members is sufficiently guaranteed. However, the danger with a delegation of Chapter VII powers is that once the power is delegated then a Permanent Member could veto a proposed subsequent decision of the Council that was intended to exercize the Council's authority and control over the way in which the delegated power was being exercized. It is for this reason that the observance of the conditions that attach to a delegation of Chapter VII powers to Member States are of such importance:[156] in particular the clear specification by the Council of the objective for which powers are being delegated, the fulfilment of which will lead to the automatic termination of the delegation of powers.[157]

The additional institutional characteristic of the Council's decision-making processes that must be guaranteed when delegating Chapter VII powers is that provided for by Article 44 of the Charter, as explained above.[158]

In summary, for a delegation of discretionary Chapter VII powers to be lawful, the Council must ensure that it retains the right at all times to change the decision of its delegate so that it can exercize effective authority and control over the way in which the delegated powers are being exercized.[159]

---

[155] See *supra* notes 146–7 and corresponding text. Moreover, in the case of the veto-power in the Council, the five Permanent Members have the right initially of course to veto the decision to delegate Chapter VII powers. This is of considerable importance to Schermers and Blokker in order for the Council to have the competence to delegate these powers: Schermers and Blokker, *supra* note 34, pp. 154–5.

[156] For these conditions, see *infra* Section II in Chapter 4.

[157] See further on this requirement: *infra* notes 51–60 in Chapter 4.

[158] See *supra* notes 134–6 and corresponding text.

[159] Cf. the position in Canada where the issue of a delegation of discretionary power without the concomitant setting of limits to the exercize of that power has arisen in the Canadian Supreme Court case of *Gavin et al.* v. *The Queen* ((1956) *ILR*, p. 154). In that case, seventeen fishermen were convicted for contravening section 7(b) of the Lobster Fishery Regulations for the Maritime Provinces of Quebec. The Regulations imposed restrictions on the time and size of the lobster catch in certain areas of the Gulf of St Lawrence. (*Ibidem.*) Chief Justice Campbell upheld the validity of a delegation of discretionary powers in the following terms: 'As the Parliament of Canada has not directly passed any legislation fixing a relevant limit for fishing operations in the locality concerned, we must consider whether Parliament has effectively delegated its power in that respect to the Governor in Council, and, if so, whether the latter has effectively exercized such delegated powers so as to validate section 7(b). It cannot be disputed that Parliament had the power to delegate its legislative authority to the Governor in Council or other body of its creation. If such delegation has taken place, the depository of the powers and authority of Parliament can exercise those powers and authority, to the extent delegated, as effectively as Parliament itself could have exercized them. It may, as the appellant's counsel urges, be eminently desirable that Parliament should specifically enact as much of its substantive legislation as possible, especially on points of fundamental importance, and should entrust to the other bodies only a limited discretionary authority to provide for varying

(iii) When powers are being delegated the limitations on the exercize of the power must be imposed on the delegate

The third consequence of the application of the *delegatus non potest delegare* doctrine to the Council results in the principle that the Council cannot delegate its powers in such a way that the delegate is allowed to exercize the power in a way other than that specified by the Charter. If this were not the case then the Council would be delegating a power greater than that which it is given by its constituent treaty. As such, this principle is an important corollary to the limitation dealt with above that an organ cannot delegate powers which it does not itself possess.[160] And, moreover, to the principle that the rights a State possesses, *vis-à-vis* an international organization in the exercize of its delegated powers, are also possessed and can be exercized against the entity to which these powers have been further delegated.[161]

To put the principle in more general terms: when a principal organ delegates a power to an entity, the limitations on the exercize of this power which exist under the constituent instrument must be imposed also on the exercize of power by the delegate. This restriction on the competence of a principal organ to delegate its powers has been recognized under the general law of international institutions and in the context of the United Nations Charter.

In the law of international institutions this principle has been applied by the European Court of Justice in the case of *Meroni* v. *High Authority*.[162] The facts of the case are dealt with above.[163] For our present purposes, the Court found that the purported delegation of power was unlawful due to, *inter alia*, the fact that the High Authority had attempted to delegate powers wider than those which it possessed itself.[164] The Court found that certain obligations and restrictions which applied when the High Authority was exercizing its power to impose fines were not applicable to the two

---

details and machinery to carry them out. This, however, is a political question, and not a judicial one. As Lord FitzGerald remarked in *Hodge v. The Queen* (1993), 9 App. Cas. 117 at p. 132, "how far it [a Legislature] shall seek the aid of subordinate agencies, and how long it shall continue them, are matters for each legislature, and not for Courts of Law, to decide". I fail to see how the power to make such Regulations could be effective, especially with regard to sea-coast fisheries, unless it contained an implied authority to make the Regulations valid beyond low-water mark. Section 34 therefore appears, by necessary intendment, to confer such a delegated authority on the Governor in Council, and the remaining question is whether, or not, that authority has in turn been validly exercized.' (*Ibidem*, p. 157.)

[160] See *supra* Section III(1).

[161] For application of this principle in the context of UN subsidiary organs, see *infra* note 183 in Chapter 3.

[162] Case 9156, [1958] *ECR* 133.

[163] See *supra* notes 47–52 and accompanying text.

[164] *Meroni* case, Case 9156, [1958] *ECR* 133, p. 150.

subsidiary organs when exercising this delegated power.[165] The fact that the subsidiary organs could take decisions which were exempt from the conditions to which they would have been subject if they had been adopted directly by the High Authority gave the subsidiary organs in reality more extensive powers than those which the High Authority itself possessed under the Treaty. Accordingly, the Court found that the purported delegation of power in this case infringed the Treaty of Rome and was thus unlawful.[166] The Court held:

Even if the delegation resulting from Decision No 14/55 appeared as legal from the point of view of the Treaty, it could not confer upon the authority receiving the delegation powers different from those which the delegating authority itself received under the Treaty.[167]

In the context of the UN, the issue was raised by the representative of France in the following manner during the debate on the establishment of an interim committee by the UN General Assembly: 'the Assembly could not delegate its powers to a subordinate authority; for, if it had certain powers, it was in virtue of the guarantees provided by its constitution'.[168]

To conclude on this point, the Security Council cannot delegate a power without requiring the delegate to observe the same Charter limitations that the Council is under when exercising the power.

There is an additional consequence of the application of the object and purpose of the non-delegation doctrine to the law of international institutions. In the US context Freedman has stated the following:

The doctrine of delegation of legislative power to private parties thus rests upon fundamental concerns for the character of the delegate and for the nature of the decision Congress has committed to the delegate. . . . The doctrine of delegation of legislative power to private parties thus searches the fundamental question of

---

[165] *Ibidem*, p. 149. In particular, under Article 15 of the European Coal and Steel Community (ECSC) Treaty the High Authority must give reasons for its decisions, but this obligation was not imposed on the two subsidiary organs. Moreover, the decisions of the subsidiary organs were not made subject to review by the European Court of Justice: a condition which applied to the exercize of power by the High Authority: see *ibidem*.

[166] *Ibidem*, p. 150.

[167] *Ibidem*. Moreover, as the Advocate-General had earlier stated in his Opinion in the case: 'At the very least, however, it is necessary to require that the guarantees laid down by the Treaty as to legal protection shall continue to exist even in the case of delegation. . . . The High Authority cannot evade those guarantees by leaving it to agencies to which powers have been delegated to adopt in its own place the decisions . . .' (*Opinion of Mr Advocate-General Romer in Meroni v. High Authority* [1958] *ECR* 177 at 190.) Accordingly, the Advocate-General went on to state: 'Thus the decisive element is whether the guarantees of legal protection to be found in the Treaty also exist in the case of a delegation of powers.' (*Opinion of Mr Advocate-General Romer in Meroni v. High Authority* [1958] *ECR* 177 at 194.)

[168] 77th meeting of the General Assembly, A/C. 1/196, *GAOR*, [1947], p. 162. On the controversy surrounding the establishment of this interim committee by the General Assembly, see *infra* notes 53–60 and corresponding text in Chapter 3.

institutional competence to perform a governmental task. The doctrine's special role is to determine whether a particular delegate is competent to perform the specific task delegated to him. That determination must take account of the fact that there is a crucial nexus between the nature of the particular legislative power being delegated and the character of the private party chosen to exercize it. The relative degree of disinterestedness that the delegate can be expected to bring to the task of decision and his relative degree of expertness in performing the task are significant criteria for estimating the institutional competence, in a constitutional sense, of a private party to whom Congress has delegated legislative power.[169]

The institutional competence of a delegate to exercize the delegated power is thus of fundamental importance to the lawfulness of the delegation.[170] This issue is discussed further in Chapters 2 to 6 which examine, where relevant, the institutional competence of the UN Secretary-General, UN subsidiary organs, UN Member States, and regional arrangements to exercize delegated Chapter VII powers.

(iv) The terms of a Council resolution delegating Chapter VII powers are to be construed narrowly

The final consequence of the application of the *delegatus non potest delegare* doctrine to the Council is that the terms of a resolution which delegates Chapter VII powers are to be interpreted narrowly.

The issue of interpretation is important since the question whether a delegation of powers is so broad that its constitutionality becomes doubtful will depend on an interpretation of the exact scope of the powers conferred.[171]

The importance of construing Chapter VII powers narrowly has been recognized by, for example, the representative of Brazil in the Security

---

[169] Freedman, *supra* note 95, pp. 334–5.

[170] See also *infra* note 178 and corresponding text.

[171] It is thus possible for a judicial body examining the lawfulness of a purported delegation of powers to circumvent altogether potential problems of legality by making a narrow interpretation of the language of a resolution. This has certainly been the recent approach of the US Supreme Court when dealing with issues of delegation. Two examples suffice to illustrate the approach. In *National Cable Television* v. *United States*, the Court refused to read literally the Independent Offices Appropriations Act of 1952 when it was applied to the Federal Communications Commission (FCC) which sought to impose fees on community antenna television. The Act prescribed that in deciding, among other things, to impose fees, 'value to the recipient, public policy or interest served' should be taken into consideration. The party seeking to invalidate the provision, argued before the Supreme Court that the fixing of a fee that took into consideration public policy or interests served could be regarded as a levying of taxes. The power to tax, it was said, is one of those essential legislative functions that Congress is not allowed to delegate. The Court used statutory interpretation to sidestep the issue when it stated '[i]t would be such a sharp break with our traditions to conclude that Congress had bestowed on a federal agency the taxing power that we read 31 USC para. 438a [31 USCS para. 438a] narrowly as authorizing not a "tax" but a "fee"'. (*National Cable Television* v. *United States*, 415 US 336 at 341.) The Court found therefore that it was unnecessary to reach the

Council debates which preceded the establishment of the UN War Crimes Tribunal for the former Yugoslavia. The representative observed:

As regards the definition of the best method for the establishment of an ad hoc international criminal tribunal, it should be borne in mind that the authority of the Security Council is not self-constituted but originates from a delegation of powers by the whole Membership of the Organization. It is never too much to recall that the Security Council, in the exercize of its responsibilities, acts on behalf of the States Members of the United Nations, in accordance with Article 24, paragraph 1, of the Charter. Just as the authority of the Council does not spring from the Council itself but derives from the fact that certain responsibilities have been conferred upon it by all the Members of the United Nations, the powers of the Council cannot be created, recreated or reinterpreted creatively by decisions of the Council itself, but must be based invariably on specific Charter provisions. . . . It is precisely because the Council exercizes a delegated responsibility in a field as politically sensitive as the maintenance of international peace and security that the task of interpreting its competence calls for extreme caution, in particular when invoking language of Chapter VII of the Charter. Especially when the Council is being increasingly called upon to fully exercize the considerable powers entrusted to it, the definition of such powers must be construed strictly on the basis of the text of the relevant Charter provisions. To go beyond that would be legally inconsistent and politically unwise.[172]

Having regard to the caution called for in this statement together with the permissibility of a delegation of discretionary Chapter VII powers, as explained above, it is appropriate that the scope of delegated Chapter VII powers are to be construed narrowly. However, against the full application of the doctrine, the cogent argument can be made that broad delegations are often essential for flexible and effective decision-making in order to maintain or restore international peace and security. This argument rests partly on the notion that delegates are unable to respond adequately to new

---

delegation question and that 'the hurdles revealed . . . lead us to read the Act narrowly to avoid constitutional problems'. (*Ibidem*, 342.) The Court went on to read the challenged section of the Act as not relevant to the case. (*Ibidem*, 343.) In other words the Court, by narrowly construing the fee so as not to be a tax, thereby avoided altogether the issue of the validity of the delegation of powers. A similar approach was adopted by the US Supreme Court in the *Benzene* case, where the Court dealt with the question whether the delegation, under section 3(8) of the Occupational Safety and Health Act of 1970, of the power to 'assur[e], to the extent feasible . . . that no employee will suffer material impairment of health or functional capacity' required the agency to find a significant risk of harm before making a rule. (*Industrial Union Department* v. *American Petroleum Inst.*, 448 US 607 at 662.) In doing so, the Court rejected the opposing argument made by the Government on the basis that otherwise 'the statute would make such a "sweeping delegation of legislative power" that it might be unconstitutional. . . . A construction of the Statute that avoids this kind of open-end grant should certainly be favored.' (*Ibidem*, 646.) This approach of the Court has been fiercely criticized by Schoenbrod, D., 'The Delegation Doctrine: Could the Court Give it Substance?', *Michigan Law Review*, 83 (1985), p. 1223 at pp. 1271–4.

[172] S/PV.3175. pp. 6–7.

and unforeseen problems unless the terms of their authorization affords them considerable flexibility.[173]

Thus to summarize, there are four main effects of the application of the non-delegation doctrine on the general competence of the Council to delegate its Chapter VII powers. First, the Council is prohibited from delegating certain of its Chapter VII powers. Second, a discretionary power can only be delegated when the Council retains such a degree of authority and control over its delegate so that it can change the decision of its delegate at any time.[174] Third, when powers are being delegated the limitations on the exercize of the power must be imposed on the delegate. Fourth, the terms of a delegation of Chapter VII powers are to be construed narrowly. In addition to these limitations, we recall the more general limitation explained above that the principal organ must possess the power it is purporting to delegate. These limitations operate in any instance where the Security Council delegates its Chapter VII powers and thus they are of importance to the delegation of Chapter VII powers to the UN Secretary-General, UN subsidiary organs, Member States, and regional arrangements, examined below in Chapters 2 to 6. However, in terms of an authoritative determination of the *vires* of a particular delegation of powers, this largely depends on the International Court of Justice being able to rule on the legality of purported delegations of power by the Council.[175]

IV. THE INTERNATIONAL COURT OF JUSTICE AND THE JUSTICIABILITY OF A DELEGATION OF CHAPTER VII POWERS

It must be emphasized that the effect of an invocation by States of the elements of the legal framework governing a delegation by the Council of its Chapter VII powers will often depend on the other, often political, considerations that the Council takes into account when making decisions. This does not, however, detract from the restraints which the legal framework governing the process of a delegation of powers places on the Council when engaged in this activity. As explained above, the decision by the Security Council when and how to carry out Chapter VII enforcement

---

[173] In the US context, see, for example, Mashaw, 'Prodelegation: Why Administrators Should Make Political Decisions', *Journal of Law, Economics and Organization*, 1 (1985), p. 81 at pp. 91–2, 95–6.

[174] This is, however, subject to the *sui generis* exception in the case of UN subsidiary organs exercising functions which the Council does not itself possess: see *infra* notes 34–46 and corresponding text in Chapter 3.

[175] Cf. the views of some authors who consider that the General Assembly has a very important role to play in this respect: see *supra* notes 124–5.

powers is a matter of political discretion which the Charter leaves solely to the Council.[176] It is accepted that the International Court of Justice should not seek to interfere in the exercize by the Council of this political discretion.[177] However, it is not the exercize of political discretion which is at the heart of the determination of the legality of a purported delegation of Chapter VII powers by the Council. The Council possesses a discretion in this regard, but the point is that the exercize of this discretion does not take place outside our legal framework. As Brownlie has stated: 'there is no dichotomy involving discretionary power and the Rule of Law. A discretion can only exist within the law. . . . [The] conclusion must be that the Security Council is subject to the test of legality in terms of its designated institutional competence.'[178] As described above, the Charter and the wider law of international institutions place certain limitations on the exercize by the Council of its general competence to delegate Chapter VII powers. Moreover, there are additional limitations that exist on the specific competence

[176] See *supra* note 8 and corresponding text. Cf. the statement by the Venezuelan representative at the San Francisco Conference who claimed for the General Assembly the right to control the Security Council in order to prevent it from transgressing established legal principles: 'This section contains such a broad delegation of the powers of the International Union [the UN] to the Security Council that it appears practically unacceptable . . . such a delegation of powers can be admitted [only] if there are attributed to the central organization, that is, the General Assembly, the necessary powers of control and if the Member States are given the remedy of an appeal thereto.' (*UNCIO*, vol. 4, p. 253 (General Doc. 2, G/7(d)(1), of 5 May 1945, p. 12), and *UNCIO*, vol. 11, p. 768 (Commission III, Security Council, Doc. 360, III/1/16, 15 May 1945, p. 4).) Needless to say, this suggestion was not at the time, or subsequently, taken up by UN Member States or UN political organs.

[177] Where the judicial function was concerned in the *Haya de la Torre* case, the Court, which was asked to pronounce on various ways of determining ways of terminating diplomatic asylum, stated: 'A choice amongst them could not be based on legal considerations, but only on considerations of practicability or of political expediency; it is not part of the Court's judicial function to make such a choice.' (*Haya de la Torre Case (Colom./Peru), ICJ Reports* (1951), p. 71 at p. 79.) See generally on the issue of the review by the International Court of the legality of decisions by the Security Council: Brownlie, I., 'The Decisions of Political Organs of the United Nations and the Rule of Law', in *Essays in Honour of Wang Tieya* (Macdonald, R.St J., ed.) (1993), p. 91; Bowett, D., 'The Impact of Security Council Decisions on Dispute Settlement Procedures', *EJIL*, 5 (1994), p. 89, and Bowett, D., 'Judicial and Political Functions of the Security Council and the International Court of Justice', in *The Changing Constitution of the United Nations* (Fox, H., ed.) (1997), p. 73; Crawford, J., 'The Charter of the United Nations as a Constitution', in *The Changing Constitution of the United Nations* (Fox, H., ed.) (1997), p. 3 at pp. 11–15; Bedjaoui, M., *The New World Order and the Security Council: Testing the Legality of Its Acts* (1994); Gowlland-Debbas, V., 'The Relationship between the International Court of Justice and the Security Council in the Light of the *Lockerbie* case', *AJIL*, 88 (1994), p. 643; Alvarez, J., 'Judging the Security Council', *AJIL*, 90 (1996), p. 1; Franck, T., 'The "Powers of Appreciation": Who is the Ultimate Guardian of UN Legality?', *AJIL*, 86 (1992), p. 519; Reisman, W. M., 'The Constitutional Crisis in the United Nations', *AJIL*, 87 (1993), p. 83; Akande, D., 'The International Court of Justice and the Security Council: Is There Room for Judicial Control of Decisions of the Political Organs of the United Nations?', *ICLQ*, 46 (1997), p. 309; Watson, G., 'Constitutionalism, Judicial Review, and the World Court', *Harvard International Law Journal*, 34 (1993), p. 1; and Herdegen, *supra* note 101.

[178] Brownlie, *ibidem*, pp. 95–6.

of the Council to delegate its Chapter VII powers to UN principal organs,
UN subsidiary organs, and UN Member States whether acting nationally or
through a regional arrangement.[179] In addition to these limitations on the
general and specific competencies of the Council to delegate Chapter VII
powers, there are limitations which attach to the exercize of the power
depending on the nature of the delegate.[180] It is these sets of limitations
which provide the objective criteria by which the legality of a delegation[181]
by the Council of its Chapter VII powers is to be judged;[182] and, moreover,
may allow the Court to rule on the legality of an exercize by a delegate of
Chapter VII powers. Such review is an important way that the Court can
defend the legitimacy of the UN system for maintaining or restoring international peace and security.[183] The use of this mechanism is not, however,

---

[179] See Chapters 2–6.

[180] These are examined with respect to the Secretary-General, UN subsidiary organs, UN
Member States, and regional arrangements, in Chapters 2–6.

[181] Once the limitations which exist on the exercize of a delegation of powers have been fully
enumerated, there is no barrier to a review process which examines the compatibility of the
exercize of a discretion of the Council to delegate with these clearly specified limitations. In
other UN fora the review of the exercize of a discretionary power *vis-à-vis* its limitations has
been upheld. See, for example, the case of *Peynado* v. *Secretary-General* where the United
Nations Administrative Tribunal reviewed the validity of the exercize by the UN Secretary-
General of a discretionary power which had been delegated to him by the UN General
Assembly: see decision of 30 Oct. 1970, 47 *ILR*, p. 356. Accordingly, to deny such a power of
review in the case of the Security Council seems neither appropriate nor consonant with
established practice of the UN in other areas.

[182] Similarly, the Italian Constitutional Court can review indirectly the delegation by Parliament to the Government of a power to promulgate acts having the force of law, a delegation
provided for by Articles 76 and 77 of the Italian Constitution: see La Pergola, A., and Del
Duca, P., 'Community Law, International Law and the Italian Constitution', *AJIL*, 79 (1985),
p. 598 at p. 604; and case cited therein of *Pascolo* v. *Commissione straordinaria*, Judgment No.
3 of 26 Jan. 1957, 2 *Rac. uff.* 21 (1957), 1957 *Giur cost.* 11. The delegation, under the
Constitution, must be only for a limited time, according to specified criteria, and with a defined
purpose: *ibidem*. Moreover, as the Advocate-General stated in his Opinion in the *Meroni* case:
'Review by the Court must therefore look to the Treaty itself and the Court must
examine . . . whether the guarantees of legal protection to be found in the Treaty also exist in
the case of a delegation of powers.' (*Opinion of Mr Advocate-General Romer in Meroni
v. High Authority*, [1958] *ECR* 177 at 194.)

[183] An unchecked impermissible delegation of Chapter VII powers by the Council compromises the legitimacy of future Security Council action and represents an affront to the rule of
law in the workings of the Council. As Brownlie states: 'Even if the political organs have a wide
margin of appreciation in determining that they have competence by virtue of Chapter VI or
Chapter VII, and further, in making dispositions to maintain or restore international peace and
security, it does not follow that the selection of the modalities of implementation is
unconstrained by legality.' (Brownlie, *supra* note 177, p. 102.) On the concept of legitimacy in
the workings of the Council, Franck has stated the point when he observed: '. . . it is clear that
the Charter, an inter-state treaty, delegates only *limited* sovereign powers to the Council. The
legitimacy of such a system of delegation, and thus its permanence, depends upon visible and
effective checks on unsupportable aggrandizement by the Council. While it would be fool-
hardy—and entirely improbable—for the Court to substitute its judgment of what constitutes
a "threat to the peace" and what measures are appropriate in meeting such a threat, some
degree of competence to review Council decisions is essential to maintaining the confidence of
all the states that have freely chosen to delegate specific and limited powers to a supranational

unproblematic. The review of the legality of decisions of principal organs by the Court can only proceed once the Court has established some basis for its jurisdiction in accordance with Article 36 of its Statute.[184] If, however, the Court finds that it does and that it has some basis for asserting its jurisdiction in a particular case, then the legal framework governing the process of a delegation of powers and the exercize of these powers may well provide an important corpus of law by reference to which the Court can review the legality of action by the Security Council and its delegates.[185]

organ with restricted Membership.' (Franck, T., 'The United Nations as Guarantor of International Peace and Security', in *The United Nations at Age Fifty: A Legal Perspective* (1995), p. 25 at p. 37.)

[184] See, for example, the *Expenses* case, *ICJ Reports* (1962), p. 151; and the *Namibia* case, *ICJ Reports* (1971), p. 6.

[185] For other grounds which may constitute a basis for review by the Court, see: Brownlie, *supra* note 177; and Bowett, *supra* note 177.

2

The Delegation of Powers to the UN Secretary-General

The Security Council may possess the competence to delegate its Chapter VII powers to the other UN principal organs. However, in practice the Council has mostly delegated such powers to the UN Secretary-General (hereafter in this Chapter, 'SG').[1] It is, accordingly, the legal issues which arise from a delegation of Chapter VII powers by the Council to the SG which is the focus of this Chapter. As such, it is beyond the scope of our present enquiry to examine the full contribution of the SG to the maintenance or restoration of international peace and security.[2]

There are three main reasons why the Security Council may decide to delegate its Chapter VII powers to the SG.[3] First, where the members of the Security Council consider that a situation requiring the use of Chapter VII

---

[1] This approach of the SG constituting, for operational purposes, the Secretariat has some support: see *UNJYB* (1982), p. 190; and Kelsen, H., *The Law of the United Nations* (1951), p. 136.

[2] It suffices to note, in this regard, that the SG may operate at the following three different levels when acting to maintain or restore international peace and security: as a UN principal organ who is available, for example, to be used for his good offices or exercizing his rights under Article 99 of the Charter; exercizing delegated functions; and exercizing delegated powers: see *Repertory of Practice of UN Organs, Supplement No. 1* (1958), p. 379. See more generally on the SG: Schwebel, S., *The Secretary-General of the United Nations* (1952); Meron, T., 'Status and Independence of the International Civil Service', *Hague Recueil des Cours*, 167 (1980-II), p. 285; Franck, T., 'The Role and Future Prospects of the Secretary-General of the United Nations', in *The Adaptation of Structures and Methods at the United Nations* (Bardonnet, D., ed.) (1986), First Part Chapter 2; Szasz, P., 'The Role of the UN Secretary-General: Some Legal Aspects', *New York University Journal of International Law and Politics*, 24 (1991–2), p. 161; Gordenker, L., *The United Nations Secretary-General and the Maintenance of International Peace* (1967); Alexandrowicz, C., 'The Secretary-General of the United Nations', *ICLQ*, 11 (1962), p. 1109; and Elaraby, N., 'The Office of the Secretary-General and the Maintenance of International Peace and Security', *Revue Egyptienne du Droit International*, 42 (1986), p. 1.

[3] Whether it is the SG who has procured a delegation of Chapter VII powers or whether the Council has at its own initiative decided to delegate such powers is not the subject of this Chapter. Suffice to note, however, that Franck considers that the SG may 'solicit broad delegations of authority from the political organs'. (Franck, T., 'Finding a Voice: How the Secretary-General Makes Himself Heard in the Councils of the United Nations', in *Essays in Honour of Judge Manfred Lachs* (Makarczyck, J., ed.) (1984), p. 481. A reason for such a procurement of a delegation of powers may well be that the potentialities of the SG are limited when the Security Council is not ready to exercize its full constitutional authority: see Avakov, V., 'The Secretary-General in the Afghanistan Conflict, the Iran-Iraq War, and the Gulf Crisis', in *The Challenging Role of the UN Secretary-General* (Rivlin, B., and Gordenker, L., eds.) (1993), p. 152 at pp. 164–5.

powers is politically very sensitive[4] or even insoluble they may delegate the responsibility to use these powers to the SG. Second, the institutional characteristics of the office of the SG are better suited than the Security Council to exercize certain of the powers of Chapter VII. For example, this Chapter gave the Council and the Military Staff Committee certain powers to deploy, command, and control military forces carrying out military enforcement action. In the absence of an effective Military Staff Committee, the Council has often chosen to delegate such powers to the SG. Third, the office of the SG is perceived as being impartial and much less subject to political considerations than the Security Council and as such has often been delegated powers by the Council to retain the legitimacy of collective enforcement measures.[5]

In exploring further such delegations of Chapter VII power, this Chapter will explore three main areas: the competence of the Security Council to delegate its Chapter VII powers to the SG; the construction of the legal framework governing the exercize of Chapter VII powers by the SG; and an analysis of the practice of the Council when delegating its Chapter VII powers to the SG and the practice of the SG in exercizing these powers.

I. THE COMPETENCE OF THE COUNCIL TO DELEGATE CHAPTER VII POWERS TO THE SECRETARY-GENERAL

There is no express provision in the Charter which provides the Security Council with the competence to delegate its Chapter VII powers to the other principal organs. However, as explained in Chapter 1, the Security Council does possess a general competence to delegate its Chapter VII powers to other entities that are part of the Organization, which would of course include other UN principal organs and thus, for our present purposes, the SG.[6] In addition to this general competence, the Council's competence to delegate Chapter VII powers to the SG is supported by reference to an implied powers approach and the subsequent practice

[4] The politically sensitive nature of these decisions may provide a policy argument why these decisions should be kept within the Council, a politically accountable body. On the legal considerations relating to the competence of the Council to be able to delegate Chapter VII powers to the SG, see *infra* Section I.

[5] Cf. *infra* note 29. As to the independence of the UN SG, see *infra* notes 27–9 and corresponding text.

[6] It seems clear also that the General Assembly possesses such a general competence. As the UN Legal Counsel has observed: '. . . there would appear to be no constitutional objection to the Assembly either delegating some of its rule-making power to the Secretary-General or, having once done so, to later withdrawing or reducing his assigned normative powers'. (*UNJYB* (1982), p. 191.)

of the Security Council in consistently delegating these powers to the SG.[7]

The practice of the Council in delegating Chapter VII powers to the SG is examined in further detail below in Section III. A subsidiary source for the Council's competence in this area may be implied from the Charter, in particular Article 98. The General Assembly, Security Council, United Nations Economic and Social Council (ECOSOC), and Trusteeship Council have the express competence under Article 98 of the Charter to delegate to the SG the performance of their functions. This provision does not itself provide an express competence for the Security Council to delegate powers to the SG, since there is a distinction between the delegation of a power and the delegation of a function under the law of international institutions[8] such that, for our present purposes, when the SG is performing functions delegated by the Security Council under Article 98[9] he is not exercizing any discretionary powers but simply implementing decisions of the Council.[10] It is nonetheless contended that the Security Council can infer the competence to delegate its Chapter VII powers to the SG from the objects and purposes of Chapter VII and Article 98 of the Charter. The Council possessing a competence to delegate its Chapter VII powers is in accord with the object and purpose of Chapter VII: the object and purpose being that the Council should be able to take such action as it deems necessary to maintain or restore international peace and security.[11] The *raison d'être* of Article 98 is that it allows the other principal organs to use the SG in assisting in the discharge of their duties. Accordingly, an argument could be made that in those cases where the effective exercize by the Council of its Chapter VII powers requires a delegation of these powers to the SG then such a delegation is prima facie lawful. However, the determination of whether such a delegation is necessary can only be examined in a concrete case and not in the abstract. Accordingly, this issue is dealt with further below in the

---

[7] It is generally accepted that a source of constitutional authority for the exercize of a certain power by a UN organ may be the subsequent practice of the organ: see, for example, the *Namibia* case, *ICJ Reports* (1971), para. 22; and Rosenne, S., *Developments in the Law of Treaties* (1994), p. 237.

[8] We recall from Chapter 1 that the distinction between the delegation of a power and the delegation of a function under the law of international institutions lies in the degree to which real power—in other words effective decision-making power—has been transferred: see *supra* note 45 and corresponding text in Chapter 1. This distinction between delegated functions (tasks) and powers in the context of the SG has been implicitly recognized by Bowett: see Bowett, D., *United Nations Forces* (1964), p. 99.

[9] Article 98 provides, in part, that the SG 'shall perform such other functions' as are entrusted to him by the Security Council.

[10] Cf. Conforti who contends that Article 98 itself provides the basis for the delegation of power by the Council to the SG: Conforti, B., *The Law and Practice of the United Nations* (1996), p. 219.

[11] See also Kirk, G., 'The Enforcement of Security', *Yale Law Journal*, 55 (1946), p. 1081 at p. 1088.

section dealing with the practice of the Council in delegating its powers to the SG.

The limitations on the competence of the Council to delegate its Chapter VII powers to the SG are the same as those which have already been explained at length in Chapter 1.[12] These can conveniently be summarized as follows: the Council must possess the power it is purporting to delegate; the Council cannot delegate its Article 39 power to determine that a threat to, or breach of, international peace and security has come into existence or has ceased to exist; the Council cannot delegate an unrestricted power of command and control over a force carrying out military enforcement action; and, finally, the Council can delegate broad powers of discretion only if it imposes on the delegate exercising its powers those same restrictions which it must itself observe when exercising the specific power and if the Council retains the right at all times to change the decision of its delegate. The observance of these limitations by the Security Council in practice is dealt with in the third section of this Chapter.

The competence of the Council to delegate its Chapter VII powers to the SG does not mean, however, that there are no legal limitations on the SG when exercizing these powers. To the contrary, it is the purpose of the following section to establish the contours of the legal framework that governs the exercize by the SG of delegated Chapter VII powers. Accordingly, this next section is not concerned with the lawfulness of a delegation by the Council of its Chapter VII powers to the SG, but with the legal framework that governs the exercize of these powers by the SG once a lawful delegation of powers has taken place.

II. THE LEGAL FRAMEWORK GOVERNING THE EXERCIZE OF DELEGATED CHAPTER VII POWERS BY THE SECRETARY-GENERAL

There are three main areas which need to be addressed when constructing the legal framework governing the exercize by the SG of delegated Chapter VII powers. First, the competence of the SG to exercize delegated Chapter VII powers. Second, the limitations that restrict the exercize by the SG of delegated Chapter VII powers. Third, legal aspects of the interpretation by the SG of delegated Chapter VII powers.

1. *The competence of the Secretary-General to exercize delegated Chapter VII powers*

In theory the SG may not possess the competence under the Charter to exercize all the powers which the Security Council may wish to delegate to

---

[12] See *supra* Section III in Chapter 1.

him.[13] The delegation of Chapter VII powers to an entity does not automatically mean the entity has the competence to exercize the powers in question. This is important since we recall from Chapter 1 that the institutional competence of the delegate to be able to exercize the delegated power can affect the lawfulness of the initial delegation of power. The main objection which has been made to the exercize by the SG of delegated Chapter VII powers is that the SG does not possess the institutional competence under the Charter to exercize discretionary powers of decision making or to make 'policy decisions'.[14] However, this argument is unconvincing for the following three reasons. First, the fact is that the SG already possesses a discretionary power of decision making under Article 99 of the Charter.[15] Article 99 of the Charter provides as follows: 'The Secretary-General may bring to the attention of the Security Council any matter which in his opinion may threaten the maintenance of international peace and security.'[16] The scope of the power in Article 99 gives the SG the competence to make what are in effect 'policy decisions'. Whether a particular issue constitutes a threat to international peace and security is the same type of discretionary power of decision making which the Council possesses under Article 39 of the Charter.[17] It is just that the consequences of this decision being made by the Council as opposed to the SG are different.[18] Second, the legality of the SG exercizing a power of discretion has been upheld in express terms by the UN Administrative Tribunal in the case of, among others, *Peynado* v. *SG*.[19] Third, the view that the SG can exercize discretionary powers is validated also by UN practice.[20] Having regard to these three factors, it is contended that the SG does possess the competence to exercize delegated powers of discretion. This position does not mean,

---

[13] Moreover, in practice the SG may not possess the ability to carry out delegated powers due to lack of sufficient resources being supplied to him by the Council.

[14] See, for example, Elaraby, *supra* note 2, pp. 8–9.

[15] See also Schwebel, S., 'The Origins and Development of Article 99 of the Charter', in *Justice In International Law: Selected Writings of Judge Stephen M. Schwebel* (1994), p. 233 at pp. 238, 243; and Kunz, J., 'The Legal Position of the Secretary-General of the United Nations', *AJIL*, 40 (1946), p. 786 at pp. 790–1.

[16] See further on Article 99 the following: Schwebel, *ibidem*; 'Commentary to Article 99', in *La Charte des Nations Unies* (Cot, J-P., and Pellet, A., eds.) (1991), p. 1327; and 'Commentary to Article 99', in *The Charter of the United Nations* (Simma, B., ed.) (1994), p. 1044.

[17] See also Lash, J., 'Dag Hammarskjold's Conception of his Office', *International Organization*, 16 (1962), p. 551 at n. 39.

[18] The SG does not have recourse to the panoply of Chapter VII powers that the Council has in order to address the cause of the threat to, or breach of, the peace. See Schwebel, *supra* note 15, p. 237 *et sequentia*.

[19] *Peynado* v. *Secretary-General of the United Nations*, United Nations Administrative Tribunal decision of 30 Oct. 1970, 47 *ILR*, p. 356 at pp. 367–8. The Tribunal in *Peynado* observed that: 'The Tribunal in earlier judgments has consistently upheld the discretionary power of the SG to terminate all appointments other than permanent or fixed-term appointments if, in his opinion, such action would be in the interest of the United Nations.' (*Ibidem*.)

[20] See, for example, *SCOR*, 15th year, 856th meeting, paras. 34 and 35; and *infra* Section III.

however, that there are no limitations on the SG when exercizing delegated Chapter VII powers.

2. The limitations that restrict the exercize by the Secretary-General of delegated Chapter VII powers

The limitations that restrict the exercize by the SG of delegated Chapter VII powers are both express and implied.

The express limitations are those contained in the Security Council resolution which is the source of the delegated power.[21] The SG cannot exercize a power which he does not himself possess: this is in effect what he would be doing in many cases if he acted beyond the mandate given to him by the Security Council.

The implied or what may better be termed general limitations that restrict the exercize by the SG of delegated powers are twofold. First is the limitation that the opinions of UN Member States cannot constitute a sole basis for decision making by the SG. Second is the obligation of the SG to exercize a delegated power of discretion in good faith. Although these are general limitations on action by the SG, there is no reason why they do not apply to the exercize by the SG of delegated Chapter VII powers.

UN Member States are not prohibited from communicating information to the United Nations which is the basis for a subsequent decision by a UN organ or its delegate.[22] However, the view of UN Member States cannot constitute the sole basis for the decision by a UN organ such that it does not itself exercize its power of discretion and make a decision in accordance with its stipulated decision-making processes. This rule which exists as part of the law of international institutions flows from the independence of an international organization from its Member States. This was affirmed by the important case of *In re Rosescu* v. *International Atomic Energy Agency (IAEA)*[23] where the International Labour Organisation's Administrative Tribunal (ILOAT) held that the IAEA Director-General could not be bound by the wishes of a particular Member State (for example that of the staff member concerned) to refuse to renew an appointment.[24] The Tribunal found that the Director-General had misused his authority, since he let

---

[21] See also Elaraby, *supra* note 2, p. 11.

[22] See, for example, the case of *Crawford* v. *Secretary-General of the United Nations*, 20 *ILR*, p. 501.

[23] *In re Rosescu* v. *International Atomic Energy Agency (IAEA)*, ILOAT Judgment No. 431 (1980). For a more comprehensive discussion of this judgment, see Meron, T., 'In re Rosescu and the Independence of the International Civil Service', *AJIL*, 75 (1981), p. 910.

[24] On the issue of the influence of Member States on the appointment of UN Staff, see Meron, *supra* note 2, pp. 311–19.

the interests of a Member State prevail over that of the Agency.[25] Applying the principle, *mutatis mutandis*, to the case of the SG: the opinion of UN Member States cannot constitute a sole basis for decision making by the SG when he is exercizing a power of discretion:[26] there must be a degree of independence in the decision-making processes of the SG. Moreover, in the case of the SG, Article 100 of the Charter reiterates this conclusion by its express reference to the independence of the SG from UN Member States.[27] It is this independence which is the source of the perceived impartiality of the office of the SG. An important part of this independence is the exercize of a power of discretion having regard to what the SG considers to be in the best interests of the Organization and not solely in the interest of any particular State or group of States.[28] The observance by the SG of his independence when exercizing delegated powers of discretion thus constitutes a fundamental condition of a delegation of powers.[29]

The second obligation, or general limitation, on the SG is that the exercize of a power of discretion must be in good faith. In this regard, the UN Administrative Tribunal has observed:

Such discretionary power must, however, be exercized [by the SG] without improper motive so that there shall be no misuse of authority. In Judgment No. 54 (*Mauch* v. *SG of the United Nations*) the Tribunal stated: 'While the measure of power here was intended to be left completely within the discretion of the SG, this would not authorize an arbitrary or capricious exercize of the power of termination, nor the assignment of specious or untruthful reasons for the action taken, such as would connote a lack of good faith or due consideration for the rights of the staff member involved.'[30]

[25] ILOAT Judgment No. 431 at 8. To similar effect, see *Reznikov* v. *World Health Organization*, ILOAT Judgment No. 1249, and *Chadsey* v. *Universal Postal Union (No. 1)*, 43 *ILR*, p. 452.

[26] As Szasz states: 'With respect to states, any pressure or inducement brought to bear on the person of the Secretary-General would clearly be improper. . . . he cannot permit the importuning of any state to supersede his own independent exercize of his discretion.' (Szasz, *supra* note 2, p. 196.)

[27] Article 100 provides: '1. In the performance of their duties the SG and the staff shall not seek or receive instructions from any government. . . . 2. Each Member of the United Nations undertakes to respect the exclusively international character of the responsibilities of the Secretary-General and the staff and not to seek to influence them in the discharge of their responsibilities.'

[28] See also Hammarskjold, D., 'The International Civil Servant in Law and in Fact', *Press Release, SG/1035*, 29 May 1961, p. 17.

[29] However, in practice it may be difficult for the SG not to take account of the views of Member States: see Urquhart, B., 'The United Nations and International Law', *The Rede Lecture* (Cambridge University Press, 1985), p. 17. This influence by Member States has seen a few commentators contend that the SG should not be involved with the carrying out of military enforcement action: see, for example, Weiss, T., 'Overcoming the Somalia Syndrome—' "Operation Rekindle Hope?" ', *Global Governance*, 1 (1995), p. 171 at p. 177.

[30] *Peynado* v. *Secretary-General*, 47 *ILR*, p. 356 at p. 368.

When exercizing a delegated power of discretion the presumption must be that the SG fulfils this requirement.

3. The interpretation by the Secretary-General of delegated Chapter VII powers

The way in which delegated powers are to be exercized are rarely specified when the Council or Assembly delegate powers to the SG. The lack of clarity in Council resolutions that delegate powers arises from the fact that the resolutions often reflect a political compromise by Member States.[31] This lack of clarity means that the SG must exercize considerable powers of interpretation to implement such resolutions. Chapter 1 establishes that a delegation of Chapter VII powers must always be express and can never be inferred.[32] However, once a delegation of powers has occurred then the SG can imply certain additional powers from the terms of the delegation. This power of interpretation is necessary for the effective exercize by the SG of powers which he has been expressly delegated.[33]

In interpreting his delegated mandate, the SG often makes reports to the Security Council which are subsequently adopted by the Council in a resolution.[34] The SG assumes that the adoption of a report by the Council means that he can use the report to interpret the terms of the Security Council's earlier resolution which was the source of the delegated powers. The report is then used as an authoritative interpretation of the SG's delegated powers. Put differently, the SG's report can provide evidence of the Council's intention regarding the implementation of the terms of its resolution.[35]

A second way in which the SG interprets his delegated powers is to examine the amount of material resources which the Council has decided to give him to carry out his delegated powers. The amount of these resources provides an important indication of the Council's intention as to how the delegated powers should be carried out.

---

[31] See, for example, a rare admission in this respect made by Ceylon: *SCOR*, 16th year, 937th meeting, para. 91, in Higgins, R., *United Nations Peacekeeping* (1980), vol. 3, p. 120.

[32] See *supra* notes 34–6 and corresponding text in Chapter 1.

[33] See also Murphy, J., 'Force and Arms', in *United Nations Legal Order* (Schachter, O., and Joyner, C., eds.) (1995), vol. 1, p. 247 at p. 249; and Conforti, *supra* note 10.

[34] This may also include statements made by the SG before the Council: see, for example, Bowett, *supra* note 8, p. 183.

[35] This was the approach adopted by the Appeals Chamber of the International Criminal Tribunals for Rwanda and the former Yugoslavia, when in the jurisdiction stage of the *Tadic* case it made a particular finding on the basis that the 'interpretation is borne out by what could be considered as part of the preparatory works of the Statute of the International Tribunal, namely the Report of the Secretary-General'. *(Prosecutor v. Tadic (Jurisdiction) (Appeals Chamber),* 105 *ILR*, p. 453 at p. 498.)

The SG has stated that his interpretation of delegated Chapter VII powers can be challenged only in the Security Council. A consequence of this is that until the Security Council makes a decision which is contrary to the SG's interpretation then it is binding on UN Member States.[36] The difficulty in obtaining an express interpretation from the Security Council as to the content of the SG's delegated powers will often mean that in practice the SG exercizes a power of authoritative interpretation over his delegated powers.[37] SG Hammarskjold has explained this approach as follows:

Let me simply point out that the Security Council has asked me to implement the resolution. Implementation obviously means interpretation in the first instance. I gave an interpretation and that interpretation was challenged. I have referred the matter back to the Security Council. I have the right to expect guidance. That guidance can be given in any form. But it should be obvious that if the Security Council says nothing I have no other choice than to follow my conviction.[38]

The interpretation which the SG gives to his delegated mandate is not subject to agreement or negotiation with UN Member States. In the Congo crisis, the SG held negotiations with Mr Tshome, the President of the Katangese provincial government, in order to try and resolve the dispute which had arisen over the attempted secession of the Katanga province.[39] During the course of these negotiations SG Hammarskjold had occasion to observe the following: 'The policy line stated here, in interpretation of operative paragraph 4, represents a unilateral declaration of interpretation

---

[36] See also Bowett, *supra* note 8, pp. 214–15. It is, moreover, generally accepted that the Council could not be bound by the interpretation of individual Members regarding the relation of a decision to any particular Charter provisions and that such an interpretation must be considered as the opinion of individual Members only: see, for example, the following statements in the Security Council: *SCOR*, 2nd year, No. 68, 173rd meeting: Australia, p. 1708; Brazil, pp. 1682–3; France, pp. 1676–8; India, pp. 1683–4; former USSR, pp. 1689–92; and UK, pp. 1674–5. *SCOR*, 3rd year, No. 133, 390th meeting: Australia, pp. 5–14; and China, pp. 1–5. *SCOR*, 4th year, No. 2, 398th meeting: Belgium, p. 11; and USA, p. 3.

[37] See also Abi-Saab, G., *The United Nations Operation in the Congo* (1978), p. 20.

[38] *SCOR*, 888th meeting, 21 Aug. 1960, para. 100.

[39] The SG was also criticized in the Congo by the former Soviet Union for interpretations which he gave to his delegated powers: XV *GAOR*, 869th meeting, 23 Sept. 1960, paras. 142–53, 288. This led the former USSR to call for the replacing of a single SG by a 'troika'; a triumvirate of one Western, one Socialist, and one 'non-aligned' or 'neutral' member: see statement by Mr Krushchev, *GAOR*, 15th Session, 882nd meeting, para. 40. Abi-Saab notes that this proposal was made by the former USSR in opposition to the fact that once the Council adopted a resolution conferring a mandate on the SG, the veto could not be used to overrule his interpretation and implementation of the delegated mandate. In other words, the former Soviet Union tried to extend the veto to the level of the Secretariat itself—i.e. from the authorizing organ to the executing organ—an extension which would have destroyed the independent character of the Secretariat. (Abi-Saab, *supra* note 37, p. 115.) Importantly, this proposal failed to gain significant support amongst the generality of UN Members: the majority of UN Member States were not opposed to the SG interpreting his delegated powers.

by the SG. It can be contested before the Security Council. And it can be changed by the Security Council through an explanation of its intentions in the resolution of 9 August. However, the finding is not subject to agreement or negotiation.'[40] Moreover, the SG went on to state that any discussions he may undertake with States must be limited to facilitating the implementation of the mandate by working out the modalities and by eliminating possible obstacles, but they can never amount to renegotiating the mandate or to imposing on the SG a certain interpretation of it.[41] The importance of the authoritative nature of the SG's interpretation *vis-à-vis* UN Member States is further illustrated in practice in the case of Somalia which is examined in Chapter 5.[42]

III. THE PRACTICE OF THE SECRETARY-GENERAL IN EXERCISING DELEGATED CHAPTER VII POWERS

The Security Council has delegated to the SG its Chapter VII powers in several different cases. There have been three main types of powers the Council has delegated to the SG: the power to conduct the internal governance of a State; certain powers in respect of UN peacekeeping operations; and certain powers in respect of a military force carrying out enforcement action. The legal considerations which apply to each particular delegation of power differ according to the power which is being delegated. Accordingly, the following section examines separately the practice of the Council when delegating each particular power.

1. The delegation of Chapter VII power to the Secretary-General to conduct the internal governance of a State

The issue of a delegation by the Council of Chapter VII powers to the SG to conduct the internal governance of a State without the express consent of the State has only arisen in the case of Somalia. However, before turning to examine this case in more detail the preliminary question which needs to be determined is whether the Council itself possesses such a power. It was explained in Chapter 1 that the Council must possess the power it is purporting to delegate.[43] Accordingly, if the Security Council does not possess the power to conduct the internal governance of a State then it cannot delegate this power. There is no express provision in the Charter which

[40] S/4417/Add. 6, 12 Aug. 1960, in Higgins, *supra* note 31, vol. 3, p. 132.
[41] See also Abi-Saab, *supra* note 37, p. 35.
[42] See *infra* note 180 and corresponding text in Chapter 5.
[43] See *supra* Section III(1) in Chapter 1.

gives the Security Council the power to conduct the internal governance of a State. However, it is contended that the general powers of the Council in Article 24(1) together with the subsequent practice of the Council in interpreting this provision would seem to justify the view that the Council does possess such a power.[44] There are three instances of relevant practice which validate this position.[45]

First, there is the legal opinion of the SG on the competence of the Security Council to assume quasi-governmental responsibilities over the Free Territory of Trieste. In this opinion the SG argued that the Security Council could exercize such powers and that it was not limited to the specific powers laid down in Chapters VI, VII, VIII, and XII of the Charter. The Council had, he suggested, a power to maintain peace and security conferred upon it by Article 24 which was wide enough to enable it to assume the responsibilities arising from the agreements relating to Trieste.[46] This conclusion by the SG appeared to be accepted by almost all of the Members of the Council as the legal basis for their decision to assume the responsibilities relating to Trieste. Thus, at the 89th meeting, the representatives of the former USSR and the UK expressly referred to Article 24 as the basis of the Council's authority.[47] The representatives of France and

---

[44] Moreover, the *travaux preparatoires* of Article 42 of the Charter seems to support the view that the Security Council possesses such a power. Norway made a proposal to amend the corresponding provision of Article 42 in the draft of Dumbarton Oaks so that it would provide expressly that the Council should in special cases temporarily assume the administration of a territory in the event that the administration of this area by the occupant State represents a threat to the peace. (*UNCIO*, vol. 3, p. 365 at pp. 371–2, Doc. 2G/7 (n)(1).) The reason for the withdrawal of this amendment was not due to subsequent opposition to the substance of the proposal, but the impression which the proposed amendment may have created that other non-mentioned measures of the Council would be precluded by Article 42. (Commn. III, Ctee. 3, Session of 23 May, 1945, *UNCIO*, vol. 12, p. 353 at pp. 354–5, Doc. 539 III/3/24.) This would need, however, to be a temporary measure, since Article 78 of the Charter—which expressly prohibits the application of the Trusteeship System to UN Member States—suggests that the Council does not possess the power to impose on a State a permanent form of government. See also Gill, T., 'Legal and Some Political Limitations on the Power of the UN Security Council to Exercise its Enforcement Powers under Chapter VII of the Charter', *Netherlands Yearbook of International Law*, 26 (1995), p. 33 at pp. 74–7.

[45] There is also the case of the General Assembly exercising such a power through the United Nations Temporary Executive Authority (UNTEA) which governed Irian Jaya during its transition from Dutch to Indonesian rule. The Netherlands and Indonesia had agreed by treaty to transfer administration of the non-self-governing territory to UNTEA, which would administer it until its transfer to Indonesia. (Agreement Concerning West New Guinea (West Irian), 15 Aug. 1962, Indon.–Neth., 437 *UNTS* 274.) The General Assembly subsequently authorized the SG to perform the tasks in the Agreement. (GA res. 1752, *UNGAOR*, 17th Session, Supp. No. 17, at 70, UN Doc. A/5217 (1962).) The Agreement gave the head of UNTEA 'full authority under the direction of the SG to administer the territory'. (Agreement Concerning West New Guinea (West Irian), 15 Aug. 1962, Indon.—Neth., 437 *UNTS* 274, Art. V.)

[46] 91st meeting of the Security Council, 10 Jan. 1947 (*SCOR*, 2nd Year, No. 3, pp. 44, 45).

[47] 89th meeting, 7 Jan. 1947 (*SCOR*, 2nd Year, No. 1: USSR, p. 9; and, *ibidem*, UK, p. 10).

the US concurred in this opinion.[48] The only dissent was that of the Australian representative who argued that the Council could act only through its specific powers and not through some general power in Article 24.[49] However, it seems clear that this approach is not a correct interpretation of Article 24. The International Court of Justice rejected this type of contention in the *Namibia* Case when it stated: 'The reference in para. 2 of this Article to specific powers of the Security Council under certain chapters of the Charter does not exclude the existence of general powers to discharge the responsibilities conferred in para. 1.'[50]

The second case which supports the contention that the Security Council possesses a general power under Article 24 which enables it to perform governmental functions is the administration of Namibia by the UN Council for Namibia.[51] Suffice to note that the International Court in the *Namibia* Case observed: 'Article 24 of the Charter vests in the Security Council the necessary authority to take action such as that taken in the present case.'[52]

Finally, the case of Cambodia establishes conclusively that the UN can in certain circumstances conduct governmental functions within a State. In an attempt to resolve the conflict in Cambodia the parties concluded the Paris Peace Accords (the 'Accords').[53] These Accords created a Supreme National Council which was defined in the Accords as the 'unique legitimate body and source of authority in which, throughout the transitional period, the sovereignty, independence and unity of Cambodia are enshrined'.[54] Security Council resolution 668 confirmed the sovereign nature

[48] 89th meeting, 7 Jan. 1947 (*SCOR*, 2nd Year, No. 1: USA, pp. 11–12; and, *ibidem*, France, p. 16).

[49] This argument was also used by Australia in relation to the Iranian question in 1947 (Goodrich, L., Hambro, E., and Simons, P., *Charter of the United Nations: Commentary and Documents* (1969), p. 204), by Portugal in 1961 in relation to the situation in Angola (*Repertoire of the Practice of the Security Council, 1959–1963*, p. 304 *et sequentia*), and by South Africa in 1971 in relation to the situation in Namibia (*Repertoire of the Practice of the Security Council, 1969–1971*, p. 79). Moreover, it was contended by Australia that, even if it was accepted that the Council had a general power under Article 24, that power would not support the assumption by the Council of governmental functions in Trieste. (*SCOR*, 2nd Year, No. 3, p. 56.)

[50] *Namibia* case, *ICJ Reports* (1971), at p. 52. See also Cot and Pellet, *supra* note 16, p. 447.

[51] The UN Council for Namibia is a UN subsidiary organ which exercized broad governmental functions. See *infra* note 63 and corresponding text in Chapter 3.

[52] *Namibia* case, *ICJ Reports* (1971), at p. 52.

[53] The Paris Conference concluded the following four documents: the Accords: the Final Act of the Paris Conference on Cambodia (*ILM*, 31 (1992), p. 180); the Agreement on a Comprehensive Political Settlement of the Cambodia Conflict (*ILM*, 31 (1992), p. 183); the Agreement Concerning the Sovereignty, Independence, Territorial Integrity and Inviolability, Neutrality and National Unity of Cambodia (*ILM*, 31 (1992), p. 200); and the Declaration on the Rehabilitation and Reconstruction of Cambodia (*ILM*, 31 (1992), p. 203). See on the Accords: Ratner, S., 'The Cambodia Settlement Agreements', *AJIL*, 87 (1993), p. 1.

[54] The Agreement on a Comprehensive Political Settlement of the Cambodia Conflict, Articles 3 and 5, *ibidem*.

of the Supreme National Council when it described it as the 'unique legitimate body and source of authority in which, during the transitional period, the independence, national sovereignty and unity of Cambodia is embodied . . . the Supreme National Council will therefore represent Cambodia externally and it is to designate its representatives to occupy the seat of Cambodia at the United Nations'.[55] Then the Accords stipulate that the Supreme National Council 'delegates to the United Nations all powers necessary to ensure the implementation of this Agreement'.[56] Accordingly, Article 2 of the Accords invited the Security Council to create the United Nations Transitional Authority in Cambodia (UNTAC) 'with civilian and military components under the direct responsibility of the SG of the United Nations', 'to provide UNTAC with the mandate set forth in this Agreement', and 'to keep its implementation under continuing review'.[57]

Thus under the law of the Charter—or more specifically under the practice built up under the Charter—the Security Council possesses the competence to govern a territory or State where the express consent to do so has been granted by the authority in control. In the case where such consent is not forthcoming it may be possible for the Council to override this requirement in certain circumstances by adopting measures under Chapter VII.[58] It is thus clear that in certain cases the Security Council is able to exercize the power to conduct the internal governance of a State and can thus delegate such a power to the SG. It is now appropriate to consider the case of Somalia where the Secretary-General, through his Special Representative, exercized such a power.

The SG's Special Representative to Somalia exercized a governmental power when he promulgated the former Somali Penal Code of 1962 as the criminal law in force in Somalia. The competence of the SG's Special Representative to 'promulgate' such a code of binding legal effect within Somalia was in this case questionable[59] since there was no relevant delegation of power by the Security Council to the SG or his Special

---

[55] In respect of the Supreme National Council, see Ratner, *supra* note 53, pp. 10–12.

[56] Comprehensive Settlement Agreement, *supra* note 53, Article 6.

[57] *Ibidem*, Article 2.

[58] Thus Ratner has stated in respect of Cambodia: 'If the United Nations were to administer Cambodia, under . . . the Charter an entity authorized to represent Cambodia would need to delegate power to the Organization or otherwise indicate Cambodia's consent to the operation; or, alternatively, the Security Council would have to approve enforcement action under Chapter VII to restore international peace and security in Southeast Asia.' (Ratner, *supra* note 53, p. 9.)

[59] The Report of the Commission of Inquiry established by Security Council resolution 885 to investigate armed attacks against UNOSOM II which led to casualties stated in respect of this action the following: '[T]he promulgation of the Somali Penal Code of 1962 as the criminal law in force in Somalia by the Special Representative of the Secretary-General was capable of being interpreted by the USC/SNA as an overstepping of the UNOSOM II mandate.' (S/1994/653, p. 17.)

Representative. An examination of the relevant Council resolution, resolution 814, makes it clear that the SG's Special Representative was not delegated the power to perform a governmental function such as the promulgation of a legal code. Security Council resolution 814 only requested '. . . the SG, through his Special Representative, to direct the Force Commander of UNOSOM II to assume responsibility for the consolidation, expansion and maintenance of a secure environment throughout Somalia. . . .' The reference to the consolidation and maintenance of a secure environment throughout Somalia cannot justify the exercize of what is in effect a legislative power: the promulgation of a legal code. Regarding an issue of such importance, the Security Council would have to delegate in express terms to the SG or his Special Representative the power to conduct the internal governance of the State.[60] It may well be that the circumstances in Somalia necessitated an immediate response by the Special Representative. However, it is especially in such circumstances that strict adherence to legal requirements is required if the UN is to assist in the re-establishment of order within a country in a legitimate and thus effective fashion.

This discussion may well be of continuing practical importance since it seems likely that there will be an increase in the delegation by the Council of the power to conduct the internal governance of a State in an attempt to maintain peace. This may result from what a past SG has stated in *The Supplement to An Agenda for Peace* as a feature of the new type of intra-State conflicts: 'the collapse of state institutions, especially the police and judiciary, with resulting paralysis of governance, a breakdown of law and order, and general banditry and chaos'.[61] The SG continues: 'Not only are the functions of government suspended, its assets are destroyed or looted and experienced officials are killed or flee the country. . . . It means that international intervention must extend beyond military and humanitarian tasks and must include the promotion of national reconciliation and the re-establishment of effective government.'[62] To conclude on this issue, the Security Council can delegate the power of internal governance to the SG, but it must do so in express terms.

2. *The delegation to the Secretary-General of certain powers in respect of UN peacekeeping operations*

The Security Council has delegated these types of power to the SG in connection with UN peacekeeping forces that are under the auspices of the

---

[60] For the requirement that a delegation of powers be express, see *supra* notes 34–6 and corresponding text in Chapter 1.
[61] Boutros-Ghali, B., *Supplement to An Agenda for Peace*, S/1995/1, paras. 12–13.
[62] *Ibidem.*

Council:[63] the power to establish UN peacekeeping forces, the power to exercize command and control over these forces; and to order the use of force in their defence.

(a) The establishment of UN peacekeeping forces by the Secretary-General

The UN Charter does not provide in express terms for the establishment or use of UN peacekeeping forces. However, the International Court of Justice in the *Expenses* case did find that the Security Council has the implied power to establish UN peacekeeping forces.[64] The Court also found that the Security Council has the competence to delegate to the SG the power to establish peacekeeping forces.[65] The legality of the process of delegation of powers by the Council to the SG in respect of UN peacekeeping operations has been widely recognized.[66] These kinds of delegations of power are necessary in the case of an establishment of UN peacekeeping forces by the SG, since he does not himself possess the competence to establish such Chapter VII forces.[67] Accordingly, the establishment of UN peacekeeping forces by the SG represents the exercize of a delegated power. In every case where the Council has established a UN peacekeeping force it has been the consistent practice of the Council to delegate to the SG its Chapter VII power to establish such a force.[68]

The Security Council does not, however, usually delegate to the SG in express terms the power to determine the composition of a UN peacekeeping force.[69] This is a power which the SG implies as being necessary for the effective exercize of the delegated power of establishment. Put differently, the delegation of the power to establish a force can be said to include within

---

[63] All UN peacekeeping forces with the exception of UNEF I, established by the General Assembly in Resolution 1000, have been established by, or under the authority of, the Security Council.

[64] *Expenses case, ICJ Reports* (1962), p. 151 at p. 167.

[65] *Expenses* case, *ibidem*, p. 177.

[66] See, for example, Higgins, R., 'A General Assessment of UN Peace-Keeping', in *UN Peace-Keeping: Legal Essays* (Cassesse, A., ed.) (1978), p. 1 at p. 7; Bowett, *supra* note 8; and Abi-Saab, *supra* note 37, p. 3.

[67] See also Higgins in *UN Peacekeeping, ibidem*, p. 7; and Abi-Saab, *supra* note 37, p. 10. Thus in the aftermath of the UN authorized military action against Iraq in 1991, the SG refused calls on him to establish and deploy a peacekeeping force in Iraq to protect persecuted minorities on the basis that he lacked the constitutional authority to do so.

[68] See White, N., *Keeping the Peace: The United Nations and the Maintenance of International Peace and Security* (1993), pp. 215–56. Consider, for a more recent example, the establishment of the 'rapid reaction force (RRF)' that was part of UNPROFOR in Bosnia. The Security Council delegated to the SG the power to establish this force in resolution 998 (1995) of 16 June 1995.

[69] Cf. the case of resolution 186 in which the Security Council delegated in express terms to the SG the power to determine the size and composition of the peacekeeping force.

it the power to determine the composition of that force. The International Court upheld this approach in the *Expenses* case.[70] In so doing the Court rejected the contention of the former Soviet Union that the SG had acted illegally in determining the composition of ONUC since this was a usurpation of the Security Council's power to do so under Article 48(1) of the Charter.[71] Accordingly, the SG in the exercize of the delegated power to establish a UN peacekeeping force has the sole competence, *vis-à-vis* UN Member States, to determine the composition of a force.[72] This right

[70] *Expenses* case, *ICJ Reports* (1962), p. 151. The establishment by the SG of the UN peacekeeping force in the Congo, ONUC, was initially authorized by the Security Council in its resolution of 14 July 1960, S/4387. Similarly, in the case of the UN Emergency Force (UNEF) the *Repertory of Practice* observed: '[I]n establishing UNEF, the General Assembly delegated to its Commander, to the Secretary-General and to the Advisory Committee certain executive powers regarding the composition of UNEF and the arrangements for its functioning.' (*Repertory of Practice of United Nations Organs* (1964, v. 1).

[71] *Expenses* case, *ICJ Reports* (1962), p. 151 at p. 175. The Court found against this argument on two interrelated grounds. First, the Court found that the Council's delegation of powers to the SG was lawful, since 'under Article 29 it [the Security Council] "may establish such subsidiary organs as it deems necessary for the performance of its functions;" [and] under Article 98 it may entrust "other functions" to the SG'. (*Ibidem*, p. 177.) The Court thus found that UN peacekeeping forces are UN subsidiary organs. Second, the Court found that the 'record of reiterated consideration, confirmation, approval and ratification by the Security Council . . . of the actions of the SG in implementing the resolution of 14 July 1960' meant that 'it is impossible to reach the conclusion that the operations in question usurped or impinged upon the prerogatives conferred by the Charter on the Security Council'. (*Expenses* case, *ibidem*, pp. 176–7.)

However, it seems that an important assumption in respect of this conclusion by the Court was the finding that: 'The armed forces which were utilized in the Congo were not authorized to take military action against any State. The operation did not involve "preventive or enforcement measures" against any State under Chapter VII and therefore did not constitute "action" as that term is used in Article 11'. (*Ibidem*, p. 177.) This does not mean that the legal basis for UN peacekeeping forces is not Chapter VII of the Charter. As the International Court of Justice stated in the *Expenses* case: 'The Court cannot accept so limited a view of the powers of the Security Council under the Charter. Articles of Chapter VII of the Charter speak of "situations" as well as disputes, and it must lie within the power of the Security Council to police a situation even though it does not resort to enforcement action against a State.' (*Expenses case, ICJ Reports* (1962), p. 151 at p. 167.) (See also Higgins, *supra* note 66, p. 3; and White, *supra* note 68, p. 200.) It does mean, however, that the decision of the Court affirming the delegation by the Council of its Article 48 powers was limited to measures not involving the use of military action against a State. Nonetheless, the competence of the Council to delegate the power of composition to the SG also extends to the case of a force which is to carry out military enforcement measures. The fact that the SG would be exercizing such a power with the consent of the States contributing troops to such a force is of crucial importance to this conclusion. Accordingly, the delegation by the Security Council to the SG of a power of composition which was intended to have binding legal effect on UN Member States in the case of a force carrying out military enforcement action would be of doubtful legality.

[72] This is a different point from the historical debate between the SG and the Council as to whether it is the Council or the SG which should determine the composition of a UN peacekeeping force. The fact that the SG exercizes the power of composition of peacekeeping forces as a delegated power means that the Council has the primary competence to determine the composition of such a force, if it so wishes.

has often been asserted by the SG in the face of opposition of UN Member States who have disagreed with the composition of a particular peacekeeping force.[73]

In determining the composition of a peacekeeping force, the SG had for a long period developed a practice whereby he would observe two principles: First, in selecting national contingents the SG would exclude military personnel belonging to any of the Permanent Members of the Security Council.[74] Second, the SG used to exclude military personnel from any country which for geographical or other reasons might have a special interest in the conflict.[75] However, ever since the establishment of UNFICYP both these principles have not been strictly observed.[76] For example, in the case of UNPROFOR there are national contingents from both the UK and France: both Permanent Members of the Security Council. While in the case of UNOSOM there were national contingents participating who were of close geographical proximity to Somalia. Such principles can be changed by the SG when he deems it appropriate. The formulation of such principles are left to the discretion of the SG as part of the exercize of the delegated power. The SG can thus change these principles to reflect political realities and thereby exercize in an effective fashion his delegated powers.

In respect of composition, however, it is important to note that the Security Council has not delegated to the SG a power to require States to contribute troops to a UN peacekeeping force.[77] The reason for this clearly being that the Council does not itself possess such a power. It has been dealt with elsewhere that the non-conclusion of Article 43 agreements by the Council has meant that it does not possess the competence to require States to contribute to a UN force.[78]

---

[73] See Di Blase, A., 'The role of the host State's consent with regard to non-coercive actions by the United Nations', in Cassesse, *supra* note 66, p. 55 at p. 61.

[74] See, for example, 'Summary Study of the experience derived from the establishment and operation of UNEF: report of the SG' (1958), as contained in Higgins, R., *United Nations Peacekeeping* (1969), vol. 1, p. 486.

[75] *Ibidem.*

[76] See Siekmann, R., *National Contingents in United Nations Peace-Keeping Forces* (1991), pp. 87–9.

[77] *Ibidem*, p. 45.

[78] See, for example, *Repertory of Practice of UN Organs, Supplement No. 3*, vol. 2, p. 244; Higgins, *supra* note 66, p. 4; and Sarooshi, D., 'Humanitarian Intervention and International Humanitarian Assistance: Law and Practice', *Wilton Park Papers*, 86 (1994), p. 3. Cf. Szasz who states that the non-implementation of Article 43 does not prevent the Security Council from requiring States under Article 48 to provide troops for Article 42-type operations, although it has not yet done so. (Szasz, P., 'Centralized and Decentralized Law Enforcement: The Security Council and the General Assembly acting under Chapters VII and VIII', in *Allocation of Law Enforcement Authority in the International System* (Delbruck, J., ed.) (1995), p. 31 at pp. 27, 165–6.)

(b) The exercize of command and control powers over UN peacekeeping forces

The Charter provides a framework for decision making by the Council when exercizing command and control powers over a UN force which is to carry out military enforcement action. Articles 46 and 47 envisage an important role for the Military Staff Committee in the decision-making processes of the Council when deciding how to use and apply armed forces.[79] Moreover, Article 44 of the Charter requires the Council to give a State which has contributed troops to a military enforcement force the ability to participate in decisions of the Council concerning the use of contingents of that State's armed forces.[80] However, it seems clear that these Charter provisions do not apply in the case of UN peacekeeping forces. There is a qualitative distinction between UN peacekeeping operations and UN military enforcement action. The Court in the *Expenses* case found that since the peacekeeping operations *in casu* were not '*enforcement* actions within the compass of Chapter VII of the Charter' 'that therefore Article 43 could not have any applicability'.[81] Similarly, Articles 44, 46, and 47 of Chapter VII which relate to the use of a military force by the Council are inapplicable to the case of UN peacekeeping forces since the Charter provisions in respect of the command and control of a military force only have application where a force is carrying out military enforcement action. Accordingly, a former SG has rejected a role for the Military Staff Committee in the context of UN peacekeeping operations.[82]

The authority for the command and control of UN peacekeeping forces established by the Security Council rests solely with the Council. This derives from the fact that they are subsidiary organs under the authority and control of the Council.[83] Accordingly, Bowett has observed, in the context of UN peacekeeping forces, that 'any political control assumed by the SG will in the future be by delegation from the Council or the Assembly, and not upon his own authority'.[84] However, in all cases of UN peacekeeping by the Security Council the Council has chosen to delegate its powers of command and control to the SG. The SG exercizing these powers of command and control assumes the role of overall

[79] Articles 46 and 47 do not operate as a limitation on the powers of the Council under Chapter VII. They do, however, specify the way in which the Council should exercize its Chapter VII powers. See further on these articles: *supra* note 133 in Chapter 1.

[80] See *supra* note 136 and corresponding text in Chapter 1.

[81] *Expenses* case, *ICJ Reports* (1962), p. 166.

[82] Boutros-Ghali, B., *An Agenda for Peace* (1992), p. 25. Cf., however, the suggestion by President Mitterand of France that the Military Staff Committee could play a greater role in the deployment of peacekeeping troops: Security Council Summit of Heads of State, 31 Jan. 1992, S/PV.3046, p. 18.

[83] See *infra* notes 163 & 167 and corresponding text in Chapter 3.

[84] Bowett, *supra* note 8, p. 357.

commander of the force.[85] There can be no legal objection, as already explained, to the use by the Council of its general competence to delegate such a power to the SG.[86] There has, moreover, been a consistent course of practice where the Council has delegated its powers of command and control to the SG.

As early as 1956, in the case of UNEF, the SG exercized strategic and political control over a UN peacekeeping force.[87] Similarly, in the second case of UN peacekeeping, in the Congo, the SG exercized authority and control over ONUC.[88] The SG in the Congo crisis made it clear that control over ONUC lay exclusively in the hands of the UN and not the host State or any contributing or other UN Member State.[89] In the case of the Congo, the consequences of the broad delegation of Chapter VII powers by the Council had two major consequences. First, it led to intense criticism of the role of the SG, and even led some States, notably the former USSR, to call for the replacing of a single SG by a 'troika',[90] and a proposal to transfer operational control from the SG to a 'unified African command' directly responsible to the Security Council.[91] Both these proposals failed to gain significant support among the generality of UN Members. Second, and more serious, was the consequence that States which contributed troops to the peacekeeping force attempted to force a change of UN policy. Such an

---

[85] See *UNJYB* (1990), p. 269; and Szasz, *supra* note 2, pp. 188–9. There are three levels of authority in respect of the command and control over UN peacekeeping forces which the SG in the *Supplement to An Agenda for Peace* has identified: '(a) Overall political direction, which belongs to the Security Council; (b) Executive direction and command, for which the SG is responsible; (c) Command in the field, which is entrusted by the SG to the chief of mission (special representative or force commander/chief military observer).' (Boutros-Ghali, B., *Supplement to An Agenda for Peace*, S/1995/1, para. 37.) The SG continued on to observe: 'The distinctions between these three levels must be kept constantly in mind in order to avoid any confusion of functions and responsibilities. It is as inappropriate for the chief of mission to take upon himself the formulation of his/her mission's overall political objectives as it is for the Security Council or the SG in New York to decide on matters that require a detailed understanding of operational conditions in the field.' (*Ibidem*, para. 38.)

[86] In the specific case of the competence of the Security Council and General Assembly to delegate powers to the SG in respect of UN peacekeeping forces, see Sohn, L., 'The Authority of the United Nations to Establish and Maintain a Permanent United Nations Force', *AJIL*, 52 (1958), p. 229 at pp. 235–6.

[87] See, for example, Bowett, *supra* note 8, pp. 117–18.

[88] Regulation 11 of the ONUC Regulations stated the following: 'Command authority. The Secretary-General, under the authority of the Security Council and the General Assembly, has full command authority over the Force. The Commander is operationally responsible to the Secretary-General through the officer-in-charge for the performance of all functions assigned to the Force by the United Nations, and for the deployment and assignment of troops placed at the disposal of the Force.'

[89] See 'First Report of the Secretary-General in the Congo crises', S/4389, p. 3. Thus Miller has argued that the UN Force in the Congo (ONUC) may be characterized, in terms of the Charter, 'as a subsidiary organ of the Council acting exclusively under the command of the SG as the agent of the Council'. (Miller, E., 'Legal Aspects of the United Nations Action in the Congo', *AJIL*, 55 (1961), p. 1 at pp. 10–11.)

[90] See *supra* note 39.

[91] Statement by Nkrumah in the General Assembly, 23 Sept. 1960: *GAOR*, 15th Session, 869th meeting, para. 30.

attempt to force a change in policy is not of course objectionable when conducted within the confines of a deliberative political organ of the UN such as the Security Council. However, the attempts by States to pressure the SG either by threatening to cease to execute the orders of the UN Command, or to impose unilaterally the conditions on which their national contingents can be used, are all of dubious legality. As explained above, if a State holds a differing interpretation of the mandate of a peacekeeping force from that of the SG the appropriate forum to raise the issue is the Security Council. A State cannot instruct its national commander who is part of a UN peacekeeping force to disobey the orders of the Force Commander, the SG's delegate.[92]

The absence of a legal requirement for the SG to take into consideration the views of UN Member States in the way that he exercizes the command and control powers which he has been delegated, is subject to the consideration that UN peacekeeping forces are consent based: that is, forces are voluntarily contributed by States. Accordingly, the SG in practice will have to take into consideration the views of States that have contributed troops to such a force. This political requirement saw, in the cases of UNEF and ONUC, the establishment of 'Advisory Committees' constituted of States which had contributed troops to peacekeeping forces. These Committees were consulted by the SG on the way in which the peacekeeping forces were to be used.[93] However, there have been no Advisory Committees established since these cases. Nonetheless, the SG has continued to take account of the views of States despite the absence of a formal mechanism for these views to be expressed.[94]

---

[92] See also Annan, K., 'Peace-Keeping in Situations of Civil War', *NYUJIL&P*, 26 (1994), p. 623 at p. 627; and Seyersted, F., *United Nations Forces* (1966), p. 32. The control exercized by the SG or his designated representative over UN peacekeeping troops is considered by the SG to be of the utmost importance: see S/26470, p. 5.

[93] In the case of UNEF, the General Assembly, in response to a proposal by the SG, established by resolution 1001 a UN subsidiary organ called the 'Advisory Committee'. The main task of the Committee was 'to undertake the development of those aspects of the planning for the Force and its operation not already dealt with by the General Assembly and which do not fall within the area of the direct responsibility of the Chief of Command'. (General Assembly resolution 1001, para. 6.) A second such advisory committee was established in the case of the Congo on 23 Aug. 1960 in response to criticisms of the SG's policy of non-intervention in relation to the Katanga region. The Committee this time was made up solely of States contributing forces to ONUC in the Congo. It seems clear that the Committee was consulted on important issues involving ONUC, including the possible use of force in order to prevent a civil war in the Congo. (Siekmann, *supra* note 76, p. 103.) An analogy for such committees exists in the European Community, where the European Council when delegating powers to the European Commission requires the Commission to consult with Advisory or Consultative Committees, as they are known, before it acts: see House of Lords, Select Committee on the European Communities, *Delegation of Powers to the Commission (Final Report)*, 3rd Report, Session 1986–7, pp. 3–5.

[94] In the case of a UN peacekeeping force in Somalia (UNOSOM II), there were regular meetings between senior UN officials and representatives of troop contributing countries: see *infra* note 80 in Chapter 5.

In terms of control over peacekeeping forces, the SG usually exercizes this power delegated by the Security Council through his Special Representative and the Force Commander. These UN Officials, as part of the UN Secretariat, are under the authority and control of the SG.[95] The mandate of the Special Representative is usually formulated by the SG or, in exceptional cases, by the Security Council itself. The usual practice is that the Council simply endorses the plan put forth by the SG.[96]

The SG's Special Representative exercizes political control over UN peacekeeping troops in the field: a power which has been delegated to him by the SG. The Force Commander translates the political directives emanating from the SG or his Special Representative into military commands which are given to the national commanders of each national contingent.[97] The *Summary Study* by SG Hammarskjold in respect of UNEF states that the Force Commander has a dual responsibility: First, he is the leader of the Force, responsible, under the SG, for its day-to-day administration. Second, he is also a representative of the United Nations and is the principal agent of the SG within the area of his command.[98] In most peacekeeping operations the SG delegates many of the powers which the Assembly or Council have delegated to him to the Force Commander of the various peacekeeping forces.[99] It seems clear that such delegations of power are lawful. There are two crucial factors which militate in favour of the legality of such a delegation of power: they both derive from the status of the Special Representative and Force Commander as part of the UN Secretariat, under the authority and control of the SG. First, the Security Council, through the SG, exercizes unchallengeable authority and control over the

---

[95] Thus, for example, the SG has the power to terminate their contract of employment. This is desirable, since, as Szasz has observed, it is an essential element of the effective exercize of power by the SG that he be allowed to appoint and dismiss officials which are responsible to him in the exercize of delegated powers. (Szasz, *supra* note 2, pp. 174, 176.)

[96] This has the added effect of strengthening the hand of a Special Representative in his dealings with the parties: see Hume, C., 'The Secretary-General's Representatives', *SAIS Review* (Summer-Fall, 1995), pp. 81–2.

[97] A NATO document outlining NATO doctrine for peace support operations states: 'If the UN Secretary-General . . . appoint[s] a Special Representative, he will be responsible for all political aspects of the mission, while the Force Commander would command military operations. In this case the precise relationship between the Special Representative and the Force Commander will be determined on a case-by-case basis.' (*NATO Doctrine for Peace-Support Operations*, 20 Oct. 1993, p. 6.)

[98] See *Summary Study*, *supra* note 74, paras. 76–7.

[99] A NATO document states: 'Once the [peacekeeping] force is established, the overall direction of the operation is in the hands of the Secretary-General, acting on behalf of and being responsible to the Security Council. The Secretary-General delegates the day-to-day operational handling to the Force Commander, but usually retains direct control over policy and major decision-making. This principle, which may limit the Force Commander's freedom of action, is generally required by the Security Council.' (*NATO Doctrine for Peace-Support Operations*, 20 Oct. 1993, p. 11.)

decisions of the delegate.[100] Second, the fact that the Special Representative and Force Commander are UN Staff Members means that they are under an obligation to act solely in the interests of the Organization.[101] The competence of the SG to delegate his powers of political and military command and control over peacekeeping forces to his Special Representative and Force Commander is a necessary and important way in which the effective exercize of delegated Chapter VII powers can be carried out.[102] This is borne out by the practice of the SG in delegating general powers of command and control over UN peacekeeping forces to his Special Representatives and Force Commanders.[103] An important element of the power of command and control over a UN peacekeeping force which has been delegated to the SG's subordinates and which is the subject of our present analysis is the ordering of the use of force in defence of peacekeepers.

(c) The competence to order the use of force in defence of UN peacekeepers

It is generally accepted that the use of force by UN peacekeepers in self-defence is lawful.[104] It is not proposed to enter into discussion here of the outer limits of this right. Our present discussion is limited to examining the role of the SG when this right of UN peacekeepers to use force in self-defence has been delegated to entities external to the UN.[105] The

---

[100] A result of this authority and control, as a former SG has observed, is that '[t]here has been an increasing tendency in recent years for the Security Council to micro-manage peacekeeping operations'. (Boutros-Ghali, B., *Supplement to An Agenda for Peace*, S/1995/1, para. 39.)

[101] See further on the independence of the UN Secretariat: *supra* note 27 and corresponding text.

[102] This was of particular importance in the case of air strikes in Bosnia. See *infra* Section II(1) in Chapter 6.

[103] There has already been substantial practice in this area. For example, Regulation 12 of the UNEF Regulations provides: '12. *Chain of Command and Delegation of Authority.* The Commander shall designate the chain of command for the Force, making use of the officers of the United Nations Command and the commanders of the national contingents made available by participating governments. He may delegate his authority through the chain of command. . . . Instructions from principal organs of the United Nations shall be channelled by the SG through the Commander and the chain of command designated by him.' A similar provision which gives the SG the competence to delegate his authority through the UN chain of command appears in virtually identical terms in the Regulations of ONUC and UNFICYP. However, in the case of UNEF the General Assembly had itself appointed the Force Commander (UNEF, Regulation 5(a)); while in the case of ONUC this appointment was made by the SG. Moreover, in the case of UNEF, command authority was given to the Force Commander while in the case of ONUC this lay with the SG's Special Representative. (Bowett, *supra* note 8, p. 341)

[104] See, for example, *Summary Study*, *supra* note 74, para. 179.

[105] Accordingly, self-defence here does not just mean defence of self (i.e. of a UN force by itself), but also the defence of such a force by some other entity (e.g. NATO). Similarly, in the

Security Council has delegated the power of UN peacekeepers to use force in self-defence to entities other than the force itself in the case of the former Yugoslavia. The Council in resolution 836 stated the following:

> ... that ... Member States, acting nationally or through regional organizations or arrangements, may take, under the authority of the Security Council and subject to close coordination with the SG and UNPROFOR, all necessary measures, through the use of air power, in and around the safe areas in the Republic of Bosnia and Herzegovina, to support UNPROFOR in the performance of its mandate set out in paragraphs 5 and 9 above.

Moreover, the Council in operative paragraph 11 '*[r]equests* the Member States concerned, the SG and UNPROFOR to coordinate closely on the measures they are taking to implement paragraph 10 above and to report to the Council through the SG'.[106] What is patent from the face of the resolution is that the Council has delegated to Member States and regional organizations or arrangements the competence to use force in response to attacks on UNPROFOR. What is not so clear, however, from the terms of the resolution is who should decide when force should be used and for what purpose. The SG took this decision upon himself as, in effect, the representative of the UN. After noting that NATO had confirmed its willingness to offer 'protective air power in the case of attack against UNPROFOR in the performance of its overall mandate, if it so requests',[107] the SG further noted '[i]t is of course understood that the first decision to initiate the use of air resources in this context will be taken by the SG in consultation with the members of the Security Council'.[108] This report, and thus the SG's inter-

context of the right of States to use force in collective self-defence, they are not acting *stricto sensu* in *self*-defence but in defence of the State which has been attacked. For an excellent discussion of the term 'self-defence' and its meaning, in the context of States, in the term 'collective self-defence', see Higgins, R., 'The Legal Limits to the Use of Force by Sovereign States: United Nations Practice', *BYIL*, 37 (1962), p. 269 at p. 307. See also Kelsen, H., 'Collective Security and Collective Self-Defence under the Charter of the United Nations', *AJIL*, 42 (1948), p. 783 at p. 792.

[106] Subsequently, the SG asked NATO to prepare plans for provision of air support capacity to implement the resolution. In a letter from the SG to the President of the Security Council dated 18 Aug. 1993, the SG stated that following the necessary training exercizes in coordination with NATO, the UN now had the initial operational capability for the use of air power in support of UNPROFOR in Bosnia: S/26335.

[107] S/25939, p. 2.

[108] *Ibidem*, p. 4. The North Atlantic Council has noted in respect of the use of close air support: 'These measures will be under the authority of the United Nations Security Council and within the framework of relevant UN Security Council resolutions, and in support of UNPROFOR in the performance of its overall mandate. For that purpose, full co-ordination will be carried out with the United Nations, including appropriate arrangements between the NATO Military Authorities and UNPROFOR and consultation with UNHCR.' (*Press Statement by the NATO Secretary-General following the Special Meeting of the North Atlantic Council in Brussels on 2 August 1993*, paras. 4–5.) The 'dual-key' system was decided upon as the mechanism to make decisions about the use of air power and air strikes. Both the UN and NATO can initiate a call for air measures, but the other side must agree for the use of force to go ahead: each side has a veto power.

pretation, was expressly adopted by the Council in resolution 844.[109] This follows from the position as explained above that the adoption by the Security Council of a report by the SG where a specific interpretation is made of his delegated mandate represents an affirmation of that interpretation.[110] In any case, the consent of the SG is required by the law governing the delegation of powers in this area. The fact that the SG is the Commander-in-Chief of UN peacekeeping forces means that any use of force by peacekeepers in self-defence would require either his consent or that of his Special Representative or Force Commander who may have been delegated this power of decision making. The practice of the UN and NATO in the former Yugoslavia has been in accordance with this legal position. The use of close air support required a request by those on the ground who were the subject of an attack. The request then went to the Force Commander and finally to the SG's Special Representative for the final decision as to whether close air support should be requested from NATO.[111]

The use of force in defence of UN peacekeepers under resolution 836 is termed 'close air support'. This is to be distinguished from 'air strikes'. The SG in a letter dated 28 January 1994 to the Security Council has explained this distinction in the following terms:

> Should UNPROFOR be attacked in the implementation of the plans, I would not hesitate to initiate the use of close air support without delay. To this end arrangements have been made with NATO, which has already authorized its forces to provide close air support to UNPROFOR in cases of self-defence. It is important in this context to make clear that a distinction exists between close air support, which involves the use of air power for purposes of self-defence, and air strikes, which involves the use of air power for pre-emptive or punitive purposes. Whereas the North Atlantic Council has already authorized close air support, I have been informed by the Secretary General of NATO that NATO forces are not authorized to launch air strikes, which would require a further decision of the North Atlantic Council.[112]

Thus close air support is only to be used in defence of UN peacekeepers. Air strikes, which involve military enforcement action, are discussed further below.[113]

---

[109] Moreover, in resolution 844 the Council in operative paragraph 4 stated that it '[r]eaffirms its decision in paragraph 10 of resolution 836 (1993) on the use of air power, in and around the safe areas, to support UNPROFOR in the performance of its mandate, and encourages Member States, acting nationally or through regional organizations or arrangements, to coordinate closely with the Secretary-General in this regard'.

[110] See *supra* notes 34–5 and corresponding text.

[111] To ensure a quick NATO response to such a request by the UN, NATO liaison officers were stationed at UNPROFOR Headquarters in Zagreb and in Sarajevo. (Leurdijk, D., *The United Nations and NATO in the former Yugoslavia* (1994), p. 16.)

[112] S/1994/94, p. 2.

[113] See *infra* note 150 and corresponding text.

In the case of the former Yugoslavia, the SG decided to delegate the competence to request, or agree to, the use of close air support to his Special Representative.[114] There was no express request from the Security Council to the SG to sub-delegate this power of command and control to his Special Representative. Thus for the SG to sub-delegate these powers to his Special Representative he must possess an implied competence to do so. The main condition for the existence of such a competence to delegate powers is that the power to delegate must be necessary or essential to the performance of the duties and functions of the SG or of his representative. The determination of whether this is the case is made by the SG himself. In the case of the former Yugoslavia, the SG stated the following reason for the delegation of power to his Special Representative:

This is necessitated not only by his responsibility for the security of the personnel, including unarmed civilians, under his control, but also out of regard for the integrity of the humanitarian and other mandates entrusted to UNPROFOR by the Security Council.[115]

This approach received the express support of a few States.[116] There was, however, concern expressed about the cumbersome nature of these procedures, which, it was argued, compromised the speed of reaction to an emergency and thus the effectiveness of the use of air power as protection for UNPROFOR and the safe areas.[117] Moreover, the practice of the Force Commander and the Special Representative was to refuse to request such support from NATO if the attack had already ceased.[118] This approach was

[114] See the report of the SG dated 16 Mar. 1994, S/1994/300, p. 15.

[115] S/1994/300, p. 15. In the UN action in the Congo, the SG ordered self-defensive measures very similar to close air support measures taken in the former Yugoslavia. In response to the news that thirteen Italian peacekeepers on 11 Nov. 1961 had been surrounded and were under siege by Armée nationale congolaise (ANC) troops, the Acting SG authorized aircraft that were part of the UN force in the area to lift the siege, even to the extent of strafing to disperse the besiegers, if the ONUC Command considered that this was to be necessary and helpful. The Acting SG repeatedly stressed that in undertaking such measures ONUC was not undertaking military enforcement action. (Higgins, *supra* note 31, at p. 355.)

[116] The Spanish representative, for example, stated: 'It is clear that to achieve these objectives it is crucial that NATO guarantee the security of the personnel of UNPROFOR, of the Office of the High Commissioner for Refugees (UNHCR) and of the other international agencies . . . We therefore deem it appropriate for the SG to have delegated to his Special Representative the authority needed to approve any request which may be made in that respect by the UNPROFOR Commander, a delegation of authority which extends to operations of immediate air support in defence of United Nations personnel in any area of Bosnia and Herzegovina.' (S/PV.3336, p. 29.) See also the statement by the representative of Bangladesh: S/PV.3336 (Resumption 3), pp. 217–18.

[117] A NATO official is quoted as saying: 'We are going to make a very strong recommendation to the United Nations that it should delegate to theatre level . . .'. (*International Herald Tribune*, 26 July 1995, p. 6.)

[118] Higgins states that this is a reason why 'it may be thought [the decision-making procedures are] weighted in favour of inaction'. (Higgins, R., 'The United Nations 50 Years On, Part III: Achievements and Failures', *European Journal of International Law*, Special Issue (1995), Chapter 6, p. 14.)

also the subject of criticism.[119] However, the way in which this delegated power is exercized is solely at the discretion of the SG or his designated agents. In the context of Member States, as explained above, the appropriate forum for any such criticism is the Security Council.[120] Nonetheless, in response to such criticism the SG's Special Representative delegated the power to order the use of air power to the Force Commander who had the express authority to delegate it to the UNPROFOR Commander. The SG summarized the position in a letter to the President of the Security Council of 27 July 1995 where he stated the following:

In order to streamline decisionmaking within the United Nations chain of command . . . [a]s regards close air support to defend United Nations peacekeepers, my Special Representative has today delegated the necessary authority to the Force Commander, who is authorized to delegate it further to the Commander of the United Nations Protection Force (UNPROFOR) when operational circumstances so require. . . . I should like to stress that the above measures are all being taken with a view to implementing existing Security Council resolutions, in particular resolution 836 (1993), and are consistent with that resolution.[121]

In the context of the use of military force, it is desirable that powers are delegated to the decision maker who is most intimately informed of the facts on the ground. Thus in those cases where the SG is delegated powers in respect of the use of close air support, the distinction between military and political command and control in the chain of command when making the decision to order such action should be abolished by a delegation of powers. Accordingly, in the case of close air support in Bosnia the most desirable position was the delegation of the power of decision to call in close air support to the UN Force Commander. There was some concern expressed that there was as a result of such a delegation no UN civilian involved in the chain of UN decision making to ask NATO for close air support, and that this was not a desirable situation. However, such a contention does not take into account two important considerations. First, that the principle of unity of command in military operations is crucial.[122] Second, that the Force Commander is under the authority and control of the SG, and as such the SG can stipulate at any time the principles which the Force Commander should take into account when making a decision to call in military support to defend UN peacekeepers.[123]

---

[119] The SG in a report to the Security Council dated 30 May 1995 stated that incidents around and in Sarajevo in May 1995 caused the SG's Special Representative to consider using air power. He notes that 'the decision not to do so was criticized by some Member States'. (S/1995/444, p. 2.)

[120] See *supra* note 36 and corresponding text.

[121] S/1995/623, pp. 2–3.

[122] See Bowett, *supra* note 8, p. 342.

[123] In fact this is precisely what the SG did in the case of the former Yugoslavia, when he later specified the basis upon which such a decision should be taken: see S/1995/444, pp. 16–17.

3. The delegation to the Secretary-General of certain powers in respect of a military enforcement force

Chapter VII of the Charter provides a framework within which the Security Council can act to use forces to carry out military enforcement action.

Article 43 of the Charter provides a mechanism for the establishment of a UN force to carry out military enforcement action. However, there has been no implementation of this provision. Moreover, the Charter provisions which envisage a role for the Military Staff Committee in exercizing command and control powers over a UN force carrying out military enforcement action have also not been implemented. Non-implementation of these provisions has seen the Council carry out military enforcement measures in most cases by delegating Chapter VII powers to forces of UN Member States or regional arrangements,[124] and by delegating to the SG certain powers of command and control over these forces.

There has been considerable debate over the effect of the non-conclusion of Article 43 agreements on the competence of the Council to use forces to carry out measures to maintain or restore international peace and security. One view may be that Article 42 measures cannot be taken without the Article 43 forces which the Charter expressly states are to carry out the measures.[125] The consequence of this view is that the Council cannot use a force to carry out military enforcement action. However, this approach places too much emphasis on form. Article 43 is simply a mechanism which was to provide the Council with a way of obtaining troops to carry out military enforcement action. The non-implementation of the article does not prevent the Council obtaining and using forces in some other way: for example, by voluntary contribution of troops by States.[126]

However, the case of the SG is different. The SG cannot establish or use a UN force to carry out military enforcement measures since he does not possess any Chapter VII powers to delegate to such a force. Accordingly,

---

[124] See Chapters 5 and 6 which deal with the delegation of Chapter VII powers to UN Member States and regional arrangements, respectively.

[125] See, for example, the statement by the representative of the UK in the Security Council in 1950: S/PV.476, 5 *SCOR* (1950), pp. 3–4.

[126] The International Court in the *Expenses* case was opposed to an approach that suggested limits on the substantive powers of the Council due to non-conclusion of Article 43 agreements: 'The Court cannot accept so limited a view of the powers of the Security Council under the Charter. It cannot be said that the Charter has left the Security Council impotent in the face of an emergency situation when agreements under Article 43 have not been concluded.' (*Expenses* case, *ICJ Reports* (1962), p. 151 at p. 167.) The source of the Council's power to use a force to carry out military enforcement action can thus be implied from Chapter VII and Article 42 of the Charter. See also Higgins, R., *Problems and Process: International Law and How We Use It* (1994), p. 266; Szasz, *supra* note 2, p. 27; Bowett, D., in *Strategy of World Order: The United Nations* (Falk, R., and Mendlovitz, S., eds.) (1966), vol. 3, p. 192; Schachter, O., 'United Nations Law in the Gulf', *AJIL*, 85 (1991), p. 452 at p. 462; Weller, M., 'The Kuwait Crisis: A Survey of Some Legal Issues', *African Journal of International & Comparative Law*, 3 (1991, March), p. 1 at p. 26; and White, *supra* note 68, p. 102.

the Council must expressly delegate the powers of establishment and of command and control to the SG for him to be able to establish and use such a force.[127]

This next section examines the role of the SG in exercizing command and control powers over the following two kinds of forces mandated to carry out military enforcement action: UN peacekeeping forces and regional organizations or arrangements.

(a) The case of a UN peacekeeping force

The consensual nature of UN peacekeeping operations means that without an express change in its mandate a peacekeeping force cannot be used to carry out military enforcement action. Suffice to note for our current purposes the distinctive nature of UN peacekeeping from UN military enforcement action, as explained by a former SG:

... a wide interpretation of the right of self-defence might well blur the distinction between operations of the character discussed in this report [peacekeeping operations] and combat operations, which would require a decision under Chapter VII of the Charter and an explicit, more far-reaching delegation of authority to the SG than would be required for any of the operations discussed here. A reasonable definition seems to have been established in the case of UNEF, where the rule is applied that men engaged in the operation may never take the initiative in the use of armed force, but are entitled to respond with force to an attack with arms, including attempts to use force to make them withdraw from positions which they occupy under orders from the Commander, acting under the authority of the Assembly and within the scope of its resolutions. The basic element involved is clearly the prohibition against any initiative in the use of armed force. This definition of the limit between self-defence, as permissible for United Nations elements of the kind discussed, and offensive action, which is beyond the competence of such elements, should be approved for future guidance.[128]

Another former SG has noted, in *An Agenda for Peace* and in *Supplement to An Agenda for Peace*, that in some cases UN peacekeeping forces are delegated tasks which 'can on occasion exceed the mission of peacekeeping forces and the expectations of peacekeeping force contributors': that is, the mandate to use force in a military enforcement capacity.[129] In such cases it

---

[127] Thus Bowett states that the authority of the SG to establish a UN force to undertake military enforcement measures is exclusively a delegated authority. (Bowett, *supra* note 8, p. 300.) Accordingly, Bowett contends that the power of the SG to establish subsidiary organs does not extend to the freedom to decide that members of the Secretariat should carry out enforcement measures. (Bowett, *supra* note 8, p. 299.)

[128] See *Summary Study*, *supra* note 74, para. 179. See also *infra* note 182 and corresponding text in Chapter 3.

[129] Boutros-Ghali, B., *An Agenda for Peace* (1992), p. 26, and *Supplement to An Agenda for Peace* (1995), para. 35. For analysis of this approach, see also Reisman, M., 'Peacemaking', *Yale Journal of International Law*, 18 (1993), p. 415.

seems clear that in addition to changing the mandate of the peacekeeping force, the Council must delegate certain additional Chapter VII powers to the SG.[130] There have, however, been objections raised to such delegations of power. The main objection being that the non-implementation of Article 43 agreements has prohibited the exercize of a power of command and control by the Council itself over forces carrying out enforcement action, and thus that the delegation of such a power would be *ultra vires*.

In the Council debates during the Korean crisis, the UK representative to the Security Council argued that the non-implementation of Article 43 meant that the response of the Council could not be based on Article 42. The representative argued that the UN was precluded from itself appointing a commander, since the agreements provided for in Article 43 had not been concluded and, accordingly, the action could not be based upon Article 42.[131] However, as already explained above, the use by the Council of its powers under Article 42 does not depend on the prior fulfilment of Article 43 agreements, except to the extent that the Council purports to make such action obligatory for all Member States. Moreover, this view was based on the mistaken assumption that the powers of an organ of an international organization are those strictly limited to the express provisions of the constituent treaty of the organization. This approach has, however, been expressly rejected by the International Court in, *inter alia*, the *Reparations* case where the doctrine of implied powers of organs of an international organization was accepted.[132] It is this doctrine of implied powers which allows the Council to exercize command and control powers over a military force that is the result of voluntary contributions by States, since this is a necessary prerequisite for the exercize of its Chapter VII powers.[133] To reiterate, the non-implementation of Article 43 does not prevent the Council from using a force that is voluntarily provided to carry out enforcement action or from exercizing command and control over such a force.

More importantly, the competence of the Council to delegate the power of command and control over a military enforcement force to the SG has been questioned by the SG himself. During the Congo crisis he stated before the Council the following:

Has the Council, have you gentlemen, ever given the Secretary-General or the Force the means—I mean now the legal means—by which we could carry out a wider mandate which you believe has been given to the Force? And if so, let me ask this last question: could the Council have given such means to the Force,

---

[130] See also the statement by the SG concerning the UN Observation Group in the Lebanon (UNOGIL), *SCOR*, 13th year, 827th meeting, p. 12, in Higgins, *supra* note 74, vol. 1, p. 550.
[131] Statement by the representative of the UK, S/PV.476, 5 *SCOR* (1950), pp. 3–4.
[132] *Reparations* case, *ICJ Reports* (1949), p. 174.
[133] See also Seyersted, *supra* note 92, pp. 162–9.

through the Secretary-General, without acting against the clear injunctions of the Charter?[134]

The objection of the SG was not as such to the delegation of power to his office, but the delegation of power by the Council without observance of the Charter's provisions which govern the use of military enforcement action by the UN. This was made clear by the following, earlier, statement of the SG: 'In a police operation, the participants would in this case need the right, if necessary, to take the initiative in the use of force. Such use of force would, however, have belonged to the sphere of Chapter VII of the Charter and could have been granted only by the Security Council itself, directly or by explicit delegation, *under conditions spelled out in that chapter.*'[135] Put differently, the SG was reiterating the point that the Charter limitations on the exercize by the Council of its Chapter VII powers must be observed. Moreover, we recall from Chapter 1 that where the Council delegates Chapter VII powers it must impose on its delegate the limitations which the Charter imposes on the Council's own exercize of the powers.[136]

Let us then turn to discuss the limitations on the Council's Chapter VII powers of command and control over a military enforcement force and how these affect the exercize of the power once it has been delegated to the SG.

When the Council mandates the SG to use UN peacekeeping forces to carry out military enforcement action it is in effect delegating to the SG the power which it possesses under Article 42 of the Charter: the power to order military enforcement action to maintain or restore international peace and security. Moreover, the Council is delegating its concomitant command and control powers under Articles 46 and 47 over such a force to the SG.[137] However, the Charter prescribes certain procedures which the

---

[134] *SCOR*, 15th year, 915th meeting, para. 157. Cf. the view of Sir Anthony Parsons who states: 'When the peacekeeping force in the Congo was authorized to use force to end the civil war between 1961 and 1964, command and control was delegated to the Secretary-General, first Dag Hammarskjold and latterly U Thant.' (Parsons, A., 'The Security Council An Uncertain Future', *The David Davies Memorial Institute of International Studies, Occasional Paper No. 8* (1994), p. 8.)

[135] Emphasis added. *SCOR*, 13th year, 827th meeting, p. 12, in Higgins, *supra* note 74, vol. 1, p. 550.

[136] See *supra* Section III(2)(b)(iii) in Chapter 1.

[137] In respect of Articles 46 and 47, see *supra* note 133 in Chapter 1. The case where the SG is delegated a power of composition of a force that has a mandate to carry out military enforcement action is somewhat more problematic. This is a delegation by the Council of its power under Article 48(1) of the Charter to determine which Members shall carry out enforcement action to maintain or restore international peace and security. As explained above, the International Court of Justice found in the *Expenses* case that the determination by the SG of the composition of the peacekeeping force was lawful. (See *supra* notes 70–1 and corresponding text.) However, as also explained above, the finding of the Court in the *Expenses* case that such a determination is lawful was limited to those cases not involving the use of armed force.

Council must observe when exercizing command and control powers over a force carrying out military enforcement action. It has already been explained in Chapter 1 that the object and purpose of these provisions require the Council when delegating powers of decision making in respect of the use of military force to ensure that the delegate takes account of the views of the five Permanent Members and that those States which have contributed troops to the force are consulted on the way their troops are to be used in any enforcement action.[138] If the Security Council were to purport to delegate to the SG a power of command and control without these requirements then it would be purporting to delegate a power wider than it itself possesses.

These requirements may best be satisfied by the use of a UN subsidiary organ which is appropriately composed and which has the mandate to advise, assist, and oversee the prosecution by the SG of the military enforcement action. Such an organ would need to be composed, in part, of military experts, as opposed to composition being limited solely to political representatives. The difference between this committee and the Military Staff Committee is that it would be established on an *ad hoc* basis with the sole purpose of dealing with the case at hand: the wider mandate of the Military Staff Committee under Article 45 would not be of concern. Moreover, the membership of such an advisory committee would need to contain representatives of States which have contributed troops to the peacekeeping force. The examples of the Advisory Committees established in respect of UNEF and ONUC constitute a precedent for the establishment of an analogous committee.[139] However, the main difference which would need to exist in the case of such a committee, if it is to be used in the context of military enforcement action, is that the committee would have to be established by the Security Council and not by the SG.[140] The importance of this is that the committee would be a subsidiary organ of the Council and not

Nevertheless, it is contended that the competence of the Council to delegate the power of composition to the SG also extends to the case of a force which is to carry out military enforcement measures. The fact that the SG would be exercizing such a power with the consent of the States contributing troops to such a force is of crucial importance to this conclusion. The delegation by the Security Council to the SG of a power of composition which was intended to have binding legal effect on UN Member States would be of doubtful legality, since it is unlikely that the Council itself possesses such a power.

[138] See *supra* note 136 and corresponding text in Chapter 1.

[139] See further on these Committees: *supra* note 93 and corresponding text. In fact, in formulating a response to the Korean crisis of 1950 a suggestion was made to establish such a committee to oversee UN authorized military enforcement action. See *infra* notes 21–3 and corresponding text in Chapter 5.

[140] The fact that a subsidiary organ is established by the Council does not mean that the Council cannot ask the SG to determine the composition of the organ: see, for example, *infra* note 164 and corresponding text in Chapter 3.

the SG and as such would be under the authority and control of, and directly answerable to, the Council.[141]

The one case where the change of mandate of a peacekeeping force to military enforcement action has taken place together with a delegation of command and control powers to the SG is in the case of Somalia. This case is particularly interesting since the Council, through the SG, had already established a peacekeeping force, UNOSOM II, which it subsequently used to carry out military enforcement action in Somalia. Thus the Security Council did not delegate to the SG the power to establish a UN force to carry out military enforcement action, but simply changed the mandate of the existing peacekeeping force. As such, it would seem that the SG was implicitly entrusted with determining the composition of UNOSOM II: the force carrying out military enforcement action.[142] However, with the change in mandate of the force to enforcement action it is not appropriate for the SG to imply the power of composition. Accordingly, in the case of UNOSOM II the Council should have expressly delegated its power under Article 48(1) to the SG in order for him to have lawfully determined the composition of UNOSOM II. This flows from the requirement that a delegation of power must be express and should not be implied.[143]

The continuing deterioration of security conditions within Somalia led the SG to propose in a report to the Council in 1993 that the mandate of the second UN peacekeeping force in Somalia (UNOSOM II) should include, *inter alia*, disarmament of the organized factions, and the achievement of security at all ports and airports in order to facilitate the delivery of humanitarian assistance. Moreover, in the report the SG states that the threat to international peace and security which the Security Council had earlier ascertained continued to exist, and that '[c]onsequently UNOSOM II will not be able to implement the above mandate unless it is endowed with enforcement powers under Chapter VII of the Charter'.[144] In response, the Security Council in resolution 814 authorized this expanded mandate for UNOSOM II, and also, *inter alia*, delegated the power of command and control over this force to the SG and his Special Representative. The resolution:

Requests the Secretary-General, through his Special Representative to direct the Force Commander of UNOSOM II to assume responsibility for the consolidation,

---

[141] On the authority and control which a principal organ exercizes over its subsidiary, see *infra* Section III(2) in Chapter 3.

[142] For discussion of the delegation of Article 48(1) power to the SG in respect of a force carrying out military enforcement action, see *supra* note 137.

[143] See *supra* notes 34–6 and corresponding text in Chapter 1.

[144] S/25354, 3 Mar. 1993, p. 13.

expansion and maintenance of a secure environment throughout Somalia . . . and in this regard to organize a prompt, smooth and phased transition from UNITAF to UNOSOM II; . . .[145]

In other words, the Security Council delegated to the SG and his Special Representative the competence to delegate to the Force Commander broad powers to achieve the specified aim. However, the fact that the force was, potentially, to carry out military enforcement action requires the UN commander, as explained above, to take into account the views of States contributing troops to the force when decisions are being made as to how these forces are to be used in enforcement action. This legal requirement was complied with by the UN Force Commander of UNOSOM II as there were extensive mechanisms for coordination between the UN and troop-contributing countries that were established.[146]

The attacks against UNOSOM II which resulted in the deaths of over twenty peacekeepers on 5 June 1993 led the Security Council to pass resolution 837 which reaffirmed that:

. . . the SG is authorized under resolution 814 (1993) to take all necessary measures against all those responsible for the public attacks . . . including those responsible for publicly inciting such attacks [in order] to establish the effective authority of UNOSOM throughout Somalia, including to secure the investigation of their actions and their arrest and detention for prosecution, trial and punishment.

The Council did not consider that it was widening the mandate of the SG. The Council simply reiterated that the SG had under the terms of resolution 814 the competence to authorize, and exercize command and control over, the use of force to conduct the action stipulated in resolution 837 as it was directed at the 'establish[ment of] a secure environment throughout Somalia'. It thus seems clear that a delegation of powers by the Security Council had taken place by resolution 814, since the SG has been granted a wide discretion. Put differently, the exercize of the power is not made subject to rules laid down by the Security Council which are so restrictive that the SG's role is merely executive such that the SG is simply performing functions assigned to him under Article 98 of the Charter.[147] Thus resolution 837 represented an authoritative interpretation by the Council of the SG's mandate to order the use of force under resolution 814. It is contended that resolutions 814 and 837 confer on the SG alone the power to decide when and how to use UNOSOM II in military enforcement operations in Somalia. This is of importance to the question of the legality of the use of force

---

[145] The chain of command in UNOSOM is similar to that of previous UN peacekeeping operations. The SG in his report of 3 Mar. 1993 states that the UNOSOM Force Commander will report to the SG's Special Representative, who, it can be assumed, reports and is responsible to the SG: S/25354, p. 17.

[146] For a detailed description of these mechanisms, see S/25354, p. 3.

[147] See *supra* note 10 and corresponding text.

by Member States in Somalia that was outside the command and control of the SG's Special Representative.[148]

(b) The case of a regional arrangement: air strikes in the former Yugoslavia

The Security Council in resolution 836 delegated to UN Member States the power to carry out air strikes in the former Yugoslavia. Resolution 836 in operative paragraph 10 delegates to UN Member States acting nationally or through a regional organization or arrangement the power to use 'all necessary measures, through the use of air power' to achieve certain ends 'under the authority of the Security Council and subject to close coordination with the Secretary General and UNPROFOR'.[149] As explained above, air strikes, as distinguished from the use of air support, clearly involve military enforcement action.[150] Resolution 836 goes on to state: '[The Security Council] *[r]equests* the Member States concerned, the SG and UNPROFOR to coordinate closely on the measures they are taking to implement paragraph 10 above and to report to the Council through the SG'. As was the case with close air support, the SG interpreted the phrase 'coordinate closely' to mean that his consent must be given, as the agent of the Council, before air power can be used. Put differently, the SG interpreted the resolution to mean that the Council had delegated to him the power to take the decision whether in a particular case air strikes should be taken. The problem with this interpretation is that a delegation of such an important power should be made in express terms by the Council. Nonetheless, the approach of the SG is confirmed in this case since it seems that the Council intended such a process of decision making. As the Norwegian delegation observed in a subsequent Council debate: '. . . It is ultimately the responsibility of the SG to decide on the steps that may be taken [in respect of air strikes], as the overall political authority rests with the United Nations.'[151] Such an interpretation has, moreover, received widespread support from many other Council Members.[152] Russia,

---

[148] See *infra* notes 84–6 and corresponding text in Chapter 5. In any case, it now seems clear that the SG does not possess the ability in practice to exercize command and control powers over a military enforcement force. It is largely as a result of the experience of Somalia that the SG has stated in his *Supplement to An Agenda for Peace*: 'Neither the Security Council nor the secretary-general at present has the capacity to deploy, direct, command, and control operations for this purpose [enforcement].' (Boutros-Ghali, B., *Supplement to An Agenda for Peace* (1995), para. 77.)

[149] For the legal considerations relating to the delegation of power to NATO to carry out air strikes in the former Yugoslavia, see *infra* Section II(1) in Chapter 6.

[150] See *supra* note 113 and corresponding text.

[151] S/PV.3336 (Resumption 1), p. 94.

[152] For example, the US representative stated: 'We need to remind ourselves that the decision to initiate air strikes rests in the hands of the Secretary-General, and it was the

however, stood opposed to the interpretation that the Council had delegated such a power of discretion to the SG. In respect of UN and NATO[153]
efforts to protect UN designated 'safe areas', the SG received, on 14 and 15
January 1994, *demarches* in which Russia reiterated its position that, in the
words of the SG, 'any use of force in Bosnia and Herzegovina should be
subject to prior consultations by the SG with the members of the Security
Council and that only after such consultations should a decision be made to
seek enforcement assistance from any source, including NATO'.[154] The SG
replied to this position in a letter to the Council which states in part the
following:

As the members of the Security Council are aware, operational arrangements have
been in place since August 1993 for the provision by NATO of air power to support
UNPROFOR in defending United Nations personnel who may come under deliberate attack from one or other of the conflicting parties in Bosnia and Herzegovina.
These arrangements have been tested in a number of exercizes and are fully operational. The first decision to initiate the use of air power for this purpose would
be taken by me, on the basis of a request by my Special Representative for the
former Yugoslavia, acting on a recommendation by the Force Commander of
UNPROFOR.[155]

The 'operational arrangements' which the SG refers to here is the 'dual key'
system which controlled the use of air strikes in the former Yugoslavia. This
system stipulates that both NATO and the UN can request such action, and
that both have to give their consent.[156] The SG's interpretation of resolution
836 has seen him give consent on behalf of the UN. This approach was
accepted by the North Atlantic Council.[157] The SG has implied an additional power in exercizing his delegated power of command and control
under Security Council resolution 836. The SG has had to define the range
of actions which can justify the use of air strikes. Interestingly, it seems
that the SG views NATO air strikes to protect UN declared 'safe areas' as

---

Council that put it there.' (S/PV.3336, p. 19.) See also the statements by the representatives
of Canada (S/PV.3336 (Resumption 1), p. 137); Nigeria (S/PV.3336, p. 53); and Afghanistan
(S/PV.3336 (Resumption 1), pp. 102–3).

[153] On the status of NATO as a Chapter VIII-entity exercising delegated Chapter VII
powers, see *infra* notes 14–16 in Chapter 6.

[154] S/1994/50, p. 2.

[155] *Ibidem*.

[156] The SG in a statement dated 23 Nov. 1994 has explained further that the dual-key
approach involves the additional element of any response being proportionate: *Secretary-
General/SM/54933*, 23 Nov. 1994.

[157] The North Atlantic Council stated that it '. . . *agrees with the position of the UN SG that
the first use of air power in the theatre shall be authorised by him.* With respect to NATO, the
North Atlantic Council shall be the political authority that will decide on the conduct of air
strikes, which will be carried out in coordination with the United Nations.' (*Atlantic News*, No.
2547, 26 Aug. 1993, emphasis added.)

clearly part of the UN operation.[158] Moreover, the SG has noted that the use of air strikes cannot be limited solely to the enforcement of the express terms of the Security Council resolutions. He states that as a result of the introduction of air defence systems by Bosnian Serbs 'any use of air power at the present time must take into account the possible prior need, in advance of a contemplated air strike, to suppress air defence systems that threaten NATO aircraft. Such pre-emptive military action . . . [is] undeniably necessary to ensure the safety of the NATO aircraft . . .'[159] The legality of such an interpretation by the SG of his delegated powers can easily be justified by reference to the right to use force in self-defence.[160]

The problem, however, in the case of NATO co-operation with the UN in carrying out military enforcement measures in the former Yugoslavia has been identified by a NATO official who observed:

In our cooperation with the UN we have violated the golden military rule to have one single command structure. . . . As long as the two organizations will cooperate, a certain measure of confusion will come back on, for example, the exact interpretation of texts (resolutions) or formulas (ultimatums).[161]

The problems with the command structure led to a request by NATO officials to simplify the command procedure for the initiation of air strikes to protect UN Safe Areas in Bosnia. In response, the SG decided to delegate his power of when to order air-strikes to his Force Commander. As explained above, the SG possesses the competence to make such a delegation of powers. Moreover, as was the case with close air support, such a situation is desirable since the decision to use force is being made by the person most familiar with the situation on the ground: the military Force Commander. This does not compromise in legal terms the requirement of UN authority and control over the military enforcement action since the Force Commander is under the authority and control of the SG and ultimately the Security Council. So if the way in which a power is being used is not acceptable in political terms then the Council or the SG can alter this practice through decisions which are binding on the Force Commander.

---

[158] See the statement by the SG in a report dated 1 Dec. 1994: S/1994/1389, pp. 13–14. See also S/1994/555, pp. 4–5. This interpretation received support from UN Member States. See, for example, the statement by the representative of Turkey: S/PV.3336 (Resumption 1), p. 109. For the attempt to protect UN declared 'safe areas', see *infra* Section II(1) in Chapter 6.
[159] S/1995/444, p. 12. Such action was taken when on 10 Sept. 1995 NATO launched missiles against Bosnian Serb air-defence systems that posed a threat to NATO aircraft which were carrying out air strikes against Bosnian Serb positions in Bosnia.
[160] For further discussion of this issue in the context of Iraq, see *infra* Section IV in Chapter 5.
[161] As quoted in Leurdijk, *supra* note 111, p. 81.

3

The Delegation of Powers to
UN Subsidiary Organs

The six principal organs of the United Nations possess the authority to establish and utilize subsidiary organs in the attainment of their Charter objectives.[1] There is, however, an important distinction to be made between the legal considerations relating to the establishment and termination of a subsidiary organ and the lawfulness of the activities of a subsidiary organ. The establishment and termination of UN subsidiary organs is governed by a legal framework consisting of the relevant provisions of the UN Charter and those parts of the general law of international institutions that relate to this activity, while the lawfulness of the acts of subsidiary organs will depend on the subsidiary complying with the legal mandate conferred on it by the principal. The former deals with the competence of principal organs to establish and terminate subsidiary organs while the latter is concerned with the subsidiary remaining within the bounds of its delegated mandate. This Chapter is concerned primarily with the identification of those elements of the general legal framework that govern the processes of establishment and termination of UN subsidiary organs. This is important to our more general enquiry relating to a delegation of Chapter VII powers since the question of a lawful delegation of powers to a subsidiary organ is inextricably linked to the process of its lawful establishment. This framework applies to all UN

---

[1] Article 7(1) of the Charter establishes the following principal organs of the United Nations: the General Assembly; the Security Council; the Economic and Social Council; the Trusteeship Council; the International Court of Justice; and the Secretariat. For the scope of the authority of principal organs to establish subsidiary organs, see *infra* Section II. The literature on UN subsidiary organs has not been extensive. The main works include: Reuter, P., 'Les Organes Subsidiaires des Organisations Internationales', in *Hommage d'une Génération de Juristes au Président Basdevant* (Chaumont, C., ed.) (1958), pp. 415–30; Torres Bernardez, S., 'Subsidiary Organs', in *Manuel sur les organisations internationales* (Dupuy, R-J., ed.) (1988), p. 109; Sarooshi, D., 'The Legal Framework Governing United Nations Subsidiary Organs', *BYIL*, 67 (1996), p. 413; Ramcharan, B., 'Lacunae in the Law of International Organizations: The Relations between Subsidiary and Parent Organs with Particular Reference to the Commission and Sub-Commission on Human Rights', in *Festchrift Ermacora* (Nowak, M., et al. eds.) (1988), pp. 37–49; Klepacki, Z., *The Organs of International Organizations* (1973), p. 17 *et sequentia*; Schermers, H., and Blokker, N., *International Institutional Law* (1995), p. 152; Dutheil de la Rochere, J., 'Etude de la composition de certains organes subsidiaires récemment crées par l'Assemblée générale des Nations Unies dans le domaine économique', *Annuaire français de droit international* (1967), p. 307; and commentaries to Articles 7, 22, 29, and 68 of the Charter in the following works: Goodrich, L., and Hambro, E., *The Charter of the United Nations* (1949), Bentwich, N., and Martin, A., *A Commentary on the Charter of the United Nations* (1950), *La Charte des Nations Unies* (Cot, J-P., and Pellet, A., eds.) (1991), and Simma, B., ed., *The Charter of the United Nations: A Commentary* (1994).

principal and subsidiary organs: it is all encompassing in scope. This is attested by the fact that once subsidiary organs are lawfully established by a principal organ, they become subsidiary organs of the United Nations as a whole and not just subsidiary organs of the particular principal organ.[2] Accordingly, the practice of all UN principal organs in establishing and terminating subsidiary organs needs to be considered in order to examine fully the variety of issues that relate to a delegation of powers by the Council to its subsidiary organs. These issues include: what is meant by a UN subsidiary organ; the authority of principal organs to establish subsidiary organs; the limitations on this authority; the competence of principal organs to delegate powers of discretion to subsidiary organs, and, in the context of the Security Council, the limitations on this competence; and, finally, the preconditions for the lawful establishment of subsidiary organs.

The operation of this framework is illustrated by reference to, *inter alia*, certain cases where the Security Council has established subsidiary organs as part of its efforts to maintain or restore international peace. For example: the UN War Crimes Tribunals for the former Yugoslavia and Rwanda, and the Unified Command in the case of Korea are considered in some detail.

I. UN SUBSIDIARY ORGANS: ISSUES OF DEFINITION

Issues of form are not of major importance when considering what constitutes a UN subsidiary organ.[3] Thus although they have usually been

---

[2] In the discussion on the current Article 7(2) of the Charter at the San Francisco Conference, this argument was made by the representative of The Netherlands in the Coordination Committee: 30 May meeting, 8, UN Doc. WD 60; CO/29 vol. 17, p. 37. As a result, UN subsidiary organs enjoy, for example, privileges and immunities under the Convention on the Privileges and Immunities of the United Nations and the capacity to conclude treaties and to contract with private entities. The UN Legal Counsel has found the Convention on the Privileges and Immunities of the United Nations applicable to UN subsidiary organs in the case of, among others, the United Nations Joint Staff Pension Fund: see *UNJYB* (1978), p. 186.

[3] Moreover, issues of form should not constitute a legal bar to the effective functioning of subsidiary organs. In a memorandum to the Secretary of ECOSOC, the UN Legal Counsel pointed to the fact that there are several examples in the practice of the General Assembly and ECOSOC where subsidiary organs have met and proceeded to discharge their mandate even though for one reason or another it was not possible to appoint the full complement of members provided for in the resolution authorizing the establishment of the body concerned. The Legal Counsel continued: 'The conclusion that may be drawn from these precedents is that the fact it is not possible to secure the appointment of all the members envisaged in a resolution establishing an organ has not been considered a bar to convening the organs in question and to permitting them to proceed with their work.' (Memorandum to the Secretary of ECOSOC, *UNJYB* (1984), p. 168.) In this opinion, the UN Legal Counsel applied the principle of effectiveness, as formulated for example in Article 28(1) of the Charter in respect of the Security Council, to the context of the operation of UN subsidiary organs. The relevant section of Article 28(1) provides: 'The Security Council shall be so organised as to be able to function continuously.' Thus, the Legal Counsel stated: '[t]he fact that a particular group

composed of representatives of States,[4] in certain cases members have been appointed in their personal capacity.[5] It is not, moreover, a requirement that the membership of a subsidiary organ should reflect or draw upon the membership of the particular principal organ or even of the Organization.[6] The only requirement regarding membership is that if States are proposed to be members of the subsidiary organ, they must either be Members of the United Nations or States that are assessed contributions by the General Assembly on the basis of their participation in the activities of the subsidiary organ.[7]

The Charter nowhere defines the term 'subsidiary organ'.[8] There have,

entitled to be represented on a subsidiary organ of the United Nations does not desire to participate in the work of that organ should not have the effect of preventing the organ concerned from being effectively, albeit incompletely, constituted and from carrying out the functions entrusted to it. In our view this in effect constitutes a waiver by the group concerned of its right to be represented on the organ in question.' (Memorandum to the Secretary of ECOSOC, *UNJYB* (1984), p. 169.)

[4] In cases where a subsidiary organ is composed of States, its membership may include all Member States—as in the case of the Committee on arrangements for a conference for the purpose of reviewing the Charter (General Assembly resolution 992 (X))—or a number of specified Member States, in which case commissions or committees are often designated as special or *ad hoc* commissions or committees. There is, however, an important distinction between a subsidiary organ and a committee which is part of the principal organ: see *infra* note 14 and corresponding text.

[5] This occurred in the case, for example, of the UN Representative for India and Pakistan. (*Repertory of Practice of UN Organs* (1955), vol. 2, p. 121.) Moreover, the Council has recommended to the Secretary-General that he appoint a UN Mediator in respect of Cyprus (*Repertoire of the Practice of the Security Council, 1964–1965*, p. 71); a Personal Representative in respect of the Dominican Republic (*Repertoire of the Practice of the Security Council, 1964–1965*, p. 72), the Middle East (*Repertoire of the Practice of the Security Council, 1966–1968*, p. 76), and Liberia (Security Council resolution 788 of 19 Nov. 1992); and that he send a Special Envoy to Abkhazia, Georgia (Security Council resolution 849 of 9 July 1993). As the UN Legal Counsel has noted: '[o]ther subsidiary organs consist of several individuals, or of a single individual, appointed in their individual expert capacity. In some instances, as in the case of the Technical Assistance Board (Economic and Social Council resolution 222 A (IX)), a subsidiary organ is composed of the executive heads, or their representatives, of the United Nations and the specialized agencies. The Administrative Committee on Co-ordination established by Economic and Social Council resolution 13 (III), which is a subsidiary organ of the Council, also consists of the executive heads of the United Nations and of the specialized agencies.' (*UNJYB* (1963), p. 169.)

[6] Certain non-Member States have been included as members of a UN subsidiary organ when deemed appropriate: see, for example, the Executive Board of UNICEF (General Assembly resolution 417 (V)) or the Governing Council of the Special Fund (General Assembly resolution 1240 (XIII)): see *UNJYB* (1963), p. 169.

[7] Accordingly, the UN Legal Counsel stated, in respect of membership of the UN Environmental Programme: 'In the absence of guidance from the General Assembly there would not appear to be a sufficient basis for the Governing Council to include as members of the proposed subsidiary organ States that meet neither of these criteria.' (*UNJYB* (1983), p. 170.)

[8] The *Repertory of Practice* points out that the term 'subsidiary organ' has not been defined by any organ of the United Nations, and that, in the practice of the Organization, 'such expressions as "commissions", "committees", "subsidiary organs", and "subsidiary bodies" have been used interchangeably'. (*Repertory of Practice of United Nations Organs*, vol. 1, p. 224.) For examples of such practice, see Gordon, W., *The United Nations at the Crossroads of Reform* (1994), p. 72 *et sequentia*. Cf. *infra* note 14 and corresponding text.

however, been several attempts made at a definition. For instance, subsidiary organs were defined in a UN document as follows:

A subsidiary organ is one which is established by or under the authority of a principal organ of the United Nations, in accordance with Article 7, paragraph 2, of the Charter, by resolution of the appropriate body. Such an organ is an integral part of the Organization . . . Most subsidiary organs have in common their establishment by parent bodies which presumably may change their terms of reference and composition, issue policy directives to them, receive their reports and accept or reject their recommendations. Generally speaking, a subsidiary organ may be abolished or modified by action of the parent body.[9]

Similarly, the *Repertory of Practice of United Nations Organs* lists the following, almost identical, common features of a UN subsidiary organ:

(a) A subsidiary organ is created by, or under the authority of, a principal organ of the United Nations;
(b) The membership, structure and terms of reference of a subsidiary organ are determined, and may be modified by, or under the authority of, a principal organ;
(c) A subsidiary organ may be terminated by, or under the authority of, a principal organ.[10]

Both definitions contain two of the preconditions for the lawful establishment of a UN subsidiary organ: that it be established by a UN principal organ, and that it be under the authority and control of a UN principal organ.[11] There is, however, the additional precondition that the establishment of the subsidiary organ does not violate the delimitation of Charter powers between the principal organs.[12] The satisfaction of these preconditions of establishment is necessary before an entity can be considered as a lawfully established UN subsidiary organ. These preconditions derive from the definition of a UN subsidiary organ, and, moreover, the law of international institutions.[13] However, in defining a subsidiary organ there is an additional element which is required: that the subsidiary organ necessarily possesses a certain degree of independence from its principal organ. This is necessary since otherwise the entity in question would simply be a part of the principal organ. This degree of independence can, as a definitional element of a subsidiary organ, be used to distinguish an entity which is part of a principal organ from a UN subsidiary

---

[9] 'Summary of internal Secretariat studies of constitutional questions relating to agencies within the framework of the United Nations': this document was subsequently proposed to the 9th Session of the General Assembly. See *General Assembly Official Records*, 9th Session, Annexes, Agenda Item 67, at p. 13, A/C 1/758, paras. 1 and 2.
[10] *Repertory of Practice of United Nations Organs*, vol. 1, p. 228.
[11] For detailed consideration of these preconditions, see *infra* Sections III (1) and (2).
[12] For detailed consideration of this precondition, see *infra* Section III (3).
[13] See *infra* Section III.

organ.[14] This occurred during the debates of the 6th Committee of the General Assembly where there was discussion as to whether committees of the General Assembly should be regarded as subsidiary organs or as integral components of the Assembly itself.[15] In the ensuing debates it was accepted that a Main Committee is not usually a subsidiary organ, but a part of the General Assembly itself since the two are identical in membership.[16] It was, nevertheless, generally agreed that if a committee continued to operate during the interval between two General Assembly sessions it would probably be a subsidiary organ with the result that the Assembly would have to consider its work.[17] The test that emerged to determine

[14] Accordingly, Torres Bernardez states: ' "subsidiary organs" should be distinguished from bodies (e.g., committees, commissions, working parties, etc.) which may be set up within a given "principal organ" as integral parts thereof. These bodies are not distinct entities or distinct "organs", albeit "subsidiary", but elements of the internal organization of the "principal organ" concerned.' (Torres Bernardez, *supra* note 1, p. 130.) In such cases no delegation of power is involved from the principal organ. This approach has also been recognized in the domestic sphere. For example, in the Israeli Supreme Court case of *Attorney-General of Israel* v. *Kamiar* it was found that no delegation of power could be said to have taken place when a Minister of Foreign Affairs authorized an Ambassador to sign a treaty on his behalf since they were both part of the same integral organ of government: *Attorney-General of Israel* v. *Kamiar*, *ILR*, 44 (1972), p. 248 at p. 249.

[15] *GAOR*, 2nd Session, 6th Committee, 57th meeting, p. 143.

[16] *Ibidem*, pp. 142–4. However, the fact that the membership of an entity is identical to that of the principal organ which established it does not in itself mean that the entity is a committee of the principal organ. Many subsidiary organs established by the Security Council are recognized as such even though they mirror the membership of the Council. For example, the Sanctions Committees established by the Security Council to monitor and ensure implementation of economic sanctions imposed by the Council against the following non-State and State entities: Southern Rhodesia, the Sanctions Committee was initially established by resolution 253 (1968) in the form of a committee of limited membership of seven, but later, on 1 Oct. 1970, the membership was expanded to include all Security Council members (*Repertoire of the Practice of the Security Council, 1966–1968*, p. 78, and *Repertoire of the Practice of the Security Council, 1969–1971*, p. 63); Iraq (Security Council resolution 661 (1990)); the former Yugoslavia (Security Council resolution 724); Libya (Security Council resolution 748); Somalia (Security Council resolution 751); Haiti (Security Council resolution 841); and Angola (Security Council resolution 864). For the operations of one of these committees, see Conlon, P., 'Lessons From Iraq: The Functions of the Iraq Sanctions Committee as a Source of Sanctions Implementation Authority and Practice', *Virginia Journal of International Law*, 35 (1995), p. 633.

[17] See, for example, the statement by the representative of the USSR: *GAOR*, 2nd Session, 6th Committee, 57th meeting, p. 143. Even if this is the case, it does not follow that, if a committee meets during the period when a principal organ is in session, it cannot be considered as a subsidiary organ. As Torres Bernardez argues: 'Categorizations made in the "internal law", or in administrative internal arrangements, of some international organizations between "standing" and "special" or *ad hoc* bodies, between "sessional" and "intersessional" bodies, etc., are not always of help as criteria to determine if a given body is an integral part of a "principal organ" or a "subsidiary organ", because both such criteria are susceptible of application to both these kinds of bodies without distinction.' (Torres Bernardez, *supra* note 1, p. 131.) What if the case were such that a committee of a principal organ were assigned the performance of functions which the principal organ did not itself possess? The mere fact that such a committee met during the same period as the principal organ cannot in itself preclude such a committee being considered to be a subsidiary organ of the principal organ. Moreover,

whether an entity is a subsidiary organ is that it will depend on whether the entity is exercizing powers and functions in a manner which is distinct from the internal workings of the principal organ. An additional factor is whether the subsidiary organ is performing functions which the principal organ does not itself possess.[18]

This requirement of independence means that the establishment of sessional committees, subcommittees, and working groups of UN principal organs does not represent the establishment of subsidiary organs.[19] Similarly, the appointment of UN staff by the Secretary-General under Article 101(1) of the Charter does not represent the establishment of subsidiary organs under Article 7(2),[20] since UN staff are in legal terms considered an integral part of the UN Secretariat,[21] a UN principal organ under Article 7(1).

In conclusion, the four definitional elements of a subsidiary organ are important in determining whether a particular subsidiary organ has been lawfully established, and therefore whether a lawful delegation of powers has taken place. These preconditions stipulate the way in which a lawful exercize of the authority of establishment by a principal organ takes place. However, if a principal organ were to exceed the scope of authority which it possesses to establish a subsidiary organ then it has also acted unlawfully.[22]

It is convenient, before examining the preconditions of establishment, to determine the scope of the authority of principal organs to establish subsidiary organs.

---

the case of committees of the General Assembly is arguably unique, since the Assembly is the only principal organ that has in a decision—paragraph 34 of decision 34/401—stipulated that its subsidiary organs are not to meet during sessions of the Assembly unless explicitly authorized to do so.

[18] See further on this issue: *infra* note 28 and corresponding text.

[19] Thus the constitutional basis of such entities is not the general authority to establish subsidiary organs, but those articles in the Charter which authorize the principal organs to adopt their own rules of procedure. See also: Simma, *supra* note 1, p. 197.

[20] Cf. Kelsen, H., *The Law of the United Nations* (1951), p. 139.

[21] Article 97 of the Charter provides, in part, the following: 'The Secretariat shall comprise a Secretary-General and such staff as the Organization may require.' See also Simma, *supra* note 1, pp. 1088–9; and Alexandrowicz, C., 'The Secretary-General of the United Nations', *ICLQ*, 11 (1962), p. 1109 at p. 1112.

[22] In both cases, this does not in itself mean that the law will treat the acts of the principal organ as utterly non-existent and not attach legal consequences to its acts. See: *Expenses* case, *ICJ Reports* (1962), p. 151 at p. 168. See further on this issue: Osieke, E., 'Ultra-Vires Acts in International Organizations', *BYIL*, 48 (1976–7), p. 259, and also 'The Legal Validity of Ultra Vires Decisions of International Organizations', *AJIL*, 77 (1983), p. 239; Morgenstern, F., 'Legality in International Organizations', *BYIL*, 48 (1976–7), p. 24; Jennings, R., 'Nullity and Effectiveness in International Law', in *Cambridge Essays in International Law* (1965), p. 64; Lauterpacht, E., 'The Legal Effect of Illegal Acts of International Organizations', in *Cambridge Essays in International Law* (1965), p. 88; and Cahier, G., 'La Nullité en droit international', *Revue Générale droit International Public*, 76 (1972), p. 645.

II. THE AUTHORITY OF UN PRINCIPAL ORGANS TO ESTABLISH SUBSIDIARY ORGANS: THE COMPETENCE OF THE COUNCIL TO DELEGATE CHAPTER VII POWERS TO SUBSIDIARY ORGANS

The authority of a principal organ to establish subsidiary organs constitutes part of our discussion of a delegation of powers by the Council since an integral part of the process of establishment is the delegation of powers to a subsidiary.[23] After discussion of the nature of the authority to establish subsidiary organs, this section will then consider whether this authority of establishment includes the competence to delegate powers of discretion to the subsidiary.

1. The nature of the authority to establish subsidiary organs

The UN Charter gives the Security Council the authority to establish subsidiary organs:[24] the Council has a general authority under Article 7(2), while Article 29 provides this in specific terms.[25] What is unclear, however, is the nature of the relationship between the two types of authority, the legal consequences of the distinction that exists, and the content of any limitations that restrict their exercize.

There is an important distinction between the general and specific authority to establish subsidiary organs.[26] The general authority to establish subsidiary organs in Article 7(2) provides in a non-restrictive way for the establishment of '[s]uch subsidiary organs as may be found necessary'. It has been shown elsewhere that Article 7(2) is *per se* a source of authority to establish subsidiary organs.[27] Under the specific authority of establishment, the Council can only establish subsidiary organs to perform, in the terms of Article 29, 'its [the Council's] functions'. However, in the case of the general authority of establishment under Article 7(2) there is no such func-

---

[23] The exception to this position is where the Security Council establishes a subsidiary organ to exercize functions which it cannot itself exercize. See *infra* note 28 and corresponding text.

[24] In so doing the Charter entered new territory as compared to the League of Nations Covenant, and opened up possibilities for the institutional development of the United Nations system. The League of Nations Covenant did not expressly provide for the establishment of subsidiary organs, although in practice a large number of subsidiary organs were established by the League: see 'Commentary to Article 7' in Cot and Pellet, *supra* note 1, p. 207.

[25] Article 7(2) of the Charter provides: 'Such subsidiary organs as may be found necessary may be established in accordance with the present Charter.' Article 29 states: '[The Security Council] may establish such subsidiary organs as it deems necessary for the performance of its functions.'

[26] This distinction is of considerable practical importance. As will be seen below, where a principal organ establishes a subsidiary organ to exercize powers and functions which it cannot itself exercize there are limitations as to the degree of authority and control which the principal can exercize over its subsidiary. See *infra* Section III(2).

[27] See Sarooshi, *supra* note 1, pp. 422–5.

tional limitation: subsidiary organs may be established under Article 7(2) to perform functions which the Council cannot itself perform.[28] This was clearly established by the International Court in the *Administrative Tribunal* and the *Application for Review* cases.[29] Thus the general authority in Article 7(2) is broader than the specific authority in Article 29 which is only for the purpose of carrying out the 'functions' of the Security Council.

There is, however, a limitation on this general authority of establishment: the Council must possess either an express or implied power under the Charter to be able to establish such a subsidiary organ.[30] This follows from the position that the authority of principal organs to establish subsidiary organs is not in itself enough for the lawful establishment of a subsidiary organ. The principal organ must itself possess either the express or implied

---

[28] As Dutheil de la Rochere in Cot and Pellet's *La Charte des Nations Unies* has observed: 'A la lumière de la pratique suivie et des indications fournies par deux avis importants de la Cour Internationale de Justice, l'avis sur la *Réparation des dommages subis au service des Nations Unies* de 1949 et l'avis sur les *Effets des jugements du Tribunal administratif des Nations Unies* de 1954, il semble que la *théorie des compétences fonctionnelles* de l'organisation fournisse la meilleure explication et de l'étendue et des limites des fonctions déléguées aux organes subsidiaires des Nations Unies a l'occasion de leur création par une manifestation de volonté de l'Organisation.... De façon positive, *les organes subsidiaires peuvent assumer toutes les fonctions, toutes les missions, tous les mandats nécessaires au fonctionnement de l'Organisation* qu'un organe principal jugera nécessaire de leur confier.' (Cot and Pellet, *supra* note 1, pp. 216–17.) A similar approach was taken by Rosner when discussing the establishment of UNEF by the General Assembly, see Rosner, G., *The United Nations Emergency Force* (1964), p. 44. See also Ciobanu, D., *Preliminary Objections to the Jurisdiction of the United Nations Political Organs* (1975) p. 30.

[29] *Administrative Tribunal* case, *ICJ Reports* (1954), p. 47. See further on this case, *infra* note 35 and corresponding text. In the *Application for Review* case, the Court found that the General Assembly had the competence to operate in the area of staff administration, and therefore that it could establish a body with judicial functions which it could not itself exercize under the Charter: *ICJ Reports* (1973), p. 166. Cf., however, the following dissenting opinions of judges of the International Court of Justice: Judge Alvarez (*Application for Review* case, *ibidem*, p. 70); Judge Hackworth (*ibidem*, pp. 78–9); Judge Onyeama (*ibidem*, p. 226); and Judge Morozov (*ibidem*, p. 298). Cf., also, the opinion of the Committee on International Criminal Jurisdiction, established to make recommendations regarding the establishment of an international criminal court, which in its report to the General Assembly stated: 'Under the Charter, the court could only be established as a subsidiary organ. The principal organ would presumably be the General Assembly, but a subsidiary organ could not have a competence falling outside the competence of its principal, and it was questionable whether the General Assembly was competent to administer justice.' (*General Assembly Official Records*, 7th Session, Supplement No. 11 (A/2136), p. 3.) Thus it was argued that since under Article 22 the General Assembly was only entitled to create subsidiary organs to assist it in the performance of its functions and that since the functions of the Assembly did not include the exercize of criminal jurisdiction over individuals, it could not, therefore, delegate such functions to a subsidiary organ. (*Ibidem.*)

[30] As Dutheil de la Rochere, in *La Charte des Nations Unies*, has acknowledged, there are limitations in this area: 'La notion de compétence fonctionnelle ne légitime pas cependant toutes les créations et l'attribution de n'importe quelles fonctions par un organe principal a un organe subsidiaire. Les organes subsidiaires ne *peuvent assumer aucune tâche étrangère ou non essentielle aux fonctions de l'Organisation*. C'est la Charte elle-même qui fixe les limites de ces fonctions essentielles.' (Cot and Pellet, *supra* note 1, p. 218.)

power which it seeks to delegate to its subsidiary.[31] However, as just noted, this does not preclude a principal organ from possessing an implied power to establish a subsidiary organ to exercize functions which it does not itself possess.[32] In such a case the power to establish such a subsidiary organ may even be implied from the general competence of the principal organ to operate in the particular area,[33] and does not *per se* involve a delegation by the Council of its own powers to the subsidiary. The principal may not itself possess the competence to perform certain functions, but the establishment of, and exercize of these functions by, a subsidiary organ may nonetheless be necessary for the effective exercize by the principal organ of its powers and functions in an area in which it has the competence to operate.[34] This is what occurred in the *Administrative Tribunal* case where the International Court found that the General Assembly had the competence to establish a judicial body, the Administrative Tribunal, to perform functions in the area of staff relations.

The majority of the Court in the *Administrative Tribunal* case found that the General Assembly did not under the Charter possess the judicial function which the Tribunal was exercizing, and thus '[b]y establishing the Administrative Tribunal, the General Assembly was not delegating the performance of its own functions: it was exercizing a power which it had under the Charter to regulate staff relations'.[35] It was the opinion of the Court that the General Assembly possessed the implied power to establish such a subsidiary organ, and that this power could be implied from its competence to operate in the area concerned, the regulation of staff relations.[36] The Court then found it necessary to undertake 'the further enquiry

[31] As Bowett states: 'The establishment of a subsidiary organ simply cannot be divorced from the functions *entrusted* to the organ . . . In other words a resolution which contemplates a subsidiary organ with a given function has to find its constitutional basis first and foremost in the articles justifying the functions—and not in an article giving a general power to establish subsidiary organs.' (Bowett, D., *United Nations Forces* (1964), p. 178.) Thus Bowett points out that in the *Expenses* case the Court did not rely on Article 22 as the source of the constitutional power of establishment of UNEF, but turned to the more substantive powers of the General Assembly, in particular Article 14. (Bowett, *ibidem*, p. 178, note 46) See also Ciobanu, D., 'The Power of the Security Council to Organize Peace-Keeping Operations', in *United Nations Peace-Keeping: Legal Essays* (Cassesse, A. (ed.)) (1978), p. 19 at p. 23.

[32] See *supra* note 28 and corresponding text.

[33] The word competence is being used here to describe what an organ of an international organization is specifically empowered to do. In this way the competence of an organ refers to the range of activities which an organ is entitled to undertake, and the conditions attached thereto, in the pursuit of its Charter designated functions and purposes. See also: Bekker, P., *The Legal Position of Intergovernmental Organizations: A Functional Necessity Analysis of Their Legal Status and Immunities* (1994), p. 75.

[34] The implication of powers by an international organization from its constituent treaty is a well accepted doctrine under international law. See, for example, the *Reparations* case, *ICJ Reports* (1949), p. 174 at pp. 180, 182.

[35] *ICJ Reports* (1954), p. 61. Cf. Judge Hackworth, *ibidem*, pp. 80–1.

[36] The Court implied from Article 101(1) of the Charter the power of the General Assembly to 'establish a tribunal to do justice between the Organization and the staff members'.

as to the agency by which it may be exercized'.[37] The Court decided that the source of authority of the General Assembly to establish such a subsidiary organ was the general authority under Article 7(2) of the Charter. Accordingly, the Court found that 'the power to establish a tribunal to do justice between the Organization and the staff members may be exercized by the General Assembly'.[38]

This use of the general authority to establish subsidiary organs to perform functions which the principal cannot itself exercize is of considerable importance when determining the legality of the recent establishment by the Council of several subsidiary organs: in particular, the UN War Crimes Tribunals for the former Yugoslavia and Rwanda.[39]

The Security Council in resolution 808 determined that the establishment of the War Crimes Tribunal for the former Yugoslavia would contribute both to putting an end to the commission of war crimes and to the restoration of peace in the former Yugoslavia.[40] Resolution 808 requested the Secretary-General to make a report to the Council on how best to establish such a tribunal. In his subsequent report, the Secretary-General states that such a tribunal should be established under Chapter VII of the Charter as a subsidiary organ of the Council. Subsequently, the Security Council, in resolution 827, acting expressly under Chapter VII established the War Crimes Tribunal for the former Yugoslavia. In the *Tadic* case the lawfulness of the establishment of the Tribunal was challenged by the Defence.[41] The issues which arose from this challenge were not dealt with by the Trial Chamber in any detail.[42] However, the Appeal Chamber of the Tribunal in

---

(*Ibidem.*) See also the *Expenses* case, where the International Court of Justice—having recognized the power of the General Assembly to act in the area of maintaining and restoring international peace—recognized the power of the Assembly to establish subsidiary organs under Article 22 through which it could exercize its functions. The Court found: 'Such implementation is a normal feature of the functioning of the United Nations. Such committees, commissions, or other bodies or individuals, constitute, in some cases, subsidiary organs established under the authority of Article 22 of the Charter.' (*Expenses* case, *ICJ Reports* (1962), p. 165.) See further as to the Court's affirmation of an implication of power in the *Administrative Tribunal* case: Amerasinghe, C., *The Law of the International Civil Service* (1994), pp. 27, 34–7; Gomula, J., 'The International Court of Justice and Administrative Tribunals of International Organizations', *Michigan Journal of International Law*, 13 (1991), p. 83 at p. 93; and Campbell, I., 'The Limits of the Powers of International Organisations', *ICLQ*, 32 (1983), p. 523 at p. 524.

[37] *ICJ Reports* (1954), p. 57.

[38] *Ibidem*, p. 58.

[39] See the analogous case of the lawful establishment of the Iraq-Kuwait Boundary Demarcation Commission by the Security Council: Sarooshi, *supra* note 1, pp. 470–2.

[40] The case of the Yugoslav War Crimes Tribunal only is examined here. However, the analysis that follows applies *mutatis mutandis* to the case of the Rwandan War Crimes Tribunal.

[41] See Defence Motions in the *Tadic* case, Case No. IT-94-I-T, 23 June 1995, paras. 3–4.

[42] The Trial Chamber dismissed the Defendants arguments on this point on the basis that the objections did not go 'so much to its jurisdiction, as to the unreviewable lawfulness of the

the *Tadic* case found that it could decide the issue of the lawfulness of the establishment of the Tribunal as part of its competence to determine its own jurisdiction.[43] The Appeal Chamber found that 'the establishment of the International Tribunal falls squarely within the powers of the Security Council under Article 41'.[44] The Appeal Chamber is not, however, suggesting that Article 41 provides a basis for the exercize by the Council of the judicial functions which have been entrusted to the Tribunal. It is clear that the purely judicial function which the Tribunal is to perform—the determination of criminal liability of individuals[45]—is a function which the Council does not itself possess under the Charter. As the Appeal Chamber held:

The establishment of the International Tribunal by the Security Council does not signify, however, that the Security Council has delegated to it some of its own functions or the exercize of some of its own powers. Nor does it mean, in reverse, that the Security Council was usurping for itself part of a judicial function which does not belong to it but to other organs of the United Nations according to the Charter. The Security Council has resorted to the establishment of a judicial organ in the form of an international criminal tribunal as an instrument for the exercize of its own principal function of the maintenance of peace and security, *i.e.*, as a measure contributing to the restoration and maintenance of peace in the former Yugoslavia.[46]

---

actions of the Security Council' (*Tadic* case, Decision on the Defence Motion on the Jurisdiction of the Tribunal, Case No. IT-94-I-T, 10 Aug. 1995, para. 40).

[43] The Appeal Chamber stated that prominent among the attributes of the judicial function, which the Tribunal was exercizing, is the power known as '*competence de la competence*': the incidental or inherent jurisdiction of any judicial tribunal to determine its own jurisdiction: 'jurisdiction to determine its own jurisdiction'. (*Prosecutor* v. *Dusko Tadic*, IT-94-1-AR72, 2 Oct. 1995, *ILM*, 35 (1996), p. 32, para. 18.) See also the *Nottebohm* case, *ICJ Reports* (1953), p. 7 at p. 119. On this issue of '*competence de la competence*' as a general principle of law, see Cheng, B., *General Principles of Law as applied by International Courts and Tribunals* (1987), pp. 275–301. For an examination of the other issues dealt with in the *Tadic* case, see Greenwood, C., 'International Humanitarian Law and the *Tadic* case', *European Journal of International Law*, 7 (1996), p. 265.

[44] *Tadic* case, *ibidem*, para. 36. Moreover, in a report of a committee of French jurists set up by the French Government to examine the establishment of the War Crimes Tribunal, it was argued that the establishment of the Tribunal was based on a power implied from Chapter VII of the Charter—specifically Article 41—since the establishment of the War Crimes Tribunal would be likely to help restore international peace and security. (S/25266, pp. 12–13.) See also Szasz, P., 'The Proposed War Crimes Tribunal for Ex-Yugoslavia', *New York University Journal of International Law and Politics*, 25 (1993), p. 405 at p. 412; Shraga, D., and Zacklin, R., 'International Criminal Tribunal for the Former Yugoslavia', *European Journal of International Law*, 5 (1994), p. 360; and O'Brien, J., 'The International Tribunal for Violations of International Humanitarian Law in the Former Yugoslavia', *AJIL*, 87 (1993), p. 638 at p. 643.

[45] The Security Council in resolution 808 decided 'that an international tribunal shall be established for the prosecution of persons responsible for serious violations of international humanitarian law committed in the territory of the former Yugoslavia since 1991'.

[46] *ILM*, 35 (1996), p. 32, para. 38.

What the Appeal Chamber of the Tribunal is indicating is that the Council possesses an implied power to establish the War Crimes Tribunal to exercize judicial functions from its express powers in Article 41, since it is a measure necessary for the effective exercize of its powers to act to maintain or restore international peace. Additionally, or in the alternative, it seems clear that the Council possesses an implied power to establish the Tribunal from its competence to act to maintain or restore international peace under Article 24(1) and, more generally, Chapter VII of the Charter.[47] Accordingly, the Secretary-General in his report to the Council on the establishment of the Tribunal stated: 'the International Tribunal should be established by a decision of the Security Council on the basis of Chapter VII . . . Such a decision would constitute a measure to maintain or restore international peace and security, following the requisite determination of the existence of a threat to the peace, breach of the peace or act of aggression.'[48] The report notes that the Security Council had already made the determination that the situation of widespread violations of international humanitarian law occurring in the former Yugoslavia constituted a threat to international peace and security.[49] The Secretary-General thus contends that the establishment of the Tribunal would be justifiable both 'in terms of the object and purpose of the decision [to restore and maintain international peace] . . . and of past Security Council practice'.[50]

Once it is clear that the Council possessed the implied power to establish the Tribunal, then there is no legal objection to the Council using its authority under Article 7(2) to establish the Tribunal as a UN subsidiary

[47] See, for example, the following statements by States' representatives in the Security Council: France (S/PV.3175, p. 9); USA (S/PV.3175, p. 13); New Zealand (S/PV.3217, p. 22); and Spain (S/PV.3175, p. 22). Similarly, in the case of the Rwandan Tribunal, see the statement by the UN Secretary-General: S/1995/134, para. 6. Moreover, the Secretary-General gave more reasons than was done in the case of the Yugoslav Tribunal why the establishment of the Rwandan Tribunal should be under Chapter VII of the Charter. He stated: '[this] was necessary to ensure not only the cooperation of Rwanda throughout the life-span of the Tribunal, but the cooperation of all States in whose territory persons alleged to have committed serious violations of international humanitarian law and acts of genocide in Rwanda might be situated. A Tribunal based on a Chapter VII resolution was also necessary to ensure a speedy and expeditious method of establishing the Tribunal.' (*Ibidem.*)

[48] S/25704 of 3 May 1993, p. 7.

[49] *Ibidem.* Moreover, the Hungarian representative to the Council observed: 'On the basis of the information that has reached us from several sources, as well as from the Commission of Experts established by the Security Council, the Council, in resolution 808 (1993), noted that the violations of international humanitarian law, because of their gravity and their generalized character, constituted a threat to international peace and security, which, in our view, fully justifies the competence of the Security Council in this sphere.' (S/PV.3217, p. 20.)

[50] S/25704, p. 7. In respect of such practice, the Secretary-General stated: 'the Security Council has on various occasions adopted decisions under Chapter VII aimed at restoring and maintaining international peace and security, which have involved the establishment of subsidiary organs for a variety of purposes. Reference may be made in this regard to Security Council resolution 687 (1991) and subsequent resolutions relating to the situation between Iraq and Kuwait.' (S/25704, p. 8.)

organ.[51] The Council could not have been acting under Article 29, since, as noted above, the Council in establishing the War Crimes Tribunal is not delegating to the Tribunal the performance of its own functions.[52]

An issue which arises in the context of a delegation by the Council of its Chapter VII powers to subsidiary organs is the extent to which a principal organ possesses the competence to delegate a power of discretion to its subsidiary as part of the authority of establishment.

2. *The delegation of a power of discretion to subsidiary organs*

The earlier practice of the UN seemed to reflect an approach that a principal organ did not possess the competence to delegate its powers of discretion to a subsidiary organ. The constitutional problems raised by a delegation of discretionary powers came into focus during discussion in the General Assembly on the establishment of an Interim Committee of the Assembly. The Interim Committee was being established to deal with matters concerning international peace and security that arose when the General Assembly was not in session.[53] During the debates those Members who opposed its establishment stated that Article 22 envisaged only a subsidiary organ with special limited powers, and that by giving the Interim Committee such broad and general terms of reference the Assembly was actually delegating its prerogatives to an organ which was equal in rank with the Assembly.[54] Accordingly, the argument ran, it was not a subsidiary organ

---

[51] However, the powers of the Security Council to act to establish an international criminal court without reference to a particular situation which constitutes a threat to or breach of international peace is highly doubtful. As a report of a committee of French jurists set up by the French Minister of State and Minister of Foreign Affairs states: 'If it was a matter of establishing a jurisdiction with universal competence, however, the Committee would be very reluctant to consider the United Nations as being competent to establish an international criminal court with binding force. There are no provisions in the Charter that could be invoked as giving the Security Council or the General Assembly such powers.' (S/25266, p. 11.) See also the statement by Arangio-Ruiz in the International Law Commission, 2300th meeting, *Yearbook of the International Law Commission* (1993), vol. 1., pp. 16–17, 26. Cf. Pellet, A., *Yearbook of the International Law Commission* (1993), vol. 1., p. 17.

[52] Compare, however, the opinion of the UN Secretary-General who in his report to the Security Council on the establishment of the Tribunal states: 'In this particular case, the Security Council would be establishing, as an enforcement measure under Chapter VII, a subsidiary organ within the terms of Article 29 of the Charter, but one of a judicial nature.' (S/25704, p. 8.) The Secretary-General took the same approach in the case of the Rwanda Tribunal: see S/1995/134, para. 8. However, what the Secretary-General probably means when he says 'a subsidiary organ within the terms of Article 29 . . . but one of a judicial nature' is that the Tribunal is an Article 29-type 'subsidiary organ' of the Council—being established under Article 7(2)—and not necessarily that the Tribunal is being established under Article 29, since if the latter were the case the Tribunal would be restricted to performing only those functions which the Council itself can perform. This reflects the difference between the general and specific authority to establish subsidiary organs: see *supra* note 26 and corresponding text.

[53] See, on the powers of the Committee, *infra* note 213 and corresponding text.

[54] UN Doc. A/C1/SR 74.

and its establishment would be a violation of Article 7(1) of the Charter which named the principal organs of the UN.[55] However, in response the US representative stated: 'To avoid raising constitutional doubts, the United States proposal did not contemplate any delegation by the Assembly of a substantive discretionary authority given by the Charter.'[56] The Indian representative interpreted this statement by the US representative to mean 'that the committee's task was to be solely that of making studies and reporting to the Assembly and that it consequently did not involve any delegation of authority'.[57] In any case, several States took the opportunity to express the view that the Charter nowhere provided that the General Assembly could delegate its own powers of discretion to a subsidiary organ.[58] Moreover, the French representative made the argument that the General Assembly:

could not delegate its powers to a subordinate authority; for, if it had certain powers, it was in virtue of the guarantees provided by its constitution. [However,] [t]he committee proposed by the United States delegation, meeting in the interval between sessions, would only have the powers of a mere committee. It would therefore act on the strength neither of an extension nor of a delegation of the Assembly's powers.[59]

---

[55] UN Doc. A/C1/SR 74.

[56] *GAOR*, 2nd Session, 1st Comm., SR 131–2.

[57] *GAOR*, 76th meeting, Doc. A/C1/196, p. 129 at p. 150. An even stricter approach was taken by the representative of Uruguay who pointed out that '[t]he only point in the United States draft resolution that remained doubtful was the power given to the interim committee to decide certain matters itself'. (*GAOR*, 2nd Session, 1st Comm., SR 140.)

[58] The Bolivian representative objected to the establishment of the Committee on the following grounds: 'Article 22 really envisaged a subsidiary organ with special limited powers. How was it possible for the Assembly, deriving all its powers from Articles 11, 13, and 14, to delegate all its prerogatives to a subsidiary organ which really would be the same as the Assembly itself or its First Committee?' (*GAOR*, 74th meeting, Doc. A/C1/196, p. 129 at p. 131.) Moreover, the Mexican representative argued that 'the interim committee as a subsidiary organ in accordance with Article 22, should not be given powers of initiative'. (*Ibidem*, p. 167.) See also the statement by the representative of Poland: *GAOR*, 74th meeting, Doc. A/C1/196, p. 129 at p. 148.

[59] *GAOR*, 77th meeting, Doc. A/C1/196. Such an argument had also earlier received support when the representative of Belgium, during the debates in the Security Council concerning certain proposals made by the Sanctions Committee—established to increase the effectiveness of economic sanctions imposed against Southern Rhodesia—stated: '. . . I must now refer to the debate which was once again provoked by the extent of the mandate given to the Committee in Security Council resolutions 253 (1968) and 277 (1970). In our opinion, the Committee can only play an auxiliary role. Even if the Council would wish it so, it would not be free to delegate to a subordinate body the responsibilities which the Charter has made incumbent on it alone. Furthermore, it would not be useful either for the Committee to be simply a faithful reflection of the Council and to be competent, as the Council is, in relation to all aspects of the question of Southern Rhodesia. Conceived as it was to function as a standing body, the Security Council, unlike the General Assembly whose activities are intermittent, does not need organs to exercize its powers in its name and in its place . . .' (1654th meeting, S/PV.1654, paras. 40, 41.) See also the statements by the United Kingdom (1655th meeting, S/PV.1655, para. 15); and France (*ibidem.*, paras. 43, 44).

The approach by States in the case of the establishment of the Interim Committee relies on the view that a subsidiary organ can only be established to perform the functions of its principal organ and not its powers.[60] However, as explained above, there is no such functional limitation when a principal organ establishes a subsidiary under Article 7(2) of the Charter. This approach has received the support of the International Court in the *Administrative Tribunal*[61] and *Administrative Review* cases.[62]

It is contended that a principal organ possesses the competence to delegate powers to its subsidiary by virtue of the general authority that it possesses to establish a subsidiary organ.[63] Kelsen explains the reasoning: 'An organ can create an auxiliary organ only by delegating its power, or part of it, to the auxiliary organ . . . The provisions of the Charter authorising certain organs to establish other organs must be interpreted to imply the authorisation to delegate power.'[64] Specifically, in the context of a delegation of Chapter VII powers by the Council, the International Court has already affirmed the competence of the Council in this regard.[65] In the

---

[60] See, for example, the statement by the Costa Rican representative: *GAOR*, 78th meeting, Doc. A/C1/196, p. 164.

[61] See *supra* note 35.

[62] See *supra* note 29.

[63] In fact, the practice of the UN has seen a shift towards the delegation of greater powers of discretion to a special category of subsidiary organs known as 'exceptional subsidiary organs': policy-making subsidiary organs. As subsidiary organs, these organs are nevertheless responsible to, and under the authority of, their principal organ in the same way as any other subsidiary organ. However, unlike other subsidiary organs, organs within this category often act as a policy-making organ of its principal organ. An example is the UN Council for Namibia which the UN Legal Counsel has described as 'a policy-making organ of the General Assembly and as the legal Administering Authority of a Territory. This latter characteristic of the Council distinguishes it from other United Nations subsidiary organs and it may, therefore, be considered an organ *sui generis* for certain purposes.' (*UNJYB* (1982), p. 164.) Moreover, the Legal Counsel found that as a UN subsidiary organ the Council's treaty-making power derives from and is exercized by the United Nations. Thus the Legal Counsel noted that conference and seminar agreements are routinely entered into by the UN on behalf of the Council for Namibia. (*UNJYB* (1982), p. 164.) As the legal Administering Authority over Namibia, the Council has been expressly endowed by the General Assembly with certain competencies and functions of a representational character which are exercized by the Council on behalf of Namibia. (*UNJYB* (1982), p. 167.) This has been widely recognized through *inter alia* full membership of the Council for Namibia in a number of specialized agencies, including the ILO, and participation in such major legislative conferences as the Third United Nations Conference on the Law of the Sea. (*UNJYB* (1982), p. 165.) The Council for Namibia was delegated powers of administration, legislation, and the competence to exercize external affairs powers in respect of the territory of Namibia. Thus the UN Legal Counsel stated that the Council can, in its capacity as the internationally recognized legal Administering Authority of Namibia, sign and ratify or otherwise adhere to the United Nations Convention on the Law of the Sea. (*UNJYB* (1982), p. 168.)

[64] Kelsen, *supra* note 20, p. 142. See also Bowett, *supra* note 31.

[65] This is of importance to, for example, the legality of much of the work of the Sanctions Committees established by the Security Council to ensure the implementation of economic sanctions. As Reisman and Stevick state in the context of the Sanctions Committee established in connection with economic sanctions imposed against Iraq and occupied Kuwait: 'In Resolution 666, the Security Council delegated to the Sanctions Committee the task of determining

Expenses case, the Court upheld, in express terms, the establishment of a UN peacekeeping force by the Council and, thereby in implicit terms, the conferring of powers on that force.[66] This competence of the Council to delegate powers of discretion to a subsidiary organ is not, however, uncircumscribed. The general limitations on the competence of the Council to delegate Chapter VII powers as explained in Chapter 1 apply. The competence of a principal organ to delegate a power of discretion to its subsidiary has been affirmed in practice in the context of a delegation of a power of binding decision.

(a) The delegation of a power of binding decision

There are two aspects to a delegation by a principal organ of a power of binding decision to its subsidiary. These depend on whom the decision by the subsidiary organ is intended to bind. In the first scenario the decision may bind the principal organ and other UN organs; while the second concerns a decision that binds UN Member States.

It is correct as a general proposition that a principal organ can delegate a power of binding decision to its subsidiary such that decisions of the subsidiary bind the principal.[67] The International Court in the *Administrative Tribunal* case expressly rejected the argument that a principal organ establishing a subordinate or subsidiary organ is inherently incapable of giving this organ the competence to make decisions that bind its creator.[68] The Court found that this question cannot be determined on the basis of the nature of the relationship between the General Assembly and the Tribunal, that is 'by considering whether the Tribunal is to be regarded as a subsidiary, a subordinate, or a secondary organ, or on the basis of the fact that it was established by the General Assembly'.[69] The answer depends on the intention of the General Assembly in establishing the Tribunal.[70] Thus the relevant question is: did the principal organ intend the subsidiary to have

what constituted "humanitarian circumstances" under Resolution 661.' (Reisman, M., and Stevick, D., 'The Applicability of International Law Standards to United Nations Economic Sanctions Programmes', *European Journal of International Law*, 9 (1998), p. 86 at p. 101.)

[66] *Expenses* case, *ICJ Reports* (1962), p. 151 at p. 167.

[67] This is an example of a wider issue which arises in the context of the authority and control that a principal organ exercizes over its subsidiary: to what extent can limitations be placed upon the exercize of this authority and control?

[68] *Effect of Awards of Compensation Made by the United Nations Administrative Tribunal Case, ICJ Reports* (1954), p. 47 at p. 61.

[69] *Ibidem*. Moreover, in written pleadings submitted to the Court in the *Administrative Tribunal* case, The Netherlands, USA, and Mexico contended that the General Assembly possessed the competence to delegate to a subsidiary organ a power of decision in a matter involving finances and administration that would bind the General Assembly: Netherlands, *Written Statements, ICJ Pleadings, United Nations Administrative Tribunal* case, p. 77; USA, *ibidem*, p. 316; and Mexico, *ibidem*, p. 240.

[70] *Ibidem*.

the power to make such binding decisions? Such an intention can be inferred from a variety of indicia. In the *Administrative Tribunal* case the
Court looked primarily at the nature of the functions conferred upon the
Administrative Tribunal by its statute.[71] The fact that the Tribunal was
established as a judicial body to exercize judicial functions which the General Assembly did not itself possess[72] was of primary importance to the
Court in reaching the decision that the Administrative Tribunal was established 'not as an advisory organ or a mere subordinate committee of the
General Assembly, but as an independent and truly judicial body pronouncing final judgments without appeal within the limited field of its
functions'.[73] In reaching this decision, the Court noted that the terms 'tribunal', 'judgment', and competence to 'pass judgment upon applications',
which appeared in the Tribunal's statute, are generally used with respect to
judicial bodies.[74] The Court thus found that the decisions of the Tribunal did
in fact bind the Assembly.[75] The degree of independence required in order
to decide whether the decisions of a subsidiary can bind the principal may
also, it is contended, be indicated by such factors as the method of appointment of the members of the subsidiary organ, whether these members serve
in an individual capacity, and the degree to which the subsidiary organ is
given the power to make decisions and act on its own.[76] To summarize, the
Court established the principle that a UN principal organ which establishes
a subsidiary to exercize powers and functions that it cannot itself exercize
cannot change individual decisions of its subsidiary which are an exercize of
those unique powers and functions. This is important, since if it were
otherwise then the principal organ would in effect be performing the very
functions which it does not itself possess under the Charter. This is of
importance to the work of the UN War Crimes Tribunal for the former
Yugoslavia.[77]

    As explained above, the Security Council does not have the authority
under the Charter to perform the judicial functions entrusted to the War

---

[71] Effect of Awards of Compensation Made by the United Nations Administrative
Tribunal Case.

[72] The International Court found that the General Assembly 'was not delegating the performance of its own functions', since the 'Charter does not confer judicial functions on the
General Assembly'. (*Ibidem.*)

[73] *Ibidem*, p. 53.

[74] *Ibidem*, p. 52.

[75] The Court stated: 'The Statute has provided for no kind of review. As this final judgment
has binding force on the United Nations Organization as the juridical person responsible for
the proper observance of the contract of service, that Organization becomes legally bound to
carry out the judgment and to pay the compensation awarded to the staff member. It follows
that the General Assembly, as an organ of the United Nations, must likewise be bound by
the judgment.' (*ICJ Reports* (1954), p. 53.)

[76] See also, in the context of UN Administrative Tribunals, Gomula, *supra* note 36, p. 83.

[77] The following analysis in the text, although limited to the Tribunal for the former
Yugoslavia, applies *mutatis mutandis* to the Rwandan Tribunal.

Crimes Tribunal.[78] The Tribunal is established to determine individual criminal responsibility for violations of international humanitarian law in the former Yugoslavia.[79] The fact that the War Crimes Tribunal is exercizing a judicial function which the Council does not itself possess is of considerable importance in ascribing to the Tribunal a degree of independence which prohibits interference by the Council in the conduct of individual cases. As the Tribunal itself found at the appeal stage of the *Tadic* case:

To assume that the jurisdiction of the International Tribunal is absolutely limited to what the Security Council 'intended' to entrust it with, is to envisage the International Tribunal exclusively as a 'subsidiary organ' of the Security Council ... a 'creation' totally fashioned to the smallest detail by its 'creator' and remaining totally in its power and at its mercy. But the Security Council not only decided to establish a subsidiary organ (the only legal means available to it for setting up such a body), it also clearly intended to establish a special kind of 'subsidiary organ': a tribunal.[80]

The Statute of the War Crimes Tribunal, like the Statute of the Administrative Tribunal, refers to the terms 'tribunal' and 'judgment'. Also in the case of the Tribunal, its Statute refers to it as a 'Court' and provides for no external review over its decisions. The Spanish representative to the Council stated in the debates preceding the adoption of resolution 827 that the Tribunal exercizes a large degree of independence in the exercize of its functions. He argued that this independence derives from the following:

the qualifications required of its members and from the procedure for their selection, which includes the participation of the Security Council and the General Assembly. It derives above all from the autonomy of its machinery, which is not subject to any external review. ... We should recall that this independence is not at all incompatible with its formal character as a subsidiary organ of the Council, as is borne out by the jurisprudence of the International Court of Justice with respect to the United Nations Administrative Tribunal and its relations with the General Assembly.[81]

Accordingly, it is clear that the War Crimes Tribunal was established as an independent judicial body pronouncing final judgments without external

---

[78] See *supra* note 45 and corresponding text.

[79] In the context of the War Crimes Tribunal for the former Yugoslavia, the New Zealand representative to the Council states: 'We must remember, however, that the Tribunal is a court. Its task is to apply independently and impartially the rules of customary international law and, we believe, conventional law applicable in the territory of the former Yugoslavia.' (S/PV.3217, p. 23.)

[80] *Tadic* case, *supra* note 43, para. 15. Accordingly, the Appeal Chamber of the Tribunal in the *Tadic* case stated that prominent among these attributes of judicial function is the power known as '*competence de la competence*': see *supra* note 43.

[81] S/PV.3217, p. 39–40.

review of its decisions within the limited field of its functions.[82] This degree of independence prevents the Council from reviewing individual decisions of the Tribunal.[83] If this were not the case then the Council would in effect be exercizing judicial functions in specific cases.[84] This does not mean, however, that the Security Council could not change a statute at any time and thus change the scope of a Tribunal's delegated mandate. This competence of the Council is part of the authority and control that a principal organ possesses over its subsidiary. The point here of course is that the exercize of such a competence cannot affect individual cases already determined by the Tribunal.[85]

[82] Article 25 of the Statute of the Tribunal does, however, provide for the possibility of appellate proceedings *within* the International Tribunal. In fact, in the Appeals Chamber decision in the *Tadic* case the Tribunal found: 'This provision stands in conformity with the International Covenant on Civil and Political Rights which insists upon a right of appeal.' (*Tadic* case, *supra* note 43, para. 4.)

[83] As the Trial Chamber in the *Blaskic Subpoena* case stated: 'As a subsidiary organ of a judicial nature, it cannot be overemphasized that a fundamental prerequisite for its fair and effective functioning is its capacity to act autonomously. The Security Council does not perform judicial functions, although it has the authority to establish a judicial body. This serves to illustrate that a subsidiary organ is not an integral part of its creator but rather a satellite of it, complete and of independent character.' (*Prosecutor* v. *Tihomir Blaskic, Decision on the Objection of the Republic of Croatia to the issuance of subpoena duces tecum*, IT-95-14-PT, 18 July 1997, at p. 11.) Moreover, as Alvarez has stated: 'As the Tribunal's decisions issued to date suggest, in at least some of these instances the body is 'subsidiary' in name only and can render final judgments that even the Council is not authorized to disturb—and that in turn can disturb the Council by suggesting limits on its powers.' (Alvarez, J., 'Judging the Security Council', *AJIL*, 90 (1996), p. 1 at p. 11.)

[84] To prevent this from occurring, the Secretary-General stated in his report dealing with the establishment of the Tribunal for the former Yugoslavia: 'that it [the Tribunal] should perform its functions independently of political considerations and not be subject to the authority or control of the Council with regard to the performance of its judicial functions'. (S/25705 and Add. 1.) Similarly, in the case of the Rwanda Tribunal the Secretary-General stated: 'The International Tribunal for Rwanda is a subsidiary organ of the Security Council. . . . As such, it is dependent in administrative and financial matters on various United Nations organs; as a judicial body, however, it is independent of any one particular State or group of States, including its parent body, the Security Council.' (S/1995/134, para. 8.) This position was adopted by the Council when it adopted the Secretary-General's report in resolution 827. As such, the Security Council is bound by decisions of the Tribunals and cannot reject a decision on any grounds, including peace and security. That is, the Council could not make a finding that a decision of a Tribunal constitutes a threat to international peace and security since it has already delegated to the Tribunals a power of binding decision in respect of individual criminal liability as a measure to restore international peace and security. There is precedent for this type of approach. In the *Administrative Tribunal* case, the International Court of Justice found that the General Assembly could not itself overturn a decision of that Tribunal in a particular case since it did not itself possess judicial functions and moreover the Assembly had in any case delegated a power of binding decision to the Tribunal: see *supra* note 75 and corresponding text.

[85] This lack of competence of the Council to intervene in decisions of the Tribunal extends beyond the case of a final judgment of an individual's criminal responsibility to include the broad range of judicial powers that the Tribunals possess the competence to exercize, including the Tribunal's 'inherent powers': see Sarooshi, D., 'The Powers of the United Nations International Criminal Tribunals', *Max Planck Yearbook of United Nations Law*, 2 (1998), p. 141 at pp. 147, 150–4.

To summarize, the Council has delegated to the Tribunals a power of binding decision in respect of their judicial functions. That is, the Council could not act as a review body and change decisions of the Tribunals that are an exercize of their judicial functions.

However, this situation is *sui generis* since the Council is delegating powers to a subsidiary organ which it cannot itself exercize. The position is, however, different in the case of the Council's express powers under Chapter VII. It is contended that the Council does not possess the competence to delegate a power of binding decision in respect of its Chapter VII powers such that the decisions of the subsidiary will bind the Council. The reason for this is that the nature of the powers being exercized under Chapter VII are different from, for example, those the Court in the *Administrative Tribunal* case found that the General Assembly was delegating in respect of the UN budget. In the *Administrative Tribunal* case the Court rejected the argument that the establishment of a tribunal competent to make an award of compensation to a staff member to which the General Assembly was bound to give effect would contravene the Charter provisions under Article 17(1) conferring upon the Assembly the power to consider and approve the budget of the Organization.[86] The Court found that Article 17 conferred

---

[86] The earlier practice of the General Assembly supports this position. In fact there has always been a consistent practice of the General Assembly delegating certain of its powers of binding decision with respect to the determination and apportionment of the UN budget to its subsidiary organs. As the UN Legal Counsel has stated: '[the] General Assembly has delegated to the Advisory Committee the power of final decision in certain budgetary matters'. (*ICJ Pleadings, United Nations Administrative Tribunal* case, p. 296.) Moreover, in oral argument before the International Court in the *Administrative Tribunal* case the UN Legal Counsel points out that a category of subsidiary organs are the operational agencies which administer relief, rehabilitation, and assistance programmes involving the expenditure of large amounts of money. The UN Legal Counsel includes in this category such subsidiary organs as the United Nations Childrens Fund (UNICEF), the United Nations Relief and Works Agency for Palestine Refugees in the Near East (UNRWA), the United Nations Korean Reconstruction Agency (UNKRA), and the High Commissioner for Refugees (*ibidem*, p. 297). He states: 'These organs are of particular interest in connection with the present questions since they have been delegated certain functions with regard to financial matters by the General Assembly. . . . An examination of the terms of reference of the operational subsidiary organs of the United Nations reveals that these organs have been vested with varying degrees of financial power regarding the programmes they administer.' (*ICJ Pleadings, United Nations Administrative Tribunal*, pp. 297–8.) The Legal Counsel goes on to note that '[v]ery broad discretion with respect to disposition of funds has been granted by the General Assembly with respect to the United Nations Children's Fund, the United Nations Korean Reconstruction Agency and the High Commissioner for Refugees'. (*ICJ Pleadings, United Nations Administrative Tribunal*, p. 299.) The Executive Board of UNICEF has the power to allocate the resources of the Fund. As the UN Counsel notes, 'General Assembly resolution 417 provided that the Board should formulate the policies, determine the programmes, and allocate the resources of the Fund for the purpose of meeting, through the provision of supplies, training and advice, emergency and long-range needs of children and their continuing need. . . .' (*Ibidem*, p. 299.) The Counsel notes that similarly broad powers have been invested in the other two subsidiary organs. (*Ibidem*.) In conclusion the Counsel noted: 'The practice of the General Assembly with regard to the delegation of financial powers to these subsidiary organs would appear to indicate that the General Assembly has not considered it necessary to pass upon the disposition of every

upon the Assembly the function of approving the budget, but that it did not confer an 'absolute power to approve or disapprove the expenditure proposed to it; for some part of that expenditure arises out of obligations already incurred by the Organisation, and to this extent the General Assembly has no alternative but to honour these engagements'.[87] The Court found that these obligations comprise the awards of compensation made by the Administrative Tribunal in favour of staff members.[88] However, the exercize of the Security Council's functions and powers under Chapter VII are distinguishable from that of the General Assembly's under Article 17, since the Council in many cases does have an 'absolute power to approve or disapprove' action in respect of the maintenance or restoration of international peace and security. Under Article 39 of the Charter the decision whether a matter constitutes a threat to, or breach of, international peace and security or an act of aggression is left solely to the discretion of the Security Council.[89] Moreover, under Article 40 the decision whether the Security Council should call for the imposition of provisional measures is left solely to the Council.[90] And finally, under Articles 41 and 42 the decision to impose or authorize economic, military, or other sanctions is also solely left to the Security Council.[91] Thus due to the unlimited nature of the Council's powers under Chapter VII it is arguable that the Security Council cannot divest itself of its implied or express powers under Chapter VII by transferring them *in toto* to a subsidiary organ. The Security Council retains at all times the competence to change the way that its Chapter VII powers are being exercized by its delegate. We recall, moreover, from Chapter 1 that this is a necessary condition for a lawful delegation of Chapter VII powers.[92] Accordingly, the Security Council cannot be bound by the decision of a subsidiary organ exercizing an express Chapter VII power of the Council that has been delegated to the subsidiary. The exception to this is where the Council is delegating to the subsidiary the performance of functions which the Council itself cannot exercize, as occurred in the case of the War Crimes Tribunals, explained above.[93]

The second issue which arises in the context of a delegation of a power of binding decision is whether the Security Council can delegate its power of binding decision under Article 25 and Chapter VII to its subsidiary organs.[94]

dollar which comes into the custody of the Organization.' (*ICJ Pleadings, United Nations Administrative Tribunal*, p. 300.)

[87] *Administrative Tribunal* case, *ICJ Reports* (1954), p. 59.
[88] *Ibidem*.
[89] See *supra* note 4 and corresponding text in Chapter 1.
[90] See *supra* note 5 and corresponding text in Chapter 1.
[91] See *supra* note 7 and corresponding text in Chapter 1.
[92] See *supra* note 159 and corresponding text in Chapter 1.
[93] See *supra* note 45 and corresponding text.
[94] The Security Council has also delegated its power to issue binding decisions to UN Member States and regional arrangements: see *infra* text following both notes 43 & 70 in Chapter 6.

It is generally accepted that the Council can, under Article 25 and Chapter VII, decide to impose a binding obligation on UN Member States.[95] The separate issue of the competence of the Security Council to delegate this power of binding decision to its subsidiary organs flows from the general competence of the Council to delegate its powers.[96] The condition that would need to be fulfilled, however, is that the Council must decide that such a measure is necessary for the maintenance of international peace and security. In other words, the Council would have to decide, using its powers under Chapter VII, that the delegation of the power to a subsidiary organ to bind Member States was a measure that is necessary for the maintenance of international peace and security. Moreover, the authority and control which the Council exercizes over its subsidiary organ is also of crucial importance to the legality of such a delegation.[97]

It seems clear that if the Security Council delegates its power to issue binding decisions against States, under Article 25 and Chapter VII, to a subsidiary organ then decisions of the subsidiary may bind UN Member States. Such decisions are in effect decisions of the Security Council for the purposes of Article 25, and as such are legally binding on UN Member States.[98] Even if this were not the case, subsequent Security Council confirmation or adoption of a decision of a subsidiary organ is sufficient to make the decision in effect one of the Council's itself, and as such binding on Member States.[99]

The Council delegated its power to issue decisions that bind States to the International Criminal Tribunals. The power of the Tribunals to make decisions that bind States is in the area of providing co-operation and judicial assistance to the Tribunals. The legal basis for the imposition by the Tribunal of such an obligation on States derives, in part, from the fact that the Tribunal was set up by Council resolution 827 as a subsidiary organ by decision of the Security Council acting under Chapter VII.[100] As the Appeals Chamber held in the *Blaskic Subpoena* case:

---

[95] See further the commentaries to Article 25 in Simma, B., ed., *The Charter of the United Nations: A Commentary* (1994) p. 407; and Cot, J.-P., and Pellet, A., eds., *La Charte des Nations Unies* (1991), p. 471.

[96] See *supra* Section II in Chapter 1.

[97] See *supra* note 159 and corresponding text in Chapter 1. On the authority and control which a principal organ exercizes over its subsidiary, see *infra* Section III(2).

[98] Accordingly, Simma states: 'Subsidiary organs may be empowered to perform the functions of the SC [Security Council] even to the extent that this may have external consequences. Article 25 obliges member States to accept and execute the decisions of the Security Council. These include the decisions of subsidiary organs to the extent that they confine themselves to the scope of functions transferred by the SC.' (Simma, *supra* note 1, p. 486.)

[99] The International Court of Justice accepted this general approach in the *Expenses* case when it found that the Security Council had adopted the decisions of the Secretary-General as its own by its 'record of reiterated consideration, confirmation, approval and ratification . . . of the actions of the Secretary-General'. (*Expenses* case, *ICJ Reports* (1962), p. 151 at p. 305.)

[100] Paragraph 4 of resolution 827 provides as follows: '[The Security Council] [d]ecides that all States shall cooperate fully with the International Tribunal and its organs in accordance

the obligation [on States] to lend cooperation and judicial assistance to the International Tribunal . . . is laid down in Article 29 and restated in paragraph 4 of Security Council resolution 827 (1993). Its binding force derives from the provisions of Chapter VII and Article 25 of the United Nations Charter and from the Security Council resolution adopted pursuant to those provisions. The exceptional legal basis of Article 29 accounts for the novel and indeed unique power granted to the International Tribunal to issue orders to sovereign States (under customary international law, States, as a matter of principle, cannot be 'ordered' either by other States or by international bodies).[101]

In other words, the Council has decided that the delegation of a power to the Tribunal to impose binding obligations on Member States in respect of certain matters constitutes a measure that is necessary to maintain or restore international peace. These matters are specified in Article 29(2)[102] which provides:

States shall comply without undue delay with any request for assistance or an order issued by a Trial Chamber, including, but not limited to:

    (a) the identification and location of persons;
    (b) the taking of testimony and the production of evidence;[103]
    (c) the service of documents;
    (d) the arrest or detention of persons;
    (e) the surrender or the transfer of the accused to the International Tribunal.

The legal effect of these binding obligations that the Tribunal may impose on States in a particular case is that it activates the provisions of Article 103 of the Charter which provides: '[i]n the event of a conflict between the obligations of the Members of the United Nations under the present Charter and their obligations under any other international agreement, their

---

with the present resolution and the Statute of the International Tribunal and that consequently all States shall take any measure necessary under their domestic law to implement the provisions of the present resolution and the Statute, including the obligation of States to comply with requests for assistance or orders issued by the Trial Chamber under Article 29 of the Statute.' See also the statements by the following State representatives in the Security Council following the adoption of resolution 827: USA (S/PV.3217, p. 13); France (S/PV.3217, p. 12); and Spain (S/PV.3217, pp. 39–40, 41).

[101] *Prosecutor* v. *Tihomir Blaskic, Judgment on the Request of the Republic of Croatia for Review of the Decision of Trial Chamber II of 18 July 1997*, 29 Oct. 1997, IT-95-14-AR108 *bis*, para. 26. The Appeals Chamber found that this obligation could be accepted by States that were not Members of the United Nations by means of express acceptance of the obligation in writing: see *ibidem*.

[102] The binding nature of a decision taken by the Tribunal under Article 29(2) was confirmed by the Security Council in resolution 1037 when it '*Reaffirms* that all States shall cooperate with the International Tribunal for the Former Yugoslavia and its organs in accordance with provisions of resolution 827 (1993) . . . and the Statute of the International Tribunal and shall comply with requests for assistance or orders issued by a Trial Chamber under article 29 of the Statute.'

[103] On the content of this power, see Sarooshi, *supra* note 85.

obligation under the present Charter shall prevail'. The effect of Article 103 is clear: that any obligation on a Member State under the Charter prevails over a conflicting treaty obligation of that State.[104] The point is, for our present purposes, that the Tribunal has the power to impose such binding obligations on Member States with the consequence, by virtue of Article 103, that this obligation will prevail over a State's other treaty obligations.

It is thus arguable that States even when acting in an International Organization of which they are a Member are under an obligation to comply with a decision of the Court of the Tribunal. This view is supported by Article 48(2) of the Charter which provides:

Such decisions [by the Security Council acting under Chapter VII] shall be carried out by the Members of the United Nations directly and through their action in the appropriate international agencies of which they are members.

This is of course not, however, a direct obligation which applies to an International Organization, but an obligation on its constituent Member States. It has, however, been explained elsewhere that the Tribunal also has the competence to issue decisions that bind UN Specialized Agencies.[105]

This does not mean, however, that in every case where the Council makes a binding decision establishing a UN subsidiary organ that there will be a delegation by the Council of its power of binding decision under Article 25 to the subsidiary. We recall from Chapter 1 that a delegation of powers must take place by express decision of the delegating organ.[106] Accordingly, for our current purposes, a delegation of a power of binding decision to a subsidiary organ must be provided for in express terms by the principal organ and cannot be implied by the subsidiary.

To conclude on the more general point, the accepted competence of a principal organ to delegate a power of binding decision to its subsidiary provides evidence of the competence of a principal to delegate a power of discretion to its subsidiary.

The lawfulness of the Council being able to delegate its Chapter VII powers of discretion to a subsidiary organ is of importance to the approach taken by the UN in response to the threat to international peace posed by the invasion of North Korean forces of the Republic of Korea on 25 June 1950.

---

[104] See as an example of how this article operates, the *Lockerbie* case, *Provisional Measures Phase, ICJ Reports* (1992), p. 3 *et seq.* See further on Article 103 of the Charter: Cot and Pellet, see note 17, p. 1381; and Simma, see note 17, p. 1116.

[105] Sarooshi, *supra* note 85, at pp. 23–5.

[106] See *supra* notes 34–6 and corresponding text in Chapter 1.

(b) The case of the Unified Command in Korea

After having determined in an earlier resolution that the 'armed attack' constituted a 'breach of the peace',[107] the Security Council, in resolution 83, recommended that the Members of the United Nations 'furnish such assistance . . . as may be necessary to repel the armed attack'.[108] Subsequently, the Council, in resolution 84, recommended that 'all Members providing military forces and other assistance pursuant to the aforesaid Security Council resolutions make such forces and other assistance available to a unified command under the United States',[109] and requested the United States to designate the commander of such forces.[110] This Unified Command, or UN Command as it later became known,[111] was established by the Security Council as its subsidiary organ, since it acted on behalf of and as 'agent' for the Security Council,[112] had the requisite degree of independence

---

[107] Security Council resolution 82 of 25 June 1950.

[108] Security Council resolution 83 of 27 June 1950.

[109] Security Council resolution 84 of 7 July 1950. The recommendation by the Council that the Member States contributing forces place them under the unified command of the United States did not involve any legal obligation on the Member States to do so. The fact that this occurred was the effect of a voluntary agreement by these Members. See also Kelsen, *supra* note 20, p. 940.

[110] On 8 July 1950, President Truman announced that he had designated General MacArthur as 'the commanding general of the military forces which the members of the United Nations place under the unified command of the United States pursuant to the United Nations' assistance to the Republic of Korea in repelling the unprovoked armed attack against it'. (*Military Situation in the Far East, Hearings Before the Senate Committee on Armed Services and the Committee on Foreign Relations*, 82nd Congress, 1st Session, Part 5, p. 3373.)

[111] Higgins points out that 'the contributing governments used the term "United Nations Command" when communicating with it; the agreements between them and the United States employed the same term; and UN resolutions referred either to UN Forces or to the UN Command'. (Higgins, R., *United Nations Peacekeeping*, vol. 2. (1970), p. 197.)

[112] Thus, for example, the UK Prime Minister in the House of Commons on 28 June 1950, the day after the adoption of resolution 83, stated: 'The House will wish to know what action His Majesty's Government is taking in pursuance of the resolution of the Security Council passed yesterday calling on all Members of the United Nations to furnish assistance to the Republic of Korea. We have decided to support the United States action in Korea by immediately placing our Naval forces in Japanese waters at the disposal of the United States authorities to operate *on behalf of the Security Council* in support of South Korea. Orders to this effect have already been sent to the Naval Commander-in-Chief on the spot.' (As cited in S/PV.476, *SCOR*, 5th year, 476th meeting (1950), p. 11 (emphasis added.) The view that the US was the 'agent' of the UN was made clear by the testimony of the first UN Force Commander, General MacArthur, when he testified before the United States Senate that: 'The Agreement that was . . . made between the United Nations and the United States Government was that the . . . Government should be the agent for the United Nations in the campaign in Korea. The orders that came to me were from the American Government, but they had under that basis the validity of both the United States Government and the United Nations . . . My instructions from the Joint Chiefs of Staff acting as the agency for the United Nations, ha[d] modified the military conditions under which I operate[d].' (*Military Situation in the Far East, Hearing before the Senate Committee on Armed Services and Foreign Relations*, 82nd Congress, 1st Session (1951), Part 3, p. 1937.)

from the Council, and was under the overall authority and control of the Council.[113]

There were two main broad powers of discretion that the Council purported to delegate to the UN Command: a power of command and control over the forces carrying out military enforcement action, and the power to decide when to terminate the military action.[114]

(i) The delegation of command and control powers

The Council in resolution 84 of 7 July 1950 'recommend[ed]' that the 'military forces' provided by the Members to carry out military enforcement action should be placed under 'a unified command under the United States of America', and requested that the US designate the commander of such forces. Moreover, the Council authorized the Unified Command 'at its discretion to use the United Nations flag in the course of operations against North Korean forces concurrently with flags of the various nations participating'. Finally, the Council resolution requested the US to 'provide the Security Council with reports as appropriate on the course of action taken under the unified command'.[115] The terms of this resolution constitute in effect a delegation by the Council of, *inter alia*, a power of command and

---

[113] See more generally on this issue of authority and control as a precondition for a lawful establishment of a subsidiary organ: *infra* Section III(2). Cf. Seyersted who contends that since the States contributing troops in Korea placed their contingents under a commander appointed by the US, rather than one appointed by the UN, this meant that the force was not subject to the 'organic jurisdiction' of the UN. (Seyersted, F., 'Can the United Nations establish military forces and perform other acts without specific basis in the Charter?', *Österreichische Zeitschrift Für Öffentliches Recht*, 12 (1962), p. 188 at p. 217.) However, it is overall authority and control by the relevant principal organ which is important in terms of characterizing an entity as a subsidiary organ and not necessarily that the principal be able to exercize operational control over its subsidiary organ. Accordingly, the seeming lack of operational command and control by the Council over the UN Command is of no significance to the issue of its characterization as a UN subsidiary organ. Importantly, the establishment of the Unified Command also fulfilled the remaining precondition of establishment that there be no violation of the delimitation of powers between the principal organs. See further on this precondition of establishment: *infra* Section III(3).

[114] The distinct legal considerations relating to a delegation by the Council to Member States of the competence to use force in the case of Korea is dealt with in Chapter 5: see *infra* Section I(1) in Chapter 5.

[115] Resolution 84 (1950) of 7 July 1950, paras. 4–5. The US representative in the Council debates preceding the adoption of resolution 84 stated: 'All these things the United States, of course, will do as a Member of the United Nations. The United States accepts the responsibility and makes the sacrifices that is involved in carrying out these principles of the United Nations. As a matter of fact, this obligation has been expressed directly to the Secretary-General in a communication dated 6 July 1950 (S/1580), which recites the fidelity of the United States to the action of the Security Council in its two resolutions of 25 and 27 June. It responds directly to the inquiry of the Secretary-General regarding the forces that could be contributed by stating what had been contributed, and the formal reply concludes by stating: "The United States will continue to discharge its obligations as a Member of the United Nations to act vigorously in support of the Security Council's resolutions."' (S/PV.476, *SCOR*, 5th year, 476th meeting (1950), pp. 11–12.)

control over a force carrying out military enforcement action to a subsidiary organ, the UN Command, under the operational control of the United States[116] but the overall authority and control of the Council.[117] More specifically, the Council delegated its command and control authority that it possesses under Articles 46 and 47 of the Charter over a force carrying out military enforcement action to the United States.[118] The recommendation by the Council that the Member States contributing

[116] The United States Government carried out a number of activities on behalf of the UN Command acting as 'the executive agent of the United Nations Forces in Korea'. For example, the US Government acting as the 'executive agent' concluded formal agreements with some of the nations who contributed troops to the action in Korea. See, for example, the Agreement between the US and The Netherlands concerning participation of Netherlands Forces, 18 May 1952, 177 *UNTS* 234, contained in Higgins, *supra* note 111, pp. 204–5. Moreover, other international agreements entered into in connection with the UN action in Korea, were concluded not by the Secretary-General acting for the UN, but by the United States Government (expressly stated to be 'the executive agent of the UN Forces in Korea') or the UN Command. For example, an agreement with the UN Korean Reconstruction Agency for the Relief and Rehabilitation of Korea (UNKRA), a UN organ, was concluded by the United States acting in its capacity as UN Command pursuant to UN resolutions. (Summary contained in *US Department of State Bulletin*, 25 (1951), p. 232.) The execution of these treaties was mostly in the hands of the UN Command and the United States Government. This did not, however, prevent the UN from invoking the provisions of the treaties concluded by the UN Command when the situation called for intervention of the Organization. See Seyersted, F., *United Nations Forces* (1966), p. 104. Such action is in conformity with the legal position that the UN Command (and in some cases the US Government acting on its behalf), acting as a subsidiary organ of the Council, entered into agreements on behalf of the Council which the UN could thus rely on; the undertakings being entered into by its subsidiary organ.

[117] Goodrich and Simons note that '[t]he resolution of July 7, requesting the establishment of a unified command by the United States and recommending that Members place their forces under that command could be interpreted as a delegation of authority to the command so established to use military force to achieve the objectives set forth in the Council resolutions and the Charter'. (Goodrich, L., and Simons, A-P., *The United Nations and the Maintenance of International Peace and Security* (1955), pp. 468–9.)

[118] See in respect of Articles 46 and 47, *supra* note 133 in Chapter 1. Accordingly, a letter from President Rhee of the Republic of (South) Korea to General MacArthur dated 15 July 1950 provides in part: '. . . I am happy to assign to your command authority over all land, sea, and air forces of the Republic of Korea during the period of the continuation of the present state of hostilities; such command to be exercized either by you personally or by such military commander or commanders to whom you may delegate the exercize of this authority within Korea or in adjacent seas. . . . who also in his person [General MacArthur] possesses the delegated military authority of all the Members of the United Nations which have joined together to resist the infamous Communist assault on the independence and integrity of our beloved land.' (As contained in Higgins, *supra* note 111, p. 212.) Moreover, Cox states that in the Korean situation, 'lacking any structure to permit strategic direction, the Council effectively delegated direction to the US commander. Unlike the allied command structure in the Gulf, however, the US Commander was also the UN Commander and the multinational forces in Korea nominally constituted a Unified UN Command.' (Cox, D., 'Enforcement, Deterrence, and the Role of the United Nations: Introduction and Summary', in *The Use of Force by the Security Council for Enforcement and Deterrent Purposes: A Conference Report*, published by The Canadian Centre for Arms Control and Disarmament (Cox, D., ed.) (1990), p. 3.) The primary reason for the delegation of command and control to the US was the overwhelming contribution of forces by the United States to the UN force. (Goodrich and Simons, *supra* note 117, p. 460.)

forces place them under the unified command of the US involved <u>no legal obligation</u> on the Member States to do so. The fact that this occurred was the result of a voluntary agreement by these Members.[119] In other words, the placing of forces under the unified command of the US was not a condition that Member States had to fulfil in order to exercize the delegated powers.[120]

It has been explained in Chapter 2 that the Council possesses the power to appoint a commander of a force carrying out UN authorized enforcement action.[121] As the Council possesses this power to appoint a commander, then, as explained above, it can delegate this power of discretion to its subsidiary. That this power of appointment was delegated to the UN Command, in effect the US, in the case of Korea was made clear by the fact that no subsequent confirmation of the US appointee was required by any UN organ:[122] the US President had designated General MacArthur as the Commander of UN Forces.[123]

---

[119] See Kelsen, *supra* note 20, p. 940.

[120] However, the US did subsequently make it a condition for States to be able to participate in the enforcement action. See, for example, Article 7 of the Agreement between the US and The Netherlands relating to the contribution of Dutch forces. (As quoted in Higgins, *supra* note 111, pp. 204–5.)

[121] See *supra* Section III(3) in Chapter 2. In the context of Korea, Bowett has stated: 'The principle of appointment of the Commander by the political organs, which was assumed to be applicable during the early discussions on the implementation of Chapter VII, was undoubtedly right: the departures from that principle, notably in Korea . . . were explicable . . . by the fact that command was delegated to one State . . .'. (Bowett, *supra* note 31, p. 347.)

[122] As Higgins notes: 'All operational control for the action in Korea lay with the United States acting in her capacity of UN Command. . . . In accordance with this resolution, the United States designated General MacArthur as Commander-in-Chief of UN Forces in Korea. . . . The United States issued a communiqué announcing the establishment of a UN Command. This Unified Command was, from an operational point of view, essentially the United States Far East Command in Tokyo. . . . The appointment of General MacArthur was, under paragraph 4 of resolution S/1588, within the prerogative of the United States and not subject to subsequent confirmation by any organ of the UN. . . . At no time was it the habit of the United States to do other than inform the UN of changes in command which had been decided upon. . . . [t]herefore . . . in military and operational terms, control was firmly in the hands of the United States. However, the parties involved clearly regarded the United States as the agent of the UN and the action in which they were engaged as a UN action. The contributing governments used the term "United Nations Command" when communicating with it; the agreements between them and the United States employed the same term; and UN resolutions referred either to UN Forces or to the UN Command.' (Higgins, *supra* note 111, pp. 195–7.)

[123] On 8 July 1950, President Truman announced that he had designated General MacArthur as 'the commanding general of the military forces which the members of the United Nations place under the unified command of the United States pursuant to the United Nations' assistance to the Republic of Korea in repelling the unprovoked armed attack against it'. (*Military Situation in the Far East, Hearings before the Senate Committee on Armed Services and the Committee on Foreign Relations*, 82nd Congress, 1st Session, Part 5, p. 3373.) President Truman later replaced General MacArthur with General Ridgway as Commander of the Unified Command: see Morriss, D., 'From War to Peace: A Study of Cease-Fire Agreements and the Evolving Role of the United Nations', *Virginia Journal of International Law*, 36 (1996), p. 801 at p. 879.

An issue which arises in the context of command and control over the UN Force is the degree to which States that contributed troops to the Force had the right to participate in decisions which concern the use of their troops in military enforcement action. We recall from Chapter 1, that the Council cannot delegate to any entity an unrestricted power of command and control over a force carrying out authorized military enforcement action, since the Council itself does not possess unlimited powers of command and control over such a force. Article 44 operates as a substantive limitation on the command and control powers of the Council. Thus, even where troops are voluntarily provided by Member States, the guarantee which Article 44 provides to these troop-contributing States still applies.[124] Accordingly, the Council when delegating the power of command and control to a subsidiary organ or to a Member State must ensure that States who contribute troops to that force are given the right to be consulted on the way in which *their troops* are to be used to carry out enforcement action. This would not have required the Unified Command to allow States' to be privy to and contribute their views on the general prosecution of the war in Korea. It is restricted only to those cases where the States' troops are to be involved in a particular action. In any case, this substantive limitation was not respected by the Council in the case of Korea. The Council did not stipulate as a condition of the exercize of the delegated power of command and control that the United States consult with Member States on the way their forces were to be used in enforcement action. There was, consequently, no provision made for a formal mechanism of consultation in the treaties concluded between the US Government and troop-contributing countries. For example, in the agreement concluded between the United States and The Netherlands, the only closely relevant provision states:

Article 7 The Government of the Netherlands agrees that all orders, directives, and policies of the Commander issued to the Netherlands Forces of its personnel shall be accepted and carried out by them as given and that in the event of disagreement with such orders, directives, or policies, formal protest may be presented subsequently.[125]

It was only when the UN Forces suffered a setback due to Communist China entering the war on the side of North Korea and serious concern was expressed by States which had contributed troops, that the 'Committee of Sixteen' procedure of consultation was established.[126] However, the responsibility for establishing a formal mechanism of consultation does not rest

---

[124] See *supra* note 134 and corresponding text in Chapter 1.

[125] *Agreement between the US and the Netherlands concerning participation of Netherlands Forces*, 18 May 1952, 177 *UNTS* 234 as reproduced in Higgins, *supra* note 111, pp. 204–5. Higgins notes that this agreement is identical to that concluded by the US Government with Belgium (223 *UNTS* 3), and differed only in small respects from that concluded with South Africa (177 *UNTS* 241): Higgins, *ibidem.*

[126] See Goodrich and Simons, *supra* note 117, p. 146.

with the State or States exercizing delegated powers: it is the responsibility of the Security Council.

A power closely associated to that of command and control which was also delegated to the Unified Command was the power to determine the composition of the UN force. This power was delegated to the US as head of the UN Command.[127] This represents a delegation by the Council of its power under Article 48(1) of the Charter.[128] In the exercize of this power the US made troop contributions subject to certain conditions and even made the decision to reject several offers of troop contributions by States.[129] The general practice for making offers of troops was for a State to communicate to the Secretary-General its willingness to contribute and in turn this offer was made known to the US Government. Preliminary informal discussions were held before the US entered formal negotiations with States.[130] These resulted in treaties being concluded between the State contributing the forces and the US who was acting as the 'executive agent for the UN forces in Korea'.[131]

(ii) The purported delegation of the power to decide when to terminate military enforcement action

A major part of the Council's purported delegation to the UN Command was the power to decide when the objective specified by the Security Council, the restoration of peace and security in the region, had been satisfied: in particular, the power to decide when the threat to international peace and security had ceased to exist. It is explained in more detail in Chapter 1 that the decision as to when a threat to or breach of international peace and security has occurred and has ceased to exist is the very *raison d'être* of

---

[127] As Higgins has observed: 'The Secretary-General informed states making offers that the United States would enter into "direct consultation with Governments with regard to the co-ordination of assistance" and all offers should be communicated to the Secretary-General, though "leaving detailed arrangements for . . . an agreement between the Government and the Unified Command". It was thus left to the discretion of the United States which nations' offers to accept.' (Higgins, *supra* note 111, p. 203.)

[128] See also a possible delegation of this power to the Secretary-General: *supra* note 142 and corresponding text in Chapter 2.

[129] Higgins, *supra* note 111, p. 197. Goodrich and Simons note: '[s]ome offers [of contribution to the force] were not accepted by the United States Government . . . either because the military contingent was too small or because there was no provision for its supply and equipment. One offer, that of the Republic of China, was not accepted for reasons that were in part political.' (Goodrich, and Simons, *supra* note 117, p. 449.)

[130] Goodrich and Simons note that the US in the 'discharge of its responsibilities of unified command, entered into direct negotiations with the government of the Member state concerned regarding the details of the offer [to contribute forces], its utilization, and other effective assistance which that government might be in a position to provide'. (Goodrich and Simons, *supra* note 117, p. 458.)

[131] See, for example, the Agreement between the US and The Netherlands concerning participation of Netherlands Forces, 18 May 1952, 177 *UNTS* 234, in Higgins, *supra* note 111, pp. 204–5.

Chapter VII and that the operation of the *delegatus non potest delegare* doctrine means that it cannot be delegated to other entities.[132] Accordingly, the purported delegation by the Council to the UN Command of the power to decide when international peace and security had been restored in the area raises a serious issue as to the lawfulness of this aspect of the delegation of powers in this case. Moreover, the US considered that it was part of its delegated powers to be able to negotiate and conclude an Armistice Agreement without further Council authorization. The United States Government thus undertook armistice negotiations with no political direction being given by the Council or General Assembly.[133] It seems that the UN itself considered that the United States possessed such authority under the powers delegated. An unpublished legal memorandum prepared for Secretary-General Lie by his Legal Adviser provides, as summarized by Goodrich, the following:

(1) that the United States had the right to conclude a cease-fire or armistice without any additional authorization or instruction from the Security Council or the General Assembly; (2) that this right was restricted to military matters, negotiations on political questions requiring further decisions by the Security Council or General Assembly; (3) that any cease-fire or armistice must be reported to the Security Council which vested the Unified Command in the United States; and (4) that the 'Committee of 16' in Washington, consisting of the United States and fifteen other Members having armed forces in Korea, had a consultative status *vis-à-vis* the United States but not the status of a United Nations Organ.[134]

The final Armistice, which was signed by the Commander-in-Chief of the UN Command and the Commanders of the Korean People's Army and the Chinese People's Volunteers, was approved by the General Assembly on 28 August 1953.[135] This was approximately one month after the Armistice had already entered into force.

This assumption of power by the UN Command was to fill an important vacuum that existed, a vacuum caused by the lack of clear specification by the Council of the objective of the enforcement action.[136] It was this that led

---

[132] See *supra* Section III(2)(b)(i) in Chapter 1.

[133] Goodrich and Hambro, *supra* note 1, pp. 508–9. By this stage the Security Council was, however, paralysed by the return of the representative of the former Soviet Union whose veto precluded further Council consideration of issues relating to the enforcement action in Korea.

[134] Goodrich, L., *Korea: A Study of US Policy in the United Nations* (1956) pp. 183–4. Morriss states that ratification of the Armistice by the political organs of the opposing sides was not required since the agreement was 'purely military in character'. (Morriss, *supra* note 123, p. 881).

[135] GA Resolution 711 (VII), 28 Aug. 1953. For explanation of the provisions of the Korean Armistice and their implementation, see Morriss, *supra* note 123, pp. 882–6.

[136] As Goodrich states: 'The United States Government, in exercizing the functions of unified command, was of course expected to act in accordance with the purposes and principles of the United Nations and the resolutions of its organs. This, however, left a wide area of discretion, since even the Security Council resolution of June 27 stated the purposes of the

to problems in practice in deciding when to terminate the enforcement action. Initially, the broad objective to be sought by the joint military action in Korea was defined by the Council resolution of 27 June 1950 in terms of assistance to be given to 'repel the armed attack and to restore international peace and security in the area'. This was followed two days later by a statement by the United States Secretary of State that the collective action was 'solely for the purpose of restoring the Republic of Korea to its status prior to the invasion from the North and of re-establishing the peace broken by that aggression. The action of this Government in Korea is taken in support of the authority of the United Nations. It is taken to restore peace and security in the Pacific area.'[137] Goodrich and Simons contend that this statement appeared to express the view of other Members supporting the collective action, and from it the inference could be drawn that the Members of the United Nations, and the United States in particular, were prepared to accept the restoration of the *status quo ante* as the basis for terminating their joint military action.[138] However, the lack of adoption of this as a clear objective by the Council at the time led to problems when the UN Command having succeeded in driving North Korean forces back to the 38th parallel had to decide whether to pursue fleeing North Korean forces and attempt to carry out the programme of the General Assembly for the establishment of an independent, democratic, and united Korea.[139] President Truman was reluctant to undertake such action without some form of UN authorization. The Security Council by this time was hamstrung by the return of the Soviets and their veto. Accordingly, it was the General Assembly that passed resolution 376 (V) on 7 October 1950 which confirmed the authority of the UN Command to undertake the destruction of the North Korean forces by military operations north of the 38th

military operation in very broad terms, viz., "to repel the armed attack and to restore international peace and security in the area." Subject to such controlling influence as might be exercized through the discussions and resolutions of the Security Council and the General Assembly and through ordinary diplomatic channels, the United States Government was left to determine how military operations in Korea should be conducted.' (Goodrich, *supra* note 134, pp. 121–2.)

[137] *US Department of State Bulletin*, vol. 23 (10 July 1950), p. 46, as cited in S/PV.475, *SCOR*, 5th year, 476th meeting (1950), p. 10.

[138] Goodrich and Simons, *supra* note 117, p. 494.

[139] Goodrich and Simons note: '. . . by the time the Assembly convened in September 1950, the radical change in the military situation made a decision regarding the military objective urgent. United Nations forces, instead of being hard pressed in front of Pusan, were driving the North Korean forces in confusion to the north and were approaching the thirty-eighth parallel. It became necessary to decide whether to be satisfied with the attainment of a minimum military objective, *i.e.* driving the North Korean forces back to the thirty-eighth parallel, or to undertake a more ambitious program that might include an attempt to free all of North Korea from Communist control, thus facilitating the carrying out of the objective of the Assembly of a unified, independent, and democratic Korea as suggested in its resolution of November 1947.' (Goodrich and Simons, *supra* note 117, pp. 468–9.)

parallel.[140] The subsequent decision to undertake action north of the 38th parallel saw the entry into the war, against the UN Forces, of large numbers of Chinese troops. It seems that as a result of the forced retreat of UN Forces in the face of a combined Chinese and North Korean offensive, the US Government returned to its position of June 1950 regarding the objectives of military action and the conditions for its termination.[141] This former objective was subsequently adopted again by the UN Command when negotiating an armistice with North Korea and Communist China.[142] Thus, the UN Command during the armistice negotiations insisted on the following as one of its requirements for an acceptable armistice: '1. A line of demarcation consistent with the United Nations objective of repelling aggression, based upon military realities, and affording defensible positions for the opposing forces . . .'.[143] The main source of the problem that arose in this case was the initial lack of clear specification by the Council of the political objectives for which it was delegating its Chapter VII powers. The failure of the Council to specify clearly when delegating its Chapter VII powers to Member States the objective of the military enforcement action brings into question the lawfulness of the delegation.[144] We recall from Chapter 1 that a clear statement by the Council as to the objective of the delegation is necessary in order for the States exercizing the delegated powers to know the limits of their mandate and indeed when that mandate

[140] See Statements by the US Secretary of State, *US Department of State Bulletin*, vol. 23 (2 Oct. 1950), p. 526; and *ibidem* (9 Oct. 1950), pp. 579–80. See also statements by the representatives of Australia (*UNGAOR*, Fifth Session, First Committee, 347th meeting (30 Sept. 1950), p. 32) and Norway (*ibidem*, 351st meeting (3 Oct. 1950), p. 37).

[141] Accordingly, the Secretary of State observed: 'Our objective is to stop the attack, end the aggression on that Government [Republic of Korea], restore peace, [and] provid[e] against the renewal of aggression. Those are the military purposes for which, as we understand it, the United Nations troops are fighting. The United Nations has since 1947 and the United States has since 1943 or 1944 stood for a unified, free, and democratic Korea. That is still our purpose, and is still the purpose of the United Nations. I do not understand it to be a war aim. In other words, that is not sought to be achieved by fighting, but it is sought to be achieved by peaceful means, just as was being attempted before the aggression.' (*Military Situation in the Far East, Hearings before the Senate Committee on Armed Services and Committees on Foreign Relations*, 82nd Congress, 1st Session, Part 3, p. 1729.)

[142] In a Special Report of the UN Command on the Armistice in Korea, it states the following: 'The operations of the United Nations Command were conducted solely for the purpose of achieving the military objective of the United Nations in Korea, i.e., repelling the aggression and restoring peace and security in Korea.' (Contained in Higgins, *supra* note 111, p. 284.)

[143] UN Doc. A/2228 (18 Oct. 1952), p. 6.

[144] White, for example, states the following: 'It can be strongly argued that the UN operation in Korea was an unconstitutional delegation of authority to the United States enabling it to use the Organisation to go beyond the collective objectives of the body . . . Doubts about whether the objectives of the operation were sufficiently collective could have been allayed, either by more control of the armed forces by means of a Committee established by the Security Council, or by being much more specific in the war aims of the UN response.' (White, N., *Keeping the Peace: The United Nations and the Maintenance of International Peace and Security* (1993), pp. 107–8.)

is automatically terminated, even in the absence of an express Council decision to that effect.[145]

Returning to the more general issue of the authority of establishment of a subsidiary organ and the delegation of power, we can conclude that the general rule regarding the lawful exercize of the general authority of establishment under Article 7(2) of the Charter is that the possession of an express power or function to be delegated to a subsidiary organ is not necessary.[146] What will, however, preclude the lawful establishment of a subsidiary organ is if the principal organ does not possess the express or implied power under the Charter to establish a subsidiary organ to perform certain functions in the area. In the case of an implied power, this may depend on whether the subsidiary organ has been established in an area in which the principal organ has a competence to exercize its powers and functions. Moreover, it can be concluded that the Council does possess the competence to delegate discretionary powers to its subsidiary. The competence of UN principal organs being able to delegate a power of binding decision to UN subsidiary organs that will enable the subsidiary to bind the principal and even Member States is instructive on this point. However, in the case of a delegation of express Chapter VII powers the Security Council always retains the competence to change the way in which those delegated powers are being exercized by its subsidiary.

III. PRECONDITIONS FOR THE LAWFUL ESTABLISHMENT OF UN SUBSIDIARY ORGANS

1. Establishment must be by a principal organ

The precondition that a subsidiary organ be established by a principal organ is a requirement under the general law of international institutions.[147] Application of this precondition to the UN context enables a distinction to be made between subsidiary organs and other types of organs; in particular, auxiliary organs and organs established by intergovernmental agreement.

A distinction between UN subsidiary organs and other kinds of UN auxiliary organs was arguably envisaged at the San Francisco Conference: perusal of the *travaux preparatoires* of Article 7(2) reveals that the term initially used in the French text was 'organe auxiliaire' which was later replaced in the final text of the Charter by that of 'organe

---

[145] This latter point was of poignant relevance to the case of Korea, since the return of the former Soviet Union led to paralysis of the Council.

[146] See *supra* note 28 and corresponding text.

[147] See, for instance, Torres Bernardez, *supra* note 1; and Schermers and Blokker, *supra* note 1.

subsidiaire'.[148] This distinction is illustrated by the case of the Military Staff Committee. Article 47(1) of the Charter provides for the establishment of a 'Military Staff Committee to advise and assist the Security Council on all questions relating to the Security Council's military requirements for the maintenance of international peace and security, the employment and command of forces placed at its disposal, the regulation of armaments, and possible disarmament'. Clearly the Military Staff Committee is to assist the Security Council in the exercize of its Chapter VII powers. However, Article 47(2) of the Charter directly establishes the Military Staff Committee when it states that the Committee 'shall consist of the Chiefs of Staff of the permanent members of the Security Council or their representatives'.[149] Thus the Committee, having been established by the Charter and not by a principal organ, does not satisfy the precondition that establishment be by a principal organ.[150] Accordingly, the Military Staff Committee cannot be considered as a 'subsidiary organ' within the meaning of Article 7(2).[151] This conclusion has been affirmed by the UN Legal Counsel who stated before the Court in the *Administrative Tribunal* case that there are a few organs which cannot be characterized as either principal or subsidiary under Article 7 of the Charter, and he included in this category the Military Staff Committee which, he noted, is directly established by Article 47 of the Charter.[152] The practical consequence of this position is that the Security Council, as a UN principal organ, cannot exercise authority and control over such an auxiliary organ.[153] The control of such an auxiliary organ, where established by the Charter, is regulated by the relevant provisions of the Charter. Thus the Security Council could not, for example, terminate the life of the Military Staff Committee or *require* it to perform tasks which have not been specified in the Charter.[154]

---

[148] See also the commentary to Article 7 of the Charter in Cot and Pellet, *supra* note 1, p. 207.

[149] There are also other provisions of the Charter which authorize non-principal organs to set up auxiliary organs not designated as 'subsidiary organs'. For example, Article 47(4) provides: 'The Military Staff Committee, with the authorization of the Security Council and after consultation with appropriate regional agencies, may establish regional subcommittees.'

[150] Cf. Torres Bernardez who argues that the term subsidiary organ can cover organs which are established by the constituent instrument of an international organization. (Torres Bernardez, *supra* note 1, p. 115.)

[151] See also Kelsen, *supra* note 20, p. 138. Cf. Goodrich and Hambro who argue that the Military Staff Committee is a subsidiary organ of the Security Council: Goodrich and Hambro, *supra* note 1, p. 231.

[152] *Administrative Tribunal* case, *ICJ Pleadings* (1954), p. 295.

[153] On the authority and control which a principal organ possesses over its subsidiary organ, see *infra* Section III(2).

[154] This may not necessarily, however, preclude an auxiliary organ like the Military Staff Committee from voluntarily accepting to undertake additional tasks which the Security Council has requested it to perform. In such a case, it would seem that the Military Staff Committee would be established and acting as a subsidiary organ of the Council for the performance of these additional functions. As such, the Military Staff Committee would be subject to the

It has been explained elsewhere that the precondition of establishment by a principal organ enables a distinction also to be made between UN subsidiary organs and other entities established by intergovernmental agreement: for example, UN specialized agencies which are all established either by intergovernmental agreement or on a legal basis separate from that of the United Nations.[155] However, the case of subsidiary organs jointly established by a UN principal organ together with another international organization is somewhat different. In an opinion in 1963, the UN Legal Counsel states the general proposition that '[t]he setting up of committees jointly with other international organizations would be considered as permissible in appropriate circumstances by application of the provisions of the United Nations Charter relating to the establishment of subsidiary organs of the Organization'.[156] The reason that such an entity is classified prima

authority and control of the Council when it is acting pursuant to the discharge of these functions.

[155] See Sarooshi, *supra* note 1, pp. 433–4. There are, however, a group of organs which, though their establishment is provided for in a treaty, are so closely linked with the United Nations that they are considered organs of the Organization. The UN Legal Counsel has termed these 'treaty organs' of the United Nations: *UNJYB* (1969), pp. 207–10, and *UNJYB* (1976), p. 200. These organs are not, however, to be considered 'UN subsidiary organs'. The UN Legal Counsel notes that these include the following: the former Permanent Central Opium Board, established by an Agreement of 1925 (*League of Nations Treaty Series*, vol. 51, p. 337) but made a United Nations organ by General Assembly resolution 54(I) of 19 Nov. 1946 and the protocol of amendment annexed thereto; the former Drug Supervisory Body, established by a Convention of 1931 (*League of Nations Treaty Series*, vol. 139, p. 301) but made a United Nations organ by General Assembly resolution 54(I) of 19 Nov. 1946 and the protocol of amendment annexed thereto; the International Bureau for Declarations of Death, established by the Convention on the Declaration of Death for Missing Persons (*UNTS*, vol. 119, p. 99), adopted by a United Nations conference on 6 Apr. 1950; the Appeals Committee established under the Protocol for Limiting and Regulating the Cultivation of the Poppy Plant, the Production of International and Wholesale Trade in, and Use of Opium (*UNTS*, vol. 456, p. 56), adopted by a United Nations Conference on 23 June 1953; the International Narcotics Control Board, established under the Single Convention on Narcotic Drugs (*UNTS*, vol. 520, p. 151), adopted by a United Nations Conference on 30 Mar. 1961; and the Committee on the Elimination of Racial Discrimination (*UNJYB* (1969), pp. 207–8). The UN Legal Counsel states: 'Except for the mode of their creation, these organs are in the same position as recognized subsidiary organs of the United Nations.' (*Ibidem.*) In a separate opinion the Legal Counsel states 'It makes no difference that the treaty in this case [establishing the International Committee on the Elimination of Racial Discrimination] was itself adopted as a decision of the General Assembly; the Assembly did not directly create the Committee, as it does in establishing subsidiary organs, but the Committee came into being only when a sufficient number of States had bound themselves by the Convention to bring it into force in accordance with its terms.' (*Ibidem*, p. 200.) The Legal Counsel went on to state that the Committee on the Elimination of Racial Discrimination is not a subsidiary organ of the General Assembly, and that 'it falls into a special category of "treaty organs of the United Nations", which are organs whose establishment is provided for in a treaty, for the purpose of carrying out its provisions, but are so closely linked with the United Nations that they are considered organs of the Organization'. (*UNJYB* (1976), p. 200.)

[156] *UNJYB* (1963), p. 168. Accordingly, the UN Legal Counsel went on to note that 'the joint United Nations FAO Inter-Governmental Committee for the World Food Programme, which consists of 20 nations members of FAO and the United Nations, was established on behalf of the United Nations by General Assembly resolution 1714 (XVI)'. (*Ibidem*, p. 169.)

facie as a UN subsidiary organ is that it has resulted from an expression of the will of a UN principal organ. However, such a classification depends of course on the other preconditions of establishment also being fulfilled. This provides a good example of the way in which all the preconditions of establishment must be satisfied for a particular entity to be considered a lawfully established UN subsidiary organ. Thus these preconditions are of some importance when, for example, identifying the legal requirements which must be met when considering whether the Security Council can jointly establish a subsidiary organ with a regional organization in order to exercize command and control over a force consisting of troops from both the regional organization and other UN Member States.[157]

In those cases where there are two principal organs of the UN involved in the establishment of a subsidiary organ it may not be immediately apparent to which the subsidiary belongs. In many cases the principal organ may have chosen to delegate its power of establishment to one of the other principal organs to exercize.[158] The principal organ which appoints the members of the subsidiary organ may not necessarily be the principal organ to whom the subsidiary belongs.[159] The test to ascertain which is the establishing principal organ will depend on which principal organ possesses the authority under the Charter to establish the subsidiary organ in question.[160] In the case where both principal organs possess the authority under the Charter to establish the subsidiary organ in question then it may be a case of both principal organs being able to exercize authority and control over the subsidiary[161] or there may have been a case of subsequent adoption by one

---

[157] For an example of a subsidiary organ exercizing powers of command and control over a force carrying out military enforcement action, see the case of the Unified Command in Korea: *supra* Section II(2)(b)(i).

[158] See, for example, *infra* note 164 and corresponding text.

[159] In an opinion given on the status under the UN Charter of the Group of Governmental Experts on International Co-operation to Avert New Flows of Refugees, the UN Legal Counsel stated: 'This characterization of the Group as a subsidiary organ of the Assembly is not affected by the fact that the members of the Group are appointed by the Secretary-General . . . Nor does the characterization of the body as an "Expert Group" affect this conclusion. Members of subsidiary organs of the General Assembly have been appointed in a large variety of ways, other than directly by the Assembly, and subsidiary organs not infrequently report through other bodies to the Assembly.' *(UNJYB* (1983), p. 177.) Examples of this great variety of appointing methods, reporting procedures, and titles for subsidiary organs of the General Assembly can be found in UN Document A/AC202/1 of 28 Mar. 1980.

[160] See also the case of the United Nations Mediator for Palestine: *Repertoire of the Practice of the Security Council, 1946–1951* (1972), pp. 223–4.

[161] For example, General Assembly resolution 31/93 of 14 Dec. 1976 and ECOSOC resolution 2008 (LX) of 14 Nov. 1976 jointly established the Committee on Programme and Coordination (which was originally established as a subsidiary organ of ECOSOC only) 'as the main subsidiary organ of the Economic and Social Council and the General Assembly' for planning, programming, and coordination of UN activities with financial implications. (See also Simma, *supra* note 1, p. 204.) See further, for other examples where principal organs of international organizations have shared a subsidiary organ, Torres Bernardez, *supra* note 1, p. 134, notes 95 and 96.

principal organ of the subsidiary as its own to the exclusion of the other.[162] The determination of which principal organ is the 'establishing organ' is an important enquiry. This will determine which principal organ can exercise authority and control over the subsidiary. The issue of which UN principal organ can exercize authority and control over a subsidiary organ has arisen in the case of UN peacekeeping forces.

It is clear that UN peacekeeping forces are UN subsidiary organs.[163] In every case where the Council has established a UN peacekeeping force, it has, to date, been the consistent practice of the Council to delegate to the Secretary-General its Chapter VII power to establish and constitute that force.[164] The Secretary-General does not himself possess the authority

[162] An example of this is provided by the United Nations Trust Fund for Population Activities (as the UNFPA was originally known). The UNFPA was initially established in 1969 by the UN Secretary-General. (*UNJYB* (1979), p. 171.) However, the General Assembly in resolution 3019 (XXVII) of 18 Dec. 1972 decided to place the UNFPA under the authority of the Assembly and decided further 'without prejudice to the overall responsibilities and policy functions of the Economic and Social Council, that the Governing Council of the United Nations Development Programme, subject to conditions to be established by the Economic and Social Council, shall be the governing body of the United Nations Fund for Population Activities'. It was on this basis that the UN Legal Counsel found: 'As a consequence of the adoption of General Assembly resolution 3019 (XXVII) the Fund ceases to be a trust fund of the Secretary-General and became a Fund under the authority of the General Assembly with an intergovernmental governing body, having its own financial regulations and rules. It thus . . . became a subsidiary organ of the Assembly similar to other Funds having intergovernmental supervisory bodies such as UNICEF, the Capital Development Fund and the United Nations Special Fund. In this respect, it should be noted that Article 22 of the Charter authorizes the Assembly to create "subsidiary organs" which are to be distinguished from principal organs specified in the Charter or completely autonomous bodies which have to be established by separate intergovernmental agreement.' (*Ibidem*, p. 172.)

[163] See the *Expenses* case, *ICJ Reports* (1962), p. 151 at p. 165. See also, for example, the following: 'Article 29', *Repertory of Practice of UN Organs*, Supplement No. 3, p. 82 at p. 83; Higgins, R., *United Nations Peacekeeping*, vol. 1 (1969), p. 271; Bowett, *supra* note 31, p. 67; Simma, *supra* note 1, pp. 590–1; Draper, G., 'The Legal Limitations upon the Employment of Weapons by the United Nations Force in the Congo', *ICLQ*, 12 (1963), p. 387 at p. 392; and Sarooshi, *supra* note 1, p. 436.

[164] Two examples suffice to provide insight into this process. First, in the case of the establishment of ONUC the Security Council delegated to the Secretary-General in paragraph 2 of resolution 143 the following broad power: '[The Security Council] *Decides* to authorize the Secretary-General to take the necessary steps, in consultation with the Government of the Republic of the Congo, to provide the Government with such military assistance, as may be necessary, until, through the efforts of the Congolese Government with the technical assistance of the United Nations, the national security forces may be able, in the opinion of the Government, to meet fully their tasks.' Second, France, The Netherlands, and the UK agreed on 7 June 1995 to create a 'rapid reaction force (RRF)' to be placed at the disposal of UNPROFOR in Bosnia. It is clear that the RRF is a part of UN peacekeeping operations in the former Yugoslavia, that it is under the UN chain of command and is to operate under existing UN rules of engagement. (S/1995/470, Annex.) The Security Council delegated to the Secretary-General the power to establish this force in resolution 998 (1995) of 16 June 1995 in the following terms: '[The Security Council] 9. *Welcomes* the letter of the Secretary-General of 9 June 1995 on the reinforcement of UNPROFOR and the establishment of a rapid reaction capacity to enable UNPF/UNPROFOR to carry out its mandate; 10. *Decides* accordingly to authorize an increase in UNPF/UNPROFOR personnel, acting under the present mandate and on the terms set out in the above-mentioned letter, by up to 12,500 additional troops, the

under the Charter to establish UN peacekeeping forces:[165] it is only the Security Council and General Assembly that possess such a power. Accordingly, the establishment of UN peacekeeping forces by the Secretary-General represents the exercize of a delegated power:[166] UN peacekeeping forces are UN subsidiary organs that are established under the authority of either the Security Council or, as the case may be, the General Assembly.[167] The legal basis for, and mandate of, a UN peacekeeping force are rooted in a resolution of either the Council or the Assembly. It follows that the Secretary-General does not possess the competence unilaterally to terminate a UN peacekeeping force—a subsidiary organ under the overall authority and control of another UN principal organ—unless this power has been expressly delegated to him by the relevant principal organ.[168] Moreover, the Secretary-General cannot infer the power to terminate a peacekeeping force from the terms of the resolution which delegated to him the authority to establish the force.[169] This is confirmed in a message by the Secretary-General to the President of the Republic of Congo:

Such a determination can be made only by the Security Council itself or on the basis of its explicit delegation of authority. It is not of no special importance that only the Security Council can decide on the discontinuance of the [peacekeeping] operation, and that, therefore, conditions which, by their effect on the operation, would de-

modalities of financing to be determined later; 11. *Authorizes* the Secretary-General to carry forward the implementation of paragraphs 9 and 10 above, maintaining close contact with the Government of the Republic of Bosnia and Herzegovina and others concerned.' See further, for the practice of the Council in this area: White, N., *Keeping the Peace: The United Nations and the maintenance of international peace and security* (1993), pp. 215–56; and the commentary to Article 40 in Cot and Pellet, *supra* note 1, p. 667.

[165] As Higgins has stated: 'There is a general consensus that the Secretary-General cannot establish a force even with the consent of all the parties directly involved . . . The Secretary-General's powers under Articles 97–99 of the Charter, even where taken with the consent of the host state and all parties concerned, apparently are not a sufficient basis for a United Nations peacekeeping mission.' (Higgins, R., 'A General Assessment of United Nations Peace-Keeping', in *United Nations Peace-keeping* (Cassesse, A., ed.) (1978), p. 1 at p. 7.)

[166] See also Alexandrowicz, C., 'The Secretary-General of the United Nations', *ICLQ*, 11 (1962), p. 1109 at pp. 1122–3.

[167] See, for example, the statement by the UN Secretary-General in the 'Summary Study of the Experience of UNEF' that '[t]he Force was recognized as a subsidiary organ of the General Assembly, established under the authority of Article 22 of the Charter of the United Nations (regulation 6)'. (A/3943, 'Summary Study of the Experience of UNEF', 9 Oct. 1958, as contained in Higgins, *supra* note 163, p. 287.)

[168] Moreover, the Secretary-General does not possess the competence to change unilaterally the mandate of a peacekeeping force. In response to pressure during a phase of the operation in the Congo for the Secretary-General to use ONUC to carry out disarmament of certain rebellious groups in the Congo, he stated: 'this [the disarmament] cannot be done by me or the United Nations Force short of new instructions from the Security Council'. (S/4629, p. 4.)

[169] The issue may be raised whether the Secretary-General has emergency powers to withdraw a peacekeeping force in a situation where the position of such a force may be imperilled. However, this approach is not appropriate since, as already explained in the text, there is no legal basis for the Secretary-General to exercize such a power under either the Charter or, unless the contrary is expressly stated, the resolution that establishes a peacekeeping force.

prive it of its necessary basis, would require direct consideration by the Security Council, which obviously could not be counted upon to approve of such conditions unless it were to find that the threat to peace and security had ceased.[170]

This approach follows from the position that the legal basis for the peace-keeping force is to fulfil the mandate specified by the Council or Assembly and that some form of decision by the relevant principal organ is thus required to terminate the force.[171] Accordingly, the unilateral decision by the Secretary-General to order the withdrawal of UNEF from Egyptian territory was *ultra vires*.[172]

It is convenient to reiterate our general point, that a UN subsidiary organ must be established by some form of expression of the will of a UN principal organ.[173]

There are no strict requirements of form which a principal organ must follow in order to establish a subsidiary organ. As just noted, the *raison d'être* of the precondition is that a principal organ express its intention that it wishes to establish a subsidiary organ.[174] As the commentary to Article 7

[170] Message dated 8 Mar. 1961, *SCOR*, 16th year, Suppl. for Jan–Mar., vol. 2, S/4629, p. 35.

[171] On the question of the requirements for the effective termination of a subsidiary organ by a principal organ, see *infra* notes 200–1 and corresponding text.

[172] The Secretary-General ordered the withdrawal of UNEF from Egypt without obtaining the authorization of the General Assembly, the political organ which had established the Force. In the report of the Secretary-General on the matter, it was contended that the Secretary-General had undertaken all reasonable consultation with the Advisory Committee on UNEF and the troop-contributing States that could in the circumstances have been expected. The report points to the failure of the Advisory Committee to convene the General Assembly and the practical difficulties in so doing as a large part of the justification for the unilateral decision which was taken. (Higgins, *supra* note 163, pp. 271–3.) However, these considerations are of a pragmatic nature and do not address the relevant issue: whether the Secretary-General has the competence to terminate a UN peacekeeping mission. See also, Higgins, *ibidem*, p. 271; and Garvey, J., 'United Nations Peacekeeping and Host State Consent', *AJIL*, 64 (1970), p. 241. Cf., however, Di Blase, A., 'The Role of the Host State's Consent With Regard to Non-Coercive Actions by the United Nations', in *United Nations Peacekeeping* (Cassesse, A., ed.) (1978), pp. 70–3; and Elaraby, N., 'United Nations Peacekeeping by Consent: A Case Study of the Withdrawal of the United Nations Emergency Force', *New York University Journal of International Law and Politics*, 1 (1968), p. 149.

[173] However, even in those cases where an entity has not been initially established by a principal organ it is possible for a principal organ to subsequently adopt the entity as its subsidiary organ. An example of such adoption is illustrated by the opinion of the UN Legal Counsel in a memorandum on the status of the Ad Hoc Committee of the International Conference on Kampuchea. The Ad Hoc Committee was established not by the General Assembly but by a conference convened by the General Assembly. The UN Legal Counsel nevertheless found that the General Assembly had adopted the Ad Hoc Committee as its own subsidiary organ by approving the conference report. The Legal Counsel stated: 'In these circumstances the Committee must be considered as being an organ of the Conference which established it and also an organ of the General Assembly which was the convening authority of the Conference and which approved and gave effect to the Conference's decision to establish the Committee.' (*UNJYB* (1984), p. 160.) Moreover, Bowett has noted that the United Nations Treaty Supervision Organization (UNTSO), while initially organized and developed by the UN Mediator for Palestine, was later adopted by the UN Security Council as its subsidiary organ. (Bowett, *supra* note 31, p. 63.)

[174] See *supra* note 173 and corresponding text.

in Cot and Pellet's commentary on the Charter states: 'Un organe subsidiaire est *créé par une manifestation de volonté de l'organe principal, quelle que soit la dénomination précise de la mesure prise—résolution, recommandation, décision . . .'.*[175] The form by which a principal organ can establish a subsidiary organ will thus depend on the principal organ in question.

In the case of the Security Council the most obvious form is by a resolution.[176] This resolution may be phrased in terms of a decision or even a non-binding recommendation. In the case of a recommendation, the International Court found in the *Expenses* case that the General Assembly has the power, under Article 14 of the Charter, to recommend to States to organize peacekeeping operations—which it found were subsidiary organs—with the consent of the States concerned.[177] In fact, the non-binding nature of this form of establishment of the subsidiary organ was of considerable importance to the International Court in finding that the peacekeeping forces in question had been lawfully established.[178]

In the majority of cases of establishment of a subsidiary organ, the expression of the will of a principal organ will require that the particular voting requirements of the relevant principal organ be satisfied. The case of the Security Council is complicated due to the issue of the veto-power which Permanent Members possess when voting on questions of a non-procedural nature. Article 27(2) of the Charter requires an affirmative vote of nine Members on procedural matters for a resolution of the Security Council to be lawfully adopted, while Article 27(3) requires 'an affirmative vote of nine members *including the concurring votes of the permanent members*' on non-procedural matters (emphasis added).[179] Thus if the estab-

---

[175] Cot and Pellet, *supra* note 1, p. 212.

[176] However, it is arguably not restricted to this form. In the case, for example, of the Security Council, Wood has stated the following ways by which the Council expresses its intention: 'The Security Council acts in various ways: there are resolutions, statements made on its behalf by the President of the Council, letters from the President (normally addressed to the Secretary-General) and other decisions (generally recorded in official documents).' (Wood, M., 'Security Council Working Methods and Procedure: Recent Developments', *ICLQ*, 45 (1996), p. 150 at p. 151.) However, in the case where the Security Council is delegating a power of discretion to the organ then, as explained in Chapter 1, such a delegation of power must be by resolution to allow the potential use of the veto-power in respect of the decision: see supra notes 36–40 and corresponding text in Chapter 1.

[177] *Expenses* case, *ICJ Reports* (1962), pp. 163–5.

[178] See *infra* note 223 and corresponding text (*et sequentia*).

[179] Despite extensive practice under these provisions, their meaning remains uncertain and controversial. See 'Commentary to Article 27' in Cot and Pellet, *supra* note 1, p. 495, and in Simma, *supra* note 1, p. 430; Blum, Y., *Eroding the United Nations Charter* (1993), Chapter 9; Kelsen, *supra* note 20, pp. 245–58; McDougal, M., and Gardner, R., 'The Veto and the Charter: An Interpretation for Survival', *Yale Law Journal*, 60 (1951), p. 209; Bailey, S., *Voting in the Security Council* (1969), pp. 26–41, and *Procedure of the Security Council*, (1997); Caron, D., 'The Legitimacy of the Collective Authority of the Security Council', *AJIL*, 87 (1993), p. 552, at pp. 566–88; and Gross, L., 'Voting in the Security Council: Abstention in the Post-1965 Amendment Phase and its Impact on Article 25 of the Charter', *AJIL*, 62 (1968), p. 315.

lishment of a subsidiary organ of the Security Council is considered to be a non-procedural decision, then it is subject to the power of veto by the Permanent Members of the Council. It has already been shown elsewhere that there is a general presumption that a decision by the Security Council to create a subsidiary organ will be classified as a procedural matter and thus not be subject to the veto.[180] However, this presumption can be rebutted where it is proposed that a subsidiary organ be established to exercize powers which are non-procedural in nature. In this case the decision of the Council is non-procedural and will thus be subject to the veto. Accordingly, if the Security Council were to establish a subsidiary organ to which it purports to delegate certain of its Chapter VII decision-making powers then the establishment of the subsidiary is arguably subject to the veto of any of the five Permanent Members. This is an important check on the powers of the Council. Were it otherwise, it may have been possible for the Security Council to decide to establish a subsidiary organ to exercize its Chapter VII powers without this decision being made subject to the veto.

There is an important distinction to be made between the decision by a principal organ to establish subsidiary organs as just discussed and the role of the individual Member State in this process. In the case of UN peace-keeping, for example, it is clear that there is a distinction which must be made between the consent of the principal organ establishing the peace-keeping force and the consent of both the States which contribute troops to the force and the State where the force is to be deployed. It is a fundamental requirement of UN peacekeeping that the deployment of a peacekeeping force is conditional on the consent of both the States contributing troops to such a force and the host State where the force is to be deployed.[181] The fact, however, that a State has voted within the principal organ concerned in favour of the establishment of a peacekeeping force does not estop that State from later refusing either to allow the deployment of the peacekeep-ing force on its own territory or to contribute troops to the force.[182] The

---

[180] See Sarooshi, *supra* note 1, pp. 442–6.

[181] As the UN Secretary-General, in paragraph 9 of his second and final report on the plan for an emergency international force of 6 Nov. 1956, observed: 'While the General Assembly is enabled to *establish* the Force with the consent of the parties which contribute units to the Force, it could not request the Force to be *stationed* or *operate* on the territory of a given country without the consent of the Government of that country.' (A/3302, contained in Higgins, *supra* note 163, p. 263.) Moreover, the International Court of Justice has found in respect of peacekeeping forces: 'the way in which such subsidiary organs are utilized depends on the consent of the State or States concerned'. (*Expenses* case, *ICJ Reports*, (1962), p. 165) On the necessity and role of consent in such operations, see Garvey, J., 'United Nations Peacekeeping and Host State Consent', *AJIL*, 64 (1970), p. 241, and Di Blase, *supra* note 172, p. 55.

[182] However, the role of host-State consent in UN peacekeeping does not extend to pro-hibiting the Security Council from changing the mandate of peacekeeping troops from

participation by a State in the establishment of a subsidiary organ cannot affect the rights which a State may otherwise enjoy under the Charter.[183] For our purposes, the point is that the exercize of delegated Chapter VII powers by a subsidiary organ, and more generally a delegate, must respect the rights of Member States under the Charter.

2. A principal organ must exercize authority and control over its subsidiary organ

The *Repertory of Practice of United Nations Organs* notes that an essential characteristic of a subsidiary organ is that it be under the authority and control of a principal organ.[184] Thus, for example, the UN Legal Counsel has stated:

peacekeeping to peace enforcement. That is, to decide to delegate military enforcement powers to a peacekeeping force. (The distinction between peacekeeping operations and operations under Chapter VII was emphasized by the Secretary-General in his *Summary Study* derived from the establishment of UNEF and by the Secretary-General in the case of ONUC in the Congo (*SCOR*, 15th year, Suppl. for July–Sept., p. 45, S/4417, para. 10); in another statement by the Secretary-General in the Council (*SCOR*, 15th year, 920th meeting, para. 73, in Higgins, R., *United Nations Peacekeeping* (1980), vol. 3, p. 56); and the adoption of this approach by the Security Council in resolution 146 and by States representatives (Argentina, *SCOR*, 15th year, 887th meeting, paras. 149–52, Tunisia, *ibidem*, paras. 130–2, Ceylon, *SCOR*, 15th year, 889th meeting, paras. 45–50, China, *ibidem*, para. 114, Ecuador, *ibidem*, para. 59, France, *ibidem*, para. 138, Italy, *ibidem*, paras. 8–15, UK, *ibidem*, paras. 70–1, and USA, *ibidem*, para. 96). The consent of the former host State is no longer necessary since by definition peace enforcement is directed against a State. The use of peacekeeping forces to carry out military enforcement measures was envisaged by the Secretary General as early as UNEF in 1956. (See *Summary Study*, as contained in Higgins, R., *United Nations Peacekeeping*, vol. 1. (1969), p. 274.) However, the consent of the troops-contributing States still remains a necessary prerequisite. More specifically, with a change in the forces' mandate States would be free to withdraw their troops from what is, in legal terms, a new force. Moreover, this is in accord with the object and purpose of Article 44 of the Charter which is, as explained in Chapter 1, applicable in cases of military enforcement action undertaken by the Security Council. (See *supra* note 134 and corresponding text in Chapter 1.) Accordingly, in the case of UNOSOM II where the Security Council changed the mandate of the peacekeeping force in resolutions 814 and 837 to military enforcement action, States had the right at that stage to withdraw their troops from what was, in legal terms, a new force. (See further as to the military enforcement action carried out by UNOSOM II: *infra* Section I(3) of Chapter 5.)

[183] Moreover, the rights which States or other entities possess with regard to a principal organ of the UN they also possess in respect of its subsidiary organs. This was illustrated in a UN legal opinion on the legal status of the International Trade Centre (ITC) and the applicability to the Centre of General Assembly resolutions regarding the participation of the PLO in UN meetings. In particular the question was whether the PLO could participate as an observer in a session of the Joint Advisory Group (JAG) on the ITC. The UN Legal Counsel noted that the General Assembly in resolution 3237 (XXIX) of 22 Nov. 1974 had invited the PLO to participate as an observer in the sessions and the work of all international conferences convened under the auspices of the General Assembly. The UN Legal Counsel then found that since, *inter alia*, the ITC had been recognized by the General Assembly as a subsidiary organ of the United Nations (*UNJYB* (1990), p. 272) the PLO was accordingly able to participate as an observer in JAG meetings. (*Ibidem.*)

[184] See *supra* note 10 and corresponding text.

The Council for Namibia was established as a subsidiary organ of the General Assembly by resolution 2248 (S–V) of 19 May 1967. As a subsidiary organ, it is responsible to, and under the authority of, the General Assembly in the same way as any other subsidiary organ.[185]

This characteristic flows from the subordinate nature of a subsidiary organ in relation to its principal.[186] The notion of ultimate control of the activities of a subsidiary organ is clear: it rests with the principal organ unless the instrument establishing the subsidiary organ stipulates otherwise.[187] There are two main consequences of the precondition that a subsidiary organ be under the authority and control of a principal organ.

First, it enables a clear distinction to be made between UN subsidiary organs and other entities.[188]

[185] Memorandum to the Representative of the Director General of the International Atomic Energy Agency to the United Nations: *UNJYB* (1982), p. 164. Similarly, the Legal Counsel has observed in respect of the Committee of Contributions, 'The Committee, as a subsidiary organ of the General Assembly . . . is bound to carry out its tasks in accordance with any directives addressed to it by the Assembly.' (*Ibidem*, p. 182.)

[186] As Judge Hackworth states in his dissenting opinion (on another point) in the *Administrative Tribunal* case: 'The term "subsidiary organ" has a special and well recognised meaning. It means an auxiliary or inferior organ; an organ to furnish aid and assistance in a subordinate or secondary capacity. This is the common acceptation of the term.' (*ICJ Reports* (1954), p. 79.) However, several writers have pointed out that this subordinate nature of a subsidiary organ does not mean that there is a hierarchy of functions between principal and subsidiary organs, in the sense that the latter deal only with minor tasks: see Torres Bernardez, *supra* note 1, p. 104; and Bentwich and Martin, *supra* note 1, p. 28.

[187] This was illustrated by the opinion of the UN Legal Counsel in his memorandum to the Secretary of ECOSOC where he stated in respect of the *Ad Hoc* Committee of ECOSOC that if 'any question arises as to the composition of the *Ad Hoc* Committee, this could be settled in the first instance in the *Ad Hoc* Committee and ultimately by the parent body, the Economic and Social Council'. (Memorandum to the Secretary of ECOSOC, *UNJYB* (1984), p. 168.) Similarly, in a memorandum to the Under-Secretary-General for Political and General Assembly Affairs, the UN Legal Counsel states 'Where the terms of reference are not clear and a question arises as to the competence of a subsidiary organ to take action on a particular matter it would, in the first instance, be settled by that organ in accordance with its rules of procedure. Should the manner in which it is settled be questioned again in the parent organ it would then be for the parent organ to decide the issue, and its decision would be final.' (*Ibidem*, p. 135.) However, if the subsidiary organ wishes to take action contrary to a decision of its principal organ there is no legal impediment to the subsidiary obtaining the permission of its parent organ: permission being either express or implied. Accordingly, in a cable to the Chief of the Governing Council Secretariat of the United Nations Environmental Programme on the question whether a subsidiary organ can provide that one of its own subsidiaries use fewer languages than itself, the UN Legal Counsel stated 'If a choice of languages is desired that would contravene a General Assembly or Economic and Social Council decision, then the permission of the Assembly or Council must be secured. This can be granted by an explicit resolution or decision, or implicitly through the approval of a financial implications statement anticipating the use of fewer languages than those normally authorized.' (*UNJYB* (1983), p. 169.)

[188] Accordingly, a private corporation which is incorporated within a State cannot lawfully be established as a UN subsidiary organ, since the organ would be subject to the laws of the State in question and would thus not be under the sole authority and control of a UN principal organ. This issue arose when UNICEF asked whether it could become a shareholder in a printing company incorporated in a Member State. In reply, the UN Legal Counsel observed:

The second consequence is that the principal organ possesses the competence to determine the membership, structure, mandate, and duration of existence of its subsidiary organ.[189] The scope of the competence to terminate a subsidiary organ is the least clear and most controversial of these competencies.

There are many instances of an express termination of the life of a subsidiary organ by formal decision of the Security Council.[190] What is not so clear is whether there can be implied termination. The Security Council considered the procedure for the termination of a subsidiary organ when deciding what the effect of the liquidation of the Commission set up to investigate the Greek frontier incident would be on its sub-subsidiary organ, the 'Subsidiary Group'.[191] In this case the Greek Frontier Commission—the subsidiary organ of the Council—had set up its own subsidiary organ: the 'Subsidiary Group'. It follows from the fact that the Frontier Commission was the subsidiary organ of the Council that the latter could exercize authority and control over the 'Subsidiary Group'. At the 188th meeting of the Council, the UK representative argued that both subsidiary organs in this case 'can be terminated only by an affirmative decision of the Council'.[192] Moreover, the representative of the United States stated: 'I entirely support the President's ruling that the Group and the Commission should remain in existence until the Council takes affirmative action.'[193] The issue was resolved by the US representative who introduced at the 202nd meeting a draft resolution to remove the question from the list of matters of which the Security Council was seized. There could be no doubt, he stated,

'The participation of UNICEF as a shareholder in a private company would submit the Organization to the regulations and rules of the national law governing corporate entities, and would thus be incompatible with the character and status of the United Nations, of which UNICEF is a subsidiary organ. As a United Nations organ, UNICEF enjoys, under Article 104 of the United Nations Charter and the Convention on the Privileges and Immunities of the United Nations, certain privileges and immunities, including immunity from legal process. Yet, as a shareholder in a private corporation, UNICEF would be subject to any legislative controls imposing fiduciary duties and liabilities for the acts of the corporation.' (*UNJYB* (1990), p. 256.) See also the opinion given by the UN Legal Counsel on whether the United Nations Development Programme could become a founding member of a corporate body under the national law of a Member State: *ibidem*, p. 259. An additional consideration here is that such an entity would not be subject to the budgetary control of the General Assembly which is required by Article 17 of the Charter: see *infra* note 230 and corresponding text.

[189] As the International Court in the *Administrative Tribunal* case observed: 'There can be no doubt that the Administrative Tribunal is subordinate in the sense that the General Assembly can abolish the Tribunal by repealing the Statute, that it can amend the Statute and provide for review of the future decisions of the Tribunal and that it can amend the Staff Regulations and make new ones.' (*ICJ Reports* (1954), p. 61.) See also Simma, *supra* note 1, p. 197.

[190] For example, the termination of the United Nations Commission for India and Pakistan on 17 May 1950: see *Repertory of Practice of United Nations Organs* (1955), vol. 2, p. 21.

[191] *Repertoire of the Practice of the Security Council, 1946–1951*, pp. 207–8.

[192] *Ibidem*, p. 208.

[193] *Ibidem*.

that in taking such a decision the Council would be destroying both subsidiary organs in question.[194] At the same meeting the US draft resolution was adopted.[195] The Greek question was accordingly removed from the list of matters and the Commission of Investigation was deemed to be terminated.[196] Thus implied termination was effected in the Greek case by removing the question from the list of matters of which the Security Council was seized. What was considered important for effective termination was not the form of determination, but that the principal organ clearly evinced its intention that the subsidiary organ was to be terminated. The position is well summarized by Cot and Pellet's commentary on the Charter: '[l]es conditions de suppression d'un organe subsidiaire sont symétriques des conditions de création: la suppression résulte d'une manifestation de volonté de l'organe principal créateur'.[197] Accordingly, there cannot be implied termination of a subsidiary organ simply because the task which the subsidiary was established to carry out has been completed. This approach has been confirmed by the UN Legal Counsel. In reply to the question whether the life of the UN Council for Namibia was to be considered as automatically terminated after the achievement by Namibia of its independence, the Council's very reason for existence,[198] the Counsel stated:

While the constitutive resolution (2248 (S–V) of 19 May 1967) and subsequent resolutions of the General Assembly imply in substantive terms that the mandate of the Council is fulfilled and that, therefore, the Council ceases to exist upon Namibian independence, no automatic dissolution of the Council is foreseen in these resolutions. The independence of Namibia . . . will not, therefore, automatically trigger the dissolution of the Council, which will continue to exist from a purely legal point of view as a duly constituted subsidiary organ of the General Assembly until such time as the Assembly itself decides otherwise. . . . As far as the question of status is concerned, therefore, one may conclude that the legal status of the Council for Namibia as a subsidiary organ of the General Assembly remains unchanged until such time as the General Assembly decides otherwise.[199]

---

[194] *Ibidem.*
[195] *Ibidem.*
[196] *Ibidem.*
[197] Cot and Pellet, *supra* note 1, p. 216.
[198] The UN Council for Namibia was a subsidiary organ which was created by General Assembly resolution 2248 (S–V) of 19 May 1967 and which was endowed with broad administrative, executive, and legislative powers to help achieve the independence of Namibia. The fact that it is a subsidiary organ of the Council is affirmed by the UN Legal Counsel in a memorandum to the Officer-in-Charge of the Office of the UN Commissioner for Namibia: see *UNJYB* (1990), p. 271.
[199] *UNJYB* (1990), p. 271. The General Assembly decided to terminate the life of the Council by resolution 44/243 of 11 Sept. 1990, which states: '*Taking note* of the declaration of the United Nations Council for Namibia adopted at its special plenary meetings . . . by which the Council decided to recommend to the General Assembly its own dissolution as a result of Namibia's attainment of freedom and independence, . . . [the General Assembly] (2) *Decides*

The general rule in this area is that the fulfilment by a subsidiary organ of the task for which it was created does not automatically terminate its life.[200] The expression in some form by a principal organ that it intends the life of the subsidiary organ to be terminated is required for effective termination to occur.[201] For example, a principal organ may expressly provide in the resolution establishing a subsidiary that its life is to be terminated upon, for example, the expiration of a certain time period.[202]

This general rule is of considerable importance to the work of the UN War Crimes Tribunal for the former Yugoslavia. In the case of the War Crimes Tribunal, the Secretary-General, in his Report to the Security Council on the establishment of the Tribunal, states:

As an enforcement measure under Chapter VII, however, the life span of the international tribunal would be linked to the restoration and maintenance of international peace and security in the territory of the former Yugoslavia, and Security Council decisions related thereto.[203]

It would not be accurate to suggest that the Secretary-General means by this statement that when the determination that international peace has been restored in the former Yugoslavia is made by the Security Council that the mandate of the Tribunal would be automatically terminated.[204] There is the additional requirement which must be satisfied for effective termination to occur: *in casu*, there would need to be a clear expression of

that the United Nations Council for Namibia, having fulfilled the important mandate entrusted to it by General Assembly 2248 (S–V) relating to the Territory, is hereby dissolved.' (General Assembly Resolution 44/243 of 11 Sept. 1990, *GAOR*, 44th Session, Supplement No. 49A, A/44/49/Add. 1 (1991), pp. 2–3.)

[200] This does not, however, mean that a subsidiary organ will be able to continue carrying out functions in respect of a task which the principal organ has decided has already been completed. As the UN Legal Counsel observed in respect of the effect of Namibia attaining its independence upon the UN Council for Namibia: 'This is not to say, of course, that all of the activities of the Council will survive the independence of Namibia. Some activities of the Council will automatically lose their *raison d'être* or will by their very nature be assumed by the new Government of Namibia.' (*UNJYB* (1990), p. 271.)

[201] Accordingly, the Security Council in resolution 689 notes in respect of the UN Iraq-Kuwait Observation Mission that 'the decision to set up the observation unit was taken in paragraph 5 of resolution 687 (1991) and can only be terminated by a decision of the Council. The Council shall therefore review the question of termination or continuation every six months.' (S/RES/689 (1991).)

[202] See, for example, the establishment by the Security Council in resolution 186 (1964) of the United Nations peacekeeping force in Cyprus (UNFICYP) for an initial time period of three months. Thus the existence of UNFICYP has, to date, depended on the Council continually renewing its mandate. See further on this issue of a time limit in UN peacekeeping forces: Di Blase, *supra* note 172, pp. 75–6.

[203] S/25704, p. 8.

[204] Cf. the defence motion that was filed in the *Tadic* case which states: 'the legal ground for the Tribunal would probably fall away precisely at that moment it would be likely to be able to do most, namely when peace has returned'. (Defence motion in the *Tadic* case, Case No. IT-94-I-T, 23 June 1995, para. 3.5.5.)

intention by the Council that the Tribunal is to be terminated.[205] This does not, however, impinge on the Council's prerogative to decide to abolish the Tribunal or to exclude from the jurisdiction of the Tribunal a whole range of cases (thereby granting in effect immunity to persons falling within a specified category). There is, however, an argument that could be made that if the Tribunal had established jurisdiction in a case then the Security Council could not purport to terminate the Tribunal's consideration of those cases in which jurisdiction had already been established. This follows from the decision of the International Court of Justice in the *Lockerbie* case which states that '[i]n accordance with its established jurisprudence, if the Court had jurisdiction on that date, it continues to do so; the subsequent coming into existence of the above-mentioned [Security Council] resolutions cannot affect its jurisdiction once established (cf. *Nottebohm, Preliminary Objection, Judgment, ICJ Reports*, 1953, p. 122; *Right of Passage over Indian Territory, Preliminary Objections, Judgment, ICJ Reports*, 1957, p. 142).'[206] This approach is supported in the context of the Tribunal when one recalls the independence the Tribunal enjoys in the exercize of its judicial powers from the Security Council.[207]

In conclusion, the authority and control which a principal organ possesses over its subsidiary organ enables the principal to be able to review and change the decisions of its subsidiary organ and terminate the life of the subsidiary with immediate effect.

3. The establishment of a subsidiary organ must not violate the delimitation of powers between principal organs specified by the Charter

The UN Charter gives certain powers to certain principal organs and certain other powers to certain other principal organs. There is in many cases a good deal of overlap of powers and functions of the principal organs. However, even in these cases there are limits to when a principal organ can

---

[205] A possible reason for this may be that the Council wants to use the threat of prosecution as a bargaining chip to force the leaders in the former Yugoslavia to conclude a binding peace: see Szasz, *supra* note 44; and D'Amato, A., 'Peace vs. Accountability in Bosnia', *AJIL*, 88 (1994), p. 500. In response to D'Amato's articles, cf. the letters to the editor of the *AJIL* by Jordan Paust, Benjamin Ferencz, and Payam Akhavan: *AJIL*, 88 (1994), p. 715, *ibidem*, p. 717, and *AJIL*, 89 (1995), p. 92, respectively. The competence of the Council to terminate the life of the Tribunal, its subsidiary organ, is a cogent argument against an International Criminal Court being established, if the Council has the competence, as a UN subsidiary organ. For the various arguments surrounding the establishment of this Court, see *Yearbook of the International Law Commission* (1993), vol. 1; and *Yearbook of the International Law Commission* (1994), vol. 1.

[206] *Lockerbie* case, *Preliminary Objections Phase*, 27 Feb. 1998 (not yet published in *ICJ Reports*), para. 37. On the issue of certain judicial powers of the Tribunal compared to that of the International Court of Justice, see Sarooshi, *supra* note 85, pp. 10–14.

[207] See *supra* notes 82–3.

exercize certain powers. Under the law of the United Nations, it is not possible for UN principal organs to impinge on each other's Charter-mandated delimitation of powers.[208] Applying this principle to our enquiry, it follows that UN principal organs cannot establish a subsidiary organ whose activities would violate the delimitation of Charter powers between principal organs.[209] This section ascertains the contours of the delimitation of Charter powers between principal organs and examines how this operates as a limitation on the authority of the Council to be able to establish subsidiary organs, and therefore to delegate Chapter VII powers to such organs, in the areas of international peace and security and United Nations finances.[210]

(a) International peace and security

Article 24(1) of the Charter confers on the Council the 'primary responsibility for the maintenance of international peace and security'. However, it is well established that this does not prevent the General Assembly from exercizing a secondary responsibility for maintaining international peace and security.[211] The question which has arisen in practice is whether the General Assembly has the authority to establish subsidiary organs to perform functions in respect of the maintenance of international peace and security. This issue has been highly controversial. It was the issue of the delimitation of Charter powers that in part provided the basis for a claim in the *Expenses* case that the General Assembly did not possess the competence to establish the first UN peacekeeping force in the Middle East (UNEF I).[212] However, the first instance where this issue arose was during discussion in the First Committee of the General Assembly on the proposed establishment of an Interim Committee by the General Assembly to deal with matters relating to international peace and security.

The Interim Committee of the General Assembly was intended to func-

---

[208] See also the following: Koskenniemi, M., 'The Police in the Temple. Order, Justice and the UN: A Dialectical View', *EJIL*, 6 (1995), p. 325 at pp. 337–8; Fitzmaurice, G., *The Law and Procedure of the International Court of Justice* (1986), p. 103; Bindschedler, R., 'La Délimitation des Compétence des Nations Unies', *Hague Recueil des Cours*, 108 (1963-I), p. 312; Judge Bustamente in the *Expenses* case, *ICJ Reports* (1962), p. 151 at pp. 292–3; and the statement by Phleger (USA), *United Nations Administrative Tribunal* case, *ICJ Pleadings* (1954), p. 322.

[209] Simma's *Commentary*, although less equivocal, states: 'The exercize by one such [principal] organ of its powers [to establish subsidiary organs] should not lead to a disturbance of the balance established between principal organs by the Charter.' (Simma, *supra* note 1, p. 386.)

[210] The delimitation of Charter powers also operates as a limitation on the authority of the Council to establish subsidiary organs to exercise judicial functions in contentious cases between States: see Sarooshi, *supra* note 1, pp. 462–3.

[211] See the *Expenses* case, *ICJ Reports* (1962), p. 163; Cot and Pellet, *supra* note 1, p. 447; and Kelsen, *supra* note 20, p. 283.

[212] Cf. *infra* note 221 and corresponding text.

tion in between the sessions of the main Assembly, its purpose being to ensure continuity in the control the Assembly could exercize over major political problems. The Committee was to have the power to discuss important disputes or situations submitted to the Assembly, to conduct investigations, and to advise, if necessary, that there should be a convening of a special session of the Assembly.[213] A major objection to the establishment of the Interim Committee was the contention that the functions proposed for the Committee were those which belonged to the Security Council and not the General Assembly. It was the representative of the Soviet Union who argued that when definite measures for the solution of a problem relating to international peace and security were to be taken, Article 11(2) of the Charter required the General Assembly to submit the matter to the Security Council.[214] Moreover, he argued, the empowering of the Interim Committee to conduct investigations and to appoint commissions of inquiry was a function of the Security Council, and not the General Assembly.[215] The Soviet Representative contended that the 'true purpose' was to create a new organ 'to weaken, circumvent, and act as a substitute for the Security Council, on which the Charter placed primary responsibility for maintaining peace and security'.[216] The opposing, better, view expressed was that the Assembly, as well as the Security Council, could take certain measures in relation to the maintenance of international peace and security and that the Assembly accordingly possessed the competence to establish the Committee.[217] The arguments in favour of the establishment of the Committee prevailed and the Interim Committee was established by resolution of the General Assembly.[218] For our purposes it is significant that in the debates the UK representative argued that the Committee would be subservient to the Security Council, which had the primary responsibility for the maintenance of international peace and security.[219] This allayed fears that the Committee, as a subsidiary organ, would be used to supplant the delimitation of powers between the Security Council and the General Assembly as established by the Charter.[220] However, until the *Expenses*

---

[213] UN Doc. A/C1/SR74 and Doc. A/PV.82, p. 60. See also Bowett, D., *The Law of International Institutions* (1982), p. 49.

[214] *Repertory of Practice of United Nations Organs* (1955, v. 1), p. 675.

[215] *Ibidem.*

[216] UN Doc. A/C1/SR 74. See also Doc. A/PV.110.

[217] *Ibidem.*

[218] *GAOR*, 2nd Session, Doc. A/519, p. 15.

[219] The UK representative stated that the Committee would have no power of direct recommendation—as the Council has—nor would it be able to send a commission of inquiry to a country without the consent of the Council. (*Ibidem*, p. 159.)

[220] This point was made in somewhat more general terms by the French representative: see *ibidem*, p. 162. Moreover, the Interim Committee was required to take account of the limitations imposed upon it by Articles 11(2) and 12(1) of the Charter. This illustrates the principle that a subsidiary organ is constrained, at a minimum, by the same limitations under the Charter as its principal organ. In fact, as Goodrich and Hambro point out, Article 12(1) became a

case the exact contours of the delimitation of powers between the Council and the Assembly in the area of international peace and security remained unclear.

In the *Expenses* case, the delimitation of Charter powers between the Security Council and the General Assembly in the area of international peace and security was one of the bases upon which the constitutionality of UNEF I, which had been established by the General Assembly, was questioned. The argument made was that matters pertaining to the maintenance of international peace and security were, according to the Charter, to be dealt with solely by the Security Council and therefore only the Security Council could establish a UN peacekeeping force. The Court rejected this argument on the basis that the primary responsibility conferred on the Council by Article 24 for matters pertaining to international peace and security is ' "primary", not exclusive'.[221] The Court went on to state that '[t]he Charter makes it abundantly clear that the General Assembly is also to be concerned with international peace and security'.[222] However, the Court did find there was a delimitation of Charter powers between the two organs that would prohibit the General Assembly from exercising certain powers. The Court found that '. . . it is the Security Council which is given a power to impose an explicit obligation of compliance if for example it issues an order or command to an aggressor under Chapter VII. *It is only the Security Council which can require enforcement by coercive action against an aggressor.*'[223] Thus the Court found that the delimitation of Charter powers here means that the General Assembly could not impose a requirement on States to carry out military enforcement action. Put differently, if a force were established by the General Assembly to carry out military enforcement action that purported to require States to contribute troops to the force, then its establishment would be *ultra vires*. The International Court went on to decide, however, that this particular delimitation of Charter powers did not apply to the case in question, since contributions to the force were on a voluntary basis. Moreover, the Court rejected the argument with regard to the delimitation of Charter powers in this case by giving a narrow interpretation to the word 'action' in Article 11(2).[224] The

greater limitation upon the Interim Committee than upon the General Assembly. They stated: '[under Article 12] [t]he General Assembly, while it may not make any recommendations concerning the question of which the Council is seized, may discuss that question. However, the Interim Committee could not even discuss any question of which the Council was seized.' (Goodrich and Hambro, *supra* note 1, p. 197.)

[221] *Expenses* case, *ICJ Reports* (1962), p. 163.

[222] *Ibidem*, p. 163.

[223] *Ibidem* (emphasis added).

[224] Article 11(2) provides that certain 'action' is within the sole province of the Security Council, to the exclusion of the General Assembly. The relevant section of Article 11(2) of the Charter provides as follows: 'Any such question on which action is necessary shall be referred to the Security Council by the General Assembly either before or after discussion.'

Court found that 'action' refers to coercive enforcement action.[225] As UN peacekeeping does not in theory involve the use of coercive enforcement measures against a State,[226] the Court rejected the argument that the application of Article 11(2) of the Charter prevented the General Assembly from lawfully establishing the peacekeeping force. The delimitation of Charter powers did not prevent the General Assembly from exercizing its power under Article 14 of the Charter to recommend—such recommendations of course being non-binding—to Member States that they establish a peacekeeping force.[227]

Consideration of the above two cases reveals that, in determining the effect of the delimitation of Charter powers on the authority of principal organs to establish subsidiary organs, the Charter provisions are to be given a broad interpretation in the area of international peace and security. The possibility of the overlapping of functions of the Security Council and the General Assembly is not in itself a barrier to their possessing concurrent jurisdiction[228] and thus both possessing the authority to establish subsidiary organs to perform functions in the relevant area. However, the delimitation of Charter powers in this area is such that it does preclude the General Assembly from establishing a UN force, a subsidiary organ, that would require a contribution of troops from UN Member States to carry out military enforcement action.

(b) United Nations finances

The International Court of Justice in the *Expenses* case found that Article 17 of the Charter vested in the General Assembly the 'control over the finances of the Organization, and the levying of apportioned amounts of the

---

[225] *ICJ Reports* (1962), pp. 163–5.

[226] The Court stated: 'UNEF and ONUC were not enforcement actions within the compass of Chapter VII of the Charter'. (*ICJ Reports* (1962), p. 166.) See also the opinion by the UN Legal Counsel regarding the implementation of Article 43 of the Charter: *UNJYB* (1982), pp. 183–4.

[227] *ICJ Reports* (1962), pp. 163–5.

[228] Moreover, subsequent to the Court's decision in the *Expenses* case, the delimitation of powers between the Security Council and the General Assembly provided for in Article 12 in respect of the maintenance of international peace and security has, through practice, become even less clear. Article 12(1) of the Charter states: 'While the Security Council is exercizing in respect of any dispute or situation the functions assigned to it in the present Charter, the General Assembly shall not make any recommendation with regard to that dispute or situation unless the Security Council so requests.' However, the General Assembly, when dealing with the situation in the former Yugoslavia, passed resolution 47/121 of 18 Dec. 1992, which urges the Security Council to exempt the Republic of Bosnia and Herzegovina from the arms embargo imposed on the former Yugoslavia under Security Council resolution 713. This resolution was passed at the same time that the Council was considering the question of the former Yugoslavia: an apparent violation of Article 12 of the Charter. See on Article 12: Blum, Y., 'Who Killed Article 12 of the United Nations Charter?', Chapter V, *Eroding the United Nations Charter* (1993), pp. 103–32.

expenses of the Organization in order to enable it [the Assembly] to carry out the functions of the Organization as a whole acting through its principal organs and such subsidiary organs as may be established under the authority of Article 22 or Article 29'.[229] Moreover, the Court found that Article 17 gave the General Assembly an exclusive right to consider and approve the UN budget.[230] Accordingly, a UN principal organ cannot purport to establish a subsidiary organ which has control over its finances such that it can determine its own budget, since the subsidiary would thus be capable of usurping the power of the General Assembly under Article 17 to decide the budget of the Organization.[231] The delimitation of powers under the Charter with respect to the authority to determine and apportion the UN budget means that an essential precondition for an entity to be lawfully established as a UN subsidiary organ is that the General Assembly exercize complete control over its budget. An entity which exercizes exclusive control over its finances cannot be considered as a UN subsidiary organ.[232]

The controversial issue which arises from the consequences of this delimitation of powers is whether the General Assembly can use its exclusive control over the UN budget to limit the competence of the Council to establish subsidiary organs. Klepacki argues this in general terms when he contends that if the activity of a subsidiary organ involves costs to be borne

[229] *ICJ Reports* (1962), p. 162.

[230] The Court found: 'Article 17 is the only article in the Charter which refers to budgetary authority or to the power to apportion expenses, or otherwise to raise revenue, except for Articles 33 and 35, paragraph 3, of the Statute of the Court which have no bearing on the point here under discussion.' (*Ibidem.*) The one possible exception to this position is where the General Assembly establishes a subsidiary organ to carry out judicial functions which may lead to costs being incurred by the UN where the General Assembly has intended that the decision of the subsidiary organ is to be final and binds even itself. Thus in the *Administrative Tribunal* case the Court dismissed the argument that it was not possible to establish a subsidiary organ which could in effect impose legal limitations on the General Assembly's express Charter powers to determine the UN budget. The Court concluded on this point: 'The Court therefore considers that the assignment of the budgetary function to the General Assembly cannot be regarded as conferring upon it the right to refuse to give effect to the obligation arising out of an award of the Administrative Tribunal.' (*ICJ Reports* (1954), p. 59.)

[231] The importance of this budgetary control is emphasized when one considers that the General Assembly fully funds and, more importantly, fully controls the budget of United Nations treaty bodies: for example, the UN Human Rights Committee. See, in respect of these UN treaty bodies, *supra* note 155.

[232] This view has been confirmed by the UN Legal Counsel when determining the status of the Special Commission established by General Assembly resolution 38/161 of 19 Dec. 1983 entitled 'Process of Preparation of the Environmental Perspective to the Year 2000 and Beyond'. He observed: 'After careful consideration and largely because the Commission, once established, is to have complete control over its finances, we have come to the conclusion that the Commission, which has adopted the name 'World Commission on Environment and Development', should not be considered as having the status of a United Nations organ or as being a part of the United Nations.' (*UNJYB* (1984), p. 163.) Cf. Morgenstern who argues that often an important reason for the establishment of subsidiary bodies is to separate their finances, largely based on voluntary contributions, from those of the parent (principal) organization. (Morgenstern, F., *Legal Problems of International Organizations* (1986), pp. 23–4.)

by the whole organization, then the consent of the 'top organ is, as a rule, required. In this manner the top organ to some extent controls the setting up of these subsidiary organs.'[233] Klepacki later states that the 'top organ' is the most important of the principal organs. It is, however, unclear whether this 'top organ' is the principal organ responsible for setting the budget of the international organization. In the context of the UN it seems that this may be the case: the UN Legal Counsel has stated:

the pre-eminence of the General Assembly as the most significant of the principal organs flows from its power of the purse (Article 17) and its power to discuss 'any matters . . . relating to the powers and functions of any organ' (Article 10).[234]

If this is indeed the case, then in the context of the United Nations the consent—albeit not formally expressed—of the General Assembly would be needed every time the Council wanted to establish a subsidiary organ. It should be emphasized that there is of course no formal procedure whereby the Council must approach the Assembly for the approval of the establishment of individual subsidiary organs. However, the point is that the Assembly can, by virtue of the delimitation of Charter powers in this area, exercize a degree of control over the activities of the Security Council.[235] So that while in theory the Security Council may have unchallengeable authority to establish a particular subsidiary organ, if, however, the General Assembly does not apportion any funds for its operation out of the UN budget then in practice it will be able to survive in name only.[236] An example of how this

---

[233] Klepacki, *supra* note 1, p. 17.

[234] *UNJYB* (1982), p. 190. The fact that the General Assembly is the only plenary organ of the UN may also be of some importance in arguing that it is Klepacki's 'top organ'. Moreover, Simma's *Commentary* states: 'It may be maintained that the General Assembly enjoys a primary position among the principal organs because Article 15 [of the Charter] provides that it shall receive and consider reports from the other principal organs.' (Simma, *supra* note 1, p. 196.) However, the commentary goes on to note: 'but this right of information does not include the right of the General Assembly to issue directives to the other principal organs where there is no such authority under other articles of the Charter'. (*Ibidem.*)

[235] This is, however, qualitatively different from saying that the Assembly has the competence to question the way in which the Security Council has exercized its powers of discretion. Serge Sur, for example, argues that under the Charter the General Assembly does not have the competence to question the way in which the Security Council exercizes its competence, especially under Chapter VII. (Sur, S., 'Security Council Resolution 687 of 3 April 1991 in the Gulf Affair: Problems of Restoring and Safeguarding Peace', *UNITAR Research Paper*, No. 12 (1992), p. 7.) Cf., however, the statement by the Venezuelan representative at the San Francisco Conference in the context of matters pertaining to international peace and security who claimed for the General Assembly the right to control the Security Council in order to prevent it from transgressing established legal principles. (*UNCIO*, vol. 4, p. 253 (General Doc. 2, G/ 7(d)(1), of 5 May 1945, p. 12), and *UNCIO*, vol. 11, p. 768 (Commission III, Security Council Doc. 360, III/1/16, 15 May 1945, p. 4).) Cf. also Koskenniemi who argues that the General Assembly should use whatever powers it has at its disposal to impose restraint on the Council in order to achieve international justice in certain cases (Koskenniemi, *supra* note 208); and Alvarez, *supra* note 83, p. 10.

[236] Cf. Suy, E., 'The Role of the United Nations General Assembly', in *The Changing Constitution of the United Nations* (Fox, H., ed.) (1997), p. 55 at p. 59.

could occur nearly arose in the case of the establishment of the War Crimes Tribunal for the former Yugoslavia. The Security Council in resolutions 808 and 827 established the Tribunal as a measure to assist in the restoration of international peace and security in the former Yugoslavia.[237] However, in Article 32 of the Statute of the Tribunal the Security Council stated that the expenses of the Tribunal 'shall be borne by the regular budget of the United Nations in accordance with Article 17 of the Charter of the United Nations'.[238] A note by the UN Secretariat to the General Assembly concerning this issue provides:

In the view of the Secretary-General . . . there was no legal bar to the Security Council reaching its own conclusions as to the appropriate financing of the International Tribunal and including a provision on the matter in the Statute which it adopted. Nevertheless, such conclusions are without prejudice to the authority of the General Assembly under the Charter to consider and approve the budget of the Organization and to apportion the expenses of the Organization among its Members.[239]

However, in the view of the General Assembly this clearly impinged on its sole prerogative to make determinations regarding the UN budget. The General Assembly voiced its discontent when it '[e]xpress[ed] concern that advice given to the Security Council by the Secretariat on the nature of the financing of the International Tribunal did not respect the role of the General Assembly as set out in Article 17 of the Charter'.[240] As a result the General Assembly did not initially pledge full financing of the Tribunal.[241] Although the General Assembly subsequently agreed to continue to finance the activities of the Tribunal, the emphasis placed by it on retaining its sole prerogative over UN finances is significant. The Assembly's sole competence in respect of UN finances may in the future be used to restrict the effective establishment of subsidiary organs by the Council.

However, in the case of the exercize of Chapter VII powers by the Council this possibility seems remote due to the emphasis the Charter places on the maintenance of international peace and security and the

---

[237] See *supra* note 40 and corresponding text.

[238] The Secretary-General in his report on the establishment of the Tribunal stated that this provision is without prejudice to the role of the General Assembly in the administrative and budgetary aspects of the question of establishing the Tribunal. (S/25704, para. 21.)

[239] A/47/1002, para. 12. Note, moreover, the earlier practice of the Security Council when, while establishing subsidiary organs, it indicated the method of financing of the subsidiary: see 'Article 29', *Repertory of Practice of United Nations Organs*, Supplement No. 3 (1972), p. 81 at p. 84, para. 12.

[240] A/47/1014, para. 3.

[241] The Assembly only '[e]ndorse[d] the recommendation of the Advisory Committee on Administrative and Budgetary Questions to authorize the Secretary-General to enter into commitments in an amount not exceeding 500,000 United States dollars to provide for the immediate and urgent requirements of the Tribunal for its initial activities'. (A/47/104, para. 5.)

Council's primary role therein. This was of considerable importance to the International Court in the *Expenses* case when it found that the Security Council could establish a peacekeeping force: 'it must be within the power of the Security Council to police a situation even though it does not resort to an enforcement action against a State',[242] and, further, that the costs of such an operation would constitute 'expenses of the Organization within the meaning of Article 17, paragraph 2'.[243] Moreover, it may be argued that if the Security Council decides to establish a subsidiary organ which it deems necessary for the maintenance or restoration of international peace, then UN Member States are under an obligation under Article 25 of the Charter to carry out this decision. Thus the argument would run that when voting in the Assembly, States should vote in favour of the provision of funds to enable the effective establishment of such a subsidiary organ. In formal terms, however, there would be no obligation on the General Assembly, but only on the Member States of which it is composed. Such an idea is not new to the law of the United Nations. When the Security Council makes a decision under Chapter VII of the Charter, this does not *per se* bind other international organizations.[244] However, UN Member States are placed under an obligation by Articles 25 and 48(2) of the Charter to vote or act in these international organizations in a manner which will enable the implementation of the Council's decision.[245] It is, nonetheless, contended that the obligation under Article 25 does not apply to States when voting in the General Assembly on the question of the budget of the Organization. The obligation on States under Article 25 is that they 'carry out the decisions of the Security Council *in accordance with the present Charter*'.[246] In the case of the establishment of a UN subsidiary organ, it has already been explained that the Charter requires that the General Assembly apportion funds from the UN budget for its effective establishment. Moreover, the provisions of the Charter dealing with the right of States to vote in the General Assembly place no restriction on the exercize of a State's individual discretion, as part of its sovereign prerogative, to vote as it deems fit. Accordingly, to require States to vote in the General Assembly in a particular way would not be in accordance with the Charter. Thus States are free to vote in the General Assembly as they deem fit when deciding whether to apportion funds for a UN subsidiary organ.

---

[242] *ICJ Reports* (1962), p. 151 at pp. 165–7.
[243] *Ibidem*.
[244] See also Simma, *supra* note 1, p. 653. Cf. the case of UN Specialized Agencies, see *supra* note 105 and corresponding text.
[245] See Simma, *supra* note 1, p. 653.
[246] Emphasis added.

4

The Legal Framework Governing The Delegation Of Powers To UN Member States

Under the scheme of the Charter it was always intended that any military enforcement measures designed to maintain or restore international peace would depend on forces supplied by UN Member States.[1] Article 43 of the Charter contained provision for UN Members to contribute forces to the Council by way of formal agreement. These forces would be used for such military enforcement action as the Council deemed necessary, and they were to be under the overall authority and control of the Council. Due, however, to political considerations no agreements under Article 43 have ever been concluded,[2] the consequence of which is that the Council cannot compel States to contribute forces to carry out military enforcement action.[3] However, the question of who is to carry out military enforcement action is very different from who is to exercize command and control over such action. It was the Military Staff Committee that was to be responsible for the strategic direction and control of States' forces who were carrying out military enforcement action.[4] The intention was that national contingents would continue to remain subject to their own regulations and obey their own national commander who would take commands from a UN Force Commander who was to be under the control of the Military Staff Committee.[5] The Council would exercize its overall command authority and control through the Military Staff Committee.[6] The lack of effective

[1] See also Dinstein, Y., *War, Aggression and Self-Defence* (1994), pp. 296–7; and Kirk, G., 'The Enforcement of Security', *Yale LJ*, 55 (1946), p. 1081 at p. 1083. The reliance on the armed forces of UN Member States is a logical consequence of the decentralized nature of the international system.

[2] However, with the end of the Cold War there was renewed hope that Article 43 will be implemented: see Boutros-Ghali, B., *An Agenda for Peace* (1992), p. 25. There have also been suggestions for the creation of a UN standing force: see *An Agenda for Peace, ibidem*, paras. 42–5; and 'Creation of a Standby United Nations Military Force', *The Record of the Association of the Bar of the City of New York*, 48 (1993), p. 981.

[3] See *supra* note 78 in Chapter 2.

[4] It was not envisaged in the Charter that the Council itself would exercise military command over the force carrying out military enforcement action. (Simma, B., ed., *The Charter of the United Nations* (1994), p. 633.) In fact, Article 47(3) of the Charter expressly confers on the Military Staff Committee the strategic direction of a force carrying out such action.

[5] See the 'Report of the Military Staff Committee to the Security Council', S/336, *SCOR, Special Supplement* (1947), No. 1., Articles 36–40.

[6] The intention as expressed in Articles 46 and 47 as well as in the General Principles Governing the Organisation of the Armed Forces concluded by the Military Staff Committee seems to be that the supreme direction of the military operations shall be exclusively in the hands of the UN and that the commanders of the national contingents shall take their

functioning of the Military Staff Committee has seen the Council delegate the power of command and control to UN Member States who have volunteered their forces to carry out military enforcement action. That is, the Council has delegated to Member States the competence to carry out military enforcement action under their own command and control.[7] There is no express provision in the Charter for such a process. This does not mean, however, that the Council does not possess the competence to delegate such powers to Member States or that there is no legal framework which governs this process of delegation or authorization.[8] To the contrary, the purpose of this Chapter is to clarify the contours of the legal framework which governs this process. This requires examination of the competence of the Council to delegate Chapter VII powers to UN Member States, the limitations on this competence, and a brief discussion of who has responsibility for the acts of a force carrying out military enforcement action. The application of this legal framework to the practice of the Council and Member States in this area is undertaken in Chapter 5.

I. THE COMPETENCE OF THE COUNCIL TO DELEGATE CHAPTER VII POWERS TO UN MEMBER STATES

The UN Charter does not in express terms give the Security Council the competence to delegate its Chapter VII powers to Member States. Accordingly, any such competence must be implied from the terms of the Charter; in particular from Chapter VII. However, before ascertaining whether the Council possesses such an implied competence it is first necessary to determine whether the Charter prohibits the Council from possessing such a competence.

The Charter in Chapter VII provides the Security Council with the power to use a UN force to carry out military enforcement action. In the case where the Council delegates certain of its Chapter VII powers to another entity, either Member States or a regional organization, to carry out

operational orders from the UN, not from their national governments. (Report of the Military Staff Committee, *ibidem.*) See also Seyersted, F., *United Nations Forces* (1966), p. 32.

[7] Some States see such delegations of power—or authorizations—as a novel way to ensure that the Charter system of maintaining or restoring international peace and security remains effective. See, for example, the statement by the Federal Chancellor of Austria, Mr Vranitzky, in the Security Council Summit Meeting in 1992. (S/PV.2981, pp. 63, 64–5.) See also Miller, A., 'Universal Soldiers: UN Standing Armies and the Legal Alternatives', *Georgetown Law Journal*, 81 (1993), p. 773 at p. 776; and Weiss, T., 'Overcoming the Somalia Syndrome—Operation Rekindle Hope?', *Global Governance* 1 (1995), p. 171 at p. 177.

[8] We recall from Chapter 1 that there is a general presumption with respect to Chapter VII action that the Security Council is delegating these powers to Member States, and thus there is no difference in substance between a 'delegation' and an 'authorization' with respect to Chapter VII powers in the case of States: see *supra* notes 58–65 and corresponding text in Chapter 1.

enforcement action, the delegation of powers has, in most cases, included a power of operational command and control over the force. It is, however, this issue of command and control which has seen commentators argue that the Council cannot lawfully delegate the exercize of its Chapter VII powers to Member States. This position rests on a restrictive interpretation of Articles 42 and 43, 46, and 47(3) of the Charter. White, although in disagreement, states the case:

Although it may be argued that the agreements under Article 43 are not necessary to make the Council's military option under Article 42 a practicality, the Charter does strongly indicate that UN control of such military operations is an essential prerequisite for the legality of military action by the Security Council. This appears to be made clear by Articles 46 and 47(3) . . . Strategic control by the Military Staff Committee and overall political control by the Security Council appear necessary for the achievement of the collective security concept, in that they embody the centralisation of the collective use of force. This argument can be used to criticise the Security Council's practice in the use of the military option, when it has simply delegated authority and control to a State or group of States.[9]

However, the opposing, better, view takes account of the position that Articles 43, 46, and 47 of the Charter are not mandatory requirements for the Council to follow: they stipulate only a way in which the Council can use its Chapter VII powers. These provisions do not prescribe the only way in which the Council can use its Chapter VII powers.[10] Suffice to refer, in the context of the non-implementation of Article 43 agreements, to the previous discussion on this point in Chapter 2 above.[11] In respect of Articles 46 and 47, the aim of these provisions is not to stipulate the only way that the Council can ensure that enforcement action is taken.[12] The intention was, rather, to provide a body, the Military Staff Committee, that was to provide assistance to the Council in its work.[13] Put differently, the Council does not need to exercize operational command and control over military enforce-

---

[9] White, N., *Keeping the Peace: The United Nations and the Maintenance of International Peace and Security* (1993), p. 103. See also Freudenschuß, H., 'Between Unilateralism and Collective Security: Authorizations of the Use of Force by the UN Security Council', *European Journal of International Law*, 5 (1994), p. 492 at p. 524; Quigley, J., 'The "Privatization" of Security Council Enforcement Action: A Threat to Multilateralism', *Michigan Journal of International Law*, 17 (1996), p. 249 at pp. 250, 264; and Bothe, M., 'Les limites des pouvoirs du Conseil de sécurité', in *Peace-Keeping and Peace-Building: The Development of the Role of the Security Council* (Dupuy, R-J., ed.) (1993), p. 67 at p. 74.

[10] See also Franck, T., 'Fairness in the International Legal and Institutional System', *Hague Recueil des Cours*, 240 (1993-III), p. 9 at pp. 286–7; and Bedjaoui, M., *The New World Order and the Security Council: Testing the Legality of Its Acts* (1994), p. 423.

[11] See *supra* note 126 and corresponding text in Chapter 2.

[12] See in respect of these articles, *supra* note 133 and corresponding text in Chapter 1.

[13] See also: Pellet, A., 'The Road to Hell is Paved with Good Intentions: The United Nations as Guarantor of International Peace and Security', in *The United Nations at Age Fifty: A Legal Perspective* (Tomuschat, C., ed.) (1995), p. 113, at pp. 125–6; Scheffer, D, 'Commentary on Collective Security', in *Law and Force in the New International Order* (Fisler-Damrosch, L.,

ment action for it to be considered as part of a collective security effort under Chapter VII of the Charter.[14] In fact, we recall from above that it was never envisaged the Council itself would ever exercize direct operational command and control over a force carrying out military enforcement action.[15]

It is contended, in general, that so long as a use of force can be characterized as a collective measure then it is lawful since it is being used to carry out the collective will of the Council on behalf of the United Nations.[16] The Council was given the primary role for maintaining international peace and security under the Charter. The fact that a delegation of Chapter VII powers occurs by virtue of a decision made by the Council confers on the exercize of such powers the character of a collective security action.[17] As Dinstein has pointed out: '. . . self-defence, either individual or collective, is exercized at the discretion of a single State or a group of States. Collective security operates on the strength of an authoritative decision made by an organ of the international community.'[18] Accordingly, we note that a delegation by the Council of its Chapter VII powers to UN Member States to undertake military enforcement action represents a combination of characteristics from the two categories of collective self-defence and collective security. The Council cannot require Member States to exercize delegated Chapter VII powers: the exercize of such powers is at the discretion of Member States. Yet in the case of a delegation of Chapter VII powers by the Council there is present an 'authoritative decision made by an organ of

and Scheffer, D., eds.) (1991), p. 100 at p. 106; and Green, L., 'Iraq, the UN and the Law', *Alberta Law Review*, 29 (1991), p. 560 at p. 575.

[14] See also White, *supra* note 9, p. 103; Franck, T., and Patel, F., 'UN Police Action in Lieu of War: "The Old Order Changeth"', *AJIL*, 85 (1991), p. 66; Weller, M., 'The Kuwait Crisis: A Survey of Some Legal Issues', *African Journal of International and Comparative Law*, 3 (1991), p. 1 at pp. 25–6; Gill, T., 'Legal and Some Political Limitations on the Power of the UN Security Council to Exercise its Enforcement Powers under Chapter VII of the Charter', *Netherlands Yearbook of International Law*, 26 (1995), p. 33 at p. 60; and Kaikobad, K., 'Self-Defence, Enforcement and the Gulf Wars, 1980–88 and 1990–91', *BYIL*, 63 (1992), p. 300 at p. 360. Cf., however, Gaga, G., 'Use of Force Made or Authorized by the United Nations', in *The United Nations at Age Fifty: A Legal Perspective* (1995), p. 41; MacDougall, M., 'United Nations Operations: Who Should be in Charge?', *Revue de droit militaire et de la guerre* (1994), p. 21 at p. 42; and Djiena Wembou, M-C., 'Validité et portée de la résolution 794 (1992) du Conseil de Sécurité', *African Journal of International & Comparative Law*, 5 (1993), p. 340 at pp. 348–50.

[15] See *supra* notes 4–6 and corresponding text.

[16] See also White, *supra* note 9, p. 103.

[17] Accordingly, Mr Vranitzky of Austria at the 1992 Security Council Summit Meeting on 'The Responsibility of the Security Council in the Maintenance of International Peace' stated: 'It may also be useful to recall the Charter's ambitious goal of multilateral peace enforcement and the creation of an effective system of global collective security. The authorization given by the Security Council to a coalition of States to use all necessary means to implement the mandatory resolutions of the Council was a significant step in this direction.' (S/PV.3046, pp. 64–5.)

[18] Dinstein, *supra* note 1, p. 277.

the international community'.[19] However, this position does not preclude the necessity that for a collective security operation under the Charter any action taken must, as explained in Chapter 1, remain under the overall authority and control of the Council.[20]

In summary, the provisions of the Charter, in particular Articles 43, 46, and 47 of the Charter, do not prohibit a delegation by the Council of its Chapter VII powers to Member States. They only prescribe a way in which the Council can exercize these powers. Nonetheless, as will be seen below, there are limitations under the Charter on the competence of the Council to delegate its Chapter VII powers. It is now important, however, to establish that the Council does possess the competence to delegate Chapter VII powers to Member States.

The two main sources of this competence are, first, the subsequent practice of the Council and other UN organs,[21] and, second, an interpretation of Articles 42 and 53 of the Charter.[22]

The practice of the Council in delegating Chapter VII powers to Member States is examined in detail in Chapter 5. It is, however, relevant to discuss here the way in which other UN organs have responded to such practice. This practice of the Organization may, in addition to the practice of the relevant organ itself, be of some importance to determining the *vires* of a specific approach or interpretation of the Charter.[23]

---

[19] Weller, thus, seems to attach much weight to the legality of the delegation of powers to Member States in respect of the Gulf due to the fact that '[t]he United Nations Security Council, to which international society had delegated the highest authority in matters of peace and security, had already determined that military measures, with all their consequences, were legitimate in this case. It was only the amount of force utilised to achieve that goal which could be subject to legal dispute.' (Weller, *supra* note 14, p. 27.)

[20] See *supra* note 159 and corresponding text in Chapter 1. In the context of UN Member States, this authority and control requires that the procedural requirements for a lawful delegation of powers are satisfied. On these requirements, see *infra* Section II.

[21] See also Conforti, B., *The Law and Practice of the United Nations* (1996), p. 204. The subsequent practice of organs of an international organization has been recognized as a source of law: see *Namibia* case, *ICJ Reports* (1971), para. 22; and Rosenne, S., *Developments in the Law of Treaties* (1994), p. 237.

[22] There is also the argument that the Council has the general implied power under the Charter to authorize Member States to use force: see Gaga, *supra* note 14, p. 45; Schachter, O., 'Authorized Uses of Force by the United Nations and Regional Organizations, in *Law and Force in the New International Order* (Fisler-Damrosch, L., and Scheffer, D., eds.) (1991), p. 65; Freudenschuß, H., 'Between Unilateralism and Collective Security: Authorizations of the Use of Force by the UN Security Council', *European Journal of International Law*, 5 (1994), p. 492 at p. 526. See also the following writers who contend that Article 48 provides a basis for the competence of the Council to delegate Chapter VII powers to Member States: Greenwood, C., 'The United Nations as Guarantor of International Peace and Security: Past, Present and Future—A United Kingdom View', in *The United Nations at Age Fifty: A Legal Perspective* (1995), pp. 69–70; Weller, *supra* note 14, pp. 25–6; Kirk, G., 'The Enforcement of Security', *Yale LJ*, 55 (1946), p. 1081 at p. 1086; Scheffer, *supra* note 13, p. 104; and Kelsen, H., *The Law of the United Nations* (1950), p. 756.

[23] There is, however, a presumption that each UN organ 'must, in the first place at least, determine its own jurisdiction'. (*Expenses* case, *ICJ Reports* (1962), p. 151 at p. 168.) Moreover, it is the International Court of Justice which is the principal organ that may possess the

A variety of UN organs have certainly treated the Council as having the competence to delegate its Chapter VII powers to Member States. The Collective Measures Committee, established by the Uniting for Peace resolution of the General Assembly, envisaged that a delegation of powers by the Council to UN Member States may prove useful as a means of enhancing the role of the UN in the area of international peace and security. The Committee concluded that until such time as the Military Staff Committee could assume its responsibilities, the United Nations, when engaged in collective military measures, must provide some agency that will be responsible for the direction and conduct of its military operations and that will be empowered 'to coordinate the efforts of individual States and to organize contributions of forces, assistance and facilities in order to initiate effective military operations against the aggressor in the shortest possible time'.[24] The Collective Measures Committee went on to propose that 'the Organization should authorize a State or group of States to act on its behalf as executive military authority, within the framework of its policies and objectives as expressed through such resolutions as it may adopt at any stage of the collective action'.[25] More recently, the Secretary-General, in his report to the Council on how to deal with the situation within Haiti, stated the following as an option:

The second option would be for the Security Council, at the request of the legitimate Government, to adopt a resolution, acting under Chapter VII of the Charter, by which it would authorize a group of Member States to establish and deploy a force to carry out the tasks described in paragraph 9 above [which include possible military enforcement action]. The Member States could be either an ad hoc group formed for the purpose of creating a multinational force or the members of the OAS, who could decide to set up an inter-American force. . . . Under this option, the force would be under the command and control of the Member States contributing to it. . . .[26]

Accordingly, the Secretary-General considers that the Council possesses the competence to delegate certain of its powers to UN Member States; including powers of command and control over a force carrying out military enforcement action. In fact, the Secretary-General has stated that a delegation by the Council of its Chapter VII powers 'would conform with the Charter, with past practice and with established principles'.[27]

competence to pronounce, most authoritatively, on the *vires* of action by the other principal organs: see *supra* Section IV in Chapter 1.

[24] *UNGAOR, Supplement No. 13*, Sixth Session, 'Report of the Collective Measures Committee', p. 25.

[25] *Ibidem*. The Committee went on to express the opinion that concrete arrangements will depend on the 'political and military circumstances of the case'. (*Ibidem.*)

[26] S/1994/828, p. 6.

[27] S/1994/828, p. 6. Similarly, the US representative has suggested that the constitutional basis of the delegation is rooted in the prior practice of the Council: 'Phase one (the delegation

Moreover, the Council possessing the competence to delegate Chapter VII powers is in accord with the object and purpose of Articles 42 and 53. The object and purpose of Article 42 is that the Security Council be empowered to take action, military if necessary, to ensure the restoration or maintenance of international peace and security.[28] As Kirgis states:

... the Council's power to authorize the use of armed force under Chapter VII may be seen as an implied power that is not literally tied to Article 42, but is consistent with the purpose of that article and emanates from the functional necessity to make the Council's enforcement authority effective.[29]

That is, a delegation of Chapter VII powers may be necessary for the attainment of the Council's primary function: the maintenance or restoration of international peace and security.

The second provision of the Charter which supports the view that the Council possesses the competence to delegate its Chapter VII powers to Member States is Article 53. This provision gives the Council, as is explained in more detail in Chapter 6, an express competence to delegate Chapter VII powers to regional arrangements.[30] The Charter would be open to a serious allegation of inconsistency if the Council were able to delegate its Chapter VII powers to Member States organized as a regional arrangement, but not to Member States acting individually or jointly (that is, not organized as a regional arrangement). Put differently, there is no qualitative difference in the nature of a delegation of powers to Member States as opposed to a regional arrangement. As such, the express competence of the Council in Article 53 to be able to delegate Chapter VII powers to regional arrangements provides cogent support for the view that the Council possesses such a competence *vis-à-vis* Member States acting individually or jointly.

To summarize, there is no provision in the Charter which provides in express terms for a delegation by the Council of its Chapter VII powers to UN Member States. Neither is there such a reference in the *travaux preparatoires* of the Charter. However, as just seen, the Charter does not prohibit the Council from exercizing such a competence. The source of the Council's competence to delegate Chapter VII powers to Member States is

of Chapter VII powers to Member States in order to intervene in Haiti) builds on the precedents of Kuwait and Rwanda.' (S/PV.3413, p. 13.)

[28] Article 42 is the source of the power of the Council to ensure that such action is taken 'by air, sea, or land forces as may be necessary to maintain or restore international peace and security'.

[29] Kirgis, F., 'The Security Council's First Fifty Years', *AJIL*, 89 (1995), p. 506 at p. 521. See also Szasz, p., 'Centralized and Decentralized Law Enforcement: The Security Council and the General Assembly Acting under Chapters VII and VIII', in *Allocation of Law Enforcement in the International System: Proceedings of an International Symposium of the Kiel Institute of International Law March 23 to 25, 1994* (Delbruck, J., ed.) (1994), p. 30.

[30] See *infra* Section I in Chapter 6.

subsequent practice. Moreover, this is supported by interpretations of Articles 42 and 53 of the Charter.

The issue which remains is whether there is a certain form which such a delegation of powers must take. In other words, is a non-binding 'recommendation' sufficient for the Council to be able to delegate its Chapter VII enforcement powers to Member States or is a 'decision' of the Council required? A delegation of powers to Member States does not impose on those States an obligation to exercize the powers in question: it provides a mandate for, but does not necessitate, military enforcement action.[31] We recall from Chapter 2 that the non-implementation of Article 43 agreements means that the Council cannot require States to contribute troops to a force that is to carry out military enforcement action.[32] Thus whether the delegation takes place by a non-binding recommendation or by decision of the Council is of no legal consequence.[33]

There are, however, two issues that arise due to the non-binding nature of a delegation of Chapter VII powers.

The first is to ascertain the legal consequence of such a delegation to a Member State where the exercize of these powers may conflict with a State's other treaty obligations. As just noted, a delegation of Chapter VII powers does not impose on States an obligation to exercize these powers, and yet it is precisely this issue of obligation which is of some importance to deciding whether a Council resolution that delegates powers attracts the application of Article 103 of the Charter so that it can override a State's other treaty obligations. It is clear from the terms of Article 103 that any obligation on a Member State under the Charter prevails over a conflicting treaty obligation of that State. The question for our purposes is whether a Member State when exercizing delegated Chapter VII powers is bound by its other treaty obligations where there is a conflict between these and the effective prosecution of its delegated Chapter VII mandate. There are three

---

[31] See also the statement by the Egyptian representative in the Council debates in respect of Security Council resolution 83: S/PV.475, *SCOR*, 5 (1950), p. 13. Moreover, under international law States are under no positive obligation to take action to restore and maintain international peace and security: see Gross, L., 'States as Organs of International Law and the Problem of Autointerpretation', in *Law and Politics in the World Community* (Lipsky, G., ed.) (1953), p. 63. Cf. the moral obligation which may exist on States to take such action as the Council may recommend. Thus, the rapporteur of the drafting committee at the San Francisco Conference found that the unanimous vote adopting Article 42 of the Charter '. . . renders sacred the obligation of all states to participate in the operations'. (Doc. 881, III/3/46, 12 *UNCIO* (1945) Doc. 766.) Thus, he continued, '[m]ilitary assistance, in case of aggression, ceases to be a recommendation made to Member States; it becomes for us an obligation which none can shirk'. (*Ibidem*, Doc. 769.)

[32] See *supra* note 78 and corresponding text in Chapter 2.

[33] As Dinstein states 'The difference between authorization and recommendation . . . appears to be more verbal than real.' (Dinstein, *supra* note 1, p. 274, n. 104.) See also Kaikobad, *supra* note 14, p. 361. For application of this approach, in the context of Security Council resolution 83 in the case of Korea, see *infra* Section I(1) in Chapter 5.

approaches to this issue. The first is that since there is no obligation under the Charter on States to exercize delegated Chapter VII powers then Article 103 does not apply. This approach rests on the contention that Article 25 of the Charter, which confers a binding nature on decisions of the Security Council, stipulates that such a binding obligation will only be imposed on States when the decision is taken 'in accordance with the present Charter'. In this regard, we recall from above that the non-implementation of Article 43 means that the Council does not have the competence to impose a binding obligation on States to exercize delegated Chapter VII powers, and accordingly, it may be contended, a decision by the Council to delegate its Chapter VII powers does not fall within the scope of Article 25 of the Charter. The consequence of this approach is that even if States take up the delegation of powers then they are still bound by their treaty obligations which may even conflict with and would therefore shape the way in which the delegated powers are exercized. In this way the delegation of powers would have to be exercized within the framework of the treaty obligations which bind the States exercizing the delegated Chapter VII powers. The second view applies solely to the context of a delegation of powers. The contention is that although there is no obligation on a State to take up a delegation of Chapter VII powers, once, however, a State does take up such a delegation of powers then it is under an obligation to exercize the powers in a certain way until the objective specified by the Council has been achieved. Accordingly, for the purposes of Article 103 once a State decides to take up a delegation of Chapter VII powers then it does have an obligation under the Charter that prevails, where there is conflict, over any other treaty obligations of the State. The third, better, view is that Article 103 may also apply to non-mandatory resolutions of the Council.[34] The International Law Commission, in its Draft Articles on State Responsibility, has summarized the point in respect of sanctions in the following terms:

> sanctions applied in conformity with the provisions of the Charter would certainly not be wrongful in the legal system of the United Nations, even though they might conflict with other treaty obligations incumbent upon the State applying them . . . such measures are the 'legitimate' application of sanctions against a State which is found guilty within that system of certain specific wrongful acts. This view would, moreover, seem to be valid not only in cases where the duly adopted decision of the Organization authorizing the application of a sanction is mandatory for the Member States but also where the taking of such measures is merely recommended.[35]

[34] See also Virally, M., *L'Organisation mondiale* (1972), p. 188; and Lauwaars, R., 'The Interrelationship between United Nations Law and the Law of other International Organizations', *Michigan Law Review*, 82 (1984), p. 1604 at p. 1607.
[35] *YBILC* (1979), vol. 2 (Part II), p. 119; and *ibidem*, vol. 2 (Part I), pp. 43–4. Accordingly, Gowlland-Debbas concludes from this draft article that, in the context of resolution 221 which authorized the limited naval interdiction against Southern Rhodesia, 'the United Kingdom

Accordingly, the implementation of UN sanctioned collective measures, even if non-mandatory, should not be obstructed by treaty obligations.[36] Put differently, Article 103 applies to a non-mandatory delegation of powers. Although this approach is, to reiterate, the best one, it is, however, important to emphasize that a State exercizing delegated Chapter VII powers is still in general terms bound by its treaty obligations except to the extent that these conflict with the effective exercize of its delegated mandate.[37]

The second issue that arises from the non-binding nature of a delegation of Chapter VII powers to Member States is whether States can decide at any time to withdraw their troops from a force carrying out UN authorized military enforcement action. There are two views on this issue. Nkala, an advocate of the first view, states: '[i]t would appear that measures imposed under a recommendation of the Security Council can be terminated differently from those imposed under an "order" of the Council'.[38] According to this view, where States voluntarily take up a delegation of Chapter VII powers then they can decide at any time to terminate their participation in the operation since their participation from the beginning was always voluntary.[39]

The second, preferred, view is that the termination of enforcement action by any State depends on a decision by the Security Council. This flows from the nature of military enforcement action. The argument underlying this approach is that military enforcement action, in the context of the UN Charter, is action which is taken or authorized by the Council for the achievement of certain objectives that are necessary for the maintenance or restoration of international peace and security. Accordingly, when a State agrees to participate in an operation which involves military enforcement action the State is agreeing to assist the Council in the achievement of a particular objective. Put differently, States are under no obligation to assist in the achievement of this objective, but once they agree to do so they are under an obligation to continue until the Council decides that the objective has been attained. This is what States agree to when they agree to carry out military enforcement action. This can be seen as an implied condition of the delegation of powers. If this were not the case then States would not be

would not have been acting illegally in basing itself upon the authorization provided by SC Res. 221'. (Gowlland-Debbas, V., *Collective Responses to Illegal Acts under International Law: United Nations Action in the Case of Southern Rhodesia* (1990), p. 422.) For the legal considerations relating to this naval interdiction, see *infra* Section II(1) in Chapter 5.

[36] Cf. *infra* note 64.

[37] It is, for example, the case that States will have to abide by their international humanitarian law obligations under the relevant treaties, since it is unlikely that the Security Council will stipulate that States in exercizing their delegated mandate will have to use force in such a way that will be contrary to these obligations. See *infra* notes 64–5 and corresponding text.

[38] Nkala, J., *The United Nations, international law and the Rhodesian independence crisis* (1985), p. 194.

[39] Nkala, *ibidem*, p. 196.

under any obligations while carrying out UN authorized military enforcement action. If this were the case, States would not be restricted to achieving the Council's stated objectives and would possibly be free to achieve
their own interests while carrying out UN authorized military enforcement
action: an undesirable and untenable position. However, once States agree
to carry out UN authorized military enforcement action they are agreeing
to exercize certain of the Council's collective security powers under the
authority and control of the Council. The *raison d'être* of this authority and
control is deciding when the Council's stated objectives have been achieved
and thus when the action is to be terminated. Member States cannot arro-
gate this right to themselves.[40] This is what States in effect do when they
purport to withdraw unilaterally their troops from a force carrying out
military enforcement action before the Council has stated that its stipulated
objective has been achieved.

The Secretary-General has suggested, for purposes of clarity, formalizing
the relationship between the Council and those States that are willing to
take up a delegation of Chapter VII powers. In his report to the Council on
how to deal with the situation within Haiti, the Secretary-General stated, as
an option, the following:

The second option would be for the Security Council, at the request of the legitimate
Government, to adopt a resolution, acting under Chapter VII of the Charter, by
which it would authorize a group of Member States to establish and deploy a force
to carry out the tasks described in paragraph 9 above. The Member States could be
either an ad hoc group formed for the purpose of creating a multinational force or
members of the OAS, who could decide to set up an inter-American force. In either
case, consultations would be required between the United Nations and the Member
States concerned and the latter would need to indicate to the United Nations their
readiness to undertake this responsibility if so authorized by the Security Council to
do so.[41]

The Secretary-General has not limited the way in which the Member States
concerned would agree to undertake to take up the delegation of Chapter
VII powers. There are several ways a State can undertake an obligation
under international law to perform a particular act. The conclusion of a
treaty is only one way.[42] However, in the case under discussion it is contended that it is the most appropriate. If a State were, for example, to make
a unilateral statement indicating its intention to take up a delegation of
Chapter VII powers then the content of the obligation would not be as clear
as if the State had concluded a treaty with the Council. This treaty would be

[40] See *supra* note 130 and corresponding text *et sequentia* in Chapter 1.
[41] S/1994/828, p. 6.
[42] This would be a type of treaty envisaged by Article 6 of the 1986 Vienna Convention on
the Law of Treaties between States and International Organisations or Between International
Organisations.

in effect a kind of *ad hoc* Article 43-type agreement. If such an agreement is concluded it should include an express provision that will ensure the Member States concerned will continue to act until the Council's objective is achieved. By conclusion of this agreement, the legal obligation on States not to withdraw their troops from a UN authorized force until the achievement of the Council's stated objectives would be reinforced. This is an important safeguard which the Council may wish to use to guarantee not only the efficacy of collective action to restore or maintain international peace and security, but also its credibility.

To summarize this section, the Security Council has the competence to delegate its Chapter VII powers to UN Member States and can do so either by means of a decision or recommendation. In either case there is no obligation on States to take up this delegation of powers. This does not, however, preclude States from exercizing these powers where there is a conflict with their other treaty obligations, nor does it mean that States can withdraw their troops from a force carrying out enforcement action without Council authorization.

With an increase in the practice of the Council delegating its Chapter VII powers to Member States, it is envisaged that future challenges to the legality of such delegations will shift from the issue of the competence of the Council to do so to the non-observance by the Council of the limitations on this competence.

II. LIMITATIONS ON THE COMPETENCE OF THE COUNCIL TO DELEGATE CHAPTER VII POWERS TO MEMBER STATES

There are inherent dangers in the practice of the Council delegating Chapter VII powers to Member States.[43] The main danger is that those Member States will exercize the delegated powers to achieve their own self-interest and not that of the UN.[44] As Abi-Saab has noted, in the case of an authorization given to a group of States to undertake enforcement action, the risk

---

[43] These have been alluded to by the Secretary-General in the *Supplement to An Agenda for Peace*: 'The experience of the last few years has demonstrated both the value that can be gained and the difficulties that can arise when the Security Council entrusts enforcement tasks to groups of Member States. On the positive side, this arrangement provides the Organization with an enforcement capacity it would not otherwise have and is greatly preferable to the unilateral use of force by Member States without reference to the United Nations. On the other hand, the arrangement can have a negative impact on the Organization's stature and credibility. There is also the danger that the States concerned may claim international legitimacy and approval for forceful actions that were not in fact envisaged by the Security Council when it gave its authorization to them.' (Boutros-Ghali, B., *Supplement to An Agenda for Peace* (1995), para. 80.)

[44] A problem related to a delegation of Chapter VII powers may be that private actors will also be able to exert a disproportionate influence on the way in which this power is being

is great that it will be abused as a vehicle for the realization of the national interest of the States concerned rather than for the realization of the purposes of the Organization.[45] This is contrary to the very reason for centring in the UN the responsibility for maintaining and restoring international peace and security: to regulate the use of force by States to attain their national ends.[46]

This issue of self-interest is not, however, always antithetical to the collective security purpose for which a Chapter VII power is delegated to Member States. In many cases there may be a convergence of a State's political interests and the UN's interest in maintaining or restoring international peace and security, although the latter of course being the reason for the delegation of Chapter VII power. The development of this notion of a convergence of self-interest is of some importance to the efficacy of the UN system for maintaining international peace and security. The perception by States that their own self-interest rests in large part in terms of the interests of the international community at large will see a Security Council which is better able to maintain or restore international peace and security, since the Council will be able to delegate its Chapter VII powers to UN Member States with the security that Member States will take up the delegation of powers and that the powers will be exercized to achieve the Council's objectives. The problem, as outlined above, arises, however, when the interests of a State are in conflict with those of the UN, as defined by the Security Council. However, the existence of limitations on the competence of the Council to delegate Chapter VII powers to Member States provides a safeguard against such a potentially negative consequence of a delegation of Chapter VII powers. There are two types of limitations on the competence of the Council to delegate Chapter VII powers to UN Member States.

The first involves a limitation on the competence of the Council to be able to delegate certain of its Chapter VII powers to Member States. These

exercized. Private actors in this case could be, for example, domestic political parties, which exercize control over a domestic legislative arm of government, or large multinational companies. This has been an issue that has plagued the delegation of governmental power in the United States: see Schoenbrod, D., *Power Without Responsibility* (1993).

[45] Abi-Saab, G., *United Nations Forces in the Congo* (1978), p. 20. See also Bowett, D., *United Nations Forces* (1964), p. 338; Duke, S., 'The State and Human Rights: Humanitarian Intervention Versus Sovereignty', in *Peacemaking, Peacekeeping and Coalition Warfare: The Future Role of the United Nations* (Mokhtari, F., ed.) (1994), p. 149 at p. 168; and Ferencz, B., *Global Survival: Security through the United Nations* (1994), pp. 138–9. See for a discussion of this possibility: Second Report on UNEF, A/3302, 5 Nov. 1956, paras. 4–5.

[46] Goodrich, L., and Simons, A., *The United Nations and the Maintenance of International Peace and Security* (1955), pp. 433–4. For an excellent description and analysis of international law regulating the use of force by States, see Brownlie, I., *International Law and the Use of Force by States* (1963).

substantive limitations have already been explained in Chapter 1 and prohibit the delegation by the Council of certain of its Chapter VII powers.[47]

The second—what are termed conditions for a lawful delegation—only
regulate the way in which the Council should delegate its powers and do not
as such prohibit the delegation of a particular power. These conditions flow
from the requirement, as explained in Chapter 1, that the exercize of
delegated Chapter VII powers must always remain under the overall
authority and control of the Council. The obligation to ensure that these
conditions are imposed on the delegate rests with the Security Council, as
delegator. The failure by the Council to do so in a particular case means that
the delegation of Chapter VII powers is *ultra vires*.

There are three conditions for a lawful delegation by the Council of its
Chapter VII powers to Member States. First, there must be a certain minimum degree of clarity in the resolution which delegates the power. Put
differently, the objective for which the power is being delegated must be
clearly specified. Second, there is an obligation on the Council to exercize
some form of supervision over the way in which the delegated powers are
being exercized. Third, the Security Council must impose on Member
States a requirement to report to the Council on the way in which the
delegated power is being exercized. All three of these conditions have been
recognized by the Council itself,[48] as well as UN Member States,[49] as important conditions for a lawful delegation by the Council of its Chapter VII
powers to Member States.[50] The source of each of these requirements is

---

[47] See *supra* Section III(2)(b)(i) in Chapter 1.

[48] Thus, in response to recommendations proposed by the Secretary-General, the Security
Council provided for the following machinery in resolution 794: '[The Security Council]
<u>Requests</u> the Secretary-General and the Member States acting under paragraph 10 [the
provision delegating to Member States the power to use "all necessary means"] above, to
establish appropriate mechanisms for coordination between the United Nations and their
military forces; . . . <u>Decides</u> to appoint an ad hoc commission composed of members of the
Security Council to report to the Council on the implementation of this resolution;
. . . <u>Requests</u> the Secretary-General and, as appropriate, the States concerned to report to the
Council on a regular basis, the first such report to be made no later than 15 days after the
adoption of this resolution, on the implementation of this resolution and the attainment of
the objective of establishing a secure environment so as to enable the Council to make the
necessary decision for a prompt transition to continued peace-keeping operations.' See also
the practice of the Security Council in Chapter 5.

[49] There was considerable emphasis placed on this machinery by States when deciding to
adopt the draft version of resolution 794. All or some of these conditions appear in
the statements in the Security Council by the representatives of Zimbabwe (S/PV.3145, pp. 7,
8–10); Ecuador (S/PV.3145, pp. 13–14); Belgium (S/PV.3145, pp. 24–5); France (S/PV.3145,
pp. 29–30.); Austria (S/PV.3145, p. 32.); and Japan (S/PV.3145, p. 43.) Similarly, in the context
of the Council authorizing 'Operation Turquoise' in Rwanda, see the statements in the
Security Council by the representatives of the USA (S/PV.3392, p. 6); and Russia (S/PV.3392,
p. 2).

[50] Accordingly, Erskine Childers has called for '. . . a General Assembly resolution stating
that armed force cannot be employed using the name or authority of the United Nations unless

examined further within the context of a discussion of the constituent elements of each requirement.

The first condition imposes an obligation on the Council to ensure that it specifies in some detail the objectives for which Chapter VII powers are being delegated. The setting by the Council of detailed objectives of the military operation and the capacity to change these objectives at any time enables the Council to exercize in an effective fashion its overall authority and control over an operation.[51] This position has been reflected in numerous statements by Members of the Security Council[52] and the Secretary-General.[53] White has, accordingly, stated in the context of a delegation of Chapter VII powers by the Council:

What is required is a clear indication by the Security Council of the extent and nature of the armed force that it is requesting States to undertake. Problems of lack of continuous control can be overcome by a clear and unambiguous mandate at the outset. If States using force under this authority then wish to use more or less force, they must seek a change in the mandate from the Security Council. This seems to be an acceptable compromise between complete delegation to States and unnecessary formalities and bureaucratic control by Committee. It appears unnecessary to place military operations under the complete control of the United Nations to achieve the centralization of force necessary to fulfil the concept of collective security, if at the outset the Security Council effectively centralises the objectives of the military operation, thereby preventing the use of military action for purposes other than those of the Security Council. If the Security Council is dominated by a State or group of States and they manage to persuade it to undertake military action that fulfils the objective of that State or group of States, as well as those of the UN, then as long as the Council has defined those purposes clearly, according to this interpretation of Charter law, the Security Council, not the State or group of States, is the initiator of the use of force.[54]

---

the UN is responsible for the decision itself, for the planning, the direction and the termination of such force. This would merely re-state the actual law of the Charter . . .' (Childers, E., 'Gulf Crisis Lessons for the United Nations', *Bulletin of Peace Proposals*, 23(2) (1992), pp. 129–38.)

[51] As Davis has stated: 'The development of proper goals and objectives, and the translation of the political mandate to the military mission, are the kernels of the problem of command and control.' (Davis, D., 'The Policy Implications of Command and Control' in Mokhtari, *supra* note 45, p. 95 at p. 99.)

[52] See, for example, the statements in the Security Council by the representatives of New Zealand (S/PV.3413, p. 22); and the Czech republic (S/PV.3413, p. 24).

[53] See, for example, the Report of the Secretary-General to the Security Council, S/24868, p. 6.

[54] White, *supra* note 9, pp. 103–4. See also Borg Olivier, A., 'The United Nations in a Changing World Order: Expectations and Realities', in Mokhtari, *supra* note 45, p. 25; the statement by the Spanish representative in the Security Council (S/PV.3392, p. 8); Sewall, S., 'Peace Enforcement and the United Nations', in *Peace Support Operations and the US Military* (Quinn, D., ed.) (1994), p. 101 at pp. 106–7; and Annan, K., 'Peace-keeping in Situations of Civil War', *New York University Journal of International Law and Politics*, 26 (1994), p. 623 at p. 627. Moreover, there has been increasing

The Council's obligation to state specific objectives for which it is delegating its Chapter VII powers to UN Member States has an analogy in domestic US law which regulates a delegation of governmental power. The US Supreme Court has tried in the case of, *inter alia, J. W. Hampton & Co.* v. *United States* to reconcile the practice of delegation by the US Congress to governmental agencies with the notion of accountability in the *delegatus potest non delegare* doctrine by requiring that statutes which delegate powers of discretion to the President state an 'intelligible principle' to guide action in the exercize of the power and to allow judicial review for acts *ultra vires*.[55]

This requirement of the Council to specify in some detail the political objectives of the operation cannot be circumvented by the provision of a vague and ambiguous objective. This consideration attains even more importance when attention is paid to the fact that the delegation by the Council of its Chapter VII powers to Member States is a 'conditional delegation'.[56] We recall from Chapter 1 the legal position that the Council cannot delegate to another entity the competence to decide when a threat to, or breach of, international peace and security has come into existence or has ceased to exist.[57] It thus follows that it is not for the delegate to decide when the objective which the Council has stated has been fulfilled and therefore when the delegation of powers ceases to exist. This power of decision is within the sole domain of the Council and cannot be

---

pressure within the US for the objectives of a delegated UN mandate to be clearly specified: see the statement by Senator John McCain (McCain, J., 'The Proper United States Role in Peacemaking', in *Peace Support Operations and the US Military* (Quinn, D., ed.) (1994), p. 85); and the speech by President George Bush made at the West Point Military Academy ('Bush's Talk to Cadets: When "Force Makes Sense"', *New York Times* 6 Jan. 1993, A6).

[55] *J. W. Hampton* v. *United States*, 276 US 394. See also *Panama Refining Co.* v. *Ryan*, 293 US 388; and *Yakus* v. *United States*, 321 US 414 at 423–7 where the US Supreme Court did not insist upon absolute non-delegation but did require Congress to make primary policy choices and devise statutory standards to guide subordinate policy making by the delegate. See also Schoenbrod, D., *Power Without Responsibility: How Congress Abuses the People through Delegation* (1993), pp. 39, 45, and Schoenbrod, D., 'The Delegation Doctrine: Could the Court Give it Substance?', *Michigan Law Review*, 83 (1985), p. 1223 at pp. 1224–8, 1246–8. This approach has, however, been severely criticized as having undermined the non-delegation doctrine by allowing later Supreme Court decisions to uphold delegations 'with standards so ambiguous as to be almost meaningless'. (Taylor, C., 'The Fourth Branch: Reviving the Nondelegation Doctrine', *Brigham Young University Law Review* (1984), p. 619 at p. 625.)

Similarly, the Italian Constitution also allows a delegation of certain powers by Parliament to the Government only on the condition that the delegation is 'for a limited time, according to specified criteria and *with a defined purpose*'. (La Pergola, A., and Del Duca, P., 'Community Law, International Law and the Italian Constitution', *AJIL*, 79 (1985), p. 598 at p. 604, emphasis added.)

[56] This notion of a conditional or contingent delegation of powers is explained in more detail in Chapter 1, *supra* note 66 and corresponding text in Chapter 1.

[57] See *supra* Section III(2)(b)(i) in Chapter 1.

delegated.[58] That is, the delegation of powers continues to exist until such time as the objective which the Council has specified in the resolution which delegates powers has been fulfilled. Upon the fulfilment of this objective the delegation of powers will automatically cease.[59] Thus the Council by specifying the objective for which the power is being delegated is in fact stipulating when the delegation of power terminates. That is, when the Security Council makes a delegation of Chapter VII powers for a specific objective, once the objective has been achieved the delegation of power ceases to exist. This automatic termination of a delegation of powers is a necessary control on the exercize of delegated Chapter VII powers since it provides a convenient way of terminating a delegation without the requirement of another decision by the Council, which is of course subject to the veto. This guards against the use of a veto in the Council by a Permanent Member to prevent the termination of a delegation of powers[60] and as such is a further guarantee against a Permanent Member exercizing delegated powers to achieve its own interests. This does not of course prevent the Council from making an express decision that its objective has been fulfilled or otherwise to decide to terminate the delegation of powers. Moreover, if the Security Council wishes to specify further an additional objective and to delegate its powers to enable this to be achieved then a positive delegation of powers is required. This position is an effective safeguard against the abuse of a delegation of Chapter VII powers.

The acceptance by States of a delegation of Chapter VII powers—by agreeing to carry out the operation—assumes that States agree to exercize the powers only for the achievement of the Council's stipulated objective. In this way, the Council's stated objective operates as a limitation on the way in which the Member States exercize their delegated powers. It is inevitable that the States which are exercizing delegated Chapter VII powers will have to make their own interpretations of the Council's stated objectives. The States are, however, to be guided in this by the intention of the Council as expressed by statements of its President or by States in the debates surrounding the adoption of the resolution which is the source of the delegated powers. Moreover, we recall from Chapter 2 that the opinion of the UN Secretary-General may be authoritative in the process of interpretation of the Council's stated objective.[61] All of this does not of course

---

[58] This position was affirmed by the Chinese representative in the Council debates in respect of Operation Restore Hope in Somalia. (S/PV.3145, p. 17.) With respect to this operation, see *infra* Section III(1) in Chapter 5.

[59] Cf. the termination of UN subsidiary organs which does not automatically occur even though the mandate for which the organ was established may have been fulfilled: see *supra* note 200 and corresponding text in Chapter 3.

[60] This is an example of what Caron has termed a 'negative veto' in the Security Council: see Caron, D., 'The Legitimacy of the Collective Authority of the Security Council', *AJIL*, 87 (1993), p. 552.

[61] See *supra* note 37 and corresponding text in Chapter 2.

preclude the Council from later making an authoritative interpretation of its earlier stated objective.

The question which remains is whether the Council must specify in some detail the level of force to be used by States in order to achieve the Council's stated objectives. White is of the opinion that such a specification by the Council is necessary for the authorization to be considered as being 'adequately centralized'.[62] Requiring the Council to specify the level of the use of force to be undertaken is not, however, particularly helpful. The Council is delegating in many cases the power of command and control over the military force to the States which are supplying the forces. It must surely be left to these States to decide what degree of force should be used to attain the Council's stated objective.[63] This does not of course mean that States when carrying out military enforcement action can evade their responsibilities under customary and treaty law and not respect their international humanitarian law obligations;[64] an important one in this case being the use of a proportionate force to achieve the Council's objectives.[65]

The second condition—which is closely related to the obligation of the Council to specify the objectives of a military enforcement action—is that the Council must conduct a continuous review of the enforcement action. The obligation to undertake supervision rests primarily on the Security Council, but there is a concomitant obligation on Member States to submit themselves to such supervision. This obligation is of fundamental importance to the Council being able to ensure that it can exercize its overall authority and control over the exercize of its delegated powers, and is, moreover, necessary for the Council to be able to make, if it so wishes, the decision when its stated objective has been achieved and thus when the delegation of powers ceases to exist.[66] UN supervision is also necessary to ensure a degree of transparency in the way that the delegated Chapter VII powers are being exercized.[67] This is important for the legitimacy of any

---

[62] White, *supra* note 9, p. 105.

[63] See also Chayes, A., in '1991 Friedmann Conference on Collective Security', *Columbia Journal of Transnational Law*, 29 (1991), at pp. 510–11; and Seyersted, *supra* note 6, p. 318.

[64] See Schachter, O., *International Law in Theory and Practice* (1994), p. 401; Seyersted, *supra* note 6, p. 203; and Gardam, J., 'Legal Restraints on Security Council Military Enforcement Action', *Michigan Journal of International Law*, 17 (1996), p. 285 *et sequentia*, and 'Proportionality and Force in International Law', *AJIL*, 87 (1993), p. 391.

[65] Gardam, *ibidem;* and Bowett, *supra* note 45, pp. 54–5. For application of this requirement in practice, see, for example, *infra* notes 63 & 64 and corresponding text in Chapter 5.

[66] See also Borg Olivier, *supra* note 54, p. 25; Weiss, T., 'Overcoming the Somalia Syndrome—"Operation Rekindle Hope?"', *Global Governance*, 1 (1995), p. 171 at p. 177; and Sewall, S., 'Peace Enforcement and the United Nations', in *Peace Support Operations and the US Military* (Quinn, D., ed.) (1994), p. 101 at p. 104.

[67] See also the statement by the Russian representative in the Security Council: S/PV.3413, p. 24.

such operation.[68] Accordingly, the aim of supervision by the Council is twofold: to determine when the Council's stated objective has been attained; and to ensure the delegated powers are being exercized in an appropriate manner, that is for the attainment of the Council's stated objective. If the Council wishes to delegate this supervisory function to another entity there are certain limitations it must observe. The Council could not, as we recall from Chapter 1, purport to delegate its responsibility to exercise overall authority and control over a force carrying out military enforcement action to another entity.[69] The Council could, however, delegate a limited form of supervision to another entity. Such supervision may consist of, for example, the review of reports submitted by States in the exercize of their delegated powers. This supervisory function could be carried out by the Secretary-General or a subsidiary organ which could be delegated this function.[70] Accordingly, in his report to the Council on what action could be taken to deal with the situation in Haiti, the Secretary-General noted that if the Council were to decide to delegate certain of its Chapter VII powers to UN Member States then 'the Security Council might wish to authorize the establishment of a small group of United Nations military and police observers who would coexist with the multinational or inter-American force (as the case might be) and whose tasks would be to verify the manner in which that force carried out the mandate conferred upon it by the Council . . .'.[71]

In addition to this supervisory function, and now we come to the third condition, the Council should impose on UN Member States which are exercizing delegated Chapter VII powers the requirement to report on a regular basis back to the Council on the progress of the operation.[72] There are two reasons why the Council should impose such an obligation on Member States exercizing delegated Chapter VII powers.

First, it is necessary for the Council to be able to exercize its supervisory function which in turn is a necessary prerequisite for the Council to be able to fulfil its obligation under the Charter to exercize overall authority

---

[68]   See *supra* notes 21–3 and corresponding text in Chapter 1.

[69]   See *supra* notes 89 & 159 and corresponding text in Chapter 1.

[70]   It is important to note that this task would not include the exercize of powers of operational command and control over the force; this would be carried out by the States who are exercizing the delegated Chapter VII powers.

[71]   S/1994/828, p. 7. As a direct result of this recommendation, operative paragraph 5 of resolution 940 states the following: '[The Security Council] *Approves* the establishment, upon adoption of this resolution, of an advance team of UNMIH of not more than sixty personnel, including a group of observers, to establish the appropriate means of coordination with the multinational force, to carry out the monitoring of the operations of the multinational force and other functions described in paragraph 23 of the report of the Secretary-General of 15 July 1994 (S/1994/828) . . .' (S/RES/940 (1994).)

[72]   In some cases this obligation has been specifically entrusted to, or been taken up by, the Secretary-General in lieu of States reporting back to the Council: see, for example, *infra* notes 175 & 228 and corresponding text in Chapter 5.

and control over an authorized enforcement action. In fact in the Korean case the existence of an obligation on States carrying out delegated Chapter VII powers to report to the Council was accepted as an alternative to the Council involving itself more directly in the strategic direction of the forces. As Goodrich and Simons have observed in respect of the Korean case:

Although Secretary-General Lie had suggested that a committee on co-ordination be set up, the prevailing opinion in the Council appears to have been that additional machinery was unnecessary at this time because the United States would be submitting reports periodically, and the Council would be able to take any further action it considered necessary on the basis of these reports.[73]

In other words, the existence of a reporting requirement is an acceptable mechanism by which the Council can fulfil, in part, its obligation to exercise overall authority and control over a force carrying out authorized military enforcement action.[74]

The second reason for the existence of such a reporting obligation follows from Articles 51 and 54 of the Charter. Article 54 requires a regional organization to report to the Council when it has, *inter alia*, used force in order to maintain international peace and security.[75] The purpose of this provision is to ensure that the Council has the information that it requires to be able to exercise overall authority and control over enforcement action by the regional arrangement or agency.[76] The purpose of Article 54 is applicable to the exercize of delegated Chapter VII powers since the action taken is for the same objective: the restoration or maintenance of international peace and security. Moreover, having regard to considerations of consistency it seems clear that the content of obligations of a Member State under the Charter should in substance be the same *vis-á-vis* the Council regardless whether it is acting individually or through a regional organization when exercizing a delegated Chapter VII power.[77] If States carrying out

---

[73] Goodrich, L., and Simons, A., *The United Nations and the Maintenance of International Peace and Security* (1955), p. 468.

[74] See, for example, the Report of the Secretary-General, S/24868, p. 5. See also statements in the Security Council by, for example, the representatives of Malaysia (S/PV.2963, p. 76), and Spain (S/PV.3413, p. 20).

[75] Article 54 of the Charter states: 'The Security Council shall at all times be kept fully informed of activities undertaken or in contemplation under regional arrangements or by regional agencies for the maintenance of international peace and security.'

[76] Simma, *supra* note 4, p. 755.

[77] In the case where there may be such a conflict, it has been suggested in Simma's *Charter of the United Nations* that the obligation which guarantees the more effective control by the Council should be the one which must prevail. In resolving the situation in the case where a State is a member of a regional organization and there may be a conflict between the obligations of a State which is preparing to use force in self-defence not having to report to the Council and the obligations of the regional organization to report such measures, it has been argued 'the more far-reaching obligation to inform contained in Art. 54 must normally prevail

military enforcement action through a regional organization are required to report to the Council on a regular basis on the progress of such action, it seems clear that Member States acting individually—that is, not through a regional organization—are under the same obligation. This reporting requirement may, however, raise considerable problems in practice. The obligation to report under Article 54 includes the requirement of regional organizations to give full notification to the Council of, *inter alia*, planned military enforcement action.[78] Suffice to note that this may raise serious problems in practice since an important element of the effective use of force is secrecy of military plans.[79]

Moreover, the existence of a reporting obligation also flows from the object and purpose of the reporting requirement in Article 51 of the Charter. Article 51 imposes a legal obligation[80] on States to report back to the Council on any measures they may have taken in the exercize of their right to individual or collective self-defence. With regard to the object and purpose of this provision, Greig has stated: '. . . it would seem that the purpose of the reporting requirement [in Article 51] is to ensure that the primary responsibility of the Council for the maintenance of international peace and security is preserved'.[81] In other words, the Charter imposes an obligation on States who are lawfully using force not under the direct operational control of the Council to report on a regular basis back to the Council.[82] The rationale is that if the Council is informed of military enforcement action then it can exercize authority and control over the action in accordance with its primary responsibility as the guardian of international peace and security. Applying this object and purpose to UN authorized military enforcement action, we find that the law of the UN Charter not only mandates the Council to be able to impose on States exercizing delegated Chapter VII

as the pertinent and fundamental provision for regional agencies, *because only on the basis of the latter is effective control by the SC fully guaranteed*'. (Simma, *supra* note 4, p. 755, emphasis added).

[78] As Hummer and Schweitzer state in Simma's *Charter of the United Nations* in respect of Article 54: 'As follows from the wording of Art. 54, the SC must be kept fully informed at all times of activities undertaken or in contemplation. That undoubtedly means that the SC has to be notified and kept informed at all times of the progress of any measure planned or taken.' (Simma, *supra* note 4, p. 753.)

[79] Simma, *supra* note 4, p. 754.

[80] The obligation of States under Article 51 is a legal obligation: see Bowett, D., *Self-Defence in International Law* (1958), p. 197.

[81] Greig, D., 'Self-Defence and the Security Council: What Does Article 51 Require?', *ICLQ*, 40 (1991), p. 366 at p. 391.

[82] Thus, Lavalle makes the point that even if the Council authorizes States to continue to exercize their right to individual or collective self-defence then, as provided in Article 51, States would be required to report back to the Council on the measures taken. (Lavalle, R., 'The Law of the United Nations and the Use of Force, Under the Relevant Security Council Resolutions of 1990 and 1991, to Resolve the Persian Gulf Crisis', *Netherlands Yearbook of International Law*, 23 (1992), p. 3 at p. 44.)

powers an obligation to report to the Council on the exercize of these powers, but requires it. It is contended that from the above analysis the Council does possess the competence to *require* States to report to it on the exercize of delegated Chapter VII powers. The legal position that the Council cannot require States to contribute forces in order to carry out military enforcement action is distinct from the competence of the Council to be able to impose conditions on the exercize by States of delegated Chapter VII powers.

III. RESPONSIBILITY FOR THE ACTS OF A FORCE CARRYING OUT UN AUTHORIZED MILITARY ENFORCEMENT ACTION

The distinction between a UN force and a UN authorized force is made by examining who exercizes operational command and control over the force. If it is the Council or a UN organ which exercizes these powers then it is a UN force. If, however, it is a Member State or a regional organization then it is a UN authorized force. Some commentators have contended that this distinction is of considerable practical importance in determining which entity is responsible for the acts of a force carrying out enforcement action. Peck, for example, contends that '[t]he question of who makes the political, strategic, and operational decisions that together comprise the right to command and control United Nations forces is central to determining who is responsible for actions taken by UN soldiers, whether they be peace-keepers or peace-enforcers. . . . Who has control over United Nations forces is paramount to a discussion of whether the United Nations can be held responsible for the actions of its soldiers.'[83] However, it is contended that the question of who exercizes *operational* command and control over the force is immaterial to the question of responsibility. The more impor-tant enquiry is who exercizes *overall* authority and control over the forces. In the case of forces from Member States exercizing delegated Chapter VII powers, it is the Security Council that exercizes overall authority and con-trol over the forces. Accordingly, it is the Council which must accept pri-mary responsibility for the acts of the force.[84] This is in accord with the nature of the legal framework governing a delegation by the Council of its

---

[83] Peck, J., 'The UN and the Laws of War: How Can the World's Peacekeepers be held accountable?', *Syracuse Journal of International Law and Commerce*, 21 (1995), p. 283 at pp. 292–3. Cf. also Seyersted, *supra* note 6, p. 411.

[84] There is a secondary responsibility which UN Member States have when exercizing delegated Chapter VII powers. For the distinction between a primary and secondary respon-sibility under international law, see: Higgins, R., 'Final Report of the Legal Consequences for Member States of the Non-Fulfilment by International Organizations of their Obligations Towards Third Parties', Report of the Institut de droit International, *AIDI*, 66-I (1995), p. 251.

Chapter VII powers to Member States, as outlined above. The Security Council is placed squarely in the centre of the operation, and is under an obligation to ensure that its delegated powers are being exercized in an appropriate manner and in order to achieve its objectives. Moreover, we recall from Chapter 1, that the Council is under an obligation to ensure that it can exercize effective authority and control over the way in which its delegated powers are being exercized.[85] Thus in the case of Korea, in response to complaints by the former USSR to the US Government over specific actions of the Force, the US Government asserted that the question of a particular attack was purely a United Nations matter since it insisted that the attacking planes were under the overall authority and control of the UN, not the US, and, accordingly, the US could not be held directly respon-

---

[85] See supra note 159 and corresponding text in Chapter 1. There is a direct analogy here with the case of State responsibility. As Brownlie states on the question of State responsibility in the context of a delegation of power by a State to agencies or personnel external to the organs of the State: '[i]n the final analysis the question is one of a *duty to control and to prevent* violations of particular principles or legal standards. A State cannot by delegation (even if this be genuine) avoid responsibility for breaches of its duties under international law. . . . This approach of public international law is not *ad hoc* but stems directly from the normal concepts of accountability and effectiveness.' (Brownlie, I., 'State Responsibility: The Problem of Delegation', in *Völkerrecht zwischen normativem anspruch und politischer Realität* (Ginther, K., Hafner, G., Lang, W., Neuhold, H., & Sucharipa-Behrmann, L., eds.) (1994), p. 299 at pp. 300–1.) This approach is supported by the International Law Commission's Draft Articles on State Responsibility: in particular Article 7(2) of which states: '**Attribution to the State of the conduct of other entities empowered to exercize elements of the government authority** . . . 2. The conduct of an organ of an entity which is not part of the formal structure of the State or of a territorial governmental entity, but which is empowered by the internal law of that State to exercize elements of the governmental authority, shall also be considered as an act of the State under international law, provided that organ was acting in that capacity in the case in question.' (Report of the ILC on the work of its forty-eighth session, 6 May–25 July 1996, *GAOR, 51st Session, Supp. No. 10 (A/51/10)*.) The ILC Commentary to this draft article explains further: 'The rule laid down in article 7, paragraph 2, stems from, and is designed to cover, the need to take into account a typical phenomenon of our times: the proliferation of entities which, within a given community, are empowered to exercize some governmental authority. . . . [In the Commission's view] it is important that the State should not be able to evade its international responsibility in certain circumstances solely because it has entrusted the exercize of some elements of the governmental authority to entities separate from the State machinery proper. The Commission, for its part, feels able to conclude that there is already an established rule on the subject; but it is also convinced that, even if that were not the case, the requirements of clarity in international relations and the very logic of the principles governing them would make it necessary to affirm such a rule in the course of the progressive development of international law.' (Report of the International Law Commission on the work of its twenty-sixth session 6 May–26 July 1974, Doc. A/9610/Rev.1, *Yearbook of the ILC*, 1974, vol. 2 (Part I), p. 276 at pp. 281–2.)

There is further support for this type of approach in the decision of the US Supreme Court in *First National City Bank* v. *Banco Para El Comercio Exterior De Cuba* where the Court found that governments cannot 'avoid the requirements of international law simply by creating juridical entities [and thereby delegating certain powers to them] whenever the need arises'. (*First National City Bank* v. *Banco Para El Comercio Exterior De Cuba*, 462 US 611 at 633.)

sible.[86] The acts of forces authorized by the Council are attributable to the UN, since the forces are acting under UN authority to establish an objective stated by the Council. The importance of this position is that it iterates the fact that the forces are carrying out military enforcement action of an international nature under the overall control of the Council. There are, however, two exceptions to this general rule.

The first is those cases where the Council was prevented from exercizing overall authority and control over the force. This would occur where the procedural limitations imposed by the Council on Member States were not observed by States' forces. For example, where States did not report back to the Council or where the Council was thwarted from exercizing supervision over the operation. The Council can only be held responsible for the acts of forces authorized by it when it has the ability to exercize overall authority and control over the acts of those forces. However, there is a positive obligation on the Council to ensure that these requirements exist in formal terms in each case of a delegation of Chapter VII powers to UN Member States.

The second exception applies in the case where the States concerned exercize powers greater than what has actually been delegated to them by the Council: that is, States' forces have acted *ultra vires* when exercizing their delegated Chapter VII powers. Where the forces were not acting in reasonable pursuit of the Council's objective then it is not the UN who is liable but the Member State which contributed the forces. The situation here is analogous to that of the law of agency where the principal is not liable for the acts of its agent which are committed outside the scope of the agent's delegated mandate and authority.[87] This issue of whether forces have acted *ultra vires* their delegated mandate in particular cases is part of our enquiry in Chapter 5.

---

[86] Accordingly, the US rejected claims submitted against it by the USSR and the People's Republic of China on the ground that these should be submitted to the United Nations, whose agent the United States was. (*Annual Report of the Secretary-General* (1950–1), pp. 30, 75–9, and *Annual Report of the Secretary-General* (1952–3), pp. 21–2.) Bowett, moreover, states: 'The insistence [by the United States] that the charges [of illegal conduct] were a matter for the United Nations to consider, and the insistence on the necessity for an impartial fact-finding Commission [to be established], was undoubtedly right. Whether it was equally right for the United States to offer compensation is less sure, for there is much to be said for the view that compensation ought normally to be a matter for the United Nations—as part of the operational budget of actions by United Nations Forces—and not for individual contributing States.' (Bowett, *supra* note 45, p. 57.) See also Taubenfeld, H., 'International armed forces and the rules of war', *AJIL* (1951), p. 671 at pp. 675–6. Cf. Seyersted, *supra* note 6, pp. 111–12, 121–2.

[87] As Sereni states: 'As to the legal effects of international agency . . . the agent's acts bind the principal only in so far as they are within the authority conferred. Beyond these limits the agent's acts do not bind the principal, unless subsequently ratified by the latter.' (Sereni, A., 'Agency in International Law', *AJIL*, 34 (1940), p. 638 at p. 655.) In the domestic law context, see, for example, *Bowstead on Agency* (Reynolds, F., ed.) (1985), p. 1.

In conclusion, the determination of whether the UN is responsible in a particular case for the unlawful acts of forces exercizing delegated Chapter VII powers will thus require examination of the imposition and compliance of the conditions that attach to a delegation of these powers; and the enquiry as to whether such forces have exceeded the scope of their delegated mandate.

5

The Delegation of Powers to
UN Member States

There has been a consistent practice of the Council delegating its Chapter VII powers to UN Member States.[1] Interestingly, although the first few instances of Korea and Southern Rhodesia were seen at the time as being exceptional *sui generis* cases, they only now, however, appear as part of a continuum in this practice. The Council has delegated its Chapter VII powers to Member States for the attainment of the following five objectives: to counter a use of force by a State or entities within a State; to carry out a naval interdiction; to achieve humanitarian objectives; to enforce a Council declared no-fly zone; and to ensure implementation by parties of an agreement which the Council has deemed is necessary for the maintenance or restoration of peace. These five objectives provide convenient headings for examination of the practice in this area. In many of these cases, the focus of any discussion in the literature has been centred on the constitutional basis of the particular power which the Council has delegated to Member States. This issue is relevant to our enquiry in two ways. First, to decide in a particular case whether there has been a delegation of Chapter VII powers by the Council. Second, the constitutional basis of the particular power will affect the content of the limitations which the Council must impose on the exercize of the delegated power. However, in most cases the particular constitutional basis of the delegated power is only a preliminary issue. The more important enquiry, once it is determined that there has been a delegation of Chapter VII powers, is whether the Council has complied with the

---

[1] Accordingly, Sir Anthony Parsons states: 'When the United States secured a resolution, in the absence from the Security Council of the Soviet Union, to react militarily to the North Korean invasion of South Korea in 1950, command and control was delegated to Washington.... When the United Nations faced its first major post-Cold War test, the Gulf crises of 1990, ... the resolution which authorized the use of force, "all necessary means", was on the lines of the Korean resolution in that it delegated full responsibility to a coalition of states led in practice by the United States. At that point, the Security Council moved out of the act and did not reconvene until Operation Desert Storm was complete and conditions governing the cease-fire had to be formulated. Roughly the same procedure, with rather more oversight by the Security Council, via the Secretary-General, has been followed in other recent cases. The Council authorized an American-led coalition to use force to break the warlord-induced famine in Somalia in 1992–93, and delegated authority in effect to NATO to use air strikes to defend "safe areas" in Bosnia in 1993. France sought and was ... authorized to use force for humanitarian purposes in Rwanda in 1994. "All necessary means" were approved for the ejection of the ruling junta in Haiti in the late summer of 1994 ...' (Parsons, A., 'The Security Council An Uncertain Future', *The David Davies Memorial Institute of International Studies, Occasional Paper No. 8* (1994), pp. 8–10.)

requirements that flow from the legal framework governing a delegation of Chapter VII powers as set out above in Chapter 4.

I. A DELEGATION OF POWERS TO COUNTER A USE OF FORCE BY A STATE OR ENTITIES WITHIN A STATE

There have been four instances where the Security Council has delegated its Chapter VII powers to Member States to counter a use of force by a State or entities within a State. These are the cases of Korea, Iraq, Somalia, and Bosnia. With the exception of the case of Iraq, the enforcement action was directed against non-State entities. Accordingly, a preliminary issue is the competence of the Security Council itself to be able to ensure that enforcement action is taken against such entities. This is a necessary line of enquiry since we recall from Chapter 1 that the Council cannot delegate a power which it does not itself possess.[2]

The wording of Article 39 makes the application of the enforcement measures in Chapter VII dependent upon the existence of 'any threat to the peace, breach of the peace or act of aggression'. The peace referred to in this passage need not, however, only be between States.[3] The Security Council may take enforcement measures in relation to a conflict occurring either within a State, between two groups of the population, or between a State and a group of the population of this State. That is, the Security Council can order enforcement action to be directed against a non-State entity.[4] Accordingly, the Council can, subject to the limitations explained in Chapter 4, delegate its military enforcement powers to Member States to take action against non-State entities within a country.[5]

Some commentators have put forward the view that the use of force by States in the cases of Korea in 1950 and the Gulf in 1991 were examples of authorized collective self-defence measures and as such were not UN enforcement action. If this is the case then these actions cannot be characterized as a delegation by the Council of its Chapter VII powers to Member States. It would simply be an affirmation by the Council of a course of conduct which States, in the circumstances, already had open to them: the

---

[2] See *supra* Section III(1) in Chapter 1.

[3] See also Kelsen, H., *Recent Trends in the Law of the United Nations* (1951), at p. 933; and the comment by the French Government concerning peacekeeping operations (*GAOR*, 19th Session (1964), Annexes, vol. 3, Agenda item 21, at 57).

[4] See also Higgins, R., *United Nations Peacekeeping 1946–1967: Documents and Commentary*, vol. 2. (1970), p. 176; *La Charte des Nations Unies* (Cot, J-P., and Pellet, A., eds.) (1991), p. 645; and *The Charter of the United Nations: An Article by Article Commentary* (Simma, B., ed.) (1994), pp. 611–12.

[5] See Higgins, *ibidem*.

use of force as part of measures taken pursuant to their inherent right of self-defence. Accordingly, the examination of the Korean and Gulf actions must necessarily determine whether the Council delegated its Chapter VII powers to Member States or whether the use of force is to be justified by reference to the right of collective self-defence of States. Only once this threshold issue is addressed, can an enquiry proceed as to the fulfilment of the requirements for a lawful delegation by the Council of its Chapter VII powers.

1. The case of Korea

The Korean conflict started on 25 June 1950 when armed forces from North Korea pushed south across the 38th parallel invading the Republic of Korea. The Council responded that very day by passing resolution 82 in which it made the decision that this 'armed attack' constituted a 'breach of the peace' and called upon the 'authorities of North Korea to withdraw forthwith their armed forces to the 38th parallel'.[6] The Security Council went on, in resolutions 83 and 84, to delegate to all Member States the competence to use force to repel this attack and to a Unified Command broad powers of command and control over the force. The majority of legal analysis of the Korean case has already been carried out above in Chapter 3, since the Unified Command, vested with command and control powers, is a UN subsidiary organ. However, an issue, for our purposes, that remains is the character of the mandate conferred on Member States.

The Council resolutions delegated Chapter VII powers to Member States and were not simply authorizing States to take measures in self-defence that they were already entitled to take. It has already been established in Chapter 1 that the only case in which a Council resolution that authorizes military action would be authorizing self-defence measures is where the resolution expressly refers to this right and does not authorize measures which could possibly exceed the scope of this right as it exists under international law.[7] We recall, moreover, from Chapter 1 that where the Council authorizes the use of force by States there is a presumption that this represents a delegation by the Council of its Chapter VII powers and not just a reaffirmation of States' rights to use force in self-defence. The exception to this general position is where the Council expressly states that it is

---

[6] There is debate over the legality of the Council's determinations in this resolution. See, for example, Kelsen, *supra* note 3, pp. 927–31. However, this is not of concern to our present enquiry since this resolution clearly involves no delegation by the Council of its Chapter VII powers: Security Council resolution 82 '[c]alls upon the authorities of North Korea to withdraw forthwith their armed forces to the 38th parallel . . . [c]alls upon all Members to render every assistance to the United Nations in the execution of this resolution and to refrain from giving assistance to the North Korean authorities'. (S/1501, 25 June 1950.)

[7] See *supra* notes 58–65 and corresponding text *et sequentia* in Chapter 1.

exercizing its powers under Chapter VII only to reaffirm the right of States to use force in self-defence. Accordingly, in order to characterize the nature of the military action taken in Korea it is necessary to examine the nature of the Council's authorization. In the case of Korea, the action could not be included within the rubric of self-defence, since the Council in resolution 83 recommended that Members furnish such assistance as may be necessary in order to repel the armed attack and, more importantly, 'to restore international peace and security in the area'.[8] The Council is delegating to Member States its power to take action to maintain or restore international peace and security.[9] The latter objective specified by the Council will in some cases involve Member States clearly going beyond the scope of measures which they could take acting pursuant to their right of self-defence.[10] Accordingly, the actions in Korea were not Security Council authorized measures of self-defence but Council authorized enforcement action. Put differently, the forces are exercising delegated Chapter VII powers on behalf of the Council.[11] This view is confirmed by the practice of Member States in exercising these powers in Korea under the command and control of the Unified Command.[12] A number of writers thus argue that Articles 39 and 42 provide the legal basis for the Council's resolutions.[13]

There are, however, those who contend that the action in Korea was

---

[8] Resolution 83 (1950) of 27 June 1950.

[9] See also Kelsen, *supra* note 3, p. 930.

[10] Brownlie acknowledges the existence of such a situation when he noted 'the terms of [a] resolution might seem to authorize enforcement measures which would involve measures other than those of mere assistance in defensive action terminating at the aggressor's frontier'. (Brownlie, I., *International Law and the Use of Force by States* (1963), p. 335.) Moreover, the fact that the powers delegated to Member States went beyond those of self-defence, which States were in any case allowed to use, is confirmed by Bowett who states in respect of the Council's subsequent recommendation in resolution 84: 'the recommendation operated as an authorisation to Members to take action which, without such authorisation, might have been illegal'. (Bowett, D., *United Nations Forces* (1964), p. 32.)

[11] Thus, for example, the UK Prime Minister in the House of Commons on 28 June 1950, the day after the adoption of resolution 83, stated: 'The House will wish to know what action His Majesty's Government is taking in pursuance of the resolution of the Security Council passed yesterday calling on all Members of the United Nations to furnish assistance to the Republic of Korea. We have decided to support the United States action in Korea by immediately placing our Naval forces in Japanese waters at the disposal of the United States authorities to operate on behalf of the Security Council in support of South Korea. Orders to this effect have already been sent to the Naval Commander-in-Chief on the spot.' (As cited in S/PV.476, *SCOR*, 5th year, 476th meeting (1950), p. 11.) See also the statement by the UK representative in the General Assembly. (*GAOR*, 9th Session First Committee, 738th meeting, 2 Dec. (1954), p. 478.)

[12] See *supra* Section II(2)(b) in Chapter 3.

[13] Higgins states the following: '. . . while the action in Korea was undoubtedly *sui generis*, it may properly be described as enforcement action recommended by the Security Council under Articles 39 and 42, the command of which was delegated to the United States as agent of the UN'. (Higgins, vol. 2, *supra* note 4, p. 178.) See also Kaikobad, K., 'Self-Defence, Enforcement and the Gulf Wars, 1980–88 and 1990–91', *BYIL*, 63 (1992), p. 300 at p. 357; and Bowett, *supra* note 10, p. 34.

authorized self-defence. Dinstein, a leading proponent of this view, contends that the force 'fought in exercize of collective self-defence (induced by the Council) as distinct from collective security'.[14] The reason for Dinstein why the measures could not have been UN enforcement action is that the Council could not *require* States to carry out the measures in question.[15] However, as already established in Chapter 4, the lawfulness of military enforcement action being taken under the auspices of the Council does not depend on there being an obligation on States to carry out such action.[16] Accordingly, as also explained above in Chapter 4, a nonbinding recommendation may provide a suitable basis for a delegation by the Council of its Chapter VII powers.[17] Thus, the fact that the Council in resolutions 83 and 84 'recommended' that States take certain action is not a barrier to the characterization of such measures as being delegated military enforcement powers.[18] In fact, it is a characteristic of delegated Chapter VII powers that there is no obligation on Member States to exercize these powers: the exercize of delegated powers is at the discretion of each Member State. To conclude on this point, the Member States in Korea were using military force pursuant to a delegation of Chapter VII powers by the Council.[19]

We recall from Chapter 4 that the Council must exercize a degree of supervision over the use of its delegated Chapter VII powers. We further

[14] Dinstein, Y., *War, Aggression, and Self-Defence* (1994), p. 275. Cf. also Simma, *supra* note 4, p. 614; and Schachter, O., 'United Nations Law in the Gulf', *AJIL*, 85 (1991), p. 452.

[15] Dinstein states: 'Although four decades apart temporally, and light years apart psychologically, the Korean and the Gulf Wars are similar in that the coalitions which gathered to repel armed attacks acted in the exercize of collective self-defence (in conformity with the recommendation or the authorization of the Council) rather than collective security (decreed by the Council in a legally binding fashion).' (Dinstein, *ibidem*, p. 295.)

[16] See *supra* notes 32–3 and corresponding text in Chapter 4. It was clear in the case of Korea, that the Council resolutions did not require States to take the measures recommended: see the statement by the UK representative in the Security Council: S/PV.476, *SCOR*, 5th year, 476th meeting (1950), pp. 3–4.

[17] See *supra* note 33 and corresponding text in Chapter 4.

[18] As Higgins has stated: '. . . in the Advisory Opinion on *Certain Expenses of the United Nations* the criteria adopted for enforcement action by the Court are that it should be directed against a state, and not based on its consent. The Court did not make the concept turn on whether it was authorized by a decision or recommendation. Given that the action was directed against North Korea, it may thus be deemed enforcement action, even though taken by means of recommendation.' (Higgins, vol. 2, *supra* note 4, p. 177.) See also Franck, T., and Patel, F., 'UN Police Action in Lieu of War: "The Old Order Changeth"', *AJIL*, 85 (1991), p. 66 at pp. 66, 70, and 74.

[19] Once this is accepted, the different issue of the debate over whether the force is to be characterized as a UN Force is no longer of any major importance: see also Nkala, J., *The United Nations, international law, and the Rhodesian independence crisis* (1985), p. 148. However, the belief that the action was a UN authorized action is important in terms of reinforcing the nature of the measures taken as a collective security measure. See Seyersted, F., *United Nations Forces* (1966), p. 41; Bowett, *supra* note 10, pp. 45, 47; and the statement by the President of the Security Council preceding the adoption of resolution 84 (S/PV.476, *SCOR*, 5th year, 476th meeting (1950), p. 2). Cf., Eagleton, C., *International Government*, pp. 542–3.

recall that this requirement is a necessary concomitant of the overall authority and control that the Council must exercise over any military enforcement action, and that it is an important way of conferring on a particular action the indicia of a collective security response.[20] Further supervision is necessary in order for the Council to be able to make the decision when its stated objective has been achieved and thus when the delegation of Chapter VII powers by the Council to Member States ceases to exist. It was, moreover, noted in Chapter 4 that this supervisory function could be undertaken either by the Council and the Military Staff Committee, by the Secretary-General, or by a subsidiary organ which would be delegated this function. Accordingly, in response to the Council's authorization of States to use force, the Secretary-General in the case of Korea gave prompt consideration to the establishment of machinery to coordinate the actions of Members.[21] The Secretary-General at the time, Trygve Lie, wanted some form of UN control over the force.[22] The Secretary-General, accordingly, proposed the establishment of a subsidiary organ to assist in the command and control of the forces involved: the proposed 'Committee on Coordination for the Assistance of Korea', to be composed of the Republic of Korea and the States who had contributed troops. A draft resolution was prepared and circulated to the delegations of the US, the UK, France, and Norway (the President of the Council). Goodrich and Simons state in respect of this draft resolution, '[t]his resolution, if it had been approved, would have requested the United States to assume responsibility for organizing a United Nations command, would have authorized the armed forces placed under this command to fly the

[20] Accordingly, Goodrich and Simons note that when the Charter was being formulated '[a]lthough it was decided not to establish an international force, recruited, organized, trained and equipped under international direction and control, the decision was taken to go one step beyond a simple "alliance system" and provide for national contingents to be placed at the disposal and under the direction of an international organ, the Security Council. . . . In this way, it was hoped that the effective organization and conduct of a collective military action for the maintenance or restoration of international peace and security would be assured.' (Goodrich, L., and Simons, A-P., *The United Nations and the Maintenance of International Peace and Security* (1955), pp. 452–3.)

[21] However, as Goodrich states: 'The Security Council's resolution of July 7 [1950] placed upon the United States Government the primary responsibility for directing military operations in Korea, including the determination of military objectives, subject to such supervision as the Security Council might exercize. The return of the Soviet representative on August 1, 1950, eliminated the possibility of any effective control or direction by that organ.' (Goodrich, L., *Korea: A Study of US Policy in the United Nations* (1956), p. 179.)

[22] Trygve Lie, the Secretary-General at the time, wrote about this proposed Committee: 'Its deeper purpose was to keep the United Nations "in the picture," to promote continuing United Nations participation in and supervision of the military security action in Korea of a more intimate and undistracted character than the Security Council could be expected to provide. The delegates of the United Kingdom, France and Norway liked the idea of such a committee; the United States Mission promptly turned thumbs down. The Pentagon was much opposed to such United Nations activity.' (Lie, T., *In the Cause of Peace* (1954), p. 334.)

United Nations flag, and would have established a "Committee on Coordination of Assistance for Korea", composed of Australia, France, India, New Zealand, Norway, the United Kingdom, and the United States, with the Secretary-General as *rapporteur*, and with the Republic of Korea invited to send a representative'.[23] However, this draft resolution was strongly opposed by the United States.[24] Presumably, the US wanted sole operational command and control over its own forces and not for the decisions of its designated commander to be reviewed by a UN subsidiary organ. In fact, it seems clear that the UN Command, under the operational control of the United States, considered that it was given a free rein to prosecute the war.[25] In any case, with the return of the Soviets, and their veto, to the Council, any supervision or direction was ruled out completely.[26] However, it is significant that the Council had provided, as part of the system for allowing it to exercize supervision over the use of its delegated Chapter VII powers, the following reporting requirement: '[the Council] [r]equests the United States to provide the Security Council with reports as appropriate on the course of action taken under the unified command'. Bowett notes that biweekly reports were in fact transmitted to the Council by the US Government.[27] This is of some importance in attributing to the action the nature of a collective security measure.[28] Despite the shortcomings, of these reports,[29]

[23] Goodrich and Simons, *supra* note 20, p. 455.

[24] Higgins, vol. 2, *supra* note 4, p. 179. See also Morriss, D., 'From War to Peace: A Study of Cease-Fire Agreements and the Evolving Role of the United Nations', *Virginia Journal of International Law*, 36 (1996), p. 801 at p. 877 (n. 419).

[25] Higgins notes that 'in the military field, the control of the United States government was complete; in the political field consultations with the UN and some contributing members were more frequent. . . . In the final analysis, however, a large range of political decisions [were] taken by the United States government, as the Unified Command. . . . General MacArthur clearly took the view that the Unified Command had been given a mandate by the UN to run the campaign, and that it was not subject to day-to-day direction from the UN. He subsequently stated: "my encounter with the United Nations was largely nominal . . . I had no direct connection with the United Nations whatsoever."' (Higgins, vol. 2, *supra* note 4, pp. 178–9). See also Russett, B., and Sutterlin, J., 'The Utilization of Force by the Security Council in Interstate Conflict', in *The Use of Force by the Security Council for Enforcement and Deterrent Purposes: A Conference Report* (Cox, D., ed.) (1990), p. 31; Bowett, *supra* note 10, p. 45; and Eagleton, C., *International Government*, pp. 542–3.

[26] See *supra* note 21.

[27] Bowett, *supra* note 10, p. 42.

[28] The UK representative in the debates preceding the adoption of Council resolution 84 stated: '. . . paragraph 6 requests the United States to provide the Security Council with certain reports. This is desirable since the Security Council ought to be informed of the effects of the action which we hope will now be taken. In any case, this paragraph clearly recognizes the paramount interests of the Council in the efforts which the Members of the United Nations are collectively making to restore the situation in Korea.' (S/PV.476, *SCOR*, 5th year, 476th meeting (1950), p. 4.)

[29] Higgins notes that '[t]he United States used this practice to provide information, rather than to seek political guidance. Indeed, it has been observed that the Secretary-General had difficulty in ensuring that the Security Council received these reports before they were released to the press.' (Higgins, vol. 2, *supra* note 4, p. 179). Bowett, moreover, notes the

the institution by the Council of a system for the provision of information on the war effort at such regular intervals to the Council was an important development in the legal framework governing a delegation of Chapter VII powers.

2. The case of Iraq

The collective response to the Iraqi invasion of Kuwait in August 1990 was multifaceted and comprehensive. It involved the use of the full panoply of measures under Chapter VII of the Charter. The issues which are of concern to this section, however, are those pertaining to the use of force by States against Iraq as part of the collective measures authorized by resolution 678 which were designed to achieve the expulsion of Iraqi forces from Kuwait, full compliance by Iraq with specified previous Security Council resolutions, and the restoration of international peace and security in the area.[30]

Resolution 678 was adopted by the Council acting under Chapter VII of the Charter due to the desire to take stronger measures to ensure the immediate withdrawal of Iraqi forces from Kuwait. The relevant sections of resolution 678 read as follows:

Acting under Chapter VII of the Charter [the Security Council],

1. *Demands* that Iraq comply fully with resolution 660 (1990) and all subsequent relevant resolutions, and decides, while maintaining all its decisions, to allow Iraq one final opportunity, as a pause of goodwill, to do so;
2. *Authorizes* Member States co-operating with the Government of Kuwait, unless Iraq on or before 15 January 1991 fully implements, as set forth in paragraph 1 above, the foregoing resolutions, to use all necessary means to uphold and implement resolution 660 (1990) and all subsequent relevant resolutions and to restore international peace and security in the area; . . .
4. *Requests* the States concerned to keep the Security Council regularly informed on the progress of action undertaken pursuant to paragraphs 2 and 3 of the present resolution; . . .

---

following: 'these were factual statements of events that had occurred and were not of the character to allow the Council to know in advance of the military planning of the United Nations Command. There seems to have been not only a reluctance on the part of the United States to take the Security Council into its confidence (understandable enough in the circumstances) but an equal reluctance to consult with the participating States . . . Thus it was that political and strategic control of the United Nations Command vested, effectively, in the United States Joint Chiefs of Staff in Washington rather than in a United Nations organ or even in a body representative of the contributing States.' (Bowett, *supra* note 10, p. 42.)

[30] Analysis of the legal issues relating to another of these measures, the enforcement of economic sanctions by naval interdiction, is dealt with below. See *infra* Section II.

It is commonly accepted that resolution 678 involved some kind of authorization by the Council of the use of force by States against Iraq.[31] Assuming, then, that the action taken pursuant to resolution 678 was Security Council authorized action the issue becomes a question of the character of the Council's authorization: was it authorized military enforcement action or authorized self-defence measures?

(a) The nature of the Security Council's authorization in resolution 678

The debate over the characterization of the authorized measures is of some importance, since this will determine whether there has been a delegation of powers. If the Council is only authorizing measures to be taken in self-defence then it is in fact not delegating any powers at all to Member States since they already have the right to use such measures under Article 51 of the Charter. Once the nature of the power being exercised by Member States is ascertained, this will allow the determination of how far States may go when acting pursuant to their authorization.[32]

The first view is that the action taken to repel Iraq's invasion was, in legal terms, justifiable under the law of collective self-defence. It is clear that the attack by Iraq against Kuwait constituted an armed attack sufficient to invoke the Article 51 self-defence exception to the proscription of the use of force contained in Article 2(4) of the Charter.[33] Accordingly, the argument runs, Kuwait and Member States acting pursuant to Kuwait's right to individual and collective self-defence could use force to ensure the withdrawal of Iraqi forces and the return to power of the 'legitimate Government' in Kuwait.[34] The Council can decide to authorize States to use force in self-defence as an exercize of its collective security response in a case. However, we recall from Chapter 1 that this authorized collective self-defence will only occur when the Council expressly states that it is limiting its authorization to such measures.[35] This did not occur in the case of resolution 678 and thus the better legal view is that the passage of resolution 678 is an exercize by the Council of its collective security function.

---

[31] See, for example, Higgins, R., *Problems and Process: International Law and How We Use It* (1994), p. 255; Schachter, *supra* note 14, pp. 402–3; Dinstein, *supra* note 14, p. 273; and Pyrich, A., 'United Nations: Authorizations of Use of Force', *Harvard International Law Journal*, 32 (1991), p. 265 at p. 268.

[32] As Greenwood states: 'The question is by no means academic, since the answer has important implications for another difficult issue, namely the extent of the authorisation to use force and whether the resolution permitted the coalition to go beyond the objective of liberating Kuwait.' (Greenwood, C., 'New World Order or Old? The Invasion of Kuwait and the Rule of Law', *The Modern Law Review*, 55(2) (1992), p. 153 at p. 167.)

[33] See, for example, Dinstein, *supra* note 14, p. 272; and Schachter, *supra* note 14, p. 402.

[34] Moreover, Dinstein argues that self-defensive action would allow, in the case of the Gulf, the extension of hostilities across the Iraqi border: see *infra* note 43.

[35] See *supra* notes 59–65 and corresponding text *et sequentia* in Chapter 1.

Moreover, it is contended that resolution 678 was a delegation by the Security Council of certain of its Chapter VII powers to Member States, since the objectives specified in resolution 678, the use of 'all necessary means to uphold and implement resolution 660 (1990) and all subsequent resolutions and to restore international peace and security in the region', are considerably broader than the objectives which would be allowed by reference to the law of self-defence under international law.[36] The military action taken should thus be characterized as an exercize of Chapter VII powers delegated by the Council to Member States.

This type of approach has been the subject of criticism by some commentators who argue that the armed forces of the coalition did not constitute a United Nations force predicated on genuine collective security, but was authorized self-defence. Dinstein, a leading proponent of the self-defence view, contends that the lack of a legally binding obligation on States to carry out action, the fact that the 'command was American', and that the financing of the operation formed no part of the UN budget, meant that in legal terms the military action was based on 'collective self-defence (induced by the Council) as distinct from collective security'.[37] However, we recall from Chapter 4 that the Security Council can carry out military enforcement measures by means other than by binding decision, and that, moreover, the Council can delegate operational command and control to Member States.[38] In addition the argument that since the operation was not financed from the UN budget it was not a UN authorized military enforcement measure can be dismissed. The force carrying out the military enforcement measures was not a UN force *per se* and thus did not require funding from

[36] As Greenwood has stated: '. . . the present writer regards Resolution 678 as providing for enforcement action rather than giving a blessing (of political, not legal, significance) to an action in self-defence which could lawfully have been mounted without the authorisation of the Council. Following the adoption of Resolution 678, the coalition States repeatedly pointed to that Resolution as their legal authority. The reference in paragraph 2 of the resolution to restoring international peace and security would sit very uneasily in a resolution based upon the right of self-defence and suggests that the States were being authorised to exercize some of the powers of the Security Council rather than merely being encouraged to exercize their own inherent rights.' (Greenwood, *supra* note 32, p. 169.) See also Russett, B., and Sutterlin, J., 'The Utilization of Military Force by the United Nations', in *The Use of Force by the Security Council for Enforcement and Deterrent Purposes: A Conference Report* (Cox, D., ed.) (1990), p. 33; Penna, D., 'The Right to Self-Defense in the Post-Cold War Era: The Role of the United Nations', *Denver Journal of International Law and Policy*, 20 (1991), p. 41 at p. 50; Freudenschuß., 'Between Unilateralism and Collective Security: Authorizations of the Use of Force by the UN Security Council', *European Journal of International Law*, 5 (1994), p. 492; and the statement by the UK Minister of State at the Foreign and Commonwealth Office: *HC Debs.*, vol. 184, cols. 525–6, 22 Jan. 1991.

[37] Dinstein, *supra* note 14, p. 275. It was also this lack of UN direction and control that, for Eugene Rostow, meant the allied action to counter Iraqi aggression was not 'UN authorised enforcement action', but collective self-defence. (Rostow, E., 'Until What? Enforcement Action or Collective Self-Defense?', *AJIL*, 85 (1991), p. 506 at p. 508.) See also Schachter, *supra* note 14, p. 459 and Chinkin, C., *Third Parties in International Law* (1993), p. 339.

[38] See *supra* notes 27 & 33 and corresponding text in Chapter 4.

the UN budget. It is a concomitant of forces being supplied by Member States on a voluntary basis that, in general, the cost of these forces will be paid by the States in question and not from the UN budget.[39] This position does not, however, prevent the force from being able to exercize delegated Chapter VII powers.[40] In summary, there are no valid arguments against characterizing the military action in Iraq as an exercize of delegated Chapter VII powers. Accordingly, a number of writers conclude that the action in Iraq was military enforcement action authorized by the Security Council pursuant to Article 42 of the Charter.[41] Having established that resolution 678 can be characterized as a delegation of Chapter VII powers, it is now appropriate to examine the content of the powers delegated to Member States by the resolution.

(b) The powers delegated to Member States by resolution 678

The passage of resolution 678 saw the delegation to Member States of the power to use force to achieve the Council's stated objective, and the power of command and control over the forces carrying out the military enforcement action.[42]

---

[39] In fact, in the case of Rwanda, the Security Council made express reference in resolution 929 to the costs being borne by the Member States that take up the delegation of Chapter VII power: see text following *infra* note 225.

[40] In this respect, Warbrick states: 'In explaining why the funding of the coalition force should not be distributed among the whole of the UN membership on the ordinary budgetary formula, a British official told the Foreign Affairs Committee: "it is a United Nations operation in the sense that it takes place under the authority of the Security Council but it is a rather special kind of UN operation in the sense that it is not a blue beret type of operation with the United Nations command . . . it is a slightly special UN operation" acting, he added, under Chapter VII of the Charter.' (Lowe, V., and Warbrick, C., eds., 'Current Developments: Public International Law', in *ICLQ*, 40 (1991), p. 965 at p. 966.)

[41] See Higgins, *supra* note 31, p. 266; Weller, M., 'The Kuwait Crisis: A Survey of Some Legal Issues', *African Journal of International and Comparative Law*, 3 (1991), p. 1 at pp. 25–6; Simma, *supra* note 4, p. 634; Shearer, I., 'International Law and the Gulf War', in *Whose New World Order: What Role for the United Nations?* (Alston, P., and Bustelo, M., eds.) (1991), p. 73; Warbrick, C., 'The Invasion of Kuwait by Iraq,' *ICLQ*, 40 (1991), p. 965; Kaikobad, *supra* note 13, p. 361; and Borg-Olivier, A., 'The United Nations in a Changing World Order: Expectations and Realities', in *Peacemaking, Peacekeeping and Coalition Warfare: The Future Role of the United Nations* (1994), p. 19 at p. 21. There are other writers, however, who consider that resolution 678 was not adopted under Article 42, but rather on the basis of the Security Council's general powers under Chapter VII. However, this does not detract from their acceptance that it was a UN authorized enforcement action as opposed to authorized collective self-defence measures: Fleischhauer, C., 'Compliance and Enforcement in the United Nations System', in *Proceedings of the 85th Annual Meeting of the American Society of International Law*, 17–20 Apr. 1991, p. 431; and Szasz, P., 'Centralized and Decentralized Law Enforcement: The Security Council and the General Assembly Acting under Chapters VII and VIII', in *Allocation of Law Enforcement Authority in the International System*, Proceedings of an International Symposium of the Kiel Institute of International Law, 23–25 Mar. 1994 (Delbruck, J., ed.) (1995), p. 30.

[42] This approach was the subject of criticism by, *inter alia*, Weston who states: '[T]he Security Council, though clearly mindful of its duty to suppress acts of aggression and other

(i) The delegation to Member States of the power to use force

Article 2(4) of the Charter proscribes the threat or actual use of force by States against the territorial integrity or political independence of any State. However, a delegation by the Council of its military enforcement powers has an empowering effect that operates to allow States to use force to achieve the Council's stated objectives. This represents a delegation by the Council to Member States of its powers under Article 42 to 'take such action by air, sea, or land forces as may be necessary to maintain or restore international peace and security. Such action may include demonstrations, blockade, and other operations by air, sea, or land forces of Members of the United Nations.'

The issue of greatest concern with respect to this delegation of Chapter VII power is that the Council is purporting to delegate to Member States a very broad power of discretion to use force without specifying clearly the objectives for which it is delegating its powers. We recall that resolution 678 states '[the Council authorizes] Member states co-operating with the Government of Kuwait . . . to use all necessary means to uphold and implement resolution 660 (1990) and all subsequent relevant resolutions and to restore international peace and security in the area'. The objectives specified by the Council thus include the implementation of resolution 660 (the immediate and unconditional withdrawal by Iraq of 'all its forces to the positions in which they were located on 1 August 1990') and all subsequent resolutions; and the restoration of international peace and security in the area.[43] The first objective is relatively clear and seems to have operated as a substantive limitation on action by Member States in their exercize of delegated powers.[44] The decision to end hostilities was made when Iraq had

breaches of the peace, paid insufficient heed to the most overriding of UN Charter purposes and principles: the pacific settlement of international disputes and, failing that, a genuinely collective assertion of authority and control dedicated to the restoration of international peace and security.' (Weston, B., 'Security Council Resolution 678 and Persian Gulf Decision Making: Precarious Legitimacy', *AJIL,* 85 (1991), p. 516 at p. 518.)

[43] Accordingly, the argument that the Security Council in resolution 678 'authorized force only to liberate Kuwait' can be rejected. See also O'Connell, 'Enforcing the Prohibition on the Use of Force: The UN's Response to Iraq's Invasion of Kuwait', *Southern Illinois University Law Journal,* 15 (1990–1), p. 453, at p. 479. Dinstein dismissed this argument for other reasons. He contends that in the exercize of self-defence an action by a State or coalition of States 'need not be terminated at the point when the aggressor is driven back, and it may be carried on by the defending State until final victory. Particularly when engaged in a successful response to a large-scale invasion, the defending State—far from being bound to stop at the frontier—may pursue the retreating enemy forces, hammering at them up to the time of their total defeat.' (See Dinstein, *supra* note 14, p. 234; and also Zourek, J., 'La Notion de Légitime Défense en Droit International', *AIDI,* 56 (1975), p. 1, at pp. 49–50.) Accordingly, he rejects the argument that the Member States could not pursue Iraq over the border. (Dinstein, *supra* note 14, p. 235.)

[44] See, for example, the statement by the representative of Malaysia (S/PV.2963, pp. 76–7), and the statement by the UK Secretary of State (*HC Debs.,* vol. 216, col. 917: 13 Jan. 1993).

been driven out of Kuwait and had agreed to accept all relevant UN resolutions.[45]

The second objective, however, is of considerable more concern. It seems clear that the Council is purporting to delegate to Member States the competence to decide when international peace and security in the region has been restored. However, as pointed out above in Chapter 1, the Council does not possess the competence to delegate to Member States the power to decide that a threat to, or breach of, international peace and security has either started or has ceased to exist.[46] The decision whether a particular matter constitutes a threat to the peace and the decision when to terminate military enforcement action must always rest with the Security Council. This is an important safeguard for ensuring that States exercize delegated Chapter VII powers only in order to achieve the objectives of the United Nations and not solely their own self-interest in a particular situation. Moreover, we further recall from Chapter 1 that if States are given the competence to determine when a threat to, or breach of, international peace and security has ceased to exist they are being delegated the power to determine when the delegation of Chapter VII powers is to be terminated.[47] The purported delegation by the Council of this broad power to Member States is unlawful. It is on the basis of this unrestricted character of the power delegated by resolution 678 that commentators have correctly questioned the lawfulness of the resolution.[48] This does not, however, render the whole of resolution 678 unlawful, but only the delegation of powers to

---

[45] Chayes observes: 'The Security Council Resolution obviously delegated a good deal of discretion to the parties—the countries who were cooperating with Kuwait in its defense—to decide what means were necessary to enforce the sanctions. . . . With the ground war itself, the question of our objectives came up in the beginning. What were our aims in the ground war given the calls for the overthrow of Saddam and the questions regarding the extent to which the Iraqi government and military machine would have to be destroyed? On the other hand, the UN Resolutions had rather specific aims: the expulsion of Saddam [by this is meant, of course, Iraqi troops] from Kuwait, the restoration of the previous government, and the establishment of peace and stability in the area. The establishment of peace and stability in the area was a somewhat elastic element of the Resolution, and I think there was actually one critical moment when, as General Schwartzkopf said, the western troops turned towards the Euphrates rather than to the North towards Baghdad. Nonetheless, there remained questions and ambiguities about the extent to which the demands and position of the coalition were fully justified under the Council Resolution . . . Was it a UN action in the classic sense? Was the UN acting in the form that it was intended to act in 1945 or was it essentially an action by the United States and other countries associated with it to further their own interest, operating under the UN cloak?' (Chayes, A., in '1991 Friedmann Conference on Collective Security', *Columbia Journal of Transnational Law*, 29 (1991), at p. 511.) McCausland notes that 'President Bush ordered an end to the hostilities because the publicly stated goals of the coalition had been achieved.' (McCausland, J., 'Coalition in the Desert', in *Peacemaking, Peacekeeping and Coalition Warfare: The Future Role of the United Nations* (Mokhtari, F., ed.) (1994), p. 232.)

[46] See *supra* Section III(2)(b)(i) in Chapter 1.

[47] See *supra* notes 129–32 and corresponding text in Chapter 1.

[48] See, for example, Weston, *supra* note 42, p. 516 at pp. 525–6.

Member States for the objective of restoring international peace and security in the region.

In practice, however, the Security Council did play an important role in the termination of the delegation of powers. The success of the coalition force in expelling Iraq from Kuwait saw the US command declare a temporary ceasefire after the full retreat of Iraqi forces from Kuwait and the restoration to power of the legitimate Government of Kuwait. The Council subsequently passed resolution 686 which, *inter alia*, affirmed that all twelve prior resolutions continued to have full force and effect, and demanded that Iraq cease hostilities and designate military commanders to meet with counterparts from the coalition forces 'to arrange for the military aspects of a cessation of hostilities at the earliest possible time'. The Council continued by expressly stating in operative paragraph 4 that it '[r]ecognizes that during the period required for Iraq to comply with paragraphs 2 and 3 above, the provisions of paragraph 2 of resolution 678 (1990) remain valid'. This provision is clearly intended as an affirmation by the Council that the delegation of military enforcement powers to Member States continues to have force. It places the legality of any subsequent use of force to achieve the objectives of the Council in its previous resolutions, including resolution 678, and the conditions stated in resolution 686 beyond any doubt.[49] However, the terms of resolution 686 were superseded by the terms of the formal ceasefire of the Council in resolution 687. The terms for a permanent ceasefire were stated by the Council in resolution 687 and these were accepted by Iraq.[50] It is beyond the scope of this present work to examine the various legal issues which pertain to Council resolution 687.[51] However, the issue which is of concern to our present discussion is whether the conclusion of the ceasefire and acceptance of its terms by Iraq terminates the delegation of military enforcement powers to Member States.

The legal argument which supports the subsequent use of force by Member States to enforce the terms of the ceasefire, posits that resolution

---

[49] See also the statement by the US representative in the Council: S/PV.2978, p. 43; and Lavalle, R., 'The Law of the United Nations and the Use of Force, Under the Relevant Security Council Resolutions of 1990 and 1991, to Resolve the Persian Gulf Crisis', *Netherlands Yearbook of International Law*, 23 (1992), p. 3 at p. 52. Cf., however, Gray, C., 'After the Ceasefire: Iraq, The Security Council and the Use of Force', *BYIL*, 65 (1994), pp. 138–9; and also the statements in the Security Council by Ecuador (S/PV.2978, p. 82), and Yemen (S/PV.2978, p. 27). This is of course subject to the contention made with respect to the dubious legality of the delegation of powers to 'restore international peace and security': see *supra* note 48 and corresponding text.

[50] Letters of 6 Apr. 1991 from Iraq addressed to the Security Council and to the Secretary-General, S/22456.

[51] These are covered in a comprehensive fashion in Gray, *supra* note 49, p. 135; Sur, S., 'Security Council Resolution 687 of 3 April 1991 in the Gulf Affair: Problems of Restoring and Safeguarding Peace', *UNIDIR Research Paper No. 12* (1992); and Morriss, *supra* note 24, pp. 892–7.

678 was suspended by resolution 687 only to the extent that Iraq complied with the terms of the ceasefire.[52] In other words, the delegation of powers in resolution 678 continues to have effect to the extent that Iraq does not comply with the terms of the ceasefire specified in resolution 687. This approach assumes that the delegation of powers to Member States in resolution 678 remains valid until the Council makes an express decision that peace has been restored in the region, thereby terminating the delegation. This position seems to have received the support of the UN Secretary-General who, following military action taken against Iraq on 13 January 1993, stated:

The raid yesterday, and the forces that carried out the raid, have received a mandate from the Security Council, according to resolution 678, and the cause of the raid was the violation by Iraq of resolution 687 concerning the cease-fire. So, as Secretary-General of the UN, I can say that this action was taken and conforms to the resolutions of the Security Council and conforms to the Charter of the United Nations.[53]

Similarly, this seems to be the approach adopted by the majority of Council members. Johnstone, although in disagreement, summarizes the position:

The vague warning of 'serious consequences' issued in January 1993 and the silence in the Council after the military strikes suggest an attitude of passive acquiescence. This attitude is consistent with the initial authorization in Resolution 678, which can be viewed as either 'delegated enforcement action' pursuant to Article 42, an act of collective self-defense pursuant to Article 51, or a hybrid of the two based on the general powers of the Security Council to maintain and restore international peace and security. In any case, the authorization supports the argument that only an explicit repeal of Resolution 678 would deprive members of the allied coalition of the authority to act unilaterally. By tacitly endorsing the argument that a new

---

[52] It was certainly the view of the US representative, Mr Pickering, that Iraq had to fulfil certain additional conditions before the coalition would decide that a threat to international peace and security ceased to exist and, therefore, that there would be a termination of the delegation of Chapter VII powers under resolution 678 to Member States. He states: 'Since the end of November and the adoption of resolution 678 (1990), the Council has focused on its implementation. Now key goals it adopted have been achieved. . . . Now the Council turns its attention to the restoration of peace and security in the area, as resolution 678 (1990) recognized would be required. The present resolution points the way. We seek as soon as possible a definitive end to hostilities. The resolution sets out the measures which Iraq must take and the arrangements which must be put in place to bring this about. Iraq has much to account for, and there is much yet to be done to fulfil the resolutions of the Council and the requirements of international law. . . . Until it is clear that Iraq has complied with these requirements, the provisions of resolution 678 (1990) authorizing Kuwait and those cooperating with Kuwait to use all necessary means to ensure Iraqi compliance with the United Nations resolutions clearly will remain in effect . . .' (S/PV.2978.) Cf. the statement by India that resolution 687 did not authorize the use of force by coalition States under the continued authority of resolution 678: S/PV.2981, p. 78.

[53] UN Department of Public Information (DPI) Briefing, 14 Jan. 1993, p. 2.

resolution was not required, Council members in effect accepted the continued delegation of military responsibility to the United States, the United Kingdom and France.[54]

However, it is contended that this is not the appropriate approach. The better legal view is that, despite the purported delegation by the Council to Member States of the power to take military enforcement action until 'international peace and security has been restored in the region',[55] the delegation of Chapter VII powers to Member States was terminated by conclusion of the formal ceasefire between Iraq and the UN, the terms of which were specified in resolution 687.[56] Nowhere in its terms, unlike resolution 686, does resolution 687 expressly preserve the right of Member States to use force under resolution 678. In fact, the conclusion of the ceasefire, of which resolution 687 was an essential part, terminated the delegation of powers in resolution 678 to Member States of the competence to use force. However, the terms of resolution 687, which sets out the conditions for a formal ceasefire and the framework for implementing those conditions, did not by itself terminate the delegation, it was, rather, the acceptance by Iraq of those terms which gave effect to the terms of resolution 687 and thus terminated the authorization to coalition States to use force.[57] This is confirmed when one considers that the effect of the opera-

---

[54] Johnstone, I., *Aftermath of the Gulf War: An Assessment of UN Action*, International Peace Academy, Occasional Paper Series (1994), p. 41. However, Johnstone questions the legality of such an approach when he states: 'The claim that every breach of Resolution 687 automatically reopens the door to unilateral military action has potentially far-reaching consequences. How serious must the breach be, and which states are allowed to respond? Force cannot be used to compel compliance with a resolution per se, even one adopted under Chapter VII. Who should decide which breaches are serious enough, either in isolation, or as part of a pattern, to constitute a threat to or breach of the peace?' (*Ibidem.*)

[55] We recall from above that this is an unlawful delegation of Chapter VII powers: see *supra* note 48 and corresponding text.

[56] As Gray states: '. . . because the Security Council imposed a ceasefire in Resolution 687 and terminated its authorization to use force under Resolution 678 and 686, the coalition States were no longer entitled to use force against Iraq without further Security Council permission. That is, violations of Resolution 687 by Iraq would not themselves justify the coalition in ending the ceasefire or in unilaterally using force.' (Gray, *supra* note 49, p. 143.) Accordingly, in the absence of an express Council authorization of further military enforcement action, the US action, on 17 and 18 Jan. 1993, which involved the launching of 40 cruise missiles against a nuclear weapons facility on the outskirts of Baghdad is legally difficult to justify: see also Gray, *supra* note 49, pp. 154–5. As noted in Chapter 1, there can be no implied delegation of powers, even to enforce Council resolutions. See also *infra* note 59. Accordingly, both Higgins and Gray dismiss the argument that the 'serious consequences' warning given in this case by the President of the Security Council can be interpreted as a valid delegation to Member States to use force without further authorization from the Council even despite repeated Iraqi interference with the UN weapons inspection programme: Higgins, *supra* note 31, p. 259; and Gray, *ibidem*, p. 155.

[57] Operative paragraph 33 of resolution 687 states that the resolution will have legal effect once Iraq has given its consent to the terms of the resolution and then 'a formal cease-fire is effective between Iraq and Kuwait and the Member States co-operating with Kuwait'. As Gray has observed: 'Although Resolution 687 "Affirms all thirteen resolutions noted above" [in-

tion of the *delegatus non potest delegare* doctrine, as explained further in Chapter 1 above, is that the terms of resolutions pertaining to a delegation of powers are to be construed in a narrow fashion.[58] Accordingly, in the absence of a Council resolution which expressly delegates powers of military enforcement to Member States, action to enforce the terms of resolution 687, although possibly desirable, would be legally doubtful.[59] This problem is a symptom of the deeper issue of the lack of clear specification by the Council of the goals for which it was delegating its Chapter VII powers to Member States.

cluding Resolution 678], it continues "except as expressly changed below to achieve the goals of this resolution, including a ceasefire." Paragraph 33 declares that a formal ceasefire is effective upon official acceptance by Iraq. [Due to this acceptance] [t]he authorization to use force in Resolution 678 is therefore no longer in force.' (Gray, *supra* note 49, p. 155, n. 119.) See also Johnstone, *supra* note 54, p. 40.

[58] On the narrow interpretation to be given to a Council resolution that delegates Chapter VII powers, see *supra* Section III(2)(b)(iv) in Chapter 1. Johnstone states the following slightly different reason for the narrow construction of the resolution delegating military enforcement powers: 'Given the ambiguous language and uncertain intent, the objective and purpose of the resolution must be considered in light of the collective security scheme embodied in the UN Charter. The Charter assigns primary responsibility for the maintenance of international peace and security to the Security Council. With Resolution 678, the Council exercized this responsibility by delegating its enforcement power to the allied coalition, but because the use of force is normally a contravention of the Charter, any ambiguity about the scope and duration of the delegation should be construed narrowly.' (Johnstone, *supra* note 54, p. 40.)

[59] For the requirement that a delegation of power be by express resolution of the Council, see *supra* notes 34–40 and corresponding text in Chapter 1. This legal position has been adopted by the Security Council in its resolution 1154 which deals with Iraq's non-compliance with the terms of resolution 687. The Security Council adopting resolution 1154 under Chapter VII '[s]tresses that compliance by the Government of Iraq with its obligations, repeated again in the memorandum of understanding, to accord immediate, unconditional and unrestricted access to the Special Commission and the IAEA in conformity with the relevant resolutions is necessary for the implementation of resolution 687 (1991), but that any violation would have severest consequences for Iraq; . . . [and further] Decides, in accordance with its responsibility under the Charter, to remain actively seized of the matter, in order to ensure implementation of this resolution, and to secure peace and security in the area.' In other words the Council is giving a warning to Iraq that non-compliance with its obligations as interpreted by the Council will result in further action by the Security Council. This may of course involve another delegation of Chapter VII powers to Member States to ensure that Iraq complies with its obligations, but the point is that such a delegation will be by a further resolution of the Council. This view was clearly stated by the representatives of States in the Security Council debates concerning the adoption of resolution 1154. For example, the representative of Brazil stated that the question of the implementation of the conditions of the ceasefire with Iraq remained firmly under the wing of the United Nations and the Security Council, and that only the Council had the authority to determine if, when, and under which conditions the formal ceasefire in resolution 687 held or not. (Security Council Press Release SC/6483 (containing record of statements by State representatives in Security Council Meeting 3858), p. 8.) The Brazilian representative went on to state that the co-sponsors of the draft resolution had given assurances that it was not their intention to imply any automaticity in the authorization for the use of force, in the case of a possible violation by Iraq, and that, after changes to the text, Brazil was satisfied that nothing in the draft resolution delegated away the Council's authority under the Charter. (*ibidem.*) See also the statements by the representatives of Kenya (*ibidem*, pp. 9–10); Japan (*ibidem*, p. 10), a co-sponsor of the resolution; China (*ibidem*, p. 12); France (*ibidem*, p. 12); Russia (*ibidem*, p. 14); and Gambia (*ibidem*, p. 14).

It has been established in Chapter 4 that the Council must impose a reporting obligation on Member States when exercizing delegated Chapter VII powers.[60] This obligation was complied with by the Council when, in paragraph 4 of resolution 678, the Council '[r]equests the States concerned to keep the Council regularly informed on the progress of actions undertaken pursuant to paragraphs 2 and 3 of the present resolution'. This reporting requirement saw various members of the coalition forces submit regular reports to the Council on the way in which they were exercizing their delegated Chapter VII powers.[61] The detailed reporting of military action that was made in these reports was sufficient to satisfy the reporting requirement that attaches to the exercize of delegated Chapter VII powers,[62] since the reports *in casu* provided the Council with sufficient information so that it could effectively supervise the exercize of its delegated Chapter VII powers. Thus, for example, Member States made it clear that they were complying with 'the applicable law of armed conflict',[63] and, as part of this, the *jus in bello* requirement of proportionality.[64]

To reiterate, in the case of the Gulf the purported delegation by the Council to Member States of the power to decide when a threat to, or breach of, international peace and security has started or when such a

---

[60] See *supra* note 72 and corresponding text in Chapter 4.

[61] For the view that paragraph 4 required Member States exercizing the delegated powers to report to the Council, see Warbrick, C., 'The Invasion of Kuwait by Iraq—Part II', *ICLQ*, 40 (1991), p. 965 at p. 967. For these reports by Member States, see: S/22090, 17 Jan. 1991; S/22100, 17 Jan. 1991; S/22106, 18 Jan. 1991; S/22115, 21 Jan. 1991; S/22126, 22 Jan. 1991; S/22130, 22 Jan. 1991; S/22131, 22 Jan. 1991; S/22153, 25 Jan. 1991; S/22156, 28 Jan. 1991; S/22164, 28 Jan. 1991; S/22169, 29 Jan. 1991; S/22180, 31 Jan. 1991; S/22192, 4 Feb. 1991 S/22194, 4 Feb. 1991; S/22199, 5 Feb. 1991; S/22200, 6 Feb. 1991; S/22210, 11 Feb. 1991; S/22216, 13 Feb. 1991; S/22217, 13 Feb. 1991; S/22218, 13 Feb. 1991; S/22227, 15 Feb. 1991; S/22239, 19 Feb. 1991; S/22248, 20 Feb. 1991; S/22251, 21 Feb. 1991; S/22258, 23 Feb. 1991, S/22259, 23 Feb. 1991; S/22292, 1 Mar. 1991 S/22341, 8 Mar. 1991 S/22350, 14 Mar. 1991 S/22358, 18 Mar. 1991 S/22413, 28 Mar. 1991 S/22522, 23 Apr. 1991 (these are reproduced in Weller, M., ed., *Iraq and Kuwait: The Hostilities and their Aftermath* (1993)).

[62] Cf. the following statement by Secretary-General Javier Perez de Cuellar: '. . . in Resolution 678 (1990) the Security Council authorised certain states to use military force instead of acting directly under Article 42. The way in which that resolution has been implemented shows that there is a need for an improved and more institutionalized mechanism for reporting to the Council by the concerned states. The Security Council needs to preserve for itself the authority to exercize guidance, supervision or control with respect to the carrying out of actions authorised by it.' (Secretary-General Javier Perez de Cuellar, 22 Apr. 1991, at the University of Bordeaux, France, UN Press Release, SG/SM/4560 (24 Apr. 1991), taken from Alston and Bustelo, *supra* note 41, Appendix A, p. 141 at p. 146.) The Secretary-General further remarked: 'What we know about the war . . . is what we hear from the three members of the Security Council which are involved—Britain, France, and the United States—which every two or three days report to the Council, after the actions. The Council, which has authorised all this, is informed only after the military action has taken place.' (Doyle, L., 'UN Has No Role in Running War', *Independent*, 11 Feb. 1991, p. 2 (Interview with Perez de Cuellar).)

[63] See the report of the US Government, S/22090, 17 Jan. 1991; and the UK Government, S/22115, 21 Jan. 1991.

[64] See, for example, the report of the Government of the UK: S/22156, 28 Jan. 1991.

situation has ceased to exist was unlawful. This is an exclusive power which UN Member States have delegated to the Council through the Charter on the condition that it is the Council alone which makes such decisions. However, this does not detract from the position that the delegation by the Council of its Chapter VII powers to Member States to ensure the immediate withdrawal by Iraq from Kuwait and the implementation of the twelve prior resolutions was a lawful exercize of its competence to delegate Chapter VII powers.

(ii) The command and control of forces in the Gulf War

It seems clear that in resolution 678 the Council delegated to Member States operational command and control over their own forces carrying out military enforcement action.[65] The resolution does not require or envisage any form of operational command or control being exercized by the Security Council over the forces from Member States.[66] This represents a delegation of the Council's power of command and control under Article 46 of the Charter to Member States. This is in contradistinction to the provisions of resolution 665 which request the States concerned to co-ordinate their actions in implementing a naval interdiction by 'using as appropriate mechanisms of the Military Staff Committee'.[67] Moreover, the Council did not specify in resolution 678 any form of command structure. Accordingly, the coalition forces were free to identify their own military commander and command structure. The Member States participating in the action decided to form a coalition with the United States in overall command.[68] The only

[65] As Chayes states: 'Resolution 678 in effect was a delegation to the President of the United States of the discretion to decide, on the basis of circumstances as he appreciated them and with such consultation of the states associated with him as he deemed necessary, when to use force. Given that the vast bulk of the financial and military costs of the operation were being borne by the United States, it was hard for the Security Council to decline to make such a delegation. The grant, however, did not eliminate but heightened the necessity for judgment in the exercize of discretion. As with all such delegations, not the existence of discretion but the wisdom of the judgment determines the quality of the outcome.' (Chayes, A., 'The Use of Force in the Persian Gulf', in *Law and Force in the New International Order* (1991), p. 3 at p. 10.) See also the speech delivered by Secretary-General Javier Perez de Cuellar, 22 Apr. 1991, at the University of Bordeaux, France, *supra* note 62.

[66] As Sir Brian Urquhart states: 'The very idea of a United Nations command under the Security Council, though traditionally accepted for peace-keeping operations, was never seriously considered for enforcement operations in the Gulf.' (Urquhart, B., 'Learning from the Gulf', *Whose New World Order: What Role for the United Nations?*, in Alston, and Bustelo, *supra* note 41, p. 13.)

[67] However, for discussion of the lack of use of the Military Staff Committee in the context of the naval interdiction imposed against Iraq, see *infra* note 156.

[68] In what was known as 'Operation Desert Shield', the operation to protect Saudi Arabia from Iraqi attack, forces from Member States were largely under national command and control. (See McCausland, *supra* note 45, p. 219.) However, in the case of 'Operation Desert Storm', the Member States whose forces were part of the coalition force to expel Iraq from Kuwait, accepted overall US command and control through 'CENTCOM'. (See McCausland, *supra* note 45, p. 219.)

substantive requirement which the resolution specifies is that the Member States must co-operate with the Government of Kuwait. It is clear that this condition was satisfied. As explained above and in Chapter 4, it is not necessary for the Council to exercize operational command and control over the exercize of its delegated Chapter VII powers for there to be a lawful delegation of powers or for the action to be characterized as United Nations authorized military enforcement action.[69] This does not mean, however, that the exercize of the delegated powers is left solely to the discretion of Member States. The contention that the measures taken under resolution 678 (1990) were not subject to the overall authority and control of the Council since there was no such role envisaged in the resolution must be rejected.[70] The lack of resolution 678 mentioning in express terms that action was to be 'under the authority of the Security Council', in contradistinction to resolution 665, does not affect the fact that this is an implied term of the resolution as required by the law governing a delegation of Chapter VII powers.[71] The Security Council will always retain overall authority and control over the exercize of Chapter VII powers it has delegated to UN Member States. Accordingly, the Council could at any time decide to terminate the delegation of powers or even decide that the powers should be exercized in another way. This has particular relevance, for example, in the context of a proportionate use of force being used to attain the Council's stated objectives.[72] The Council could at any time have, for example, required States to change the level of force being used by Member States in the Gulf in the exercize of their delegated powers.[73]

In conclusion, the Council's delegation of its operational power of command and control to Member States in the Gulf was legally acceptable. Accordingly, the argument by States that there had been a delegation of authority 'without accountability'[74] is inaccurate in the sphere of command and control powers.

[69] See *supra* notes 14 & 15 and corresponding text in Chapter 4.

[70] Cf. Lavalle, *supra* note 49, p. 33.

[71] On the general requirement of the Council to exercize authority and control over an operation, see *supra* note 159 and corresponding text in Chapter 1.

[72] Cf. Weston who states: 'The unrestricted character of Resolution 678 does not stop here. In addition to leaving the precise source of its authority unstated, the resolution neglected to restrict the destructive weaponry and any other means of warfare that might have been relied upon, and did not require any meaningful accounting to, or guidance from, the Security Council, the Military Staff Committee, or any other UN institution that might have been appropriate (requiring merely that "the states concerned . . . keep the Council regularly informed").' (Weston, *supra* note 42, pp. 525–6.) Cf. also Chayes, *supra* note 45, p. 511.

[73] Cf. *supra* notes 62–5 and corresponding text in Chapter 4.

[74] The representative of Yemen stated in the Council preceding the adoption of resolution 678: '. . . the draft resolution before us is not related to a specific article of Chapter VII of the Charter; hence the Security Council will have no control over those forces, which will fly their own national flags. Furthermore, the command of those forces will have nothing to do with the United Nations, although their actions will have been authorized by the Security Council. It is a classic example of authority without accountability.' (S/PV.2963, p. 33.)

3. *The case of Somalia*

The UN became involved in the crisis in Somalia in January 1992 when the Somali permanent representative to the UN requested assistance from the Organization.[75] In response, the Security Council passed resolution 733 which, *inter alia*, called for a ceasefire between the warring factions, imposed an arms embargo against Somalia, called for an increase in the amount of humanitarian assistance being sent to Somalia, and requested the Secretary-General to send a fact-finding mission to the country. Subsequently, in resolution 751, the Security Council set up a peacekeeping force, the United Nations Operation in Somalia (UNOSOM), which had as one of its main objectives the protection of humanitarian assistance operations. However, the lack of safe conditions for the delivery of humanitarian assistance in Somalia led the Security Council in resolution 794 to authorize the Secretary-General and any co-operating Member States to use 'all necessary means to establish as soon as possible a secure environment for humanitarian relief operations in Somalia'. This resolution provided the legal basis for 'Operation Restore Hope', carried out by UNITAF (United States marines and forces from other Member States), which had the limited objective of providing a secure environment for the delivery of humanitarian assistance in Somalia.[76] However, it was the opinion of the Secretary-General that when Operation Restore Hope came to an end a 'secure environment' had not yet been established in Somalia.[77] Accordingly, the Secretary-General recommended that the mandate of UNOSOM II would have to include enforcement action and would be the first such operation of its kind carried out by a peacekeeping force.[78] The Security Council expressly adopted this recommendation when it stated in resolution 814 the following:

Acting under Chapter VII of the Charter of the United Nations, [the Security Council] Requests the Secretary-General, through his Special Representative, to direct the Force Commander of UNOSOM II to assume responsibility for the consolidation, expansion and maintenance of a secure environment throughout

---

[75] For a brief history of the Somali dispute see Sarooshi, D., 'Humanitarian Intervention and International Humanitarian Assistance: Law and Practice', *Wilton Park Papers*, 86 (1994), pp. 25–7.

[76] For the legal considerations relating to this delegation of power by the Council, see *infra* Section III (1).

[77] The Secretary-General stated in a report of 3 Mar. 1996: 'It is clear to me that the effort undertaken by UNITAF to establish a secure environment in Somalia is far from complete and in any case has not attempted to address the situation throughout all of Somalia. Moreover, there have been, especially recently, some disheartening reverses. Accordingly, the threat to international peace and security which the Security Council ascertained in the third preambular paragraph of resolution 794 (1992) is still in existence. Consequently UNOSOM II will not be able to implement the above mandate unless it is endowed with enforcement powers under Chapter VII of the Charter.' (S/25354, p. 13.)

[78] *Ibidem*.

Somalia . . . in accordance with the recommendations contained in his [the Secretary-General's] report of 3 March 1993, and in this regard to organize a prompt, smooth and phased transition from UNITAF to UNOSOM II; . . .

Two features of this resolution are relevant for our present discussion. First, the resolution established two objectives for the peacekeeping force to achieve: the 'consolidation, expansion, and maintenance of a secure environment throughout Somalia' and 'the rehabilitation of the political institutions and economy of Somalia'. Second, this resolution provided for the replacement of UNITAF forces with a UN peacekeeping force that, for the first time in UN history, was established with a Chapter VII mandate:[79] that is, it could carry out military enforcement action. Moreover, the Council delegated command and control of UNOSOM II to the Secretary-General's Special Representative for Somalia. Accordingly, the procedural requirements for a delegation of powers, set out in Chapter 4, did not have to be met, since the force was under the direct operational command and control of the UN through the Secretary-General's Special Representative. However, the fact that the force was, potentially, to carry out military enforcement action requires the UN commander, as explained in Chapter 4, to take into account the views of States contributing troops to the force when decisions are being made as to how these forces are to be used in enforcement action. This legal requirement was complied with by the UN Force Commander of UNOSOM II, as there were mechanisms for coordination between the UN and troop-contributing countries that were established.[80]

The major problems which came to beset UNOSOM II started on 5 June 1993 with the attack on UN peacekeepers by Somali forces which resulted in the deaths of over twenty UN peacekeepers. This led the Security Council to pass resolution 837 which authorized the Secretary-General to take all necessary measures to arrest and detain for prosecution those responsible for the attack. The relevant section of the resolution states:

Acting under Chapter VII of the Charter of the United Nations, . . . [the Security Council] Reaffirms that the Secretary-General is authorized under resolution 814 (1993) to take all necessary measures against all those responsible for the armed attacks referred to in paragraph 2 above, to establish the effective authority of UNOSOM II throughout Somalia, including to secure the investigation of their actions and their arrest and detention for prosecution, trial and punishment;

This resolution was the legal basis for subsequent military enforcement action taken by UNOSOM II in their attempts to arrest General Aidid who was widely believed to have ordered the attack.[81] Moreover, military en-

[79] See, for example, Bothe in Simma, *supra* note 4, p. 589.
[80] For a detailed description of these mechanisms, see S/25354, p. 3.
[81] The US representative, for example, stated: 'Today's draft resolution reaffirms the existing authority of UNOSOM II to take strong and forceful action to safeguard international

forcement action was carried out by UNOSOM II in order to achieve, *inter alia*, disarmament of militia loyal to General Aidid.[82] For our present purposes, the major legal issue concerning UNOSOM II was the relationship between the UN Command and the forces from Member States which composed the peacekeeping force. It appears that the Force Commander was not in effective control of several national contingents which, in varying degrees, persisted in seeking orders from their home authorities before executing orders of the Force Commander.[83] It is clear that in such cases, these forces were acting in contravention of resolutions 814 and 837 which expressly delegated the power of command and control over these forces to the Secretary-General's Special Representative.

Moreover, there were forces from UN Member States operating in Somalia who were not, in formal terms, part of UNOSOM II and not therefore under formal UN command or control.[84] The legality of these operations by forces not under the operational command and control of the

forces, to punish those who attack them and to restore security. Appropriate measures include the disarming and detention of persons posing a threat to United Nations forces or obstructing their operations.' (S/PV.3229, p. 8.)

[82] See the Report of the Secretary-General on the implementation of Security Council Resolution 837 (1993), S/26022, 1 July 1993. On 12 June 1993, UNOSOM II initiated military action in south Mogadishu. In a series of air and ground military actions, UNOSOM II removed Radio Mogadishu from control of the United Somali Congress/Somali National Alliance (USC/SNA) who are led by General Mohammed Aidid, and disabled or destroyed militia weapons and equipment in three previously authorized storage sites and a related clandestine military facility. (S/26738, p. 15.) These actions undertaken by UNOSOM II were strongly supported by the Security Council in a Presidential statement issued on 14 June 1993. There was moreover subsequent military enforcement action, using both air strikes and ground forces, which was undertaken by UNOSOM II against USC/SNA militia forces and positions in an attempt to disarm Mogadishu South. (For a detailed description of these actions, see the Report of the Secretary-General on the implementation of Security Council resolution 837 (1993), S/26022, pp. 2–9.)

[83] For a description of such cases, see: S/1994/653, pp. 28–9, 45; and Hirsh, J., and Oakley, R., *Somalia and Operation Restore Hope: Reflections on Peacemaking and Peacekeeping* (1995), p. 119.

[84] As Hirsh and Oakley note: 'When six more Americans were wounded by a landmine explosion on August 22, President Clinton ordered Delta Force commandos, Army Rangers, and a helicopter detachment airlifted to Mogadishu. Though acting in support of the UNOSOM II mandate, they operated under separate US command, reporting to Major General William Garrison of the Joint Special Operations Command, who reported to CENTCOM directly. Their orders were to capture Aidid and senior SNA officials whenever the opportunity arose. Montgomery [Commander of US Forces in Somalia and Deputy UN Force Commander] was to be informed but had no authority over the operations.' (Hirsh and Oakley, *supra* note 83, p. 122.) See also the Report of the Special Commission established pursuant to Security Council resolution 885: S/1994/653, p. 32. Moreover, Lorenz notes that: 'During the last two months of 1993, there were four active military chains of command in Somalia. UNOSOM II reported to UN Headquarters in New York. Three independent US commands reported to USCINCENT at McDill AFB, Florida: US Forces Somalia, JTF Somalia, and the Joint Special Operations Task Force (JSOTF) which reported to the CINC through USSOCCENT. This situation did not lend itself to clear lines of command and control, and made coordination and implementation of ROE difficult.' (Lorenz, F., 'Rules of Engagement in Somalia: Were They Effective?', *Naval Law Review*, 42 (1995), p. 62 at p. 67.)

Secretary-General's Special Representative is highly questionable.[85] The delegation of Chapter VII powers in resolution 837 to carry out military enforcement operations in order to capture and try those responsible for the 5 June action and to carry out disarmament in Somalia was given exclusively to the Secretary-General's Special Representative and the UN Force Commander solely in respect of UNOSOM II. In order for the Special Representative to use forces external to UNOSOM II to carry out military enforcement action, an express delegation of power would be required: to the Secretary-General or his Special Representative to exercize command and control over such a force and to the force itself to enable it to carry out such action.[86] However, nowhere in resolutions 814 or 837 was there such a delegation of power to the Secretary-General or his Special Representative or a delegation of powers to UN Member States to take enforcement action to arrest and detain for trial General Aidid. The Special Representative could not imply the power to use forces external to UNOSOM II from the terms of either resolution, since it involves an implication of power to exercise command and control over a force which does not itself have a legal basis to use force. Moreover, as explained further below, Member States do not possess the competence to use force

---

[85] On 3 Oct. 1993, US Rangers launched an operation in south Mogadishu aimed at capturing a number of General Aidid's senior aides who were suspected of complicity in the 5 June attacks as well as subsequent attacks on UN personnel and facilities. The operation succeeded in apprehending twenty-four suspects, including two key aides to General Aidid. (S/26738, p. 17.) However, during the course of the operation, two US helicopters were shot down by Somali militiamen, and while evacuating the twenty-four USC/SNA detainees the US Rangers came under concentrated fire. Eighteen US soldiers lost their lives and seventy-five were wounded. The Secretary-General noted that the planning and execution of the Ranger operation was decided by US commanders and carried out by US forces that were deployed in support of the UNOSOM II mandate, but who were not under UN command or authority: S/26738, pp. 17–18. Following these events the US reinforced its Quick Reaction Force with a joint task force consisting of air, naval, and ground operations equipped with tanks and armoured vehicles. Subsequently, the US announced its intention to withdraw its forces from Somalia by 31 Mar. 1994. Following this lead, European Governments with contingents serving in UNOSOM II also announced their intention to withdraw their troops by the same date. This effectively saw the end of military enforcement action in Somalia. Subsequently, the Security Council in resolution 885 requested 'that the Secretary-General, under his authority in resolutions 814 (1993) and 837 (1993) . . . suspend arrest actions against those individuals who might be implicated but are not currently detained pursuant to resolution 837 (1993), and make appropriate provision to deal with the situation of those already detained under the provisions of resolution 837 (1993)'. On 17 Jan. 1994, the Secretary-General gave instructions to his Special Representative for Somalia to release the remaining eight detainees. He ordered their release based on a peace agreement reached on 16 Jan. in Mogadishu between the Habr Gedir and Abgal sub-clans, as well as the written and oral reports he received from the independent jurist and former Chief Justice of Zimbabwe, who had been asked to review the cases of the detainees.

[86] In order for such a delegation to have occurred to the Quick Reaction Force and the US Rangers the Council would have had to pass a resolution similar in terms to resolution 794. The one difference would be the purpose for which the powers were being delegated. For the content of resolution 794, see *infra* note 171 *et sequentia* and corresponding text that follows.

under resolution 794, since the passage of resolution 814 terminated the delegation of powers to Member States in this resolution.[87] The external forces in this case would have had to have been contributed to UNOSOM II as an integral part of the force in order for the Force Commander to use them to carry out the objectives specified in resolutions 814 and 837. Accordingly, to the extent that these forces carried out enforcement action under the direction of the Secretary-General Special Representative,[88] or unilaterally, both the Special Representative and UN Member States were acting without a legal mandate. In order to conform with the law in similar situations in the future, either the Security Council would have to delegate Chapter VII enforcement powers directly to UN Member States or Member States would have to contribute their troops to the UN force under, in this case, the UN chain of command.[89]

In any case, the delegation of powers to UNOSOM II under resolution 837 continued until the Council decided in resolution 897 to restrict the mandate of UNOSOM II to more traditional peacekeeping functions thereby terminating its mandate to carry out military enforcement action.

4. The case of Bosnia: the Rapid Reaction Force

The decision to establish a Rapid Reaction Force (RRF) for Bosnia was taken in response to the seizure of 300 UN peacekeepers as hostages at the end of May 1994. The Secretary-General states that the proposal for a RRF would address several aspects of the predicament in which UNPROFOR currently finds itself:

It would in particular provide the Commander of UNPROFOR with well-armed and mobile forces with which to respond promptly to threats to United Nations personnel. It would thus reduce the risk that increasing casualties and harassment might cause the troop-contributing Governments and the Security Council to consider withdrawal. . . . On balance . . . I believe that the proposed reinforcement of UNPROFOR will enhance the Force's ability to continue its humanitarian efforts, with less danger to its personnel than at present, and it is on this basis that I recommend that the Security Council accept the proposal put forward by France, the Netherlands and the United Kingdom.[90]

However, the Secretary-General made clear that the RRF should not be considered as an attempt by the Council to enforce peace in the former

---

[87] See text following *infra* note 188.

[88] In an action on 12 July 1993, the US Quick Reaction Force, in this instance under the direction of UNOSOM II, took part in a disarmament operation together with UNOSOM II: S/26738, p. 16.

[89] Significantly, the US stated, in a change of policy towards participation in UN peacekeeping, that it was willing to keep on some US troops in the UNOSOM II force that was to follow the UNITAF force: see Hirsh and Oakley, *supra* note 83, p. 46.

[90] S/1995/470.

Yugoslavia and that the RRF would be an integral part of UNPROFOR which, as a peacekeeping force, does not have the capacity to carry out military enforcement action.[91] The Secretary-General noted that the UK, France, and The Netherlands had all agreed that the 'RRF would be an integral part of the existing United Nations peace-keeping operation (UNPF/UNPROFOR)'.[92] Accordingly, the 'RRF would be under the existing United Nations chain of command; it would operate under the operational command of the United Nations military commanders in the theatre, who would continue to be under the overall direction of the Secretary-General and his Special Representative'.[93] It was in resolution 998 that the Security Council decided in response to the Secretary-General's proposal 'to authorize an increase in UNPF/UNPROFOR personnel, acting under the present mandate and on the terms set out in the above-mentioned letter [of the Secretary-General]' and further 'authorize[d] the Secretary-General to carry forward the implementation of' the establishment of a RRF to enable UNPF/UNPROFOR to carry out its mandate 'maintaining close contact with the Government of the Republic of Bosnia and Herzegovina and others concerned'.

However, despite these statements it seems clear that the RRF in Bosnia subsequently undertook action that can only be characterized as military enforcement action following the deaths of two French peacekeepers in Sarajevo on 23 July 1994.[94] Units of the RRF—which had earlier established themselves in offensive positions overlooking Sarajevo in order to launch a military response against Bosnian Serb forces should they fire upon UN

---

[91] The Secretary-General states that the mission of the RRF could include: 'emergency actions/responses to assist isolated or threatened United Nations units; helping redeployment of elements of UNPROFOR; and facilitating freedom of movement where necessary'. (S/1995/470.) Specifically, the Secretary-General states '[t]he purposes of the RRF would be to give the commander a capacity between "strong protest and air strikes"; it would increase tactical operational flexibility and would be intended to have a deterrent effect but it would not change the United Nations role to peace-enforcement; the status of UNPROFOR and its impartiality would be unaffected'. (S/1995/470.) Accordingly, the Russian representative expressed the following concern in the Council debates preceding the adoption of the resolution that established the RRF: 'strengthening UNPROFOR's ability to protect the lives and safety of its peace-keepers should in no way make United Nations forces a party to the conflict. It is of paramount importance that the draft resolution clearly calls for the maintenance of UNPROFOR's impartial, peace-keeping nature and for the retention of present decision-making procedures and rules of engagement'. (S/PV.3543, p. 10.) Moreover, the Honduran representative at the same Security Council meeting stated: '[m]y delegation supports this proposal [the establishment of the RRF] not only because its objective is to strengthen UNPROFOR's capacity to fulfil its mandate while reducing the risk to its personnel, but also because, above all, it will continue to be a peace-keeping operation'. (S/PV.3543, p. 12.)

[92] S/1995/470.

[93] *Ibidem.*

[94] This was supported by the Turkish representative who stated in the Security Council: 'The United Nations Force [RRF] in Bosnia and Herzegovina was established as a protection force and has never, from the very outset, been a traditional peace-keeping force.' (S/PV.3543, p. 7.) See also the statement by the representative of Botswana: S/PV.3543, p. 15.

positions or convoys in and around the city[95]—took offensive action as part of a co-ordinated action taken also by NATO airplanes in order to respond to attacks on UN declared safe areas: an operation known as 'Deliberate Force'.[96] RRF artillery and mortar units fired at Bosnian Serb targets, including heavy weapons sites.[97] This provoked a strong reaction by the Russian Government whose representative stated in the Council:

... the active participation of the Rapid Reaction Force in neutralizing Serbian positions clearly exceeds its mandate as set out in resolution 998 (1995). This is no longer about protecting United Nations personnel and humanitarian convoys; it is a virtual participation in military action against one side. I wish to quote from a document distributed by the NATO secretariat at a meeting of the Political Committee of the North Atlantic Cooperation Council:

'In the evening of 5 September, firing was observed in Sarajevo. According to the United Nations evaluation, an exchange of fire, initiated by the forces of the Bosnian Government, had taken place between the two belligerent parties. The Rapid Reaction Force fired warning shots towards the forces of the Bosnian Serbs. The commander of the local forces of the Bosnian Government received a letter containing a warning.'

This approach, I think, very clearly illustrates the fact that the Rapid Reaction Force is no longer impartial, although it remains an integral part of the United Nations peace-keeping operation in Bosnia.[98]

However, this view ignores the fact that the Council in resolution 836 had delegated to UNPROFOR a mandate that included the use of force to protect UN declared safe areas.[99] Thus it was that the US representative stated '[w]hile my Government regrets that air strikes are necessary, we fully support the action taken by the United Nations and NATO to deter further attacks on the safe areas. Those actions are fully authorized by existing Security Council resolutions. It was the Security Council which created the safe areas, and it was the Council that gave the United Nations Protection Force (UNPROFOR) the mandate to deter attacks against them. We believe that the Council must now support UNPROFOR's efforts to implement that mandate.'[100] This is a justifiable approach, since, as

---

[95] Dodd, T., 'War and Peacekeeping in the Former Yugoslavia', *House of Commons Research Paper, 95/100*, 12 Oct. 1995, pp. 15–16.

[96] See *infra* note 50 *et sequentia* and corresponding text in Chapter 6.

[97] Dodd, *supra* note 95. These weapons were used to retaliate against Bosnian Serb positions in mid-August. (*Ibidem,* pp. 15–16.) At the end of the operation approximately 1,000 shells had been fired. (*Ibidem,* p. 18.)

[98] S/3575, pp. 3–4.

[99] See *infra* Section II(1) in Chapter 6.

[100] S/PV.3575, p. 6. More specifically, with regards to the RRF, the representative of Turkey stated: 'For a long time now, the blatant violations of relevant Security Council resolutions on Bosnia and Herzegovina, in particular resolutions 824 (1993) and 836 (1993), have remained unchallenged. ... The long-awaited appropriate response to the aggressor came only after

explained above, Security Council resolutions 836 and 998 do provide a
legal basis for the Rapid Reaction Force being able to participate in military
enforcement action to protect UN declared safe areas.

II. A DELEGATION OF POWERS TO
CARRY OUT A NAVAL INTERDICTION

The delegation by the Council of military enforcement powers to UN
Member States to carry out a naval interdiction is necessary for such action
to be lawful,[101] since, in the absence of such an express authorization, the
threat or actual use of force or even interference against foreign shipping on
the High Seas would in peacetime involve a State's responsibility for the
breach of its obligation to respect the rule of the freedom of the High Seas
as set out, most recently, in Article 87 of the 1982 UN Concretion on the
Law of the Sea (UNCLOS) as well as a violation of Article 2(4) of the
Charter.[102] A violation of Article 2(4) would also take place where the naval
interdiction was being carried out within the territorial sea of the target
State. An express authorization is required to carry out a naval interdiction
even where the Council may have imposed economic sanctions against a
State, since States do not have a right to enforce a Security Council resolution, where such action would be contrary to international law, simply by
virtue of the existence of the resolution.[103] In order for the Council's authorization to confer legality on States' actions when carrying out a naval
interdiction, the authorization will either have to override the State's treaty

another marketplace massacre in Sarajevo. We see the United Nations–North Atlantic Treaty
Organization (NATO) joint operation, belated as it may be, as a very important step in the
right direction. . . . We hold the view that the operation should not be terminated until its
objectives are fully met. The involvement of the Rapid Reaction Force in the operation is also
totally in conformity with the mandate as set out in various Security Council resolutions, in
particular resolution 998 (1995).' (S/PV.3575, p. 16.)

[101] The carrying out of a naval interdiction is only one of a wide range of measures for which
naval forces of Member States may be utilized in order to maintain or restore international
peace and security. See Sands, J., 'Blue Hulls: A Maritime Agenda for Peace', in Mokhtari,
supra note 45, p. 111 *et sequentia*. The Security Council has also delegated its Chapter
VII powers to carry out a naval interdiction to a regional arrangement: see *infra* note 76 in
Chapter 6.

[102] See also Gowlland-Debbas, V., *Collective Responses to Illegal Acts Under International
Law: United Nations Action in the case of Southern Rhodesia* (1990), p. 410; Jones, T., 'The
International Law of Maritime Blockade—A Measure of Naval Economic Interdiction',
Howard Law Journal, 26 (1983), p. 761; and Politakis, G., 'UN Mandated Naval Operations
and the Notion of Pacific Blockade: Comments on Some Recent Developments', *African
Journal of International and Comparative Law*, 6 (1994), p. 173 at p. 193.

[103] As Higgins states: 'There is no entitlement in the hands of individual members of the
United Nations to enforce prior Security Council resolutions by the use of force.' (Higgins,
supra note 31, p. 259.)

law obligations or constitute a valid exception to both Article 2(4) of the Charter and Article 87 of the 1982 UNCLOS.[104]

We recall from Chapter 4 that if a State takes up a delegation of Chapter VII powers, then, in the exercize of these powers, it is not bound by its treaty obligations that conflict with what the Council has mandated.[105] Additionally, or in the alternate, it is contended that States implementing a Council authorized naval interdiction fall, in any case, within the exceptions to the relevant treaty provisions. In the case of Article 87 of the 1982 UNCLOS relating to the freedom of the High Seas, the exception is contained in Article 110(1) which provides: 'Except where acts of interference derive from powers conferred by treaty'. As the States carrying out a naval interdiction are exercizing powers which have been delegated by the Council, under the Charter, then they fall within this exception. Accordingly, Fawcett had earlier argued that the powers of the Council under Chapter VII of the Charter are among the treaty powers envisaged in the exception to the corresponding provision of the 1958 High Seas Convention, Article 22.[106] Moreover, with regard to Article 2(4) of the Charter, the taking of military enforcement action by States pursuant to a Council authorization under Chapter VII of the Charter constitutes an exception to the general prohibition on the use of force by States. The question here, accordingly, is whether the Council has the competence to delegate such powers to Member States, and not whether Member States can lawfully use force pursuant to such a delegation. It is pertinent to recall in this context that, as has already been explained in Chapter 4 above, the Council does possess such a competence. In any case, there has not been an extensive practice of the Council delegating its Chapter VII powers to Member States to carry out a naval interdiction. This has only occurred in three cases: where the Council sought to ensure the implementation of economic sanctions against Southern Rhodesia, Iraq, and Haiti.

1. The case of Southern Rhodesia

An oil embargo was among the measures imposed by Security Council Resolution 217 (1965) in response to the Unilateral Declaration of Independence by the Smith Regime in Southern Rhodesia. This embargo was not mandatory but only recommendatory.[107] After the passage of this

[104] For the latter proposition, see also Gowlland-Debbas, *supra* note 102, p. 410.

[105] See *supra* note 36 and corresponding text in Chapter 4.

[106] Fawcett, J., 'Security Council Resolutions on Rhodesia', *BYIL*, 41 (1965–6), p. 103 at pp. 120–1.

[107] Nkala argues, accordingly, that this embargo was largely ignored. (Nkala, *supra* note 19, p. 91.)

resolution there were unconfirmed reports that two Greek-registered tankers, the *Arietta Venizelos* (later renamed *Joanna V*), and the *Charlton Venus* (later renamed *Manuela*), were being chartered to carry oil to be secretly pumped through the Mozambique–Rhodesia pipeline at Beira.[108] When this became public knowledge, the Greek Government attempted to place pressure on the captain of the *Joanna V* to stop her from proceeding to Beira. Nkala notes that the British Government lost patience with the fact that the Greek Government's efforts were to no avail, and suggested that the ship be stopped by force from reaching Beira, presumably by British naval forces.[109] The Greek Government refused stating: 'no Government would consent to a foreign power intercepting or intimidating merchant ships under its flag'.[110] The Greek Government did, however, state that 'if the United Nations authorizes the British Government to intercept the vessel, we shall respect the decision. However, we cannot give our permission without a United Nations ruling.'[111] Despite the Greek Government's position, a British frigate intercepted the *Joanna V* on the High Seas when it became clear that it was heading towards Beira.[112] Nevertheless, the *Joanna V* was allowed to continue on to Rhodesia since her captain claimed that he would not be discharging his cargo in Beira. Simultaneously, the Greek-registered tanker, *Manuela*, was also heading for Beira.[113] The British Government, determined that a major breach of the oil embargo should not occur, requested that an emergency meeting of the Council be called.

At this meeting, the United Kingdom introduced a draft resolution, adopted as resolution 221 (1966), which '[c]alls upon the Government of the United Kingdom of Great Britain to prevent, by the use of force if necessary, the arrival at Beira of vessels reasonably believed to be carrying oil destined for Southern Rhodesia, and empowers the United Kingdom to arrest and detain the tanker known as the Joanna V upon her departure from Beira in the event her oil cargo is discharged there.' This authorization was sufficient to deter the *Joanna V* from discharging her cargo of oil in Beira, and thus she was not subsequently arrested or detained by the British Navy. It was certainly the view of the UK representative that the authorization of the Council was necessary for the UK to carry out lawfully the naval interdiction. He states:

What I am doing is to seek your authority to respond to that challenge [to the economic sanctions] with vigorous and forthright action. . . . Without that authority,

---

[108] (1965–6) *Keesings Record of World Events*, 21417.
[109] Nkala, *supra* note 19, p. 93.
[110] (1965–6) *Keesings Record of World Events*, 21417.
[111] *Ibidem.*
[112] Nkala, *supra* note 19, p. 93.
[113] *Ibidem*, p. 94.

the United Kingdom Government has to face defiance of the United Nations with its hands tied. The Royal Navy undoubtedly had the physical power to prevent the Joanna V, for instance, from entering Beira. But in this matter my Government has been anxious that at all times its actions should be lawful actions and that it should not risk acting in breach of the law of nations. . . . I therefore ask the Council now, by adopting the draft resolution I propose, to enable the United Kingdom to carry out without fear of illegality the responsibilities which in the Rhodesian situation are ours. I ask the Council, in furtherance of our common cause, and to meet the threat which I have described, to enable the United Kingdom Government to take within the law all steps, including the use of force as the situation may demand, to stop the arrival at Beira of ships taking oil to the rebel regime.[114]

This is consistent with the legal position explained above that Member States cannot seek to carry out a naval interdiction without Council authorization. *In casu*, the Council resolution, as noted above, was necessary for the UK to be able to arrest and detain vessels on the High Seas.[115]

This legalizing effect of the resolution assumes, of course, that the resolution is lawful. The issue of the constitutional basis of the resolution requires, however, further analysis. The authorization in resolution 221 was not mandatory. However, this in itself was not a problem. As explained in Chapter 4 above, the Council can delegate its Chapter VII powers by means of a non-mandatory resolution.[116] The more contentious issue arose from the recommendatory nature of the oil embargo in resolution 217 which resolution 221 sought to enforce. In other words, is it lawful for the Council to delegate Chapter VII powers to a Member State to enforce an oil embargo which other States were not, in strict legal terms, obliged to respect? The simple answer to this apparent dilemma is that such a decision is within the Council's prerogative under the Charter. The Council has a broad (political) discretion under Chapter VII of the Charter to take measures that it deems are necessary for the maintenance or restoration of

---

[114] S/PV.1276, para. 21, *SCOR*, 21st year (1966), pp. 4–5. The notion of a delegation of powers in this case was indicated by the representative of The Netherlands who stated that, in order to enforce the oil embargo, the Council can do no better than 'to confer upon the Government of the United Kingdom the mandatory power and authority it seeks to intercept all vessels that attempt to defy the oil blockade. This specific power is asked by the United Kingdom delegation in the draft resolution now before us . . .' (*Ibidem*, p. 9.)

[115] Accordingly, Nkala states that the British action in seeking a mandate from the Security Council 'was not only desirable, but also probably the only legally correct course of action in the circumstances'. (Nkala, *supra* note 19, p. 113.) See also the statement by the US Government: S/PV.1276, para. 19.

[116] See *supra* note 33 and corresponding text in Chapter 4. Thus Nkala and Akehurst take the view that resolution 221 was only a recommendation which Britain could apply at her discretion: Nkala, *supra* note 19, p. 105; and Akehurst, M., *A Modern Introduction to International Law* (1982), p. 184. Moreover, resolution 221 represents a specific delegation, as opposed to a general delegation, by the Council of its Chapter VII powers to the United Kingdom. This specific delegation of powers is in contradistinction to the general delegation of powers which occurred in the cases of Iraq, the former Yugoslavia, and Haiti which are examined below.

international peace and security. An important feature of these powers is the flexibility that the Council has to move from the use of one power to another within Chapter VII as it deems fit and proper to address a threat to, or breach of, the peace in the circumstances of a particular case. Accordingly, the non-mandatory nature of the oil embargo was not a barrier to the Council subsequently deciding that, in the circumstances, it was necessary to enforce this embargo by military means.[117]

A discussion of the constitutional basis of resolution 221 continues by examining whether resolution 221 represents a delegation by the Council of its powers under Article 42 of the Charter or whether it is part of the implementation of Article 41 measures imposed by the Council against a State. Article 41 of the Charter involves the use of measures 'not involving the use of armed force'; while Article 42 envisages enforcement action that may include 'blockade, and other operations by . . . sea . . . forces of Members of the United Nations'. In order to ascertain which power a resolution falls under will thus depend on whether the resolution envisages the threat or use of force. It seems clear that resolution 221 envisaged the use of force by the United Kingdom in order to arrest and detain, if necessary, those vessels reasonably believed to be carrying oil destined for Southern Rhodesia and is thus most consistent with Article 42 which envisages such action.[118] Accordingly, such action, whether a blockade or not, involves at least the threat of the use of force, and is, thus, not a matter which falls within the purview of Article 41, since this article applies only to 'measures not involving the use of armed force'.[119] It is thus contended that resolution

[117] Higgins justifies the Council resolution in the following manner: 'Quite apart from the Charter, nations are under a general legal obligation not to support unrecognized governments in their rebellion. It can be argued that the sending of oil to the Smith regime, contrary to the express wishes of the constitutional authority, was an international wrong done to the UK. The question then was whether the UK could take action to redress and prevent this third-party support of the illegal government. Since the inception of this Charter—and this has been made clear by the International Court of Justice—unilateral forcible self-help by wronged nations is not permitted. The United Kingdom therefore sought the authorization of the relevant international organ—the Security Council—for such action. Effectively, what happened with the passing of the so-called Beira resolution was that the Security Council authorized an individual nation to take action against third parties supporting a regime in rebellion against its authority; and the means by which this was done was by designating such support of the rebel authorities—especially should it be successful—as a threat to peace.' (Higgins, R., 'International law, Rhodesia, and the UN', *The World Today*, 23 (1967), p. 94 at p. 96.)

[118] See also, for example, the statement by the representative of Argentina: S/PV.1276, *SCOR*, 21st year (1966), p. 11. Moreover, Fawcett states that 'Resolution 221 was unique in expressly authorizing a use of force by a member State outside its jurisdiction and in itself unlawful.' (Fawcett, *supra* note 106, p. 118.) Fawcett argues that under the UN Charter the UK action by the frigate which sent an armed boarding party onto the *Manuela* and compelled her to alter her course away from Beira was no other than the use of armed force. (*Ibidem*, p. 119.)

[119] The Charter also in Article 2(4) makes no distinction between the threat or actual use of force. Cf. Politakis, *supra* note 102, p. 197; and Fielding, L., 'Maritime Interception: Centrepiece of Economic Sanctions in the New World Order', *Louisiana Law Review*, 53 (1993), p. 1191 at p. 1241.

221 represents a delegation by the Council of its powers under Article 42 of the Charter. As Higgins has stated: 'It is hard to see that the action by the United Kingdom at Beira and the action of the US fleet in the Gulf are not "blockade . . . or other operations" within the meaning of Article 42.'[120] Moreover, the *Repertory of Practice of United Nations Organs* states that the authorization of the use of force in resolution 221 'might be deemed as implicitly referring to Article 42'.[121] However, Fawcett argues that the Council could not have invoked Article 42 before applying its mandatory measures under Article 41 and testing their efficacy and thus ascertaining that non-military measures under Article 41 would be inadequate to restore peace in the particular situation.[122] After reviewing the relevant articles of Chapter VII, Fawcett concludes that '[t]here remains, as the basis for it [resolution 221], a recommendation under Article 39'.[123] However, this is not the correct legal view, since, as we have already noted, the Council enjoys a broad prerogative under the Charter to move from the use of one Chapter VII power to another. *In casu*, the Council may, if it wishes, resort to military measures under Article 42 at any time if it is satisfied that the situation calls for the immediate use of force.[124]

Nevertheless, other commentators argue that resolution 221 could not have been based on Article 42, since the Security Council Members firmly rejected the inclusion of any specific references to either Articles 41 or 42 in the resolution itself; and that whilst collective action under Articles 41 and 42 is usually associated with mandatory action, resolution 221 clearly places no such obligation on Member States. The conclusion from this, according to a leading commentator, is that resolution 221 is based on a recommendation under Article 39.[125] However, the fact that States rejected the inclusion of an express reference being made to Article 42 in the resolution and that the resolution cannot require the United Kingdom to take up the delegation of power, does not constitute a barrier to the constitutional basis of resolution 221 being grounded in Article 42. The lack of an express reference to an article of the Charter does not mean the Council did not adopt a resolution on the basis of that article. In fact Article 42 has never been expressly referred to in any Council resolution, despite having been the

---

[120] Higgins, *supra* note 31, p. 260. See also Kaikobad, *supra* note 13, p. 358.

[121] *Repertory of Practice of United Nations Organs, Supp. No. 3*, vol. 2, p. 238. Similarly, Nkala concludes that '[t]he most likely basis for paragraph 5 seems to have been Article 42 which deals with military enforcement measures'. (Nkala, *supra* note 19, p. 103.)

[122] Fawcett, *supra* note 106, p. 120. See also Szasz, *supra* note 41, p. 26.

[123] Fawcett, *supra* note 106, p. 120.

[124] See also Nkala, *supra* note 19; and Simma, *supra* note 4, p. 628 at p. 631.

[125] Gowlland-Debbas, *supra* note 102, pp. 417–18. Gowlland-Debbas had, however, earlier stated: 'The resolution plainly authorizes the United Kingdom to utilize coercive or enforcement measures in the form of a limited use of force, measures similar to those envisaged in Article 42, particularly since the objective, as seen below, is to end the threat to international peace.' (Gowlland-Debbas, *supra* note 102, p. 408.)

constitutional basis for several resolutions. Moreover, in the case of Article 39 the Council has made numerous resolutions based on this article without making an express reference to the article.[126] With regard to the second point of objection, the lack of an obligation to carry out military enforcement action does not in itself mean, as noted above in Chapter 4, that such action could not be authorized under Article 42.[127]

Even if the contention that resolution 221 is based on Article 42 is not accepted and it is found that resolution 221 was based on Article 39, this does not change the consequence that the resolution represents a delegation by the Council to a State of its power to carry out military enforcement action. A competence that the Council, as explained in Chapter 4 above, does possess.[128] Importantly, the Council complied in substance with the conditions for a delegation of Chapter VII powers. The Council specified clearly the objective for which powers were being delegated: 'to prevent, by the use of force if necessary, the arrival at Beira of vessels reasonably believed to be carrying oil destined for Southern Rhodesia'. Although the Security Council did not in the case of Southern Rhodesia impose an obligation on the UK to report back to the Council on the exercize of the delegated powers, the UK Government did, in any case, keep the Council sufficiently informed so that the Council could exercize supervision over the way in which the delegated powers were being used.[129] What the example of a delegation by the Council of its Chapter VII powers in the case of Southern Rhodesia shows is that the broad political discretion the Council possesses in respect of the way it may choose to exercize its Chapter VII powers also applies to its decision to delegate these powers.[130]

2. The case of Iraq

In response to Iraq's invasion of Kuwait on 2 August 1990, the Council, in resolution 661, imposed mandatory economic sanctions against Iraq and occupied Kuwait. The Council established a sanctions committee to monitor the implementation of the sanctions regime by States. Subsequently, the US and UK, whose naval forces were already deployed in the Gulf, stated that their warships would be used to prevent any violations of UN sanc-

---

[126] See 'Commentary to Article 39', in Cot and Pellet, *supra* note 4, p. 651 *et sequentia*.

[127] See *supra* note 33 and corresponding text in Chapter 4.

[128] See *supra* Section I in Chapter 4. Accordingly, the arguments against the British draft resolution did not in any way challenge the competence of the Council to delegate the power to carry out a naval interdiction to the UK: they were political and not legal objections: see S/PV.1276 and S/PV.1277.

[129] See, for example, the following provisional verbatim records of Security Council meetings: S/PV.1274–7.

[130] Moreover, the proposed amendments to the British draft which would have called upon Britain to use force to deal with the situation in Rhodesia were rejected by the Council. (S/PV.1277, paras. 174–8, *SCOR* (1966), pp. 36–8.)

tions. The US Government stated that the legal basis of the action would be the right of self-defence: in particular, the right of collective self-defence being exercized at the request of the legitimate Government of Kuwait.[131] The examination of the lawfulness of such action is beyond the scope of this present study.

However, in any case the legality of the naval interdiction in order to enforce resolution 661 was put on firm ground with the passage of Security Council resolution 665. The initial US draft resolution which proposed that resolution 665 should include a reference to such 'minimum use of force as may be necessary to prevent maritime trade in breach of the embargo' was rejected by the Soviets and the Chinese.[132] Freedman and Karsh note that the Chinese and the Soviets 'refused to accept a reference to the "minimum use of force" which could be a matter for interpretation ... Instead, they preferred to spell out precisely the nature of the authority given by the UN.'[133] Moreover, the 'non-aligned members' prepared a draft which would have in express terms mandated the 'active involvement of the Secretary-General' and required 'accountability to the Security Council'.[134] All of these concerns were reflected to a degree in the adoption by the Security Council of resolution 665 which provides, in relevant part, the following:

[The Security Council] [c]alls upon those Member States co-operating with the Government of Kuwait which are deploying maritime forces to the area to use such measures commensurate to the specific circumstances as may be necessary under the authority of the Security Council to halt all inward and outward maritime shipping in order to inspect and verify their cargoes and destinations and to ensure

---

[131] Contained in UN Doc. S/21537, 16 Aug. 1990. The Kuwaiti Government notified the Secretary-General of its request for assistance in the following terms: 'In the exercize of its inherent right of individual and collective self-defence and pursuant to Article 51 of the Charter of the United Nations, Kuwait should like to notify you that it has requested some nations to take such military or other steps as are necessary to ensure the effective and prompt implementation of Security Council resolution 661.' (S/21498, 13 Aug. 1990.) The Kuwaiti request for assistance satisfies the requirement stated in the *Nicaragua* case that for States to be able to exercize their right to collective self-defence on behalf of another State, there must be an express request for assistance: *Nicaragua* case, *ICJ Reports* (1986), p. 14 at pp. 104–5. See also the statement by the US Government: S/21537.

[132] Freedman, L., and Karsh, E., *The Gulf Conflict 1990–1991* (1993), p. 146.

[133] *Ibidem*, p. 149. Moreover, these States rejected the following recommendation of paragraph 1 of the initial draft resolution proposed by the US: 'that Member States should take all necessary action in accordance with the Charter (i.e. under Article 51) including use of such air, sea or land forces as may be necessary to ensure complete compliance (with Resolution 660–664)'. As Freedman and Karsh stated: 'Since this would essentially mean [the first US draft proposal] a UN umbrella for national actions, the American initiative soon ran into difficulties. China was unhappy with this formula, which seemed designed to give the Americans carte blanche to take whatever military action they chose. If the Administration wanted to avoid a Chinese veto—or even abstention—then some limits on its freedom of action were to be accepted.' (*Ibidem*, p. 146.)

[134] Freudenschuß, *supra* note 36, p. 496.

strict implementation of the provisions related to such shipping as laid down in Resolution 661 (1990).

This resolution represents a delegation by the Council to Member States of its power under Article 42 to 'take such action by . . . sea . . . forces as may be necessary to maintain or restore international peace and security. Such action [including] . . . blockade . . . by sea . . . [by] forces of Members of the United Nations.' It seems clear from the debates in the Council meeting when the resolution was adopted, that the Members of the Council considered that they were acting under Article 42 of the Charter, and thus that force may be used to achieve the objectives stipulated in the resolution.[135] For example, the Colombian representative in the debate preceding the adoption of resolution 665 stated the following:

We are under no illusion that when the Council comes to vote on this draft resolution it will be establishing a naval blockade, even though it may not say so, and that—though the Council may not say so either—it is acting pursuant to Article 42 of the Charter.[136]

Accordingly, Murphy contends that 'the statements of most of the Security Council members during the passage of Resolution 665 reveal a belief that the Security Council was either delegating a power to states or authorizing enforcement measures. Consequently, Resolution 665 is probably best viewed not as an affirmation of an independent right to self-defense, but rather as itself generating a right to take forcible action.'[137]

There is, nonetheless, a cogent argument made by several authorities that the constitutional basis of resolution 665 is found not exclusively in either Articles 41 and 42. Ralph Zacklin, for example, states:

la résolution 665 (1990), pourrait-on dire, est délibérément ambiguë et semble indiquer que, dans cette résolution, le Conseil de sécurité a combiné d'une manière

---

[135] See, for example, the statement by the US representative: S/PV.2938, p. 26; and Weller, *supra* note 41, p. 22. Cf., however, the Chinese in accordance with their traditional approach to issues relating to the use of force: S/PV.2938, pp. 53, 54–5.

[136] UN Doc. S/PV.2938, p. 21. Cf. Fielding in respect of the classification by the Colombian representative of the authorized action as a blockade. Fielding contends that the interception in the Gulf was not a blockade for its objective was not to block the enemy coast 'for the purpose of preventing ingress and egress of vessels. The interception was directed at cargo, not ships, and may be considered a use of the right of visit and search in the further development of the law of contraband.' (Fielding, *supra* note 119, p. 1218.)

[137] Murphy, S., 'Collective Security After the Cold War', *Columbia Journal of Transnational Law*, 32 (1994), p. 201 at p. 228. Cf. the statement by the British representative after the adoption of resolution 665: 'Tonight the international community has chosen the best course for dealing with such maritime breaches of economic sanctions, but I must remind the Council that sufficient legal authority to take action already exists under Article 51 of the Charter and the request which we and others have received from the Government of Kuwait. If necessary, we will use it.' (S/PV.2938, p. 48.) It seems that the point being made is that sufficient authority existed in any case to carry out such naval interdiction regardless of the additional basis under resolution 665.

novatrice les diverses possibilités offertes par le Chapitre VII, aboutissant ainsi à une mesure qui se situe entre les Articles 41 et 42.[138]

Whatever, the exact constitutional basis, it seems clear that a delegation of certain of the Council's powers under Article 42 were involved with the passage of resolution 665. Lavalle, however, takes the contrary view when he states:

But this liberal interpretation of the Charter [that there can be a delegation by the Council of its Chapter VII powers] cannot provide a basis for the use of force under Resolution 665 (1990). For one thing it is doubtful that the interpretation is intrinsically sound. Coercive action involving the use of force pursuant to a delegation of authority by the Security Council based on Article 48 would amount to an intermediate category between the decentralized (but provisional) system of Article 51 and the largely centralized scheme that is the subject of the first sentence of Article 42. A construction of the Charter allowing such action would have such far-reaching implications that it does not appear reasonable to accept it in the absence of perfectly explicit language supporting it. Particularly since the construction is by no means the only way to give effect to Article 48, which can very well be taken to be no more than a complement to Article 42 as a whole and to Article 43, from which provisions it could accordingly not be separated.[139]

Moreover, Lavalle argues that 'even if the validity of the interpretation were assumed, it would be difficult to rely on it to demonstrate that the use of force under Resolution 665 (1990) is constitutional. For this resolution provides that measures taken under it by the armed forces to which it refers are subject to the authority of the Council, which, even if that authority could properly be characterized as nominal, is hardly consistent with the view that the Council meant to delegate its power to use force.'[140] However, this position is unpersuasive, since, as already explained in some detail above in Chapter 4, the Council does posses the competence to be able to delegate its Chapter VII powers to Member States.[141] Interestingly, one of

---

[138] Zacklin, R., 'Les Nations Unies et la crise du Golfe', in *Les aspects juridiques de la crise et de la guerre du Golfe* (Stern, B., ed.) (1991), at pp. 67–8. Moreover, Politakis impliedly adopts this position when he states: 'The UN-authorised naval action was aimed solely at the strict implementation of trade sanctions. The purpose was to discourage sanctions-breaking, not to engage the aggressor. It was all about certifying global compliance with UN decisions rather than setting up an offensive against the international wrongdoer. Yet, military means were mobilised and armed force was occasionally used. In that sense, it should cause little wonder if the embargo-enforcing resolutions were found to venture in uncharted waters halfway between economic sanctions and military enforcement. Enforcing a maritime embargo simply shares elements of both, without being squarely identifiable with either. It possesses an intrinsically dual character as the term economic warfare *per se* amply denotes.' (Politakis, *supra* note 102, pp. 197–8.) See also: Verhoeven, J., 'Etats allies ou Nations Unies? L'O.N.U. face au conflit entre l'Irak et le Koweït', *Annuaire Français Droit Internationale*, 36 (1990), p. 167.

[139] Lavalle, *supra* note 49, pp. 24–6.

[140] *Ibidem*, p. 26.

[141] See *supra* Section I in Chapter 4.

the essential characteristics of the process of delegation of powers, which Lavalle uses as an argument against the Council's competence to delegate such powers, is that the action is collective and centralized in nature, but decentralized in implementation.[142] In fact, as also explained in Chapter 4, one of the important safeguards on such a delegation of powers is that the exercize of those powers should always be subject to the overall authority and control of the Council,[143] yet this is identified by Lavalle as a reason why resolution 665 could not be considered as a delegation of powers.

There was, nevertheless, considerable opposition expressed to the resolution by Cuba and Yemen.[144] There were two main arguments put forward. First, that the commander of the forces carrying out the naval interdiction should have been appointed by the Security Council. Second, the objective of the Council is vague and that when this is combined with the lack of specification of the area of operation, it could mean that enforcement action may be undertaken anywhere in the world.[145]

As to the first contention, the fact that the Council did not appoint the commander of forces exercizing delegated powers is not a legal barrier to the lawful delegation of Chapter VII powers. As explained in Chapter 4 above, the Council can delegate to Member States the competence to use force as well as command and control powers over a military enforcement force; leaving it up to those States which take up the delegation of powers to appoint a commander. In such a resolution the Council implicitly delegates to Member States the power to assume command and control of their forces when carrying out the military enforcement action. If Member States then decide to delegate, in turn, this command and control to a single Member State this is within the scope of their delegated powers. What is, however, necessary is that the Council retain overall authority and control of the operation: a requirement which is adequately provided for, in fact in express terms, by resolution 665.[146]

The argument that the area in respect of which the naval interdiction is imposed is 'so ill-defined that the zone could extend all round the world' is far-fetched. The resolution states in express terms that measures taken must be 'commensurate to the specific circumstances'. In any case, it would seem that Security Council resolutions authorizing the use of force must be

---

[142] See *supra* notes 16–19 and corresponding text in Chapter 4.

[143] See *supra* note 20 in Chapter 4.

[144] Unsurprisingly, the Iraqi representative also argued that resolution 665 was unlawful: S/PV.2938, p. 71.

[145] S/PV.2938, pp. 13–15, 16. See also the statement by the representative of Yemen in the Council. (S/PV.2938, pp. 8–10, 11.)

[146] See, for example, the statement by the representative of Ethiopia. (S/PV.2938, p. 52.) See also Weller who contends that resolution 665 makes it clear that 'the operation was undertaken under the authority of the United Nations, rather than in the exercize of the right of individual and collective self-defence'. (Weller, *supra* note 41, p. 22.) Cf. Freudenschuß, *supra* note 36, p. 524.

interpreted having regard to the requirements of proportionality as it exists in both *jus ad bellum* and *jus in bello*.[147] This element of proportionality restricts in this case both the scope of measures and the area of operation in which force may be used: the latter being limited to the region which is the subject of the Council resolution. This was the approach taken by the US Government which chose unilaterally to restrict the area of operations to,

include the Strait of Hormuz, Strait of Tiran, and other choke points, key ports and oil pipeline terminals. Specifically Persian Gulf interception efforts will be concentrated in international waters south of 27 degrees north latitude; Red Sea interception efforts will be conducted in international waters north of 22 degrees north latitude.[148]

Accordingly, Fielding argues that the measures taken to enforce interception as part of the Persian Gulf interception process satisfy the 'commensurate to the specific circumstances' requirement in resolution 665,[149] since controls were built into the process to allow the minimum possible application of force needed.[150]

Nonetheless, there was legitimate concern expressed in the Council that the delegation of powers conform with the requisite legal requirements. Accordingly, the Finnish representative emphasized in the Council the importance of the delegation being exercized only to attain the Council's stated objectives:

The new resolution now adopted . . . is a decision without precedent and with far-reaching implications. Therefore any concrete action by the naval forces concerned will require close attention to ensure that they serve the purposes intended by the Council. We see the new measures as strictly limited to the framework of resolution 661 (1990), strengthening its implementation.[151]

However, in the case of resolution 665, the objective was adequately specified: it was limited to enforcement of the economic sanctions imposed by resolution 661.[152] This designation of a clear objective was of considerable

---

[147] See also Greenwood, C., 'The relationship between ius ad bellum and ius in bello', *Review of International Studies*, 9 (1983), p. 221 at p. 223.

[148] Special Warning No. 80 issued by the United States Department of the Navy, 17, Aug. 1990, as reproduced in Lauterpacht, E., Greenwood, C., Weller, M., and Bethlehem, D., eds., *The Kuwait Crisis: Basic Documents* (1991) p. 248. Interestingly, it was precisely the fact that the zone of operations was not specified by the Council which Fielding identifies as an advantage of the resolution: *ibidem,* p. 1222.

[149] *Ibidem,* p. 1227. Moreover, Fielding states: 'The interception provides a controlled, limited, and highly precise enforcement tool which is reasonable and acceptable to the world community. Regardless of the discretion given to intercepting nations under Resolution 665 as to the area, time, and use of force, the interception was in form designed to apply the least possible use of force in the least offensive and most controlled manner possible.' (*Ibidem.*)

[150] *Ibidem,* p. 1219.

[151] S/PV.2938, p. 47. See also the statement by the representative of France: S/PV.2938, p. 32.

[152] The practical consequences of this were important. Accordingly, Fielding states: 'The objectives were clarified, publicized to the target state and its citizenry, and presented as the

importance in rendering the delegation of powers in this case as being in conformity with the legal framework that governs a delegation of powers.

The source of concern for the Colombian representative was the apparent lack of accountability for the exercize of the delegated powers.[153] However, this concern was in theory addressed adequately by paragraph 4 of resolution 665 which provides:

[The Council] [f]urther requests the States concerned to co-ordinate their actions in pursuit of the above paragraphs of this resolution using as appropriate mechanisms of the Military Staff Committee and after consultation with the Secretary-General to submit reports to the Security Council and its Committee established under resolution 661 (1990) to facilitate the monitoring of the implementation of this resolution; . . .

The Council thus indicated in express terms that it would be monitoring the implementation of the resolution and that in order to facilitate this it required the States exercizing the delegated Chapter VII powers to make reports to the Council on the exercize of delegated power.[154] However, the States carrying out the naval interdiction did not as such submit reports to the Council. This represents a breach of a condition of the delegation. This

quid pro quo for termination of the interception. The objectives designated were short, quickly attainable, and within the power of Iraq, the target state. There was a clear relationship between the sanction and the remedy, with the onus clearly upon the target state. The burden and the blame for the deprivation under the interception operation was shifted to Iraq for it was made clear to Iraq that upon the withdrawal of forces and the restoration of the legitimate Government of Kuwait, the interception operation would be discontinued. This strategy made the exercize more palatable to the world at large and was beneficial for publicity or propaganda purposes. Further, while the goals were multiple, they were of a limited nature and remained focused on an immediate primary purpose, the liberation of Kuwait.' (Fielding, *supra* note 119, pp. 1228–9.)

[153] After noting that the resolution authorizes the use of force, the Colombian representative stated: 'That neither worries nor frightens us, but we wish to be candid: We feel concern about other points of the draft resolution; we share some of the anxieties expressed by the Permanent Representatives of Yemen and Cuba over the fact that in this draft resolution the Security Council is delegating authority without specifying to whom. Nor do we know where that authority is to be exercized or who receives it. Indeed, whoever does receive it is not accountable to anyone.' (S/PV.2938, pp. 22–5.)

[154] Moreover, the US representative sought to allay these fears by stating in the Council the following: 'The United States has vigorously sought and fully supports collective efforts to respond to this crisis. It supports collective efforts to enforce the trade sanctions strictly. United States naval forces, in co-ordination with other naval forces in the area, would use such minimum force only as necessary to accomplish that purpose. In accordance with its responsibilities under this resolution and at the request of the legitimate Government of Kuwait, the Government of the United States will co-ordinate its actions with those of the many other nations that have sent naval forces to the region. . . . We are also ready to discuss an appropriate role in this process for the Military Staff Committee. This new resolution—665 (1990)—addresses the application of the mandatory sanctions of resolution 661 (1990), specifically against maritime shipping. It lends the full weight and authority of the Security Council and, through it, the community of nations to the efforts of States that are deploying maritime forces to ensure that the sanctions are respected. (S/PV.2938, p. 31.)

is of considerable concern, since the reporting requirement was intended as the main way by which the Council could be kept sufficiently informed of the exercize of its delegated powers so that it could, if it wished, change the way in which these powers were being delegated.[155]

The provision in resolution 665 that States co-ordinate their actions with the Military Staff Committee was not mandatory. This is indicated by the use of the phrase 'using as appropriate' in the resolution when referring to the use of the mechanisms of the Military Staff Committee, which gives the Member States concerned considerable discretion in terms of deciding whether these are to be used at all. The use of the Military Staff Committee was not a condition specified by the Council for the lawful exercize by Member States of its delegated Chapter VII powers. The language in the resolution was broad enough to give the US and UK the discretion to use force without having to resort in legal terms to direction from the Military Staff Committee.[156]

3. The case of Haiti

In response to the *coup d'état* in Haiti, which saw the overthrow of the democratically elected Government of President Aristide, the Security

---

[155] Accordingly, Lavalle is highly critical of the naval interdiction operation in the Gulf. He states: 'But not only has neither the Council nor the Committee received any report under Resolution 665 (1990); the Council has not even received full information as to which States have deployed naval forces in the area and how those forces coordinated their activities. In addition, neither the composition of the naval forces deployed nor particulars as to what they have done have been brought to the Council's notice.' (Lavalle, *supra* note 49, pp. 24–5.)

[156] Cf. the initial view of the French Government which took the position that each act of 'coercion' would require resort to the Security Council and presumably the Military Staff Committee: see 'Naval Blockade Endorsed', *UN Chronicle*, 17 Dec. 1990. It thus seems clear that the express reference to a role for the Military Staff Committee was the result of a political compromise between States which desired full UN control, such as the former Soviet Union and Malaysia (see, for example, the statement by the Malaysian representative: S/PV.2938, p. 37), and States which preferred forces deployed unilaterally under national command. Fielding states: 'Even though the military staff committee never became active, the contemplated use of these structures permitted compromises to be made and maintained the fragile coalition by allowing the Security Council a continuing role of monitoring, reviewing, and advising regarding use of force.' (Fielding, *supra* note 119, p. 1231.) In any case, the mention by the resolution of an appropriate role for the Military Staff Committee was of no consequence. Although the Military Staff Committee met, they did not attempt to interfere or in any way exert control over the US-led Coalition Command Structure regarding naval operations in the Gulf. (See also White, N., *Keeping the Peace* (1993), p. 105.) The representative of the former Soviet Union stated: '. . . Our unambiguous support for the resolutions of the Security Council reflects the Soviet Union's intention to act exclusively within the framework of collective efforts to settle this crisis. . . . It is also important that the Security Council make full use of the opportunities afforded by the machinery of the Military Staff Committee and of the Committee established under resolution 661 (1990).' (S/PV.2938, p. 43.) Significantly, however, at the end of a routine fortnightly meeting of the Military Staff Committee held the next day, the Soviet delegate merely distributed copies of this statement and asked his colleagues to reflect on it. (Freudenschuß, *supra* note 36, p. 492 at p. 494.)

Council in resolution 841 imposed economic sanctions against Haiti. The Council, acting under Chapter VII, made the determination that 'in these unique and exceptional circumstances, the continuation of this situation threatens international peace and security in the region' and then imposed economic sanctions against Haiti which were consistent with those imposed earlier by the Organization of American States.[157]

The subsequent conclusion of the New York Island Agreement, between President Aristide and the leader of the *coup*, saw the Council in resolution 861 suspend with immediate effect the oil and arms embargo against Haiti. The Council did, however, state in this resolution that it would reimpose sanctions if the terms of the Governors Island Agreement were not fully implemented.[158] The Secretary-General, in a report to the Security Council dated 13 October 1993, pointed to a number of violations of the undertakings entered into by the *coup* leaders and their general unwillingness to fulfil the commitments of the Governors Island Agreement.[159] Accordingly, the Secretary-General states: 'I consider it necessary, in accordance with resolution 861 (1993), to terminate the suspension of the measures set out in paragraphs 5 to 9 of resolution 841 (1993).'[160] The Security Council adopted this recommendation when in resolution 873 it decided to re-impose its oil and arms embargo against Haiti. The Council in resolution 875 provided for the implementation of these sanctions when, acting under Chapters VII and VIII of the Charter, it '[c]alls upon Member States, acting nationally or through regional agencies or arrangements, cooperating with the legitimate Government of Haiti, to use such measures commensurate with the specific circumstances as may be necessary under the authority of the Security Council to ensure strict implementation of the provisions of resolutions 841 (1993) and 873 (1993) relating to the supply of petroleum or petroleum products or arms and related materiel of all types, and in particular to halt all inward maritime shipping as necessary in order to inspect and verify their cargoes and destinations'.

The reason for the imposition of this naval interdiction is, as stipulated by the resolution, the effective enforcement of the economic sanctions imposed earlier by the Council which are aimed at ensuring the implementation by the military authorities in Haiti of the terms of the Governors Island Agreement.[161] The clear stipulation of the reason for the delegation of powers is important when ascertaining the lawfulness of the delegation.

---

[157] The earlier OAS sanctions were not binding on Haiti: see Sarooshi, *supra* note 75, p. 16.

[158] For measures taken by the Council to ensure implementation of this agreement, see *infra* Section V(1).

[159] See S/26573, 13 Oct. 1993.

[160] *Ibidem*, para. 10.

[161] See statement by the representatives of Spain (S/PV.3293, p. 12) and Brazil (S/PV.3293, p. 23). See in respect of further Security Council action to ensure implementation of this Agreement, *infra* Section V(1).

Moreover, we recall from Chapter 4 that upon the fulfilment of this objective the delegation of powers will be automatically terminated. This conditional nature of the delegation of powers was reiterated by the representative of Brazil who stated in the Council:

The decision taken today can be understood only as a means to ensure the strict implementation of the sanctions measures previously imposed by this Council with relation to the supply to Haiti of petroleum, petroleum products, arms and related material. It is thus clear that the authorization given in operative paragraph 1 of the resolution adopted today is restricted in scope, space and time by the clearly limited purpose which constitutes its *raison d'être* and is intended to have effect only until those sanctions measures are suspended or terminated.[162]

The express statement by the Council that the exercize of delegated powers are under the 'authority of the Security Council' is important in finding that the resolution is a lawful exercize by the Council of its competence to delegate its Chapter VII powers. An important element of this authority and control is the imposition of a reporting requirement on the States exercizing delegated powers. There is no reporting requirement stipulated in resolution 875. However, this is, it may be argued, an implicit condition of the delegation of powers, since it is necessary for the Council to be able to exercize effective command and control over the use of its delegated Chapter VII powers. This was recognized by the representative of China who stated in the Council after voting in favour of the adoption of resolution 875: 'in carrying out measures authorised by the resolution, countries should take only action commensurate with the specific situations prevailing at the time, strengthen coordination with the efforts of the Secretary-General and his Special Representative and keep the Security Council informed on a regular basis'.[163] This was subsequently recognized by the Council in resolution 917.

In resolution 917 the Security Council decided to expand the sanctions regime imposed against Haiti, in particular the 'illegal authorities' in the country. The Council in reaffirming the delegation of powers to Member States in resolution 875 to carry out a naval interdiction added two elements to the delegation. First, it authorized States to halt outward shipping, as necessary, to ensure compliance with the expanded sanctions regime: resolution 875 only gave States the power to halt inward bound maritime shipping. Second, the Council in resolution 917 expressly provides for a reporting requirement when it *'calls upon* Member States . . . to ensure that the Committee established pursuant to resolution 841 (1993) [the Sanctions Committee] is kept regularly informed'. Accordingly, the Council has in this case delegated part of its supervisory function to its subsidiary organ, the Sanctions Committee. However, the appropriateness of such a body

---

[162] S/PV.3293, p. 24.   [163] S/PV.3293, p. 18.

carrying out such a supervisory function in the light of its general mandate is questionable. In any case it is unclear to what extent resolution 917 envisages that the Committee should carry out such a supervisory role in respect of the naval interdiction. Paragraph 14 of resolution 917, which sets out the tasks the Sanctions Committee is to perform, nowhere mentions the supervision of the carrying out, on behalf of the Security Council, of the naval interdiction. In terms of the supervision of the carrying out of the naval interdiction, it suffices to note that the Council made provision in resolution 917 such as to ensure that it possessed sufficient information to be able to effectively excercize its authority and control when it deems necessary. In such a case it is to be expected that the Secretary-General would inform the Security Council of any issues, in his opinion, that arise concerning the naval interdiction. The Security Council, by use of these two channels of reporting, seemed to be aware of the measures being taken and by whom in carrying out the naval interdiction.[164]

III. A DELEGATION OF POWERS TO ACHIEVE HUMANITARIAN OBJECTIVES

A delegation by the Council of its Chapter VII powers for the achievement of humanitarian objectives constitutes, in legal terms, a form of UN authorized humanitarian intervention. It is not, however, always going to be the same as traditional humanitarian intervention, since this is defined as military and non-military action 'to stop the gross and widespread violation of human rights occurring within a state; and for that reason it has traditionally been directed against the authority in control of the country in question'.[165] While in the case of a Security Council delegation of Chapter VII powers action may be taken against an authority in control of a certain territory, the objectives, however, which have been specified by the Council often do not involve the stopping, as such, of the cause of the gross and widespread violation of human rights but have been for other humanitarian purposes; for example, ensuring the delivery of humanitarian assistance.

Nonetheless, the Council has attempted to deal with humanitarian crises by using the common technique of delegating its Chapter VII powers to Member States to carry out and command military enforcement action in order to achieve a variety of objectives. For this to occur, the Council needs

---

[164] See also the 'Report by the Secretary-General to the Security Council', dated 20 June 1994, S/1994/742, para. 10.

[165] Sarooshi, *supra* note 75, p. 1. The legality of such unilateral humanitarian intervention by States is doubtful. (See Brownlie, I., 'Humanitarian Intervention', in *Law and Civil War in the Modern World* (Norton-Moore, J., ed.) (1974), p. 217 at pp. 217–18; and Sarooshi, *ibidem,* p. 2.) However, what is clear is that the Council has the competence to render humanitarian intervention by States lawful. (Sarooshi, *ibidem,* pp. 2–4.)

to link gross violations of human rights occurring within a country to a threat to, or breach of, international peace and security. In other words, the Council must make an Article 39 determination:[166] a necessary prerequisite for the Council to be able to use or even delegate its Chapter VII powers.[167]

This section will examine those cases in which the Council has made such an Article 39 determination and has delegated its Chapter VII military enforcement powers to Member States to achieve a humanitarian objective within a State.

1. The delivery of humanitarian assistance in Somalia

The lack of law and order in Somalia meant that humanitarian assistance was not being delivered effectively to the civilian population. Thus in resolution 751 the Security Council set up a peacekeeping force, the United Nations Operation in Somalia (UNOSOM), which had as one of its main objectives the protection of humanitarian assistance operations. However, the continuing lack of safe conditions for the delivery of humanitarian assistance in Somalia saw the Secretary-General in a letter to the Security Council make five alternative proposals in order to enable the establishment of a secure environment for humanitarian relief operations in Somalia as soon as possible.[168] The first proposal of the Secretary-General involved the delegation by the Security Council of its Chapter VII powers to Member States to establish a secure environment within Somalia. The Secretary-General mentioned in connection with his first proposal the offer by the United States to organize and lead such an operation. However, he contends in his report that if this option were to be favoured by the Council then his 'advice would be that the Council should seek to agree with the Member States who would undertake the operation on ways of recognizing the fact that it had been authorized by the Security Council and that the Security Council therefore had a legitimate interest in the manner in which it was carried out'.[169] There was some emphasis placed by the Secretary-General on the Council making clear that the operation would be under the Council's overall authority and control.[170]

It was in essence this first proposal of the Secretary-General that was given express endorsement by the Security Council in resolution 794, which, in operative paragraph 10, states:

---

[166] See also Higgins, *supra* note 31, p. 255; and Alston, P., 'The Security Council and Human Rights', *Australian Year Book of International Law*, 13 (1992), p. 107 at pp. 130–4.
[167] See *supra* note 43 and corresponding text in Chapter 1.
[168] S/24868.
[169] *Ibidem*, p. 5.
[170] *Ibidem.*

Acting under Chapter VII of the Charter of the United Nations, [the Security Council] Authorizes the Secretary-General and Member States cooperating to implement the offer referred to in paragraph 8 above to use all necessary means to establish as soon as possible a secure environment for humanitarian relief operations in Somalia; . . .

The Council, in accordance with the requirement that it make an Article 39 determination before it can exercize or delegate its Chapter VII powers, determined in resolution 794 that 'the magnitude of the human tragedy caused by the conflict in Somalia, further exacerbated by the obstacles being created to the distribution of humanitarian assistance, constitutes a threat to international peace and security'. Moreover, in this resolution, the Council requested the Secretary-General to submit a plan to ensure that UNOSOM would be able to fulfil its mandate upon the withdrawal of the authorized force.

In response to resolution 794, the first elements of the Unified Task Force (UNITAF), spearheaded by the US to its credit, were deployed in Mogadishu on 9 December 1992.[171] The mandate of UNITAF under Security Council resolution 794 (1992) was to use all necessary means to establish as soon as possible a secure environment for the humanitarian relief operations in Somalia. Resolution 794 envisaged a large degree of UN command and control over any enforcement action when it stated the following in operative paragraphs 12, 13, and 15:

[The Security Council]

12. Also authorizes the Secretary-General and the Member States concerned to make the necessary arrangements for the unified command and control of the forces involved, which will reflect the offer referred to in paragraph 8 above;
13. Requests the Secretary-General and the Member States acting under paragraph 10 above to establish appropriate mechanisms for coordination between the United Nations and their military forces;
15. Invites the Secretary-General to attach a small UNOSOM liaison staff in the field headquarters of the unified command.

Some members of the Council attached considerable importance to the fact that the UN would have a large degree of command and control over the operation through the Secretary-General. For example, the representative of Zimbabwe stated the following in the Security Council meeting prior to the adoption of resolution 794:

---

[171] In addition to the US force, UNITAF included military units from Australia, Belgium, Botswana, Canada, Egypt, France, Germany, Greece, India, Italy, Kuwait, Morocco, New Zealand, Nigeria, Norway, Pakistan, Saudi Arabia, Sweden, Tunisia, Turkey, United Arab Emirates, United Kingdom, and Zimbabwe. (UN Department of Public Information, 'The United Nations and the Situation in Somalia', *Reference Paper, DPI/1321/Rev.3*, 1 May 1994, p. 29, note 2.)

An effort can be construed as international only if the United Nations is at its centre. It is therefore in this context that my delegation welcomes the draft resolution before us in document S/24880. This draft resolution, which we are about to adopt, places the Secretary-General of the United Nations at the controlling centre of the operation. . . . Zimbabwe attaches a lot of importance to the idea that in any international enforcement action the United Nations must define the mandate; the United Nations must monitor and supervise its implementation; and the United Nations must determine when the mandate has been fulfilled. My delegation is happy that the draft resolution before us meets these very important requirements. This sets an important precedent for future operations under equally unique circumstances.[172]

Moreover, the Belgian representative stated:

. . . the draft resolution makes it quite clear that the operation in Somalia will be under the political control of the United Nations. The coordinating machinery to be set up between the States participating in the operation and the Secretary-General, and the decision-making powers granted to the Secretary-General concerning the duration of the operation, are, in my delegation's opinion, key elements in this draft resolution. For these reasons, Belgium will vote in favour of the draft resolution before us . . .[173]

However, despite these provisions and pronouncements, the Secretary-General did not exercize any effective command and control powers over UNITAF.

Moreover, the Council complied with the reporting requirement which must be imposed on States exercizing delegated Chapter VII powers, when, in paragraph 18 of resolution 794, it

Requests the Secretary-General and, as appropriate, the States concerned to report to the Council on a regular basis, the first such report to be made no later than fifteen days after the adoption of the present resolution, on the implementation of the present resolution and the attainment of the objective of establishing a secure environment so as to enable the Council to make the necessary decision for a prompt transition to continued peace-keeping operations; . . .

As already explained in Chapter 4, the reporting requirement is an essential component of the Council's exercize of its overall authority and control over the use of its delegated Chapter VII powers. In accordance with this requirement, the US Government submitted two reports to the Council in

---

[172] S/PV.3145, pp. 7, 8–10. Similarly, the Ecuadorean representative stated the following: 'All of this, in Ecuador's view, recognizes the fundamental role of the United Nations . . . in that the Security Council is the body that will authorize start-up, continued execution and termination. Moreover, the unified command and control of the military forces will be subject to arrangements between the Secretary-General and the Member States contributing contingents. Those arrangements will reflect the reality of the contributors' participation.' (S/PV.3145, pp. 13–14.) Moreover, for the Chinese representative the fact of UN control over the operation was decisive in terms of an affirmative vote for the resolution: S/PV.3145, p. 17. [173] S/PV.3145, p. 24.

compliance with paragraph 18 of Security Council resolution 794.[174] The content of these reports, together with the reports of the Secretary-General,[175] were sufficient as to allow the Council to be able to exercize overall authority and control of the operation: in particular, to decide when its specified objective had been achieved and thus when the delegation of powers was to be terminated.

However, the issue of the objective of the operation was a matter of some controversy. It is clear that by the use of the 'all necessary means' formula in resolution 794 the Security Council envisaged the taking of military enforcement action, if necessary, by UN Member States to achieve the Council's stated objective of providing a secure environment for the delivery of humanitarian assistance.[176] The exact content of this objective was, however, somewhat vague, and became the source of a difference of interpretation between the US Government and the UN Secretary-General.[177] The US Government maintained that this contemplated the use of force only in order to overcome obstructions to humanitarian operations. It was the view of the US Government that its mission was the establishment by US forces of a secure environment for the delivery of relief supplies and the consolidation of the security framework so that it could be handed over to regular UN forces.[178] However, the Secretary-General contended that disarmament of the militias of the Somali factions was an essential part of the attainment of the objective of a secure environment.[179] Accordingly, in his

---

[174] S/24976, and S/25126.

[175] S/24992, S/25168, and S/25354.

[176] As the French representative clearly stated in the Council after the adoption of the resolution: 'We hope that the Somali parties and all who possess weapons in Somalia will take due note of the international community's determination and that they will choose to cooperate in ensuring that the humanitarian goal of our action may be achieved without resort to force. However, it is always possible that such force may be required, and that is why the resolution makes reference to Chapter VII of the Charter of the United Nations.' (S/PV.3145, p. 30.) See also the statements by the representatives of the US (S/PV.3229, p. 8); Spain (S/PV.3229, p. 23); and Venezuela (S/PV.3229, p. 16). See also Joseph, H., 'Humanitarian Assistance Operations Challenges: The Centcom Perspective on Somalia', *Joint Forces Quarterly*, vol. 1, no. 2 (Nov. 1993); and Hirsh and Oakley, *supra* note 83, p. 43.

[177] See Augelli, E., and Murphy, C., 'Lessons of Somalia for Future Multilateral Humanitarian Assistance Operations', *Global Governance*, 1 (1995), p. 339, at p. 353; and Gendron, M., 'The Legal and Strategic Paradigms of the United Nations' Intervention in Somalia', in Mokhtari, *supra* note 45, p. 71 at p. 84.

[178] Hirsh and Oakley, *supra* note 83, p. 46. The first report of the US Government to the Council as required by resolution 794 thus did not include disarmament as part of the mission. The report states: 'In response to Security Council resolution 794 (1992), the President directed the execution of Operation Restore Hope on 4 December 1992. The United States central command (USCENTCOM) was given the mission of conducting joint and combined military operations in Somalia, under United Nations auspices, to secure major airports and seaports, key installations and food distribution points, to provide open and free passage of relief supplies, provide security for convoys and relief organizations and to assist United Nations and non-governmental organizations in providing humanitarian relief.' (S/24976, p. 2.)

[179] S/24868, p. 5. Moreover, UNOSOM II under resolution 837 interpreted the part of its mandate involving the establishment of a 'secure environment' as not merely authorizing but

report to the Council of 19 December 1992, the Secretary-General stated that his interpretation of the mandate was that it included disarmament of the factions.[180] In a letter to President Bush of 11 December 1992, the Secretary-General called for the US-led forces to conduct a full-scale total disarmament programme for the whole country using whatever force might be required.[181] The rationale for this approach was that in order to create any sense of lasting security in Somalia, it was necessary to drain the large reserves of weapons which had flooded the country. It was felt that only the US could carry out the kind of comprehensive disarmament and stabilization that would enable a UN peacekeeping force to operate effectively when US forces departed. There was apprehension that without such action the security situation would deteriorate quickly once the bulk of US Marines had left Somalia. Interestingly, the Secretary-General sought to impose his interpretation on UN Member States taking part in Operation Restore Hope by use of the powers delegated to him by the Security Council in resolution 794. The Secretary-General did not want to start the transfer from UNITAF to UNOSOM II, a power delegated to him by resolution 794, until the US had accepted and carried out his broader interpretation of the mandate.[182] This failure to clarify the relationship between the UN and UNITAF, which translated into practical problems in the theatre,[183] is the result of the Council failing to specify in greater detail the objective of the delegation of powers. What is of interest to our enquiry is which interpretation in legal terms is the more authoritative: that of the Secretary-General or that of the United States' Government?

requiring it to disarm the militias. UNOSOM II was, however, under the direct command and control of the Secretary-General's Special Representative: see text following *supra* note 86.

[180] S/24992. During subsequent informal consultations between Council Members, France, Ecuador, and Zimbabwe were the only States who supported complete disarmament. (Freudenschuß, *supra* note 36, p. 515.)

[181] As cited by the Secretary-General in his report to the Council of 3 Mar. 1993, S/25354, p. 12.

[182] Report of the UN Secretary-General of 19 Dec. 1992, 'The Situation in Somalia', S/24992. The Secretary-General stated that he had attempted to implement the wish of the Council that a transition back to peacekeeping operations be achieved promptly by imposing two 'conditions' on the exercize of the power delegated to UNITAF by resolution 794 of the Council. These were: 'First, UNITAF should take action to ensure that the heavy weapons of the organized factions were neutralized and brought under international control and that the irregular forces and gangs were disarmed before it withdrew. Second, and equally essential, the authority entrusted to UNITAF should be exercized throughout Somalia.' (As noted in the Secretary-General's report of 12 Nov. 1993, S/26738, p. 15.)

[183] The rules of engagement of UNITAF forces were accordingly drawn up by US Commanders on the basis that their mandate was to ensure the delivery of humanitarian relief: see Lorenz, *supra* note 84, p. 63. These rules of engagement gave UNITAF Commanders a very limited authority to use 'all necessary force' in the context of disarmament: 'UNITAF Commanders could use such force to confiscate and demilitarize crew served weapons in their area of operations. . . . [Moreover] Commanders are authorized to use all necessary force to disarm individuals in areas under the control of UNITAF.' (*Ibidem*, p. 64.)

In the case of resolution 794 there was no control mechanism specified by which the use of force by States was to be under the operational command and control of the Council or the Secretary-General. The command and control of UNITAF was firmly in the hands of the US military. This was envisaged by paragraph 12 of resolution 794 where the Council: 'Also <u>authorizes</u> the Secretary-General and the Member States concerned to make the necessary arrangements for the unified command and control of the forces involved, which will reflect the offer referred to in paragraph 8 above'. Thus the Secretary-General states: 'Although the United Nations established UNITAF's mandate, the Organization neither organized nor commanded the troops that were sent to fulfil it. The operational command of UNITAF forces was assumed by the United States forces, which had the largest contingent.' [184] Moreover, as Lorenz, writing in the US *Naval Law Review*, states: 'UNITAF was under the operational control of USCINCENT, and all US forces, with the exception of a handful of UN staff, were under the control of the UNITAF commander.'[185] However, the resolution does envisage the Secretary-General operating as the link between the Security Council and the States carrying out the authorized action.[186] We recall from Chapter 4 that States exercizing delegated Chapter VII powers do so under the overall authority and control of the Council, and that it flows from this that the Council can at any time give a further interpretation of the objective to be achieved, change this objective, or even decide to terminate the delegation of powers. The Secretary-General in the case of resolution 794 was acting as the agent of the Security Council. He was delegated powers, together with Member States, to 'use all necessary means to establish as soon as possible a secure environment for humanitarian relief operations in Somalia'. Accordingly, the resolution allows for auto-interpretation of the delegation of powers by both the Secretary-General and the Member States that took up the delegation. The fact that the operation is being carried out under the overall authority and control of the Council means that the view of the Secretary-General as the UN organ exercizing delegated powers is that which shall, in legal terms, prevail. This does not mean, however, that this approach will not encounter considerable political difficulties.[187] This illustrates a potential problem with a delegation of Chapter VII powers to Member States, that the Security Council, or its designated UN delegate, may be forced to accept a narrower interpretation

---

[184] Boutros-Ghali, B., *The United Nations and Somalia, 1992–1996*, p. 33.

[185] Lorenz, *supra* note 84, p. 67.

[186] As the French representative noted: 'the role devolving upon the Secretary-General throughout the operation, in terms of its establishment, its follow-through and its implementation through UNOSOM—which will eventually take it over—is essential'. (S/PV.3145, p. 29.)

[187] See Gendron, M., 'The Legal and Strategic Paradigms of the United Nations' Intervention in Somalia', in Mokhtari, *supra* note 45, p. 71 at p. 84.

of a delegated mandate simply because this may be the only basis on which States will take up the delegation.[188] In any case, *in casu*, this controversy was resolved by resolution 814 where the Council delegated Chapter VII powers solely to the UN Secretary-General and his Special Representative, and thereby terminated the delegation of powers to Member States under resolution 794. We recall that this approach was confirmed in resolution 837 where the Council:

Requests the Secretary-General, through his Special Representative to direct the Force Commander of UNOSOM II to assume responsibility for the consolidation, expansion and maintenance of a secure environment throughout Somalia ... in accordance with the recommendations contained in his report of 3 March 1993, and in this regard to organize a prompt, smooth and phased transition from UNITAF to UNOSOM II; ...

From the terms of this paragraph it is clear that the Security Council has delegated to the Secretary-General the discretion as when to deploy UNOSOM II and the notion of what a 'secure environment' is can only be decided by the Secretary-General.[189] The reference by the Council to the report of the Secretary-General dated 3 March 1993 is of some significance, since in that report the Secretary-General indicated that a 'secure environment' includes, *inter alia*, disarmament of the organized factions.[190] This represents the adoption by the Security Council of the Secretary-General's interpretation.

2. The delivery of humanitarian assistance in Bosnia

The first time that the UN Security Council delegated Chapter VII enforcement powers in the case of the former Yugoslavia was in resolution 770. The Security Council expressly stated in the preamble to resolution 770 that 'the provision of humanitarian assistance in Bosnia and Herzegovina is an important element in the Council's effort to restore international peace and security in the area'. This provided the requisite Article 39 determination for the delegation by the Security Council of its Chapter VII powers.[191]

---

[188] As Thakur states: 'Nations are unwilling to authorise and arm international soldiers unless assured that they will fight *their* battle.' (Thakur, R., 'From Peace-Keeping to Peace-Enforcement: the UN Operation in Somalia', *The Journal of Modern African Studies,* 32 (1994), p. 387 at p. 397.)

[189] This is confirmed when recourse is made to the Secretary-General's report on the transition from UNITAF to UNOSOM where he states: 'One further point would need to be clarified in any Security Council resolution authorizing the deployment of UNOSOM II under the new mandate, namely that the deployment will be at the discretion of the Secretary-General, his Special Representative and the Force Commander acting under the authority of the Security Council.' (S/25354, p. 21.)

[190] S/25354, p. 13.

[191] On this general requirement, see *supra* note 43 and corresponding text in Chapter 1.

Frustrated at the lack of success of UNPROFOR's attempts to ensure the safe delivery of humanitarian assistance, the Council, in resolution 770, '[a]cting under Chapter VII . . . Calls upon States to take nationally or through regional agencies or arrangements all measures necessary to facilitate in coordination with the United Nations the delivery by relevant United Nations humanitarian organizations and others of humanitarian assistance to Sarajevo and wherever needed in other parts of Bosnia and Herzegovina'. The Council was well aware that it was delegating a coercive power to use military force.[192] The Indian representative in the Council emphasized the importance of such a delegation of powers being subject to the operational command and control of the Council: it was the view of the Indian Government that this operational command and control was required by Chapter VII of the Charter.[193] In fact it was because of this issue of 'command and control' that India abstained in the vote in the Council on resolution 770.[194] This issue also saw two other States abstain in the voting on resolution 770: Zimbabwe and China.[195] The representative of Zimbabwe proposed, instead of the delegation of military enforcement power to UN Member States, the 'deployment of a security force to protect humanitarian operations, fully controlled by and fully accountable to the United Nations, as that contemplated for Somalia'.[196] However, this approach fails to take into account that the Council always retains, as explained in Chapter 4,[197] overall authority and control over the use of its delegated powers, and as such operational command and control is not a legal requirement. Importantly, in the case of resolution 770, the Council provides for the effective exercize of its authority and control when it requires States to report back to it, through the Secretary-General, on the action taken.[198] Moreover, the specification by the Council of the objective to ensure the delivery of humanitarian assistance is relatively clear and unobjectionable. It would soon become clear if States were carrying out military action not directly related to the attainment of this objective. Accordingly, it would seem from the terms of the resolution that the Council has satisfied this condition for a delegation of its Chapter VII powers. The enquiry as to whether States

---

[192] See the statement by the representative of Ecuador: S/PV.3106, p. 9.

[193] See the statement by the representative of India: S/PV.3106, p. 12.

[194] S/PV.3106, pp. 13, 14–15.

[195] See the statements by the representatives of Zimbabwe (S/PV.3106, p. 17), and China (S/PV.3106, p. 51).

[196] S/PV.3106, p. 18.

[197] See *supra* note 20 in Chapter 4.

[198] In the relevant sections of resolution 770, the Council: 'Acting under Chapter VII of the Charter of the United Nations, . . . Calls upon States to report to the Secretary-General on measures they are taking in coordination with the United Nations to carry out this resolution, and . . . Requests the Secretary-General to report to the Council on a periodic basis on the implementation of this resolution'. This obligation on States was emphasized by the Belgian Government, a co-sponsor of resolution 770: S/PV.3106, p. 45.

have complied with the other conditions in practice is not possible, since the delegation of powers in resolution 770 was not taken up by UN Member States. The Secretary-General notes in a report dated 30 May 1995 that '[f]ollowing the adoption of that resolution, a number of Member States proposed that the function identified in it could be added to the mandate of UNPROFOR, operating in accordance with the established principles and practices of United Nations peace-keeping operations. After the London Conference of August 1992, it was agreed by potential troop contributors that, instead of proceeding with the implementation of resolution 770 (1992), they would contribute troops to UNPROFOR for this purpose under a new resolution.'[199] The Secretary-General made it clear that the adoption by the Council of resolution 770 did not create any additional mandate for UNPROFOR since it 'was directed at Member States'.[200] Thus a new Security Council resolution would be required to expand the mandate of UNPROFOR. Moreover, the Secretary-General made it clear that the troops which UN Member States were to contribute to UNPROFOR for the purpose of providing protective support for humanitarian relief convoys in Bosnia would be under his command and control. In effect these additional troops were being treated by the Secretary-General as a contribution to the UN peacekeeping force (UNPROFOR) which were to be used for a specific purpose. Accordingly, when the Secretary-General in a report to the Council dated 10 September 1992 requested an expanded mandate for UNPROFOR to provide protective support for humanitarian relief convoys throughout Bosnia, he stated that this approach is desirable since '[i]t would assure the Security Council's control of the operation, while at the same time avoiding the imposition of additional financial burdens on the Organization'.[201] This proposal was approved and adopted by the Security Council in resolution 776. The Council states that it '[a]uthorizes, in implementation of paragraph 2 of resolution 770 (1992) the enlargements of UNPROFOR's mandate and strength in Bosnia . . . recommended by the Secretary-General . . . to perform the functions outlined'. Thus the UN retained operational command and control over any possible use of force which was to occur in Bosnia.[202] The UN Secretary-General exercized his command and control when he stated that UNPROFOR, as a UN peacekeeping force, should not undertake military enforcement action under Chapter VII of the Charter.[203] Accordingly, the

---

[199] S/1995/444, p. 7.   [200] *Ibidem.*   [201] S/24540, p. 5.

[202] Cf. statements by the representatives of Zimbabwe (S/PV.3114, pp. 3–4); and India (S/PV.3114, pp. 6–8).

[203] The reluctance of the Secretary-General for UNPROFOR to use force was based on his view that 'I do not believe it to be in the interests of the United Nations for a peace-keeping force to be converted into one which, by mandate and composition, becomes a party to the conflict it was originally deployed to help the parties to bring to an end.' (S/1994/1067, para. 44.) In a report to the Security Council, the Secretary-General notes: 'In providing protective

Secretary-General notes that '[t]he Security Council approved my report in its resolution 776 (1992) and authorized the enlargement of UNPROFOR, without citing Chapter VII of the Charter or authorizing "all measures necessary"'.[204] This represents a termination by the Council of the delegation of Chapter VII powers contained in resolution 770.

This case illustrates the important difference between a delegation of powers to a UN authorized military enforcement force and a delegation of powers to a UN peacekeeping force: a distinct set of legal considerations apply to each force. Although both are composed of troops from UN Member States, their legal status, mandate, chain of command, and *modus operandi* all may differ substantially.[205]

3. The delivery of humanitarian assistance and the creation of a secure environment in Albania

In response to the rapidly deteriorating humanitarian situation in Albania in March 1997, the Government of Italy in a letter to the Secretary-General offered to take the lead in organizing and commanding a force to address the situation.[206] The Security Council provided the legal framework for such action when it passed resolution 1101. This resolution makes the requisite Article 39 determination by stating that 'the present situation of crisis in Albania constitutes a threat to peace and security in the region' and as such allows the Council to have recourse to the full panoply of its Chapter VII powers. The resolution goes on to establish a 'temporary multinational protection force' (MPF) under the command of Italy in order to achieve two objectives: 'to facilitate the safe and prompt delivery of humanitarian assistance, and to help create a secure environment for the missions of international organizations in Albania, including those providing humanitarian assistance' (paragraph 2). The Council went on to authorize 'the Member States participating in the MPF to conduct the operation in a neutral and impartial way to achieve the objectives set out in paragraph 2 above and, acting under Chapter VII of the Charter of the United Nations, further authorizes these Member States to ensure the security and freedom

---

support to UNHCR-organized convoys, the UNPROFOR troops concerned would follow normal peace-keeping rules of engagement. They would thus be authorized to use force in self-defence. It is to be noted that, in this context, self-defence is deemed to include situations in which armed persons attempt by force to prevent United Nations troops from carrying out their mandate. These considerations are particularly relevant in the current tense situation in the proposed area of operations.' (S/24540, p. 2.)

[204] S/1995/444, p. 7.

[205] In respect of UN peacekeeping forces, see *supra* Section III(2) in Chapter 2.

[206] Letter from the Permanent Representative of Italy to the United Nations to the Secretary-General, 27 Mar. 1997, S/1997/258.

of movement of the personnel of the said multinational protection force' (paragraph 4). Accordingly, the Council delegated to the Member States' forces who were participating in the MPF the competence to use force, if necessary, to carry out their mandate. The Member States who took up the mandate delegated by the Council in resolution 1101 have, however, stated in clear terms that they consider the mission to be purely humanitarian in nature. They state: 'The mission of the force, in accordance with Security Council resolution 1101 (1997), is to facilitate the safe and prompt delivery of humanitarian assistance and to help create a secure environment for the missions of international organizations in Albania, including those providing humanitarian assistance. The purpose of the multinational protection force as set out in resolution 1101 (1997) is therefore a strictly humanitarian one.'[207] Even though the Member States participating in the mission may intend that it will be strictly humanitarian in nature, this does not mean, however, that there has not been a delegation to the MPF of the competence to carry out military action, if necessary, to achieve its designated objective. An important part of the objective of the MPF is to establish a secure environment in the country such that the delivery of humanitarian assistance can proceed unimpeded. This may in some cases involve the use of force. This interpretation is validated by the earlier case of Somalia where the Security Council in resolution 794 delegated Chapter VII powers to Member States for the achievement of the same objective: the creation of a secure environment throughout the country in order to ensure the delivery of humanitarian assistance.[208] We recall from our earlier discussion on this resolution that the delegation of power in resolution 794 to achieve and maintain a secure environment included the competence to use force.[209] This eventuality seems in fact to have been considered by the States who were members of the MPF.[210]

The countries which contributed troops to the MPF established a Steering Committee, consisting of State representatives and the Commander of

---

[207] 'Report to the UN Security Council on the operation of the multinational protection force for Albania', as contained in S/1997/296, Annex, para. 15.

[208] See *supra* note 76 and corresponding text.

[209] See *supra* note 176 and corresponding text.

[210] They state: 'Taking into account the prevailing conditions throughout the country and the fact that the force acts under Chapter VII of the Charter of the United Nations, the force has been provided with rules of engagement in accordance with its mandate to ensure the security and freedom of movement of its personnel. These rules include self-defence, limited use of force, identification and warning before using force, proportionality in the use of force, need to prevent collateral damage, prohibition of retaliation and the right to position defence.' (See 'Second report to the Security Council on the operation of the multinational protection force for Albania', as contained in S/1997/335, Annex, para. 12.) See also the 'Report to the UN Security Council on the operation of the multinational protection force for Albania', as contained in S/1997/296, Annex, para. 11.

the operation. The role of this Committee was to provide 'political guidance' to the force.[211] This is a positive development since it fulfils the obligation, as discussed in Chapter 1, that the lead-State who exercizes overall command over the force is to take into account the views of those States who have contributed troops to the force on the way in which their forces may potentially be used.[212] This initiative is also desirable since a stated objective of the Steering Committee was to monitor the activities of the force to ensure full compliance of its activities with the delegated mandate of the Security Council.[213] In its final report to the Council, the Italian Government, on behalf of the States participating in the MPF, noted in respect of this Committee: 'The Steering Committee drafted its own decision-making and procedural rules, which proved to be effective. In addition to giving political guidance to the force, it reported regularly to the Security Council on the progress of the operation and was a useful forum for consultation on the international effort for Albania. The Steering Committee operated by consensus. This mechanism proved to be a political asset, since all countries shared responsibility for the Committee's decisions, reinforcing cohesion and solidarity.'[214]

In accordance with the Council's obligation to impose a reporting requirement on States exercizing delegated Chapter VII powers, resolution 1101 '[r]equests the Member States participating in the multinational protection force to provide periodic reports, at least every two weeks, through the Secretary-General, to the Council, the first such report to be made no later than 14 days after the adoption of this resolution, inter alia, specifying the parameters and modalities of the operation on the basis of consultations between those Member States and the Government of Albania'.[215] Although the Council has used the term 'request', it has, however, clearly been accepted by the States participating in the operation that this constitutes an obligation. In the first report by the MPF to the Security Council, it states that '[t]he countries contributing to the force will continue to

---

[211] 'Report to the UN Security Council on the operation of the multinational protection force for Albania', as contained in S/1997/296, Annex, para. 6. This Steering Committee met on a weekly basis: see, for example, the 'Fifth report to the Security Council on the operation of the multinational protection force in Albania', contained in S/1997/440, Annex, para. 3.

[212] On this requirement, see *supra* note 136 and corresponding text in Chapter 1.

[213] 'Report to the UN Security Council on the operation of the multinational protection force for Albania', as contained in S/1997/296, Annex, para. 6.

[214] See the 'Eleventh and final report to the Security Council on the operation of the multinational protection force', S/1997/632, Annex, para. 17.

[215] The same obligation was imposed by the Security Council on the MPF when the Council extended the duration of the operation in resolution 1114. This obligation was complied with by the MPF under both resolutions: the Italian Government undertaking to submit the reports to the Security Council on behalf of the States participating in the MPF. The reports submitted to the Council were as follows: S/1997/296, Annex; S/1997/335, Annex; S/1997/362, Annex; S/1997/392, Annex; S/1997/440, Annex; S/1997/460, Annex; S/1997/501, Annex; S/1997/513, Annex; S/1997/551, Annex; S/1997/601, Annex; and S/1997/632, Annex.

provide, pursuant to their obligations under resolution 1101 (1997), timely reports to the Security Council on the implementation of the resolution'.

The MPF contributed significantly to improving security within Albania and to restoring stability to the country,[216] to such an extent that the Albanian authorities requested that the MPF remain in the country during the electoral process to help ensure a secure environment for the conduct of the elections and in particular to protect the Organization for Security and Cooperation in Europe (OSCE) electoral monitoring mission.[217] The Steering Committee accepted this role for the force, subject of course to a Security Council resolution extending the duration of the MPF operation.[218] It was, thus, implicitly considered that since the MPF mandate included the ensuring of a secure environment and protecting the work of international organizations, protection of the OSCE Office for Democratic Institutions and Human Rights would fall within the MPF's current mandate and as such no expansion of mandate was required. The Security Council adopted this approach when in resolution 1114 it did not expand the mandate of the MPF but simply expanded the duration of the operation for a further forty-five days. In carrying out this aspect of its mandate, the MPF had to use varying degrees of force in order to protect OSCE monitors.[219] The elections in Albania were held and the OSCE was able to report that the elections were, in the circumstances, acceptable and could constitute the foundation for a strong democratic system.[220] The Security Council by delegating its Chapter VII powers to Member States in compliance with the legal framework governing this process contributed significantly to the restoration of peace and security within Albania.

4. The establishment of a safe haven in Rwanda

The humanitarian situation in Rwanda from mid-1994 was, by all accounts, appalling.[221] There was a massacre of civilians from particular ethnic groups

[216] See, for example, the following reports by the MPF to the Security Council: S/1997/362, Annex; S/1997/392, Annex; S/1997/440, Annex; and S/1997/460, Annex. See also the statement by the representative of Albania in Security Council Meeting 3791: Security Council Press Release SC/6385, p. 5.

[217] See the 'Sixth report to the Security Council on the operation of the multinational protection force in Albania', S/1997/460, Annex, paras. 4–11.

[218] See the 'Sixth report to the Security Council on the operation of the multinational protection force in Albania', S/1997/460, Annex, para. 12.

[219] See, for example, the following reports of the MPF to the Security Council: S/1997/501, Annex, para. 18; S/1997/513, Annex, para. 18; and S/1997/551, Annex, para. 14.

[220] See the 'Ninth report to the Security Council on the operation of the multinational protection force in Albania', S/1997/551, Annex, para. 15.

[221] See 'Report of the Secretary-General on the Situation in Rwanda', S/1994/640 (1994). For a concise description of the political developments in the late eighties which led to this humanitarian crisis, see Tyagi, Y., 'The Concept of Humanitarian Intervention Revisited', *Michigan Journal of International Law*, 16 (1995), p. 883 at pp. 902–4. For a more detailed description, see Prunier, G., *The Rwanda Crisis: History of a Genocide* (1995).

on a genocidal scale. The Council in resolutions 918 and 925 gave the United Nations Assistance Mission for Rwanda (UNAMIR) a mandate to intervene in order to end the massacres. It was nonetheless the opinion of several States that the inevitable delay involved with the expansion and effective operation of UNAMIR would cost even more thousands of lives in Rwanda.[222] Accordingly, the Governments of France and Senegal volunteered in June 1994 to send immediately a force to establish and maintain safe humanitarian areas in the country to try and prevent further genocide from occurring.[223] The Government of France, in a letter addressed to the Secretary-General, requested express authorization for this action in the following terms:

In the spirit of resolution 794 (1992) of 3 December 1992, our Governments would like, as a legal framework for their intervention, a resolution under Chapter VII of the Charter of the United Nations giving them a mandate to act until the expanded UNAMIR is deployed. As we see it, the interim force should be able to withdraw towards the middle of August at the latest, after handing over to UNAMIR when its reinforcements have been deployed.[224]

As a result of this offer, the Secretary-General stated in a letter addressed to the President of the Security Council the following:

In these circumstances, the Security Council may wish to consider the offer of the Government of France to undertake, subject to Security Council authorization, a French-commanded multinational operation in conjunction with other Member States, under Chapter VII of the Charter of the United Nations, to assure the security and protection of displaced persons and civilians at risk in Rwanda. Such an operation was one of the options envisaged in my letter of 29 April (S/1994/518) and a precedent exists for it in the United States-led operation Unified Task Force in Somalia (UNITAF) which was deployed in Somalia in December 1992. If the Council decides to authorize an operation on these lines, I consider it would be necessary for it to request the Governments concerned to commit themselves to maintain their troops in Rwanda until UNAMIR is brought up to the necessary strength to take over from the multinational force and the latter has created conditions in which a peace-keeping force operating under Chapter VI of the Charter would have the capacity to carry out its mandate. This would imply that the multinational force should remain deployed for a minimum period of three months.[225]

The Security Council provided this 'legal framework' by passing resolution 929. To understand this legal framework it is necessary to see the relevant sections of resolution 929 in their entirety:

---

[222] Letter dated 20 June 1994 from the Permanent Representative of France to the United Nations addressed to the UN Secretary-General, S/1994/734, 21 June 1994.
[223] *Ibidem.*
[224] *Ibidem.*
[225] Letter dated 19 June 1994 from the Secretary-General addressed to the President of the Security Council, S/1994/728, 20 June 1994, p. 4.

Noting the offer by Member States to cooperate with the Secretary-General towards the fulfilment of the objectives of the United Nations in Rwanda (S/1994/734), and stressing the strictly humanitarian character of this operation which shall be conducted in an impartial and neutral fashion, and shall not constitute an interposition force between the parties, . . .

Determining that the magnitude of the humanitarian crisis in Rwanda constitutes a threat to peace and security in the region, . . .

2. Welcomes also the offer by Member States (S/1994/734) to cooperate with the Secretary-General in order to achieve the objectives of the United Nations in Rwanda through the establishment of a temporary operation under national command and control aimed at contributing, in an impartial way, to the security and protection of displaced persons, refugees and civilians at risk in Rwanda, on the understanding that the costs of implementing the offer will be borne by the Member States concerned;

3. Acting under Chapter VII of the Charter of the United Nations, authorizes the Member States cooperating with the Secretary-General to conduct the operation referred to in paragraph 2 above using all necessary means to achieve the humanitarian objectives set out in subparagraphs 4 (a) and (b) of resolution 925 (1994);

4. Decides that the mission of Member States cooperating with the Secretary-General will be limited to a period of two months following the adoption of the present resolution . . .;

10. Requests the States concerned and the Secretary-General, as appropriate, to report to the Council on a regular basis, the first such report to be made no later than fifteen days after the adoption of the present resolution, on the implementation of this operation and the progress made towards the fulfilment of the objectives referred to in paragraphs 2 and 3 above; . . .

This resolution has several salient features. First, the Council made the requisite Article 39 determination that the humanitarian crisis constituted a threat to peace and security in the region. Second, the Council delegated the power of command and control over the operation to the Member States undertaking the operation. Third, the costs of the force are expressly stated to be borne by the Member States supplying the forces. Fourth, the Council specified the objective of the operation by referring back to its previous resolution 925. This objective being to contribute to the security and protection of displaced persons, refugees, and civilians through, among other means, the establishment and maintenance of secure humanitarian areas, and the provision of security and support for the delivery of humanitarian assistance. Fifth, the Security Council limited the operation to an initial period of two months. Sixth, the Council specified an obligation on France or the Secretary-General, 'as appropriate', to report back to the Council on the exercize of the delegated Chapter VII powers.

Subsequently, French forces, exercizing these delegated powers, carried out an operation that became known as 'Operation Turquoise'. Moreover, in a letter dated 1 July 1994 addressed to the Secretary-General, the French representative explained that an increase in the level of fighting which occurred outside the capital was going to create a humanitarian disaster that would soon be uncontrollable. As a result, France proposed the organization of a 'safe humanitarian zone' where the civilian population would be protected from the conflict. It was the opinion of the French Government 'that, on the basis of resolutions 925 (1994) and 929 (1994), it is authorized to organize such a safe humanitarian zone. Nevertheless, it is the wish of France that, through you, the United Nations should indicate its support for the establishment of such a zone.'[226] It would seem from the objective specified by the Council in resolution 929 that this is a valid interpretation by France of its delegated mandate. Nevertheless, the French Government was seeking an affirmation by the Security Council, through the Secretary-General, of its interpretation: an affirmation which it subsequently received. This is a desirable practice, since it reiterates the overall authority and control that the Security Council exercizes over its Chapter VII powers.

This overall authority and control of the Council was further ensured by the Secretary-General and the French Government reporting to the Council in compliance with the reporting requirement specified in resolution 940 that allows either the Secretary-General or the French Government to fulfil this requirement.[227] The Council did not, justifiably in this case, impose an obligation solely on the States exercizing delegated powers to report to it on the exercize of the delegated powers, since there was an express requirement, in paragraph 3 of resolution 929, for these States to co-operate with the Secretary-General in the conduct of the operation. It was thus appropriate to impose this obligation jointly on the Member States concerned and the Secretary-General. In practice there was close co-operation between the French forces and the UN which allowed the Secretary-General to exercize adequate supervision over the fulfilment by the French forces of the objective specified by the Council in resolution 929.[228]

5. The establishment of a safe area in Iraq

The end of hostilities in the Gulf War saw rebel groups try and overthrow the Government of Saddam Hussein. However, Iraqi forces brutally

---

[226] Letter dated 1 July 1994 from the Permanent Representative of France to the United Nations addressed to the Secretary-General, S/1994/798, Annex.

[227] The UN Secretariat presented an oral report to the Security Council on 7 July 1994 (as stated in S/1994/924) and there was a report of the Secretary-General dated 3 Aug. 1994 (S/1994/924). The French Government submitted four reports to the Council during the operation: S/1994/795, S/1994/799, S/1994/933, and S/1994/1100. The French Government stated in its final report that a decisive factor in the success of the operation was the strict observance of neutrality. (S/1994/1100, p. 5.)

[228] See the report of the Secretary-General to the Security Council, 6 Oct. 1994. See also Tyagi, *supra* note 221, p. 905.

crushed the rebellions by Shia groups in the South and Kurdish separatists in the North. As a result, large numbers of refugees tried to flee into neighbouring countries to escape retribution by Iraqi forces. Subsequently, and in response to this humanitarian crisis, the Security Council passed resolution 688 which condemned 'the repression of the Iraqi civilian population in many parts of Iraq . . . the consequences of which threaten international peace and security'.

It was thus clear that the Security Council had found the consequences of the repression of Iraqi civilians to constitute a threat to international peace and security. However, having made an Article 39 determination, the Council did not, in express terms, provide a way to deal with the threat to the peace. Nonetheless, on 16 April 1991, the US, the UK, and France, under the code name 'Operation Provide Comfort', sent troops into Northern Iraq to establish a small triangle security zone. This security zone was to provide a safe area for the return of fleeing Iraqi citizens and was under the protection of the allied forces: no access was, understandably, granted to Iraqi forces.[229] This safe haven was created by forcing Iraqi troops to cease operations north of the 36th parallel.[230] The UK House of Commons was told that this was 'a temporary measure to meet an immediate and overwhelming humanitarian need and to allow the refugees to return to their homes in conditions of safety. . . . [O]ur actions in the conflict with Iraq and in establishing safe havens in northern Iraq have been consistent with, and have derived support from United Nations resolutions.'[231] Iraq opposed at first the establishment of the safe havens, but said later that it would not hinder them in order to allow the humanitarian relief efforts to proceed. Iraq did, however, call on the UN to assume responsibility for the safe-haven operations.[232]

It is not proposed here to examine all the legal considerations relating to this action. Our discussion will be limited to the issue whether the action of coalition forces can be characterized, and thus justified, in legal terms as an exercize of delegated Chapter VII powers. There are two possibilities: first, that Security Council resolution 688 delegated Chapter VII powers to Member States in order to address the humanitarian crisis in Iraq; second, that the delegation to Member States in resolution 678 to use all necessary measures to restore international peace and security continued to exist and that since Iraq's repression constituted a threat to international peace, Member States were, accordingly, justified in militarily intervening to stop the source of the threat to international peace.

---

[229] Malanczuk, P., 'The Kurdish Crisis and Allied Intervention in the Aftermath of the Second Gulf War', *European Journal of International Law*, 2 (1991), p. 114 at p. 121.

[230] Greenwood, *supra* note 32, p. 176.

[231] *HC Debs.*, vol. 192, cols. 500–1 (6 June 1991).

[232] UN Doc. S/22513.

The refugee relief effort was announced by Bush as 'an humanitarian effort under the auspices of UN Security Council Resolution 688' that needed no further authorization.[233] However, it is clear that resolution 688 was not intended to delegate to Member States the exercize of any Chapter VII powers to alleviate the human suffering of Iraqi citizens. The express reference in the resolution and in the Council debates preceding the resolution to the restrictive effect of Article 2(7) of the Charter provides ample evidence in favour of this view against construing the resolution as a delegation of Chapter VII powers. Article 2(7) is clear when it states that an express exception to the prohibition on the UN intervening in the internal affairs of Member States exists where the Council takes enforcement action under Chapter VII of the Charter. Accordingly, by mention of the operation of Article 2(7) it seems clear that this exception, Chapter VII enforcement action, was not envisaged by the resolution.[234] This approach is substantiated by the Memorandum of the Foreign and Commonwealth Office submitted to the UK House of Commons Foreign Affairs Committee in respect of Operation Provide Comfort which provides:

Resolution 688, which applies not only to northern Iraq but to the whole of Iraq, was not made under Chapter VII. Resolution 688 recognized that there was a severe human rights and humanitarian situation in Iraq and, in particular, northern Iraq; but the intervention in northern Iraq 'Provide Comfort' was in fact, not specifically mandated by the United Nations . . .[235]

The remaining possible legal basis for the allied action, in terms of a delegation of powers, was that it was an exercize of those powers delegated under resolution 678. This depends on whether the delegation of powers in resolution 678 continued up until the relevant time. However, as noted above, the adoption of the formal ceasefire in Security Council resolution 687 and its subsequent acceptance by Iraq terminated the delegation of powers by the Council to Member States to carry out military enforcement action.[236] Accordingly, the legal basis of the coalition action remains un-

---

[233] Cf. the Secretary-General who criticized the coalition's unilateral action stating that Iraq's consent, which was not given, was necessary for such an intervention in its territory to be legal. (*Keesings Record of World Events* (1991), p. 38126.)

[234] Accordingly, Gray states that resolution 688, 'although referred to at the time by the States involved, clearly does not authorize forcible humanitarian intervention. It was not passed under Chapter VII and did not expressly or implicitly allow the use of force.' (Gray, *supra* note 49, p. 162.)

[235] See 'UK Materials in International Law', *BYIL*, 63 (1992), p. 824. Moreover, the UN Legal Division later agreed that Resolution 688 was 'humanitarian in intention and not enforceable, since it did not cite Chapter VII of the UN Charter'. (Quoted in Spielman, J., 'The Middle East and the Persian Gulf', in *A Global Agenda: Issues Before the 48th General Assembly of the United Nations* (Tessitore, J., and Woolfson, S., eds.) (1993), p. 43.)

[236] See *supra* note 57 and corresponding text.

clear.[237] The UK Foreign Office holds the view that the action is justified by reference to 'the customary international law principle of humanitarian intervention'.[238] Legal analysis may well prove this is the accurate position. However, whether this is the case is beyond the scope of our current enquiry. All that can be said at present is that the action cannot be justified by reference to an exercize of delegated Chapter VII powers.

IV. A DELEGATION OF POWERS TO ENFORCE A COUNCIL DECLARED NO-FLY ZONE: THE CASE OF IRAQ

The Council has, under Chapter VII of the Charter, imposed constraints on the movement by a State or a combatant of its military and civilian aircraft in areas within a State: these are commonly referred to as 'no-fly zones'. This requires, of course, that the Council make a determination under Article 39 of the Charter that such aviation activity within these zones constitutes a threat to international peace and security in order for the ban on flights to be a measure lawfully adopted under Chapter VII. Moreover, such a characterization is necessary for such a ban not to violate the provisions of Article 2(7) of the Charter relating to non-interference by the UN in the internal affairs of a State. The Council has expressly declared a no-fly zone and delegated Chapter VII military enforcement powers to enforce its ban in the cases of Iraq and Bosnia. The case of Bosnia, however, is dealt with in Chapter 6 since it involves a delegation of power to States acting through regional arrangements.

In the case of Iraq, Member States, acting in the aftermath of the Gulf War, sought to impose no-fly zones within the country to protect minority groups from persecution. The issue which is the subject of our present discussion is whether such action can be justified by reference to a delegation by the Council of its Chapter VII powers.

It was in response to the persecution of minority groups within Iraq by

---

[237] See also Greenwood, *supra* note 32, p. 176; Schachter, *supra* note 14, p. 452; Gray, *supra* note 49, p. 163; Warbrick, C., 'The Invasion of Kuwait by Iraq—Part II', *ICLQ*, 40 (1991), p. 965 at p. 973; and Malanczuk, P., 'The Kurdish Crisis and Allied Intervention in the Aftermath of the Second Gulf War', *EJIL*, 2 (1991), p. 114.

[238] See 'UK Materials in International Law', *BYIL*, 63 (1992), p. 824. Moreover, in answer to the question 'Does Her Majesty's Government regard it as essential that it should only intervene in another country when invited to do so by the government of that country? Was this principle breached in the case of the Iraq Kurds?' the following answer was given by the UK Foreign and Commonwealth Office: 'We believe that international intervention without the invitation of the government of the country concerned can be justified in cases of extreme humanitarian need. This is why we were prepared to commit British forces to Operation Haven, mounted by the Coalition in response to the refugee crisis involving the Iraqi Kurds.' (*Ibidem.*) See also Teson, F., 'Collective Humanitarian Intervention', *Michigan Journal of International Law*, 17 (1996), p. 323 at pp. 343–8.

the Iraqi regime in the aftermath of the Gulf War, that the US, the UK, and France declared 'no-fly zones' to prevent Iraqi air force and armed helicopters from bombing these minority groups.[239] The UK Secretary of State stated: 'We believe that the no-fly zone should include, [sic] well it's a ban obviously on Iraqi helicopters or fixed wing planes and so they will be deterred from flying but they would be excluded if they did fly.'[240] As to the legal basis of the action, a UK Foreign and Commonwealth Office spokesman stated that 'the measures proposed were justified under international law in response to a situation where there was demonstrably overwhelming humanitarian need. This action was in support of UN SCR 688 which demanded that the Iraqi Government cease its repression of the civilian population and demanded that it cooperate with the United Nations humanitarian relief programmes.'[241] The US Government announced the imposition of the 'no-fly zone' in Southern Iraq on 26 August 1992 when it stated that coalition aircraft would begin flying surveillance missions in southern Iraq on 27 August.[242] The US Government sought to justify its decision to impose the no-fly zone on the basis of this issue of surveillance. President Bush, when announcing the imposition of the zone, stated:

We now know of Saddam's use of helicopters and, beginning this spring, fixed wing aircraft to bomb and strafe civilians and villages, there in the south . . . These reports are further confirmation that the government of Iraq is failing to meet its obligations under UN Security Council resolution 688. . . . By denying access to human rights monitors and other observers, Saddam has sought to prevent the world from learning of his brutality. It is time to ensure the world does know. And therefore, the United States and its coalition partners have today informed the Iraqi government that 24 hours from now coalition aircraft, including those of the United States, will begin flying surveillance missions in southern Iraq, south of the 32 degrees North latitude to monitor the situation there. This will provide coverage of the areas where a majority of the most significant recent violations of resolution 688 have taken place. . . . The coalition is also informing Iraq's government that in order to facilitate these monitoring efforts, it is establishing a no-fly zone for all Iraqi fixed and rotary-wing aircraft. . . . It will remain in effect until a coalition determines that it is no longer required. . . . I want to emphasize that these actions are designed to enhance our ability to monitor developments in southern Iraq.[243]

However, in a joint statement issued by Members of the Coalition, resolution 688 was relied upon to a greater degree as a justification for the imposition of the no-fly zone. The Coalition Members state:

---

[239] There were no-fly zones imposed in the north of Iraq to protect the Kurds and in the south to protect the Shia Muslims.

[240] UK Secretary of State's interview on the BBC World Service, 20 Aug. 1992, in Weller, *supra* note 61, p. 723.

[241] Statement by UK FCO Spokesman, 20 Aug. 1992, in Weller, *ibidem*, p. 724.

[242] US Press Release: Coalition to impose 'no-fly' zone in southern Iraq, 26 Aug. 1992, in Weller, *ibidem*.

[243] *Ibidem*, pp. 724–5.

In view of these failures to comply with UNSCR 688, the coalition has concluded that it must itself monitor Iraqi compliance with UNSCR in the south. Coalition aircraft will therefore begin flying surveillance missions over Iraqi territory south of 32 degrees north to monitor and report on the state of Iraqi compliance with the provisions of the resolution. In support of this monitoring effort a no-fly zone for all Iraqi fixed and rotary wing aircraft—military and civilian—will be established south of 32 degrees north. This no-fly zone will go into effect twenty-four hours from now and will remain in effect until further notice. To be clear: Iraq may not fly military . . . aircraft . . . south of the 32nd parallel. We will respond appropriately and decisively to any Iraqi failure to comply with this requirement.[244]

The relevant part of resolution 688 provides the following: 'The Security Council . . . *Condemns* the repression of the Iraqi civilian population in many parts of Iraq, including most recently in Kurdish populated areas, the consequences of which threaten international peace and security in the region . . . [and] *Demands* that Iraq, as a contribution to removing the threat to international peace and security in the region, immediately end this repression . . . [and] . . . *Insists* that Iraq allow immediate access by international humanitarian organizations to all those in need of assistance in all parts of Iraq and to make available all necessary facilities for their operations'. It seems clear that this resolution decided that the Iraqi repression constitutes a threat to international peace and security. However, it is also clear, as explained earlier, that the resolution does not delegate to Member States any Chapter VII powers to take action to stop the repression of minority groups within Iraq.[245] We recall, moreover, from Chapter 1 that the Council can only delegate its Chapter VII powers to Member States by express decision:[246] a delegation of powers cannot be implied by Member States from very general terms in a Council resolution. Accordingly, the Secretary-General did not seek to rely on resolution 688 as the legal basis for the imposition and enforcement of the no-fly zone. Instead, the Secretary-General sought to rely on resolution 687 when providing a justification for a coalition air strike against Iraqi anti-aircraft missile sites moved into the southern no-fly zone.[247] This strike was made only after Iraq had failed to comply with a request from the coalition partners to withdraw the missiles which were perceived as a threat against coalition aircraft patrolling the no-fly zone.[248] Interestingly, the UK did not seek to rely on

---

[244] Statement issued by the Members of the Coalition at New York, 26 Aug. 1992, in Weller, *ibidem*, p. 725.

[245] See *supra* note 234 and corresponding text.

[246] See *supra* notes 34–7 and corresponding text in Chapter 1.

[247] Moreover, in Dec. 1992, Iraq provoked further retaliation when an Iraqi warplane flew within the no-fly zone area in the south of Iraq. The Iraqi plane was shot down by a US plane. ((1992) *Keesings*, 39247.)

[248] (1993) *Keesings*, 39291. The Secretary-General stated the following in respect of this incident: 'The raid yesterday, and the forces that carried out the raid, have received a mandate from the Security Council, according to resolution 678, and the cause of the raid was the violation by Iraq of resolution 687 concerning the cease-fire. So, as Secretary-General of the UN, I can say that this action was taken and conforms to the resolutions of the Security Council

resolution 688 in respect of this action, invoking, instead, self-defence as its justification for the air strikes.[249] However, self-defence would only be available as a legal justification for such action if coalition members had a valid legal basis for their aircraft to be patrolling the zone. Accordingly, we return to the main issue: is there a legal justification for a no-fly zone being imposed and the enforcement of such a zone by coalition members, the reason for coalition aircraft being within Iraqi territory. The only possible legal justification for the imposition and enforcement of a no-fly zone in this case is by reference to the notion of humanitarian intervention.[250] The fact that the members of the coalition took it upon themselves to determine when they should terminate their action provides evidence that these States considered they were acting on the basis of humanitarian intervention and were not exercizing delegated Chapter VII powers. In this regard we recall the statement by President Bush and the later statement by the coalition that the 'no-fly zone will go into effect twenty-four hours from now and will remain in effect until further notice'.[251] States that are exercizing delegated Chapter VII powers do not, as we recall from Chapter 1, have the competence to decide when the delegation of powers is terminated. However, whether the concept of unilateral humanitarian intervention operates so as to justify the imposition and enforcement of what was a desirable, in humanitarian terms, no-fly zone is beyond the scope of this present work.[252] Suffice, however, to note for our current purposes that to the extent the coalition action in imposing the no-fly zone rests on Security Council resolution 688 it is on unstable legal ground.

V. A DELEGATION OF POWERS TO ENSURE IMPLEMENTATION BY PARTIES OF AN AGREEMENT WHICH THE COUNCIL HAS DEEMED IS NECESSARY FOR THE MAINTENANCE OR RESTORATION OF PEACE

The recent practice of the Council has seen it delegate Chapter VII enforcement powers to Member States in order to ensure compliance by parties to

and conforms to the Charter of the United Nations.' (UN Department of Public Information (DPI) Briefing, 14 Jan. 1993, p. 2.)

[249] It was accordingly stated by a member of the UK Government in the House of Commons: 'Iraq has been warned frequently not to interfere with allied aircraft in the zones. Such aircraft have the inherent right of self-defence against Iraqi threats to their safety. Attacks against Iraqi missile systems and associated command and control centres were necessary and proportionate responses in self-defence to such threats.' (*HC Debs.*, vol. 217, Written Answers, col. 514.)

[250] See also Johnstone, *supra* note 54, pp. 38–9.

[251] US Press Release: Coalition to impose 'no-fly' zone in Southern Iraq, 26 Aug. 1992, in Weller, *supra* note 61, p. 725.

[252] On humanitarian intervention more generally, see: Teson, F., *Humanitarian Intervention: An Inquiry into Law and Morality* (1994); Brownlie, *supra* note 165; and Sarooshi, *supra* note 75.

an agreement which the Council has decided is necessary to maintain or restore peace. The implementation by the Council of agreements which have already been concluded by parties to a conflict has two main advantages. First, it allows the Council to specify in some detail the objective for which the Council is delegating its Chapter VII powers, since the implementation of an agreement already concluded by the parties will usually contain limited, specific, objectives. Accordingly, this nullifies to a large extent the criticism that States who are exercising delegated powers may do so in an attempt to implement their own political interests in a matter. The second advantage is that it gives the Council a greater degree of legitimacy, both local and international, when acting under Chapter VII. This is of considerable importance to the long-term effectiveness of any military enforcement action that may subsequently be taken.[253]

The Council has delegated its Chapter VII powers to Member States to ensure the implementation of agreements between parties in the cases of Haiti, Bosnia, and the Central African Republic. The case of the Dayton Peace Agreement in Bosnia is, however, dealt with in Chapter 6 since it involves a delegation of powers to States to act through a regional arrangement.

1. The Governors Island Agreement: the restoration of democracy in Haiti

On 29 September 1991, the democratically elected government of Haiti was overthrown in a violent *coup* by members of the Haitian armed forces. The response of the international community was immediate. The Canadian, French, United States, and Venezuelan ambassadors to Haiti successfully intervened by persuading the *coup* leaders to allow President Aristide, who was at the time under arrest, to leave the country. The OAS response to the *coup* saw a meeting of OAS Foreign Ministers resolve to recognize President Aristide and his government as Haiti's only 'legitimate' government and to recommend that all OAS Member States take specific action to isolate economically and diplomatically the '*de facto*' government which had seized control.[254] The OAS imposed a non-mandatory trade embargo

---

[253] This is well illustrated by the case of Somalia, where the Secretary-General, in his report to the Council assessing the achievements of the UN in Somalia, stated the following: 'The experience of UNOSOM II has thus confirmed the validity of the point that the Security Council has consistently stressed in its resolutions on Somalia, namely that the responsibility for political compromise and national reconciliation must be borne by the leaders and people concerned. It is they who bear the main responsibility for creating the political and security conditions in which peacemaking and peace-keeping can be effective. The international community can only facilitate, prod, encourage and assist. It can neither impose peace nor coerce unwilling parties into accepting it.' (S/1995/231, 28 Mar. 1995, para. 64.)

[254] While non-recognition has been used by the United Nations, for example in the case of Southern Rhodesia, this was the first time it had been used by the OAS. This policy of

against Haiti which included the freezing of Haitian assets, the banning of arms sales, and the diplomatic isolation of the '*de facto*' government. With the failure of these and subsequent efforts of the OAS to dislodge the *coup* leaders in Haiti from political power,[255] the matter was taken to the United Nations. Subsequently, in response to a request from the 'legitimate' government of Haiti, the UN Security Council passed resolution 841. Acting under Chapter VII, the Security Council imposed a universal arms embargo against Haiti; froze all overseas assets controlled by the '*de facto*' government; and threatened to impose a worldwide trade embargo against Haiti to come into force on 23 June 1993 unless the UN Secretary-General advised otherwise.[256] The effect of these sanctions and growing international pressure, saw the head of the '*de facto*' authorities in Haiti conclude with President Aristide the Governors Island Agreement under the auspices of both the OAS and the United Nations. It was primarily the signing of this accord and the New York Pact of June 1993, which generated hopes for a possible peaceful transition to the restoration of democracy and prompted the Security Council in resolution 861 to suspend the economic sanctions imposed by resolution 841. The Governors Island Agreement provided for the return to Haiti of President Aristide, his designation of a Prime Minister, and the eventual return to democracy in Haiti. Subsequently, however, in the light of persistent breaches by the *de facto* authorities in Haiti of their obligations under these accords, the Secretary-General concluded that there was a serious and persistent lack of implementation of the Governors Island Agreement, and considered, in the light of the opinions expressed also by the Secretary-General of the Organization of American States (OAS), that it was necessary to revoke the suspension of the measures set forth in resolution 841 (1993).[257] Accordingly, the Council decided in reso-

collective non-recognition is legally important, as it represents a common refusal to validate an illegal act, see: Gowlland-Debbas, *supra* note 102; and Dugard, J., *Recognition and the United Nations* (1987).

[255] A meeting of Foreign Ministers in May 1992 recommended to OAS Member States that they, *inter alia*, deny vessels that violate the embargo access to their port facilities, monitor compliance with the embargo, and refuse entry to their territories of persons who were involved in any way with the *coup*. (Sarooshi, *supra* note 75, p. 15.)

[256] On the delegation by the Council of its Chapter VII powers to enforce this embargo, see *supra* Section II(3).

[257] The Secretary-General, in a report to the Council dated 13 Oct. 1993, states: 'I must inform the Council that the Commander-in-Chief of the Armed Forces of Haiti, as one of the parties to the Agreement, and the police chief and commander of the Port-au-Prince metropolitan area, as one of the 'authorities in Haiti' have failed to fulfil the commitments entered into by General Cedras in his capacity as co-signatory of the Governors Island Agreement.' (S/26573, para. 9.) Accordingly, the Secretary-General decided '[i]n the light of all the foregoing facts, which reflect serious and consistent non-compliance with the Governors Island Agreement, and having regard to the views of the Secretary-General of the Organization of American States, I consider it necessary, in accordance with resolution 861 (1993), to terminate the suspension of the measures set out in paragraphs 5 to 9 of resolution 841 (1993)'. (S/26573, para. 10.) The Council in resolution 867 decided to authorize the establishment and immediate

lution 873 to reimpose the sanctions set forth in resolution 841, unless the parties complied with their commitments.[258] In its resolution 917 of 6 May 1994, the Council imposed additional sanctions against Haiti and decided that the sanctions regime would not be lifted until the following events had taken place: the creation of a proper environment for the deployment of UNMIH, the retirement of the Commander-in-Chief of the Armed Forces of Haiti, and the resignation or departure from Haiti of the Chief of Staff of the Armed Forces of Haiti and the Chief of the Metropolitan Zone of Port-au-Prince.

The Council had earlier, in resolution 867, decided to establish a peace-keeping force (UNMIH) in Haiti to assist in the transition to democracy. However, the Secretary-General in his report of 28 June 1994 stated that due to a further deterioration of the situation in Haiti the circumstances under which the original UNMIH was planned had substantially changed. Accordingly, the Secretary-General in his report of 15 July 1994 stated that the original size of the force should be expanded and that the deployment of any force to Haiti would be likely to take place 'in a disturbed and violent environment'.[259] Accordingly, the Secretary-General stated that '[i]t cannot therefore be excluded that the expanded force would have to use coercive means in order to fulfil its mandate. Given these law-and-order aspects of the expanded force's tasks, it would be necessary for the Security Council to act under Chapter VII of the Charter in authorizing its mandate.'[260] The Secretary-General recommended to the Council an expanded force 'with a mandate from the Security Council, acting under Chapter VII of the Charter, that would permit the force to use coercive means as necessary in assisting the legitimate authorities to carry out various support functions'.[261] The Secretary-General then proposed three possible options to the Council in order to establish an expanded force. The first option was for the Council to expand the existing force (UNMIH) and give it a revised mandate under Chapter VII covering the additional tasks envisaged in resolution 933.[262]

dispatch of a United Nations Mission in Haiti (UNMIH) for a period of six months to help implement the Governors Island Agreement. The Secretary-General stated in successive reports that the mandate entrusted to UNMIH by resolution 867 could not be implemented because of various developments in Haiti which constituted non-compliance by the Armed Forces of Haiti with the relevant provisions of the Governors Island Agreement. (See the following reports of the Secretary-General: 13 Oct. 1993 (S/26573), 11 Nov. 1993 (S/26724), 26 Nov. 1993 (S/26802), and 19 Jan. 1994 (S/1994/54).)

[258] The Secretary-General in his report to the Council of 15 July 1994 confirmed the absence of any fundamental improvement in the situation in Haiti. (S/1994/828)

[259] S/1994/828, p. 2.

[260] *Ibidem*, p. 3.

[261] *Ibidem*, p. 5.

[262] S/1994/828, p. 5. The Secretary-General did not recommend this proposal, on the basis that the contributions of troops for the required expansion in UNMIH would not be forthcoming as well as the fact that even if enough troops could be found their deployment would be too slow. (S/1994/828, pp. 5–6.)

The second option was for the 'Security Council, at the request of the legitimate Government, to adopt a resolution, acting under Chapter VII of the Charter, by which it would authorize a group of Member States to establish and deploy a force to carry out the tasks described in paragraph 9 above'.[263] The Secretary-General stipulated that:

consultations would be required between the United Nations and the Member States concerned and the latter would need to indicate to the United Nations their readiness to undertake this responsibility if so authorized by the Security Council to do so. Under this option, the force would be under the command and control of the Member States contributing to it and those Member States would be responsible for financing it, with the help of such voluntary contributions as other Member States might wish to make available. This option has the advantage of not requiring any limit on the proportion of the force to be contributed by a single country.[264]

The third option was to entrust phases one and two of the operation to different forces. This option combines in effect elements of options one and two. Phase one is to be undertaken by a multinational or inter-American force authorized under Chapter VII of the Charter with the mandate of establishing a secure environment. Phase two would be entrusted to UNMIH under Chapter VI of the Charter at the level of strength authorized by the Council in resolution 867. Once the multinational or inter-American force had established a safe and secure environment within Haiti then the main body of UNMIH would be deployed to Haiti as soon as possible to begin work on implementing the relevant provisions of the Governors Island Agreement. The Secretary-General states in respect of this third option 'that the multinational or inter-American force should not be withdrawn without an agreement having been concluded between the Member States concerned and the United Nations on the timing and modalities of its withdrawal'.[265] The reason for this suggestion by the Secretary-General is presumably as a result of the experience of Somalia where troops were withdrawn from 'Operation Restore Hope' before the Secretary-General thought that the situation within Somalia was safe and secure and thus appropriate for the deployment of UNOSOM II.[266] The Secretary-General states that if the Council decides to choose the second or third option then it might wish to authorize the establishment of a small group of UN military and police observers 'who would coexist with the multinational or inter-American force (as the case might be) and whose tasks would be to verify the manner in which that force carried out the mandate conferred upon it by the Council . . .'.[267]

---

[263] S/1994/828, p. 6.
[264] *Ibidem.*
[265] *Ibidem.*
[266] See *supra* note 182 and corresponding text.
[267] S/1994/828, p. 7.

The Council decided that economic sanctions were not sufficient to dislodge the *coup* leaders from Haiti when it passed resolution 940 which adopted in effect the third proposal of the Secretary-General[268] and decided the following:

4. *Acting* under Chapter VII of the Charter of the United Nations, [the Security Council] authorizes Member States to form a multinational force under unified command and control and, in this framework, to use all necessary means to facilitate the departure from Haiti of the military leadership, consistent with the Governors Island Agreement, the prompt return of the legitimately elected President and the restoration of the legitimate authorities of the Government of Haiti, and to establish and maintain a secure and stable environment that will permit implementation of the Governors Island Agreement, on the understanding that the cost of implementing this temporary operation will be borne by the participating Member States; . . .
6. *Requests* the Secretary-General to report on the activities of the team within thirty days of deployment of the multinational force; . . .

There were considerable doubts expressed by some Governments as to the lawfulness of the measures contained in resolution 940. There were three main arguments. First, that the crisis in Haiti was not such as to constitute a threat to international peace and, accordingly, sufficient as to justify the delegation by the Council of its military enforcement powers to States to resolve the crisis.[269] This contention, however, lacks cogency. It was explained in Chapter 1 that under Article 39 the Council has a broad discretion to decide that a particular issue constitutes a threat to, or breach of, international peace and security and thus deserves attention under Chapter VII.[270] Accordingly, the determination by the Council in resolution 940 that the situation in Haiti continued to constitute a threat to international peace and security was well within its powers. In fact, as noted in Chapter 4 above, such a determination under Article 39 is a precondition for a delegation by the Council of its Chapter VII powers. Once this decision is made, it is, under Chapter VII, within the sole discretion of the Council, again, to

[268] Accordingly, the US representative stated the following at the Council meeting at which resolution 940 was adopted: 'The resolution we have adopted today authorizes a two-phased approach. In the first phase, a multinational force, acting under Chapter VII of the Charter, is empowered to restore legitimate authority to Haiti. The United States is prepared to organize and lead such a force. We seek, and anticipate, that others will join. . . . We hope that the current military leaders in Haiti will depart voluntarily and that the multinational force will not be opposed. But this resolution authorizes action whether or not our hopes are realized. . . . The timing of the transition from phase one to phase two will be determined by the Security Council after appropriate consultation and after a stable and secure environment has been established and the means for fulfilling the United Nations mission are at hand. . . . Phase one builds on the precedents of Kuwait and Rwanda.' (S/PV.3413, p. 13.)
[269] See the statements by the representatives of Brazil (S/PV.3413, pp. 9–10); Mexico (S/PV.3413, pp. 4–5); and Uruguay (S/PV.3413, p. 7).
[270] See *supra* note 4 and corresponding text in Chapter 1.

decide whether to use military enforcement measures to achieve certain objectives:[271] *in casu*, the delegation to States of the competence to use force to achieve the restoration of democracy in Haiti and the return of its 'legitimate President'. Accordingly, States can voice their individual opinion that a particular situation does not constitute a threat to, or breach of, the peace for the purposes of Article 39 or that the Council should not delegate its military enforcement powers to Member States to address the cause of the threat to the peace, but this does not detract from the competence of the Council to take lawfully such decisions.[272] To conclude, the doubts expressed by several countries as to whether the situation within Haiti constituted a threat to international peace under Article 39 of the Charter can be dismissed.

The second argument against the validity of resolution 940 was that the Council should have defined the forces which it was authorizing to carry out the military enforcement action.[273] There is, however, no prohibition in law from the Council making a general delegation of its powers as opposed to a specific delegation.[274]

The third objection to the resolution was that there should have been a time limit specified for the operation.[275] The stipulation of time limits is a desirable condition for a delegation by the Council of its Chapter VII powers, but it is not a necessary one.[276] The fundamental requirement for the lawful delegation of powers is that the exercize of delegated Chapter VII powers remains under the overall authority and control of the Council. This is maintained by the Council specifying certain procedural guarantees

---

[271] See also the 'Commentary to Article 39' in Cot and Pellet's commentary on the Charter which states that the initiation of an enforcement action results from the Security Council's discretionary power: the Council being the sole judge of the appropriateness and timing of enforcement measures, and the sole judge of the type of measure to take under Chapter VII. (Cot and Pellet, *supra* note 4, p. 645.)

[272] This is well illustrated by the position of the New Zealand Government which expressed its opposition to the choice of approach taken by the Council but not to the legality of such an approach: S/PV.3414, pp. 21–2.

[273] See, for example, the statement by the representative of Mexico: S/PV.3413, p. 5.

[274] On the difference between these two types of delegation, see *supra* note 44 and corresponding text in Chapter 1.

[275] See the statements by the representatives of Mexico (S/PV.3413, pp. 4–5); and Cuba (S/PV.3413, p. 6).

[276] In any case, the argument that the failure of the resolution to specify a time frame meant that it was an open-ended authorization was refuted by the New Zealand representative who stated: 'In conclusion, I want to refer to the question that was raised in the debate today by the representative of Mexico. He argued that the Security Council was writing a blank cheque with this resolution. I would like to say that while this may perhaps have been an understandable criticism of earlier versions of the draft resolution, the resolution adopted today contains some elements—which I am pleased to say were introduced in part as a result of proposals from my delegation—which clearly indicate that the operation would be of a temporary nature and would be focused specifically on a specific point in history. We do not believe, therefore, that it is an open-ended 'blank cheque', and we believe that the resolution reflects this.' (S/PV.3413, p. 22.)

which attach to the exercize of delegated Chapter VII powers: the conditions of delegation. *In casu*, these are satisfied, since the Council in resolution 940 specified a clear objective for which the Chapter VII powers were being delegated to Member States, imposed on the States exercizing the delegated powers a requirement to report to the Council on the conduct of operations, established a subsidiary organ to monitor the exercize of power, imposed an obligation on the Secretary-General to report to the Council on the conduct of the activities, and reserved for itself the exclusive competence to determine when the objective had been attained and therefore when the delegation of Chapter VII powers to Member States was to be terminated.

It seems clear from the resolution that the objective for the exercize of delegated Chapter VII powers was the provision of a safe and secure environment that would allow the full implementation of the Governors Island Agreement.[277] The stipulation by the Council of the objectives for which Chapter VII powers have been delegated is of considerable importance, as explained in Chapter 4, in conferring legality upon the delegation of powers.[278]

We recall from Chapter 4 that the imposition of a reporting requirement on States exercizing delegated Chapter VII powers is a necessary condition for the exercize by the Council of its supervisory role over the delegated powers and is thus a precondition for a lawful delegation by the Council of these powers. This is satisfied by the Council, which, in paragraph 13 of resolution 940, states the following reporting requirement:

[The Council] [r]equests the Member States acting in accordance with paragraph 4 above to report to the Council at regular intervals, the first such report to be made not later than seven days following the deployment of the multinational force.

We recall from Chapter 4 that the Council has the competence to require such a reporting requirement from States. However, the question which arises is whether the reporting requirement specified by the Council in resolution 940 is mandatory or only recommendatory in nature. The language used, 'the Council ... requests', may be viewed as being recommendatory in nature and thus non-binding. However, the fact that the Council stipulates that the first such report is to be made 'not later than seven days following the deployment of the multinational force' would seem to indicate that the Council requires States exercizing the delegated powers to make such reports. Nevertheless, even if the language were considered to be recommendatory, the use of such language is not in itself conclusive. The language of the resolution of a Security Council only provides part of the evidence in ascertaining the intention of the Council and

---

[277] See, for example, the statement by the representative of Djibouti: S/PV.3413, p. 23.
[278] See also the statement by the representative of the Czech Republic: S/PV.3413, p. 24.

thus the interpretation to be given a Security Council resolution. An examination of the statements by State representatives in the Council debates is also of considerable importance in ascertaining this intention. *In casu*, these statements indicate that the reporting requirement is a condition of the delegation of powers. It was this requirement, as part of the exercize by the Council of its authority and control over the operation, that proved important for the support by, for example, the Spanish Government, the representative of which stated:

Spain, which attaches great importance to the principle of non-intervention, especially on the American continent, supported resolution 940 (1994) because of the singular and exceptional circumstances of this case, because of the clear position taken by the legitimate authorities of Haiti and because the action to be initiated will not be carried out unilaterally but, rather, within a multilateral and institutional framework, under the authority and control of the United Nations. Had it been otherwise, we should not have been able to support such an action. . . . the Member States participating in the multinational force will, for their part, keep the Council informed at regular, frequent intervals. Similarly, the Secretary-General himself will report periodically to the Council on the implementation of the resolution. The Council's follow-up mechanism does not end there. In accordance with resolution 917 (1994) of May 1994 and until President Aristide returns, the Secretary-General will continue to report every month on all aspects of the situation in Haiti so that the Council can keep this matter under constant consideration.[279]

The US Government, in accordance with the reporting requirement stipulated in resolution 940, submitted regular reports to the Security Council on the activities of the Multinational Force (MNF).[280] These reports proved important for the Council to be able to exercize its overall authority and control over the exercize of its delegated Chapter VII powers.[281] Moreover, these reports illustrate the importance that the Force itself placed on restricting themselves to the attainment of the objectives stipulated by the Council: in all of these reports the US Government states that it 'reports on the coalition's progress towards achieving the objectives laid down in paragraph 4 of resolution 940 (1994)'.[282]

---

[279] S/PV.3413, p. 20.

[280] For the reports of the MNF, see: S/1994/1107, Annex; S/1994/1148, Annex; S/1994/1208, Annex; S/1994/1258, Annex; S/1994/1321, Annex; S/1994/1377, Annex; S/1994/1430, Annex; S/1995/15, Annex; S/1995/70, Annex; S/1995/108, Annex; S/1995/149, Annex; S/1995/183, Annex; and S/1995/211, Annex.

[281] As the representative of the Czech Republic stated in the Council: 'By successfully completing the task it was authorized to undertake by paragraph 4 of resolution 940 (1994), the multinational force has demonstrated the usefulness, in some circumstances, of the Security Council entrusting groups of States with enforcement action. . . . In following the progress of the MNF, the Security Council benefited from frequent, detailed and on-the-record reports provided on behalf of the MNF by the United States delegation. We are grateful for this reporting effort.' (S/PV.3496, p. 9.)

[282] S/PV.3429, p. 3.

The Council adopted in resolution 940 the additional safeguard that the Secretary-General is required to report on the implementation of the resolution. This is not strictly required as a legal requirement for a delegation by the Council of its Chapter VII powers, but it is an additional safeguard which contributes to the effectiveness of UN supervision and control over the operation.[283] Moreover, the degree of United Nations supervision over the conduct of the operation was bolstered by the Council establishing in resolution 940 a subsidiary organ to monitor the operations of the MNF.[284]

The provision of paragraph 8 of resolution 940 was of considerable importance in enabling the Security Council to exercize effective authority and control over the exercize of its delegated powers. It provides:

[The Security Council] [d]*ecides* that the multinational force will terminate its mission and UNMIH will assume the full range of its functions described in paragraph 9 below when a secure and stable environment has been established and UNMIH has adequate force capability and structure to assume the full range of its functions; the determination will be made by the Security Council, taking into account recommendations from the Member States of the multinational force, which are based on the assessment of the commander of the multinational force, and from the Secretary-General; . . .

The express statement by the Council that the mission of the MNF will be terminated upon the achievement of a secure and stable environment, as determined by the Security Council, reiterated the sole discretion the Council enjoys in determining when the delegation of powers is to be terminated. The retention of this power of determination by the Council is an important legal requirement for a lawful delegation of Chapter VII powers; as explained above in Chapter 1.[285] This is precisely the process by which the delegation of powers to Member States in the case of Haiti was terminated by the Council. The Commander of the MNF in Haiti made the declaration that a secure and stable environment had been established in Haiti so as to permit full implementation of the Governors Island Agreement and, moreover, that the MNF had facilitated the departure of the *coup* leaders from Haiti and the return of President Aristide.[286] The Member

---

[283] This safeguard was proposed by the Secretary-General in his earlier report of 15 July 1994 to the Security Council: S/1994/828, para. 23.

[284] Para. 5 of resolution 940.

[285] See *supra* notes 129–32 and corresponding text *et sequentia* in Chapter 1.

[286] The Commander of the MNF in Haiti made the following statement to the Security Council: 'Security Council resolution 940 (1994) sets conditions for the transition from the multinational force to the United Nations Mission in Haiti (UNMIH) based upon the assessment of the Commander of the multinational force, and allows the transfer of the multinational force functions to UNMIH when (a) a secure and stable environment has been established and (b) UNMIH has adequate force capability and structure to assume the full range of its functions. In accordance with resolution 940 (1994), the multinational force Commander in Haiti, in conjunction with subordinate multinational contingent commanders,

States participating in the MNF recommended, accordingly, that the Council determine that it is now appropriate for the United Nations Mission in Haiti (UNMIH) to assume the full range of its functions.[287] Acting pursuant to these recommendations, the Security Council in resolution 975 terminated the delegation of Chapter VII powers to the MNF.[288] The official transfer of responsibilities from the MNF in Haiti to UNMIH took place at the National Palace at Port-au-Prince on 31 March 1995.[289]

A condition of the delegation of Chapter VII powers in resolution 940 was that States exercising the delegated powers do so under 'unified command and control'. It is within this framework that States are authorized 'to use all necessary means' to achieve the specified objectives. Accordingly, no State could act independently to use force in order to achieve the objectives set out in resolution 940. However, the Council did not specify who should lead the MNF. Put differently, to whom the Council intended to delegate its powers of command and control over a military force carrying out military enforcement action was unclear. In legal terms, the Council, in resolution 940, left it up to States that wished to participate in the multinational operation to agree on a State to appoint the 'unified command'. There is nowhere an express statement as to which State or authority should designate the force commander. This lack of clarity is, however, undesirable, since it could lead to possible division and contention between States as to the interpretation of who has the competence to exercize the delegated

declares that a secure and stable environment has been established in Haiti, attaining the first of two requirements to satisfy the conditions for transition to UNMIH. The multinational force has facilitated the departure of the coup leaders from Haiti and the return of President Aristide . . . and established the secure and stable environment necessary to permit full implementation of the Governors Island agreement.' (S/1995/55, p. 4.)

[287] S/1995/55, p. 3.

[288] The relevant part of Security Council resolution 975 provides the following: 'Noting in particular the MNF commander's statement of 15 January 1995 and the accompanying recommendation, based on the MNF commander's report, of the States participating in the MNF (S/1995/55), regarding the establishment of a secure and stable environment in Haiti, Noting the recognition in these reports and recommendations that a secure and stable environment has been established in Haiti, . . . 5. Determines, as required by resolution 940 (1994) and based on the recommendations of the Member States participating in the MNF and in concurrence with paragraph 91 of the report of the Secretary-General of 17 January 1995 (S/1995/46), that a secure and stable environment, appropriate to the deployment of UNMIH as foreseen in the above mentioned resolution 940 (1994), now exists in Haiti; 6. Authorizes the Secretary-General, in order to fulfil the second condition specified in paragraph 8 of resolution 940 (1994) for the termination of the mission of the MNF and the assumption by UNMIH of its functions specified in that resolution . . . 7. Further authorizes the Secretary-General, working with the MNF commander, to take the necessary steps in order for the UNMIH to assume these responsibilities as soon as possible, with the full transfer of responsibility from the MNF to UNMIH to be completed by 31 March 1995'. Accordingly, in the Thirteenth and final report of the Multinational Force to the Council, the US Government stated that '[a]s the United Nations will assume responsibility for the mission in Haiti on 31 March 1995, this will be the final report of the multinational force'.

[289] S/1995/305, para. 3.

power of command and control. The Council should, as it did in the case of Korea, indicate with a degree of specificity the 'lead State' who is authorized to exercise delegated powers of command and control over the force carrying out military enforcement action.[290] In political terms, it was, nonetheless, clear that this lead State was assumed to be the United States.[291] It can be assumed that there was general agreement that the US, as the lead country, had the prerogative to appoint the Force Commander. Accordingly, the US Government appointed Lt. Gen. Hugh Shelton of the US Army as the commander of the MNF. This assumption by the US as the role of the lead country is confirmed when one considers that all the reports of the MNF to the Council were conveyed to the Council by the US Government. This represents a positive development in this area compared, for example, to the case of Iraq where Member States reported individually to the Security Council on their exercize of delegated Chapter VII powers.[292]

In terms of the effectiveness of the exercize of these delegated Chapter VII powers, early diplomatic efforts by the US saw the '*de facto* military authorities in Haiti' agree to give up their control, thus allowing the democratically elected authorities of Haiti to resume governance of the country and the MNF to enter Haiti unopposed. These forces, spearheaded by the US, entered Haiti on 19 September 1994. Accordingly, in the majority of the reports of the MNF to the Council there are statements to the effect that the threat to the MNF was low.[293] In fact, according to some of the reports, the gradual expansion of the MNF was 'welcomed into the outlying areas by the local population'.[294] This is the major reason for the relative success of the operation in Haiti as compared to that which took place in Somalia. The difference being that the local population was not hostile to the foreign intervention and in fact perceived the foreign forces as carrying out desirable and legitimate objectives on behalf of the international community which were of benefit to the Haitian population as a whole.[295]

---

[290] Cf. the view of the Government of Honduras: S/PV.3496, pp. 7–8.

[291] A UN Department of Public Information Document states '[o]n 19 September 1994, in a first phase of the military operation authorized by Security Council resolution 940 (1994), the lead elements of the 28-nation multinational force, spearheaded by United States troops, landed in Haiti without opposition'. (DPI/1306/Rev.4 (95.VII.I), p. 201; see also S/1994/1107, p. 2.)

[292] See *supra* note 61 and corresponding text.

[293] For example, the Eighth report states: 'The threat to multinational forces remains low.' (S/1995/15, Annex, p. 3).

[294] S/1995/15, Annex, p. 3. See also the Ninth report (S/1995/70, Annex, p. 2), and the Thirteenth and final report (S/1995/211, Annex, p. 3).

[295] Brownlie had earlier emphasized the importance of 'local legitimacy' when he stated: 'Once the local form of legitimacy has been destroyed, it is very difficult to restore a government with a credible legitimacy internally or externally.' (Brownlie, I., 'International Law in the Context of the Changing World Order', in *Perspectives on International Law* (Jasentuliyana, N., ed.) (1995), p. 48 at p. 54.)

Moreover, the ability of the MNF in Haiti to work with a government perceived as legitimate by the majority of the population in Haiti was of crucial importance.

Interestingly, it seems that the Member States exercizing delegated Chapter VII powers to establish a secure situation within Haiti considered that disarmament was a necessary activity to achieve such a situation. This is in contradistinction to the determination by Member States as how best to establish security in the case of Somalia. Accordingly, in its second report to the Council on the operations of the MNF, the US noted that the force 'continues to search aggressively for and seize weapons caches, to protect public safety and to expand its presence in the countryside'.[296] This auto-interpretation by States of their delegated mandate is within their prerogative. However, it remains unclear whether a particular interpretation of a phrase in one case may in the future estop the States concerned from interpreting the identical phrase with respect to another, though similar, case so as to justify fundamentally different action.[297]

2. The Bangui Agreements in the Central African Republic

In 1996 there were in the Central African Republic (CAR) three successive mutinies by elements of the CAR Armed Forces which led to a politico-military crisis in the country.[298] There was a subsequent conference between President Patassé of the CAR and the rebel forces in Bangui which resulted in the 'Bangui Agreements' which included the elements necessary for a comprehensive settlement of the crisis.[299] In response to a request by letter from President Patassé,[300] an inter-African force was established by the States of Burkina Faso, Chad, Gabon, Mali, Senegal, and Togo with the mandate of restoring peace and security in the CAR by monitoring the implementation of the Bangui Agreements and conducting operations to disarm the former rebels, the militia, and all other unlawfully armed individuals: this force was named the Inter-African Mission to Monitor the Implementation of the Bangui Agreements (MISAB).[301] The Security Council subsequently adopted as its own these actions when in resolution 1125 it approved the conduct of Member States participating in MISAB in order to achieve the objective of facilitating the return to peace and security in the CAR by monitoring the implementation of the Bangui Agreements. The Security Council, moreover, delegated a limited competence to carry

---

[296] S/1994/1148, Annex, p. 3.

[297] See, more generally, on the role of estoppel in international law: Brownlie, I., *Principles of Public International Law* (1994), pp. 640–2.

[298] See the 'Report of the Secretary-General Pursuant to Resolution 1136 (1997) Concerning the Situation in the Central African Republic', S/1998/61, 23 Jan. 1998, paras. 4–13.

[299] See S/1997/561, Annex, Appendices III–VI.

[300] See S/1998/61, para. 5.   [301] See S/1998/61, para. 5.

out military enforcement action to these States when, acting under Chapter VII, in resolution 1125 it authorized the Member States participating in MISAB and those States providing logistical support to ensure the security and freedom of movement of their personnel. Accordingly, the Council delegated to the States' forces who were participating in the operation the competence to use force if necessary to carry out their mandate. The MISAB was, however, under the authority and control of an International Monitoring Committee which exercized political command and the MISAB Command which exercized military command, both of which were not UN bodies.[302] Accordingly, the Council, in conformity with its obligation to do so,[303] required the States who were exercizing this delegated mandate to submit reports to it on a regular basis. The Council decided, moreover, that this delegation of power would be limited to an initial period of three months, after which the Council would assess the situation on the basis of the reports submitted to the Secretary-General at least every two weeks by the Member States participating in MISAB.

The first report by Member States participating in MISAB to the Security Council through the Secretary-General as required by Council resolution 1125 indicates that MISAB had to use enforcement action in some circumstances to achieve its mandate.[304] However, it is clear from a perusal of the reports subsequent to the first report that there were no further casualties or injuries sustained by the MISAB force.[305] This would seem to imply, in the absence of any other evidence to the contrary, that there was no further enforcement action carried out by the Member States who were part of MISAB. In any case, by the time of the fourth report it was clear that MISAB had achieved very substantial improvements in the security situation in the CAR and that it had contributed significantly to the restoration of peace to the country.[306] Due to this contribution, the Security Council, acting under Chapter VII, decided in resolution 1136 to extend for a further three months its authorization of the Member States participating in MISAB and those States providing logistical support to ensure the security and freedom of movement of their personnel.[307] The Member States participating in MISAB were requested to provide periodic monthly reports to the Council on the way in which they were supervising and assisting in the

---

[302] S/1997/652, para. 5.

[303] See *supra* note 72 and corresponding text in Chapter 4.

[304] The first report states: '[i]n the course of the various operations conducted by MISAB, and particularly during the confrontations of 22 and 23 March and 20 to 26 June, the force suffered the following losses: 6 dead . . . [and] 20 wounded . . .'. (S/1997/652, Annex.)

[305] S/1997/684, Annex, para. 34; S/1997/716, Annex, para. 49; S/1997/759, Annex, para. 52; S/1997/795, Annex; & S/1997/828, Annex.

[306] See S/1997/759, Annex, paras. 53–9. See also the fifth (S/1997/795, Annex) and sixth reports (S/1997/828, Annex); and the Report of the Secretary-General (S/1998/61, para. 23).

[307] This authorization was extended further in subsequent Security Council resolutions 1152 (5 Feb. 1998) and 1155 (16 Mar. 1998).

implementation of the Bangui Agreements;[308] while the Secretary-General was requested to provide a report on the implementation of the resolution, including recommendations on further international support for the CAR.

The Secretary-General in his subsequent report of 23 January 1998 noted that France was preparing to withdraw its force of 1,400 troops that had been providing invaluable logistical support to MISAB, and that '[s]ince MISAB would not be able to maintain its presence in Bangui without adequate financial and logistical support, the only viable option for the maintenance of stability in the Central African Republic appears to be the establishment and deployment of another peace-keeping operation authorized by the international community'.[309] The mandate of such a force would be '. . . similar to that of MISAB. The primary purpose would be to maintain stability in Bangui so that the peace process could continue to move forward. Through its presence throughout the city and regular patrolling, a United Nations stabilization force would seek to maintain the security established by MISAB and to create an environment conducive to the holding of free and fair legislative elections scheduled to be held in August/ September 1998.'[310] The Secretary-General envisaged that such a force would be under his operational command and control, and that the head of mission would be a Special Representative appointed by the Secretary-General.[311]

The Security Council in resolution 1159 decided to adopt the recommendation of the Secretary-General and to establish a UN peacekeeping force in the CAR (UN Mission in the CAR: 'MINURCA') from 15 April 1998. The Council stated in resolution 1159 its affirmation 'that MINURCA may be required to take action to ensure security and freedom of movement of its personnel in the discharge of its mandate'.[312] In so doing, the Council decided in express terms that its Chapter VII authorization to Member States participating in MISAB and those States providing logistical support to ensure the security and freedom of movement of their personnel was to end on 15 April 1998. At the time of writing, MINURCA was still in operation in the CAR.

[308] These reports were in fact submitted to the Security Council, see: S/1997/954, Annex; S/1998/3, Annex; and S/1998/86, Annex.

[309] S/1998/61, para. 29.

[310] S/1998/61, para. 30. The mandate and concept of operations of the proposed UN mission in the CAR were set out in further detail in a subsequent report of the Secretary-General: S/1998/148, Annex.

[311] S/1998/61, para. 32. On 3 Apr. 1998, the Secretary-General appointed his Special Representative (S/1998/297), and on 14 Apr. 1998 his MINURCA Force Commander (S/1998/320).

[312] As part of this mandate, the Council stated that MINURCA was, among other things, to 'assist in maintaining and enhancing security and stability, including freedom of movement, in Bangui and the immediate vicinity of the city'. (Security Council resolution 1159, para. 10(a).) The rest of the mandate as specified by the Council is contained in para. 10(b)–(f) of resolution 1159.

6

The Delegation of Powers to Regional Arrangements

The remaining entity to which the Council has delegated Chapter VII powers is regional arrangements or agencies ('regional arrangements').[1] The examination of this particular delegation, which is the focus of this Chapter, is divided into three main parts: First, the competence of the Council to delegate Chapter VII powers to regional arrangements. There are two issues which arise in such cases. The first is the legality of a delegation to a regional arrangement from the perspective of the United Nations; the second is the legal implications of such a delegation from the perspective of the regional arrangement. As to the first issue, the legal points in play are in substance the same as those relating to a delegation to individual Members as will be demonstrated. The second issue is concerned with the question whether regional arrangements have the competence to exercize delegated Chapter VII powers. This latter issue arises since, as we recall from Chapter 1, the competence of the Council to delegate Chapter VII powers to an entity does not in itself mean that the entity has the institutional competence to be able to exercize those powers. The second part of this Chapter is concerned with the legality of the practice of the Council in delegating Chapter VII powers to regional arrangements, in

---

[1] There is an extensive literature concerning the general subject of the use of enforcement powers by regional organizations or arrangements. This includes: Gray, C., 'Regional Arrangements and the United Nations Collective Security System', in *The Changing Constitution of the United Nations* (Fox, H., ed.) (1997), p. 91; Akehurst, M., 'Enforcement Action by Regional Agencies with Special Reference to the Organization of American States', *BYIL*, 42 (1967), p. 175; Wolfrum, R., 'The Protection of Regional or Other Interests as Structural Element of the Decision-Making Process of International Organizations', *Max Planck Yearbook of United Nations Law*, 1 (1997), p. 259; Walter, C., 'Security Council Control over Regional Action', *Max Planck Yearbook of United Nations Law*, 1 (1997), p. 129; Norton-Moore, J., 'The Role of Regional Arrangements in the Maintenance of World Order', in *The Future of the International Legal Order*, vol. 3 (Falk, R., and Black, C., eds.) (1971), p. 122; Nolte, G., 'Restoring Peace by Regional Action: International Legal Aspects of the Liberian Conflict', *ZaöRV*, 53 (1993), p. 603; Schreur, C., 'Regionalism v. Universalism', *EJIL*, 6 (1995), p. 477; Rivlin, B., 'Regional Arrangements and the UN System for Collective Security and Conflict Resolution: A New Road Ahead?', *Foreign Relations*, 11 (1992), p. 95; Boutros-Ghali, B., *Contribution a' l'étude des ententes régionales* (1949); 'Commentary to Article 52', in *The Charter of the United Nations* (Simma, B., ed.) (1994), p. 679; 'Commentary to Article 53', in *The Charter of the United Nations* (Simma, ed.) (1994), p. 722; 'Commentary to Article 52', in *La Charte des Nations Unies* (Cot, J-P., and Pellet, A., eds.) (1991), p. 797; and 'Commentary to Article 53', in Cot and Pellet, *ibidem*, p. 817; and Société Française pour le Droit International Colloque de Bordeaux, *Régionalisme et Universalisme dans le Droit International Contemporain* (1977).

particular to the North Atlantic Treaty Organization (NATO), and the legality of the exercize of these powers by the regional arrangement concerned. The third part is concerned with a brief discussion of the policy considerations relating to a delegation of Chapter VII powers to regional arrangements.

I. THE COMPETENCE OF THE COUNCIL TO DELEGATE CHAPTER VII POWERS TO REGIONAL ARRANGEMENTS

The starting point for any discussion of the delegation of enforcement powers to regional arrangements is Chapter VIII of the Charter. Article 53(1), which is the *raison d'être* of Chapter VIII, provides as follows:

> The Security Council shall, where appropriate, utilize such regional arrangements or agencies for enforcement action under its authority. But no enforcement action shall be taken under regional arrangements or by regional agencies without the authorization of the Security Council . . .

The authorization by the Security Council of a regional arrangement to take military enforcement action under Chapter VIII represents the delegation of Chapter VII powers by the Council.[2] Chapter VIII of the Charter does not provide the Council with any substantive powers of enforcement to maintain peace in addition to the powers the Council already possesses under Chapter VII.[3] Article 53(1) only gives the Council the competence to delegate Chapter VII powers to regional arrangements. Accordingly, the provision in Article 53(1) for the Council to utilize regional arrangements to carry out military enforcement action does not change the position that the powers which the Council is delegating to these arrangements, by virtue of its competence under this Article, are Chapter VII powers. The delegation of Chapter VII powers to a regional arrangement thus takes place by the Council using its competence so to delegate under Chapter VIII.

However, it is clear from Article 53(1) that regional arrangements are not empowered to take enforcement action without prior Council authorization, that is without a delegation by the Council of its Chapter VII powers.[4] Accordingly, in this way the position of UN Member States acting

---

[2] The process of delegation of Chapter VII powers to a regional arrangement is, thus, different than to other entities, since there is an express provision for such a process in the Charter.

[3] Moreover, Ress notes in Simma's commentary on the Charter, after citing relevant authority, that 'it is widely accepted that Art. 53(1) cl. 1 and cl. 2 do not confer any additional authority on the SC [Security Council]'. (Ress in Simma, *supra* note 1, p. 731.)

[4] See, for example, Ress in Simma, *supra* note 1, p. 733 and citations contained therein; and Sarooshi, D., 'Humanitarian Intervention and Humanitarian Assistance: Law and Practice',

individually or through a regional arrangement is the same. In both cases, with the exception of military action taken in self-defence, a delegation of powers by the Council is necessary for military enforcement action to be lawful. This position derives from the general prohibition in Article 2(4) of the Charter on the use of force by States,[5] and relies on the position that there are no additional rights to use force which States derive by virtue of their membership in a regional arrangement, even if the arrangement possesses independent legal personality.[6] Just as there are no such additional rights, there are in general terms no additional obligations on States when exercizing delegated Chapter VII powers through the framework of a regional arrangement. Accordingly, the Security Council cannot require a regional arrangement, composed of UN Member States, to carry out military enforcement action under Chapter VIII of the Charter. This position is, moreover, supported when one recalls the position that a delegation of powers to States is permissive but not mandatory.[7]

In addition to the prior authorization of the Security Council being necessary for enforcement action by a regional arrangement, the Council must be able to exercize overall authority and control over the use of its delegated powers. The fact that these powers are being exercized through the mechanisms of a regional arrangement does not alter the legal position that the Council must ensure that it can exercize its overall authority and control, as distinct from operational command and control, over the

---

Wilton Park Paper, 86 (1994). Cf. the case of military enforcement action by the Economic Community of West African States (ECOWAS) in Liberia, as explained in Sarooshi, *ibidem*; and Kufuor, K., 'The Legality of the Intervention in the Liberian Civil War by the Economic Community of West African States', *African Journal of International & Comparative Law*, 5 (1993), p. 525. But cf. Gray, *supra* note 1, p. 107. However, in its response to the *coup* which overthrew the democratically-elected Government in Sierra Leone, the Security Council did delegate to ECOWAS by resolution 1132 the power to carry out a naval interdiction against that country, and in the Council debates concerning the adoption of the resolution the representative of the Russian Federation stated that enforcement measures should not be taken by regional organizations without Security Council authorization. (Security Council Press Release, SC/6425, 8 Oct. 1997, p. 10.) On the delegation of power to ECOWAS to carry out a naval interdiction, see *infra* note 76.

[5] See more generally on this prohibition: Brownlie, I., *International Law and the Use of Force by States* (1963); and Dinstein, Y., *War, Aggression and Self-Defence* (1994).

[6] In addition, a cogent argument can be made that the members of a regional arrangement are fully subject to the obligations undertaken by their membership in the UN and cannot avoid these obligations by invoking the constitution of the regional organization or arrangement. (See also *UNCIO XII*, pp. 771, 812; and Simma, *supra* note 1, p. 697.) Moreover, this approach is fully endorsed by Article 48(2) of the Charter which states: 'Such decisions shall be carried out by Members of the United Nations directly and through their action in the appropriate international agencies of which they are members.' The thrust of this provision is that States are not relieved of their obligations by virtue of their membership in another organization or arrangement which may happen to possess international legal personality. The application of Article 103 leads to the same conclusion; see with respect to Article 103: *infra* note 17 and corresponding text *et sequentia*.

[7] See *supra* note 31 and corresponding text in Chapter 4.

action.[8] This flows from the position that there is no qualitative difference in the nature of a delegation of powers to Member States as opposed to a regional arrangement.[9] This position is recognized by Article 53(1) of the Charter which stipulates that a condition of a delegation of Chapter VII powers to a regional arrangement is that the operation remain under the 'authority of the Council'.

In summary, the fact that initiation of military enforcement measures by a regional arrangement is subject to prior authorization[10] and that the arrangement must comply with a reporting requirement is sufficient indication that the Charter envisages the start-up, supervision, and termination of enforcement action by a regional arrangement to be carried out by the Security Council. In this way a delegation by the Council of its Chapter VII powers whether to a UN Member State or a regional arrangement is identical: it is an exercize by the Council of its collective security function under the Charter. In legal terms, this authority of the Council requires, as in the case of UN Member States, conditions to be imposed on the regional arrangement for there to be a lawful delegation of Chapter VII powers. We recall that these three conditions are the specification of a clear objective for which the power is being delegated; the exercize of supervision over the use of the delegated powers; and the imposition of a reporting requirement. The observance of these conditions in practice is examined in Section II of this Chapter.

The Security Council by delegating Chapter VII powers to a regional arrangement may be authorizing, depending on the terms of the delegated mandate, the use of military enforcement action against a State that is not a member of the regional community. This is consistent with the purpose of a delegation of Chapter VII powers—to maintain or restore peace by achieving the Council's stipulated objectives—and the provisions of Chapter VIII of the Charter. Article 52(1) of the Charter provides that regional arrangements can deal with 'such matters relating to the maintenance of international peace and security as [is] appropriate for regional action'. It is in this context that Article 53(1) goes on to state that the Council 'shall, where appropriate, utilize such regional arrangements or agencies for enforcement action under its authority'. The power of deciding whether it is 'appropriate' for the carrying out of enforcement action in a particular case is left to the Security Council. The Council has been given the primary responsibility for the maintenance of international peace and security.

---

[8] It follows from the exercize of this overall authority and control that the Council, as in the case of UN Member States, is accountable and, in legal terms, responsible for the exercize of its delegated powers by a regional arrangement. In the case of UN Member States, see *supra* Section III in Chapter 4.

[9] See *supra* note 77 in Chapter 4.

[10] The Charter does not allow a regional arrangement to be proactive in the taking of military enforcement action without the authorization of the Council: see *supra* note 4.

Accordingly, the Council possesses the competence to authorize a regional arrangement to carry out enforcement action against a State that is not a member of the particular regional arrangement if it deems that this is necessary for the maintenance of international peace and security.[11] This competence of the Council to use regional arrangements with an external focus is an important feature of the delegation of powers to such arrangements. This is also of significance to the use of collective self-defence organizations such as NATO for the carrying out of military enforcement action under the auspices of the Council, since NATO has not until now been regarded as a regional arrangement for the purposes of Chapter VIII of the Charter: it has been seen as a collective self-defence pact.[12] A major reason why NATO sought to characterize itself as a collective self-defence alliance was to avoid the obligation in Article 53(1) to seek prior permission from the Security Council before it could act in a particular case.[13]

The combination, however, of the Council delegating tasks in the area of peace and security to NATO and the self-redefinition of NATO to carry out tasks which are in addition to its original mandate under the NATO Charter,[14] allow it to fit within the rubric of a Chapter VIII regional arrangement. This approach was certainly adopted by the German Constitutional Court—the *Bundesverfassungsgericht*—in its decision that NATO can be classified as a type of collective security system, and thus that German troops could participate in NATO actions that were directed at the implementation of Security Council resolutions.[15] In any case, it is certainly clear that the Security Council has treated NATO as a Chapter VII regional

---

[11] See also Kelsen, H., *The Law of the United Nations* (1951), p. 327; and Simma, *supra* note 1, p. 731. Cf. the opposing view that a regional arrangement should only be concerned with the keeping of peace within the arrangement and cannot as such be utilized to take measures outside the regional community: see Vellas, P. , *Le Régionalisme International et l'Organisation des Nations Unies* (1948), p. 206.

[12] See, for example, Kelsen, H., 'Is the North Atlantic Treaty a Regional Arrangement?', *AJIL*, 45 (1951), pp. 162–6.

[13] A possible additional reason for such a legal characterization was to avoid the more onerous reporting obligation of a regional arrangement under Article 54. The obligation on a regional arrangement to report to the Security Council is broader than the reporting obligation on States exercizing self-defence under Article 51 of the Charter. Article 54 requires a regional arrangement to inform the Council not only of measures already undertaken, but also those being contemplated: an *ex ante* obligation to inform; while the reporting obligation in Article 51 is less stringent, since it only requires States to report to the Council those self-defence measures already taken: it is an *ex post* obligation to inform. See also *supra* notes 78–9 and corresponding text in Chapter 4.

[14] See, for example, the carrying out of operations outside the NATO area of operation: *infra* Section II. Cf., Zöckler, M., 'Germany in Collective Security Systems—Anything Goes?', *EJIL*, 6 (1995), p. 274 at p. 279.

[15] *Adria-, AWACS- und Somalia-Einsaetze der Bundeswehr, Entscheidungen des Bundesverfassungsgerichts, BVerfGE,* 90 (1994), p. 286. Cf. Zöckler, M., 'Germany in Collective Security Systems—Anything Goes?', *EJIL*, 6 (1995), p. 274 at p. 279.

arrangement. As Simma's *Commentary on the Charter* states: 'These resolutions manifestly show that NATO has been considered by the SC [Security Council] as one of the regional arrangements which might be entrusted with specific enforcement actions.'[16] The practice of the Council in this regard is examined further below in Section II of this Chapter. However, this analysis is solely from the viewpoint of the United Nations. It is now opportune to discuss the issue from the viewpoint of the regional arrangement. In particular, the problems for regional arrangements of the limits of their constitutions and how this affects their competence to carry out a delegated mandate. Put differently: can the Security Council authorize a regional arrangement to carry out enforcement action that is not *per se* provided for in its constituent instrument?

We recall from Chapter 4 that States do not have to comply with their treaty obligations when these are in direct conflict with their exercize of delegated Chapter VII powers.[17] Applying Article 103 of the Charter to a State which is a member of both the UN and a regional arrangement, we find that the State may not have to comply with its treaty obligations under the constituent treaty of the regional arrangement where these are in conflict with obligations imposed on a State by the Security Council. This means that States may not have to comply with their obligations under the constituent treaty of their regional arrangement when exercizing delegated Chapter VII powers, but it does not mean that the State is put under a positive obligation to exercize these powers using the structures of the regional arrangement. We recall from above that the Security Council cannot require a State or a regional arrangement to take up a delegation of Chapter VII powers.[18] What the Security Council may do, however, is to require States, as a condition for the exercize of the delegated power, to use the mechanisms of a regional arrangement.[19]

However, the legal position of Member States in terms of being able to take up a delegation of Chapter VII powers may be different from that of regional arrangements. It may not always be legally possible for a regional arrangement under its constituent treaty to take up a delegation of Chapter VII powers. In such cases, a delegation of powers to a regional arrangement does not mean that the organs of that arrangement can exceed the powers they have been given by their constituent instrument. The delegation of Chapter VII powers to a regional arrangement gives the arrangement—and

---

[16] Simma, *supra* note 1, p. 730. See also: Gray, *supra* note 1, pp. 113, 115–16.

[17] See *supra* note 36 and corresponding text in Chapter 4. The application of Article 103 to a delegation of Chapter VII powers has already been discussed in more detail in the context of UN Member States: *ibidem*.

[18] See *supra* note 7 and corresponding text.

[19] See, for an example, *infra* note 92 and corresponding text.

thus its organs—the right to exercize those powers but not in disregard of its constituent treaty. This does not of course preclude the relevant organs of a regional arrangement from deciding, according to the relevant constitutional provisions, that the arrangement will take up the delegation of Chapter VII powers. In any case, for the purposes of our current enquiry, suffice to note that the internal constitutional constraints on a regional arrangement being able to exercize delegated Chapter VII powers does not affect the lawfulness of the delegation or *the exercize of delegated powers* from the perspective of the United Nations Charter.

Moreover, the issue of the organs of a regional arrangement having the competence under their constituent treaty to exercize delegated powers is different from the legal position of States that are members of both the United Nations and the regional arrangement. Having already established in Chapter 4 that the Council possesses the competence to delegate Chapter VII powers to Member States, the issue of the internal constitutional restraints of a regional arrangement becomes almost irrelevant. Member States have the competence to exercize the delegated powers whether or not the regional arrangement has the competence to do so, and, where States are Members of both organizations, they are not precluded from exercizing delegated Chapter VII powers acting nationally because of their membership in the regional arrangement. The internal structure and competence of an arrangement constituted by treaty binds only the organs of the arrangement and not necessarily, as noted above, the Member States acting in their individual capacity. However, the issue of using the organs of a regional arrangement to assist in carrying out military enforcement action remains problematic.

II. THE DELEGATION OF POWERS TO NATO

The practice of the Security Council has not been to delegate its Chapter VII powers to NATO in specific terms, but to delegate these powers more generally to UN Member States with provision for the exercize of these powers through regional arrangements. The Security Council has delegated its Chapter VII powers in such cases to achieve the following objectives that it had determined were necessary for the maintenance or restoration of international peace and security: the protection of a Security Council declared 'safe area'; the carrying out of a naval interdiction; the enforcement of a Security Council declared 'no-fly zone'; and the implementation of an agreement which the Council has deemed is necessary for the maintenance or restoration of peace.

1. The attempt to protect UN declared 'safe areas' in Bosnia

It was explained in Chapter 2 that the Security Council delegated to the UN Secretary-General the competence to exercize command and control powers over Member States carrying out air strikes in the former Yugoslavia in order, *inter alia*, to protect UN declared 'safe areas'.[20] Moreover, the Security Council in resolution 836 delegated to UN Member States, acting individually or through a regional arrangement, the power to take military action to protect these safe areas. In resolution 836 the Council, acting under Chapter VII, '*[d]ecides* that ... Member States, acting nationally or through regional arrangements, may take, under the authority of the Security Council and subject to close coordination with the Secretary-General and UNPROFOR, all necessary measures, through the use of air power, in and around the safe areas in the Republic of Bosnia and Herzegovina, to support UNPROFOR in the performance of its mandate set out in paragraphs 5 and 9 above'. Moreover, the Council in operative paragraph 11 '*[r]equests* the Member States concerned, the Secretary-General and UNPROFOR to coordinate closely on the measures they are taking to implement paragraph 10 above and to report to the Council through the Secretary-General'. There were two objectives specified in resolution 836 which would enable Member States to use force by their air capability: the defence of UN peacekeepers and the deterrence of attacks on the safe areas.[21]

These delegations of power were taken up by certain Member States who chose to act through a regional arrangement, NATO, of which they were all Members. Accordingly, the Secretary-General notes that, in a letter of the Deputy Secretary-General of NATO dated 11 June 1993, NATO had confirmed its willingness to offer 'protective air power in case of attack against UNPROFOR in the performance of its overall mandate, if it so requests'.[22] Such a decision by the NATO Council was not, *stricto sensu*, a requirement

---

[20] In resolution 819 the Security Council demanded that 'all parties and others concerned treat Srebrenica and its surroundings as a safe area which should be free from any armed attack or any other hostile act'. Moreover, in resolution 824 the Council acting under Chapter VII declared that Sarajevo, Tuzla, Zepa, Gorazde, Bihac, and Srebrenica should be 'treated as safe areas by all the parties concerned and should be free from armed attacks and from any other hostile act'. See also S/1994/300, para. 28.

[21] It is clear that resolution 836 envisaged the use of force to achieve these objectives: see, for example, the following statements by States in the Security Council debates preceding the adoption of resolution 836: France (S/PV.3228, p. 13); Hungary (S/PV.3228, pp. 52–3); and Spain (S/PV.3228, p. 59). We recall, moreover, that resolution 836 expanded the mandate of UNPROFOR to enable it to deter attacks on the safe areas by, *inter alia*, authorizing UNPROFOR, acting in self defence, to take measures necessary, including the use of force, to respond to the bombardments or armed incursions into the safe areas. (See also Weller, M., 'Peace-Keeping and Peace-Enforcement in the Republic of Bosnia and Herzegovina', *ZaöRV*, 56 (1996), p. 71 at p. 108.) However, UNPROFOR, as a lightly armed peacekeeping force, did not have the capability to carry out such action in an effective manner.

[22] S/25939, p. 2.

for UN Member States to exercize the delegated powers, since the delegation was to Member States directly and did not specify that they must act through a regional arrangement or organization.[23] However, if States are to act through a regional arrangement then the fulfilment of any necessary requirements pursuant to the particular constituent instrument of the organization in question is an obligation that must needs be satisfied by States.[24] *In casu*, this is a decision of the North Atlantic Council. Accordingly, this further decision of the North Atlantic Council was sought by the UN Secretary-General in a letter dated 6 February 1994.[25] This was in reaction to a massacre that resulted from the shelling of a Sarajevo market place on 5 February 1994 leading to stronger joint UN/NATO action to alleviate the siege of the city. The Secretary-General saw his authority to seek a NATO decision authorizing air strikes as being under Security Council resolution 836.[26] His request was made in the following terms:

I should be grateful, therefore, if you could take action to obtain, at the earliest possible date, a decision by the North Atlantic Council to authorize the Commander-in-Chief of NATO's Southern Command to launch air strikes, at the request of the United Nations, against artillery or mortar positions in or around Sarajevo which are determined by UNPROFOR to be responsible for attacks against civilian targets in that city. The arrangements for the coordination of such air strikes would be elaborated through direct contacts between UNPROFOR Headquarters and NATO's Southern Command, as has already been done in the case of close air support for the self-defence of United Nations personnel in Bosnia and Herzegovina.[27]

In a NATO Council meeting of 9 February 1994 it was decided to authorize air strikes if Bosnian Serb forces and the Bosnian Government did not, within ten days, withdraw or regroup and place under the control of UNPROFOR all heavy weapons located in an exclusion zone, described as 'an area within 20 kilometres of the centre of Sarajevo'.[28] To ensure the implementation of these measures, NATO Members decided that heavy weapons remaining within the operational area at the end of the stated time and not under the control of UNPROFOR would be subject to air strikes

---

[23] Cf. the delegation of powers in the case of the naval interdiction against the former Yugoslavia (see *infra* Section II(2)) and in the case of the Implementation Force in Bosnia (*infra* Section II(4)).

[24] See *supra* Section I.

[25] S/1994/131, Annex.

[26] This interpretation has been supported by Member States: see, for example, the statements in the Security Council by the representatives of France (S/PV.3336, p. 16); Oman (S/PV.3367, p. 52); and New Zealand (S/PV.3367, p. 56).

[27] S/1994/131, p. 2.

[28] 'Decisions taken at the meeting of the North Atlantic Council on 9th February 1994(1)', NATO Press Release (94) 15, 9 Feb. 1994.

carried out in close coordination with the UN Secretary-General. This became known as the 'Sarajevo ultimatum'.[29] NATO members also agreed to the UN Secretary-General's request to authorize the Commander-in-Chief of Allied Forces in Southern Europe to launch air strikes against artillery positions from which attacks on civilian targets in Sarajevo originated.[30] Subsequently, the Bosnian Government suggested that a meeting of the Security Council should be called to discuss NATO action. This suggestion was taken up, and the Council subsequently held a meeting on 14 February 1994. The discussion in the Council focused on, *inter alia*, NATO's ultimatum to the Serbian forces which were besieging Sarajevo. There was overwhelming support by States for the position that the NATO ultimatum was mandated by Council resolutions 824 and 836. As, for example, the representative of France stated in respect of the NATO decisions:

[They lie] squarely within the framework of Security Council resolutions 824 (1993) and 836 (1993) with respect to safe areas. Indeed, the lifting of the siege from those areas . . . is the purpose of those resolutions, which, *inter alia*, authorized UNPROFOR to use force, including air power, in fulfilling its mandate. Hence there is no need for these decisions of the North Atlantic Council to be submitted to the Security Council for any further decision. Moreover, my Government considers that in contacting NATO the Secretary-General was acting within his authority and in accordance with Security Council resolutions.[31]

Moreover, the Egyptian delegate saw the authority for the NATO ultimatum as flowing directly from the terms of Security Council resolution 836. He observed:

---

[29] Leurdijk, D., *The United Nations and NATO in Former Yugoslavia: Partners in International Cooperation*, (1994), p. 51.

[30] *Ibidem.*

[31] S/PV.3336, p. 16. Similarly, the US representative stated: 'Weapons not under United Nations control may be subject to air strikes. During the 10 days the North Atlantic Treaty Organization (NATO) will also respond, in coordination with the United Nations, to the artillery or mortar fire that has wreaked such havoc in Sarajevo. These decisions are consistent with resolutions approved by the Council. They do not require further Council action. We need to remind ourselves that the decision to initiate air strikes rests in the hands of the Secretary-General, and it was the Council that put it there.' (S/PV.3336, p. 19.) See also the statements by the representatives of The Netherlands (S/PV.3336 (Resumption 1), p. 134); Belgium (S/PV.3336 (Resumption 2), pp. 179–80); Norway (S/PV.3336 (Resumption 1), p. 94); Turkey (S/PV.3336 (Resumption 1), p. 109); Afghanistan (S/PV.3336 (Resumption 1), pp. 102–3); and Malaysia (S/PV.3336 (Resumption 1), p. 82). Cf., however, the position of the Russian Government which stated that the ultimatum was made by an organ which 'has no authority to take decisions on the substance of a settlement in Bosnia. . . . A decision on such a request [to use force] must be taken by the Secretary-General after consultation with the members of the Security Council.' (Letter dated 10 Feb. 1994 from the Permanent Representative of the Russian Federation to the United Nations addressed to the President of the Security Council, S/1994/152: see also S/PV.3336, 14 Feb. 1994, p. 39.)

The Security Council adopted resolution 836 (1993), which permits the use of air strikes to ensure the protection of the safe areas of Bosnia and Herzegovina. It permits this in two events: first, if there is a new bombardment or a new violation of the safe areas, not only of Sarajevo but of all the zones specified by the Security Council; and secondly, if the Serbs should fail to respect the ultimatum to remove their heavy weapons from Sarajevo within the prescribed deadline.[32]

Similarly, the UN Secretary-General welcomed the NATO ultimatum in respect of Sarajevo, and later relating to Gorazde, as being in accordance with paragraph 10 of resolution 836.[33] This position supported by States and the Secretary-General is accurate.

In terms of whether the imposition of the ultimatum was within the scope of the delegated powers, it would seem that the decision to impose the ultimatum is a reasonable interpretation by Member States, acting through NATO, of their mandate under resolutions 836 and 844 to protect the safe areas. It was a measure necessary to achieve the objective specified in these resolutions: the protection of the safe areas. In this way, the NATO ultimatum can be conceived of as an exercize of Chapter VII powers on behalf of the international community. In fact, the representative of Tunisia in a statement in the Security Council seemed to adopt the NATO ultimatum as that of the international community. He observed: 'Today, after the warning issued by NATO, the international community is demonstrating a firm will to put an end to the massacres and to find the ways and means to do so.'[34]

In political terms, the even-handed nature of the ultimatum was important for several States.[35] Moreover, there was some value placed on the contribution such an ultimatum could make to a successful peace process:[36] once the contentious issue of Sarajevo was resolved it was assumed there would be a much greater chance for a negotiated settlement.[37]

---

[32] S/PV.3336 (Resumption 1), p. 97.

[33] S/1994/444, para. 49.

[34] S/PV.3336 (Resumption 2), p. 161.

[35] The German representative in the Council stated that '[t]he decision of the Council of the North Atlantic Treaty Organization (NATO) is balanced because it also calls upon the Government of Bosnia and Herzegovina, within the same period, to place under UNPROFOR control its heavy weapons within the Sarajevo exclusion zone and to refrain from attacks launched from within the current confrontation lines in the city'. (S/PV.3336 (Resumption 1), p. 77.) Moreover, the aim of the air strikes as being a political tool to be used in negotiations with the warring factions is a common element of many of the statements by States in the Security Council: see, for example, Italy (S/PV.3336 (Resumption 1), p. 118).

[36] See, for example, the statement by the Government of Sweden in the Security Council: S/PV.3336 (Resumption 1), p. 113.

[37] Cf., however, the position of the Government of the Federal Republic of Yugoslavia which, in a letter to the UN Secretary-General, states, unsurprisingly, that it considers in mandating the NATO air strikes the UN was 'behaving like a belligerent party'. (S/1994/418, p. 2.)

The involvement of the UN, in particular the Secretary-General, was also of particular importance for many other States, since they considered it as a necessary prerequisite for the Council to be able to exercize its overall authority and control over the action. As the Norwegian Government stated in the Council debates: '[i]t is ultimately the responsibility of the Secretary-General to decide on the steps that may be taken, as the overall political authority rests with the United Nations'.[38] In accordance with this approach, the Secretary-General notes in respect of air strikes by NATO '[i]t is of course understood that the first decision to initiate the use of air resources in this context will be taken by the Secretary-General in consultation with the members of the Security Council'.[39] This report of the Secretary-General was expressly adopted by the Council in resolution 844.[40] Similarly, in a report dated 2 August 1993, the Secretary-General stated that:

the purpose of the use of air power . . . is to promote the fulfilment of objectives approved by the Security Council . . . It follows that the general authority granted in Resolution 770 in this respect must be interpreted in the context of the modalities

---

[38] S/PV.3336 (Resumption 1), p. 94. See also the statements by the representatives of Canada (S/PV.3336 (Resumption 1), p. 137); and Tunisia (S/PV.3336 (Resumption 2), p. 161).

[39] S/25939, p. 4. Similarly, in an earlier NATO Council meeting of 4 Aug. 1993, Canada (together with the UK, Belgium, and France) in particular stressed the need for UN control over events while the US seemed prepared to concede such a UN role only in cases where aircraft were called upon to protect UNPROFOR but not with regard to other uses against Serb targets. (Freudenschuß, H., 'Between Unilateralism and Collective Security: Authorizations of the Use of Force by the UN Security Council', *European Journal of International Law*, 5 (1994), p. 492 at p. 511.) Freudenschuß, states that '[i]n the course of the next few days, the US—under strong pressure from its allies—first conceded that the choice of targets for air strikes must be approved by both NATO and the UN and ultimately agreed that the first such attack required approval by the Secretary-General'. (*Ibidem.*) Leurdijk states that in respect of the NATO 'ultimatum' there are the following three possible answers to the question of who would give the order to launch an air operation: '1) in the event of an attack or threat of attack against UNPROFOR, the UN Secretary-General had already delegated this power to his representative in former Yugoslavia, who could also ask for close air support from NATO's CINCSOUTH [Commander-in-Chief of NATO's Southern Command]; 2) in the event of further artillery or mortar attacks against the civilian population of Sarajevo, CINCSOUTH had received authority from the NAC on 9 February to act at the request of the UN, so that the UN special representative and the UNPROFOR commander could ask him for air strikes; 3) NATO, in coordination with UN Secretary-General Boutros-Ghali, would take decisions regarding the control of heavy weapons after the expiry of the 'ultimatum'. In this respect, an additional issue arose with respect to the interpretation of the phrase in NATO's "ultimatum", "putting under the control of UNPROFOR". Would this imply "physical control" by UNPROFOR personnel in a number of assembly points, requiring the displacement of cannons, or just the technical incapability of shelling Sarajevo, leaving the heavy weapons on their original sites without direct control?' (Leurdijk, *supra* note 29, p. 55.)

[40] Moreover, the Council in operative paragraph 4 of resolution 844 stated that it '[r]eaffirms its decision in paragraph 10 of resolution 836 (1993) on the use of air power, in and around the safe areas, to support UNPROFOR in the performance of its mandate, and encourages Member States, acting nationally or through regional organizations or arrangements, to coordinate closely with the Secretary-General in this regard'.

established pursuant to Resolutions 816 and 836. For this as well as pragmatic reasons, I have consistently taken the position that the first use of air power in the theatre should be initiated by the Secretary-General . . . In approving the report of the Secretary-General of 14 June 1993 in its Resolution 844, the Security Council has endorsed this approach . . . It is therefore my understanding that the decision to use air power in Bosnia and Herzegovina pursuant to UN resolutions must continue to rest with the Secretary-General . . . You may recall that action by NATO to enforce the no-fly zone was subject to specific authorization by the Force Commander of UNPROFOR.[41]

Accordingly, the use of the 'dual-key' approach, as explained in more detail in Chapter 2, was employed by the Secretary-General and NATO in respect of the use of air strikes.[42] This operational command and control by the Secretary-General, representing the exercize of authority and control by the Council, over the use of such military force is an important factor that militates in favour of the lawfulness of the delegation of powers in resolution 836.

The Members of the Security Council who affirmed the legal basis for the NATO ultimatum were clear in affirming that the Secretary-General and NATO had the power to decide whether the use of force was required and that no further recourse to the Security Council was necessary.[43] In other words, the Secretary-General and Member States, acting through NATO, had been delegated a discretionary power of decision making. Moreover, the Security Council has delegated powers of binding decision making to the Secretary-General and Member States which they can further decide to back up with military enforcement measures: namely air strikes. The imposition of the NATO ultimatum was in effect an exercize of the power of the Security Council under Article 25 of the Charter to impose a binding legal obligation, but through the mechanism of delegation. This was an exercize of the Council's power under Article 25 and Chapter VII of the Charter to make decisions that bind UN Member States. However, we recall from Chapter 1 that the lawfulness of such a delegation of power depends on the Council being able to exercize a sufficient degree of authority and control over the exercize of delegated powers such that it could decide to change at any time the way in which those powers were being exercized. *In casu*, we find that the NATO ultimatum is lawful, since the Council exercizes a

---

[41] Moreover, the North Atlantic Council subsequently affirmed in express terms the position that the first use of air power must receive the authorization of the UN Secretary-General: 'Decisions Taken at the Meeting of the North Atlantic Council on 9th Aug. 1993', Press Release (93) 52, 9 Aug. 1993, *Atlantic News*, No. 2547, 26 Aug. 1993.

[42] See *supra* note 156 and corresponding text in Chapter 2.

[43] See *supra* notes 31 & 32 and corresponding text. Cf. the earlier position of the Russian Government that the Secretary-General should consult with the Security Council before deciding to authorize the use of force under resolution 836: Letter from the Permanent Representative of the Russian Federation to the United Nations addressed to the Secretary-General, S/1994/138, 8 Feb. 1994.

sufficient degree of authority and control, through the Secretary-General, over the implementation of the decision.

Moreover, further agreement was sought by the UN Secretary-General from NATO for the carrying out of air strikes for the protection of the other five 'safe areas' in Bosnia.[44] However, an additional NATO ultimatum to besieging Serb forces was only issued in respect of Gorazde.[45] The legal considerations relating to the Sarajevo ultimatum apply equally to the imposition by NATO of an ultimatum relating to the UN declared safe area of Gorazde.[46] However, while the Sarajevo ultimatum was at least success-

[44] The UN Secretary-General in a letter to the Secretary-General of NATO dated 18 Apr. 1994 stated: 'The tragic events which are currently taking place in Gorazde demonstrate the need for the North Atlantic Council to take a similar decision with respect to the five other safe areas declared by the Security Council, namely the towns of Tuzla, Zepa, Gorazde, Bihac and Srebrenica and their surrounding areas. I should accordingly be grateful if you could take action to obtain, at the earliest possible date, a decision by the North Atlantic Council to authorize the Commander-in-Chief of NATO's Southern Command to launch air strikes, at the request of the United Nations, against artillery, mortar positions or tanks in or around the above-mentioned safe areas which are determined by UNPROFOR to be responsible for attacks against civilian targets within those areas. The arrangements for the coordination of such air strikes would be elaborated through direct contacts between UNPROFOR Headquarters and NATO's Southern Command, as has already been done in the case of close air support for the self-defence of United Nations personnel in Bosnia and Herzegovina and air strikes in and around Sarajevo.' (S/1994/466, pp. 2–3.)

[45] On 22 April 1994 the North Atlantic Council imposed two 'ultimatums' in respect of Gorazde. The first set of decisions imposing an 'ultimatum' required the following conditions to be satisfied: '(a) Bosnian Serb attacks against the safe area of Gorazde to cease immediately; (b) Bosnian Serb forces to pull back 3 kilometres from . . . Gorazde by 1 a.m. GMT on 24 April 1994; and (c) From 1 a.m. GMT on 24 April 1994, UN forces, humanitarian relief convoys and medical assistance teams are to be free to enter Gorazde unimpeded, and medical evacuations are to be permitted.' (NATO decision reproduced in Security Council document: S/1994/495, pp. 2–3.) If these conditions were not met then the NATO Council decided the following: 'The Commander-in-Chief of NATO's Southern Command is authorized to conduct air strikes against Bosnian Serb heavy weapons and other military targets within a 20 kilometre radius of the centre of Gorazde (but inside the territory of Bosnia and Herzegovina) in accordance with the procedural arrangements worked out between NATO and UNPROFOR following the Council's decisions of 2 and 9 August 1993.' (NATO decision reproduced in Security Council document: S/1994/495, pp. 2–3.) In its second set of decisions taken at the same meeting, the North Atlantic Council agreed on the following second 'ultimatum': 'that a "military exclusion zone" (within the territory of Bosnia–Herzegovina) is established for 20 kilometres around Gorazde, which calls for all Bosnian Serb heavy weapons . . . to be withdrawn by 0001 GMT on 27th April 1994; . . . that if the safe areas of Bihac, Srebrenica, Tuzla or Zepa are attacked by heavy weapons from any range or if, in the common judgment of the NATO Military Commanders and UN Military Commanders, there is a concentration or movement of heavy weapons within a radius of 20 kilometres of these areas . . . which threatens those areas they will, for the purposes of this decision and without further action of the Council, be designated individually or collectively, military exclusion zones, and due public notice to governments and to the parties will be given if and when this happens. The exact line of the perimeter of these areas will be established jointly by UNPROFOR and CINCSOUTH.' (Reproduced in S/1994/ 498, pp. 2–3.)

[46] Moreover, the lawfulness of the NATO ultimatum in respect of Gorazde was expressly affirmed by the following States in the Security Council: Turkey (S/PV.3367, p. 8); Sweden (S/PV.3367, p. 29); Spain (S/PV.3367, p. 48); Rwanda (S/PV.3367, p. 49); and New Zealand (S/PV.3367, p. 55).

ful in securing a partial withdrawal of Serbian heavy weaponry from around Sarajevo by the expiry of the deadline, the Gorazde ultimatum was not so effective.[47]

It was the opinion of the Government of Bosnia and Herzegovina that the terms of resolution 836 imposed an obligation on NATO to take the action mandated by the Council. A letter dated 8 February 1994 from the Bosnian representative to the President of the Security Council provides the following:

Pursuant to resolutions 824 (1993) and 836 (1993), the United Nations Security Council has already adopted the necessary mandate and authority for 'Member States, acting nationally or through regional arrangements' to 'take the necessary measures, including the use of force, in reply to bombardments against the safe areas'. In this context, NATO is obliged to act in accordance with the responsibilities and obligations delegated to it by the United Nations and the Member States thereof. In response to the continuing siege of Sarajevo and the unprecedented bombardments of Friday, 4 February and Saturday, 5 February, the Member States should have the opportunity to examine and evaluate, in an open debate of the Security Council, what steps have been undertaken or are contemplated by NATO having assumed the authority and responsibilities delegated to it by the United Nations.[48]

However, the content of any such 'obligation' cannot be legal, but is only political. It has already been explained in some detail in Chapter 1 that a delegation of Chapter VII powers by the Council can provide a mandate for, but does not require, military enforcement action. Thus it is inaccurate to speak in terms of an obligation, since neither NATO nor UN Member States are bound by law to carry out any action.[49]

---

[47] Press Statement on 21 Feb. 1994 by NATO Secretary-General Manfred Worner following expiry of the deadline for withdrawal of heavy weapons from in and around Sarajevo, in *NATO Review*, Apr. 1994, p. 22. See also S/PV.3344, p. 4; and Leurdijk, *supra* note 29, pp. 55–6.

[48] S/1994/134. See also the statement by the representative of Jordan (S/PV.3336 (Resumption 2), p. 155).

[49] Nonetheless, there were additional air strikes carried out by UN Member States acting through NATO in co-ordination with the Secretary-General's Special Representative. As the Secretary-General stated on 24 May 1995: '. . . the use of air power was authorized not only for the defence of UNPROFOR personnel but also to deter attacks on the safe areas. UNPROFOR has requested NATO to use its air power on nine occasions when my Special Representative has deemed such action necessary and appropriate. In all cases air power was used against Bosnian Serb targets or targets in Serb-controlled parts of Croatia that had been operating in support of the Bosnian Serbs. On 12 March 1994, close air support was requested when UNPROFOR troops came under fire near Bihac but was not implemented because of bad weather. On 10 and 11 April 1994, close air support was provided near Gorazde . . . On 5 August 1994, air strikes were made against targets in the Sarajevo exclusion zone. On 22 September 1994, an air strike was made near Sarajevo following an attack on an UNPROFOR armoured car. On 21 and 23 November 1994, air strikes were made against Udbina airfield in Croatia, which had been used to launch air attacks in the Bihac safe area, and against surface-to-air missiles in western Bosnia and Herzegovina and in the Krajina region of Croatia that had threatened NATO aircraft.' (S/1995/444, pp. 16–17.)

It was not until August 1995, in response to yet another shelling of Sarajevo, that an intensive air campaign was used against the Bosnian Serbs to protect the safe areas and force a peace settlement. This campaign was known as Operation Deliberate Force. The NATO Secretary-General announced on 30 August 1994 that NATO military aircraft had commenced attacks on Bosnian Serb military targets in Bosnia.[50] The decision to initiate operations was taken jointly by the UN Force Commander and the NATO Commander-in-Chief, Allied Forces Southern Europe.[51] The declared aim of the operation was to 'reduce the threat to the Sarajevo Safe Area and to deter further attacks there or on any other Safe Area. We hope that this operation will also demonstrate to the Bosnian Serbs the futility of further military actions and convince all parties of the determination of the Alliance to implement its decisions.'[52] The air campaign was conducted in conjunction with military action by the Rapid Reaction Force against Bosnian Serb positions that were determined to have been firing upon Sarajevo.[53] Subsequently, it became clear that there were a number of detailed conditions, fulfilment of which were necessary, for the termination of the operation. In a letter of 3 September 1995 from General Janvier to the Bosnian Serbs, the following conditions were specified: 'our objective remains attaining compliance of the Bosnian Serbs to cease attacks on Sarajevo or other Safe Areas; the withdrawal of Bosnian Serb heavy weapons from the total exclusion zone around Sarajevo, without delay; complete freedom of movement for UN forces and personnel and NGOs and unrestricted use of Sarajevo airport'.[54] There was concern expressed by the Russian representative that these air strikes were not in conformity with Security Council resolutions.[55] Subsequently, the Russian representative criticized the NATO action on, *inter alia*, the grounds that no consultations had been held with Council Members as to the decision to initiate the use of force.[56] However, the delegation of powers to Member States in resolution 836 clearly envisaged the use of force to achieve such objectives as the Secretary-General and Member States deemed necessary to protect the safe areas.[57] The operation clearly was not directed at changing the balance

---

[50] Statement by NATO Secretary-General, NATO Press Release (95) 73, 30 Aug. 1995.

[51] *Ibidem.*

[52] *Ibidem.*

[53] Transcript of News Conference with NATO Admiral Smith, 31 Aug. 1995; and US Press Release EUR503 09/01/95, Operation Deliberate Force Press Briefing, 1 Sept. 1995.

[54] As contained in Statement by NATO Secretary-General, Sept. 1995, Press Release (95)79.

[55] UN Press Release DH1969, 31 Aug. 1995.

[56] S/PV.3575, p. 3.

[57] See also, in the context of Operation Deliberate Force, the following statements by States in the Security Council: the United Kingdom (S/PV.3575, p. 4); United States (S/PV.3575, p. 6); Nigeria (S/PV.3575, p. 8); Indonesia (S/PV.3575, pp. 8–9); Italy (S/PV.3575, p. 10); and Turkey (S/PV.3575, p. 16).

of military power in Bosnia. Thus it was that the UN Secretary-General fully supported the NATO action.[58] The Russian Government, however, was also critical of the enforcement role played by the Rapid Reaction Force. It stated that its involvement in 'neutralizing Serb positions', was in excess of the mandate set out in resolution 998 and that this 'very clearly illustrates the fact that the Rapid Reaction Force is no longer impartial, although it remains an integral part of the UN peace-keeping operation in Bosnia'.[59] However, as already explained in Chapter 5, UNPROFOR, and thus the RRF, was delegated an enforcement mandate in resolution 836 in order to prevent attacks on the safe areas.[60] Accordingly, the RRF, being part of UNPROFOR, by taking part in Operation Deliberate Force was not carrying out action that was *ultra vires* its delegated mandate.[61] The separate question of whether the Security Council can delegate military enforcement powers to a UN peacekeeping force has already been dealt with above in Chapter 2.[62]

As a result of this military action, the Bosnian Serbs agreed to conclude on 14 September 1995 in Belgrade a framework agreement on compliance with NATO's conditions. Subsequently, the NATO leaders determined that the Bosnian Serbs had complied with their conditions and air strikes were suspended.[63]

2. A delegation of powers to carry out a naval interdiction: the case of the former Yugoslavia

In response to the large-scale fighting which erupted in Croatia after its declaration of independence from the former Yugoslavia, the Security Council in resolution 713 determined that the continuation of the conflict constituted a threat to international peace and security, and, accordingly, acting under Chapter VII imposed 'a general and complete embargo on all deliveries of weapons and military equipment to Yugoslavia'. Subsequently, the Council in resolution 757 imposed wide-ranging economic sanctions against the Federal Republic of Yugoslavia (Serbia and Montenegro). No express provision was made in resolution 757 for the enforcement of its own provisions. However, after the adoption of resolution 757, NATO as well as the Western European Union (WEU) examined the possibility of carrying out naval operations which would monitor

---

[58] UN Press Release DH/1971, 5 Sept. 1995.
[59] S/PV.3575, p. 4.
[60] See *supra* Section I(4) in Chapter 5.
[61] See also the statement by the representative of Turkey: S/PV.3575, p. 16.
[62] See *supra* Section III(3)(a) in Chapter 2.
[63] Joint Statement by General Janvier and Admiral Smith, NATO Press Release (95) 43, 21 Sept. 1995.

compliance with resolutions 713 and 757.[64] The North Atlantic Council subsequently worked out the operational arrangements and announced that NATO monitoring operations (code-named 'Operation Maritime Monitor') would commence. The maritime surveillance operation would be supplemented by a WEU force operating in an adjacent area of responsibility.[65] These operations were limited to tracking merchant shipping and shadowing vessels suspected of violating resolutions 713 and 757. In the absence of Council authorization, States had no legitimate legal basis upon which they could police more strongly the sanctions regime. The lack of enforcement of the sanctions regime was considered to be its major defect. Accordingly, the subsequent Security Council resolution 787 decided, in operative paragraph 12, the following:

Acting under Chapters VII and VIII of the Charter of the United Nations, [the Security Council] *[c]alls upon* States, acting nationally or through regional agencies or arrangements, to use such measures commensurate with the specific circumstances as may be necessary under the authority of the Security Council to halt all inward and outward maritime shipping in order to inspect and verify their cargoes and destinations and to ensure strict implementation of the provisions of resolutions 713 (1991) and 757 (1992).

Moreover, the Council '*[r]equests* the States concerned, nationally or through regional agencies or arrangements, to coordinate with the Secretary-General *inter alia* on the submission of reports to the Security Council regarding actions taken in pursuance of paragraphs 12 and 13 of the present resolution to facilitate the monitoring of the implementation of the present resolution'. This express role for the Secretary-General and the existence of a reporting requirement were both important for the Council to be able to exercise overall authority and control over the use of its delegated powers.[66] As already noted in Chapter 5, the fulfilment of the reporting obligation by the Secretary-General is appropriate in a case where the Secretary-General is given an important role in the exercize of the powers delegated.[67]

The Council went on in resolution 820 to impose wide-ranging economic sanctions against the Federal Republic of Yugoslavia (Serbia and Montenegro). Paragraph 29 of this resolution authorized maritime forces in the area to operate, if necessary, within the territorial sea of the Federal Republic of Yugoslavia. The resolution: '*Reaffirms* the authority of States

---

[64] Politakis, G., 'UN Mandated Naval Operations and the Notion of Pacific Blockade: Comments on Some Recent Developments', *African Journal of International & Comparative Law*, 6 (1994), p. 173 at p. 182.

[65] *Ibidem*, p. 182.

[66] The Council's authority and control over the operation was of decisive importance for the support by India of the adoption of the resolution. (S/PV.3137, p. 6.)

[67] See *supra* note 228 and corresponding text in Chapter 5.

acting under paragraph 12 of resolution 787 (1992) to use such measures commensurate with the specific circumstances as may be necessary under the authority of the Security Council to enforce the present resolution and its other relevant resolutions, including in the territorial sea of the Federal Republic of Yugoslavia (Serbia and Montenegro).' Nowhere does the resolution provide for any procedural requirements that States must satisfy to guarantee the Council's exercize of authority and control over the operation. However, by '[r]eaffirm[ing] the authority of States acting under paragraph 12 of resolution 787 (1992)', the Council impliedly recognizes that the conditions attaching to the exercize of the previously delegated authority also apply to the power delegated in resolution 820. In fact, there are not as such any powers being delegated in resolution 820 that are additional to those delegated in resolution 787: both resolutions delegate to Member States the competence to use force to carry out a naval interdiction. However, resolution 820 differs from its predecessor resolution 787 since it expands the zone of operation to include the territorial sea of the former Yugoslavia.[68]

Resolution 820 goes further to specify measures that might be taken against ships of *third States* that are suspected of having violated the economic sanctions. In the case of the Gulf crisis in resolution 670, the Council only *recommended* the detention of ships of Iraqi registry used to violate UN sanctions. However, in the case of the former Yugoslavia, the Security Council *decided* that vessels caught trying to violate the sanctions would be forfeited—in other words 'captured'—irrespective of their nationality. The Council in paragraph 24 of resolution 820 decided:

that all States shall impound all vessels, freight vehicles, rolling stock and aircraft in their territories in which a majority or controlling interest is held by a person or undertaking in or operating from the Federal Republic of Yugoslavia (Serbia and Montenegro) and that these vessels, freight vehicles, rolling stock and aircraft may be forfeit to the seizing State upon a determination that they have been in violation of resolutions 713 (1991), 757 (1992), 787 (1992) or the present resolution; [and the Council] ... *Decides* that all States shall detain pending investigation all vessels, freight vehicles, rolling stock, aircraft and cargoes found in their territories and suspected of having violated or being in violation of resolutions 713 (1991), 757 (1992), 787 (1992) or the present resolution, and that, upon a determination that they have been in violation, such vessels, freight vehicles, rolling stock, aircraft shall

---

[68] In respect of this provision, the representative of Brazil stated in the debates preceding the adoption of resolution 820: 'It is our understanding that the specific provisions of paragraph 29 of the draft resolution, as they refer to the territorial sea of the Federal Republic of Yugoslavia (Serbia and Montenegro), are of an exceptional nature, related specifically to the situation under consideration by the Security Council, and cannot be considered as a precedent that in any way alters or derogates from the regime of coastal-State rights in this territorial sea, in accordance with the 1982 United Nations Convention on the Law of the Sea and other relevant norms of international law.' (S/PV.320, p. 13.)

be impounded and, where appropriate, they and their cargoes may be forfeit to the detaining State; . . .[69]

This provision is of considerable importance. What the Council has purported to delegate to Member States is not only the power to 'capture' vessels as that term was used previously in general international law,[70] but also the competence to make decisions that can impose legal obligations on States. In other words, the Council is delegating its power under Article 25 of the Charter to make decisions that are binding on Member States. Accordingly, Politakis states, '[w]ith regard to the investigation and the determination as to whether or not the detained vessel has in fact violated the UN trade embargo, one can only presume that what is meant is an administrative inquiry involving agencies such as customs officials, port authorities or eventually the Foreign Trade and the Foreign Affairs Ministries. For all intents and purposes, however, such administrative fact-finding exercize would appear as the modern equivalent of the traditional judicial decision declaring the blockade-runner as prize.'[71] The practice of the UK in its legislation, for instance, authorizes the Secretary of State to determine whether a ship has operated in violation of the UN-imposed sanctions. The determination takes the form of a certificate the issue of which is deemed conclusive and following which the ship or its cargo may be forfeited and sold for the best available price.[72]

Subsequent to the passage of resolution 820, the NATO Council and the WEU Council in a joint session of 8 June 1993 decided to place their up-till-

---

[69] S/RES/820 (1993), p. 6.

[70] Colombo, C., *International Law of the Sea* (1967), pp. 779–88. Politakis states in respect of the enforcement of the sanctions regime: '. . . there has been a qualitative difference, in the level of escalation, between the Gulf experience and that of the former Yugoslavia as far as the enforcement of the embargo is concerned. In the context of the Gulf crisis, Res. 670 (1990) *recommended* the mere *detention* of ships of *Iraqi* registry used in violation of UN sanctions, whereas in the case of the former Yugoslavia Res. 820 (1993) *decided* the eventual *forfeiture* of *any* vessel irrespective of its nationality. Furthermore, action was to be taken against vessels found anywhere within the territorial waters and not only against those berthed in port . . . [b]oth seized and detained vessels could eventually become the property of the seizing/detaining State, if it was determined that they have violated the sanctions regime imposed by the Security Council.' (Politakis, *supra* note 64, p. 184, emphasis added.)

[71] Politakis, *supra* note 64, p. 185.

[72] Under the UK 1993 United Nations Sanctions Order, an 'authorised officer' under the Order may request ships to halt, to remain in port or to divert to another place and may authorize such steps, including the use of reasonable force, as he considers necessary to secure compliance. Fox and Wickremasinghe state in respect of further provisions of the Order: 'Where such a request has been made of ships . . . and the Secretary of State determines that they have been operated in violation of the UN resolutions, then the ship, aircraft or vehicle in question may be impounded. The Secretary of State's determination may be made by a certificate, the issue of which shall be "conclusive evidence of that matter". An impounded vessel or vehicle or its cargo or both may be forfeited by the Secretary of State and sold for the best available price that can be obtained. . . . The owner of a ship . . . may institute proceedings to set aside an order of forfeiture, on the grounds that the conditions for forfeiture set out in the Order have not been met.' (Fox, H., and Wickremasinghe, C., 'UK Implementation of UN Economic Sanctions', *ICLQ*, 42 (1993), p. 945 at p. 962.)

now separate contingents under a unified command in order to prevent unauthorized shipping from entering the territorial waters of the Federal Republic of Yugoslavia. Thus a combined NATO/WEU Task Force was established which was known as Operation Sharp Guard.[73] This joint naval interdiction operation, which began on 15 June 1993, seems to have been a success. A NATO report on the operation notes, '[a]fter the UN Security Council strengthened the embargo against Serbia and Montenegro with resolution 820 in April 1993, no ship has been able to break the embargo and six ships have been caught while attempting to do so'.[74] Following the suspension of both economic sanctions against the Federal Republic of Yugoslavia and the embargo on small arms against Bosnia and Herzegovina as instituted by Security Council resolutions 1021 and 1022, the Sharp Guard mission was restricted to heavy weapons and ammunition embargo enforcement.[75]

The case of the former Yugoslavia is not the only instance where the Council has delegated Chapter VII powers to a regional arrangement to carry out a naval interdiction in order to enforce a regime of economic sanctions, but it is the only case where the delegation of powers was taken up by the regional arrangement.[76]

---

[73] On 8 June 1993, the Councils of NATO and the WEU, at a joint session, approved a combined concept of operations in the following terms: 'The Councils approved the combined NATO/WEU concept of operations for the implementation of UNSCR 820 in the Adriatic. This includes a single command and control arrangement for combined NATO/WEU operations ('SHARPGUARD') under the authority of the Councils of both organisations. Operational control of the combined NATO/WEU Task Force (CTF) for embargo operations in the Adriatic has been delegated through SACEUR and CINCSOUTH to Commander-in-Chief Naval Allied Forces Southern Europe (COMNAVSOUTH). Acting on behalf of the North Atlantic Alliance and the Western European Union, he will exercize operational control over a combined Task Force to conduct operations to monitor and enforce compliance with UN sanctions in accordance with UNSCRs 713, 757, 787 and 820. The combined Task Force will, in particular, aim at preventing all unauthorised shipping from entering the territorial waters of the Federal Republic of Yugoslavia (Serbia and Montenegro).' (Press release, published in *Atlantic News*, No. 2533, 11 June 1993.)

[74] NATO Factsheet on NATO/WEU Operation Sharp Guard, dated 26 Apr. 1996.

[75] *Ibidem.*

[76] In response to the overthrow of the democratically-elected Government of Sierra Leone, the Security Council delegated to the Economic Community of West African States by resolution 1132 the power to carry out a naval interdiction against Sierra Leone in order to enforce an arms and petroleum embargo that was instituted against the country also by resolution 1132. The Security Council in paragraph 8 of the resolution stated: 'Acting also under Chapter VIII of the Charter of the United Nations, authorizes ECOWAS, cooperating with the democratically-elected Government of Sierra Leone, to ensure strict implementation of the provisions of this resolution relating to the supply of petroleum and petroleum products, and arms and related matériel of all types, including, where necessary and in conformity with applicable international standards, by halting inward maritime shipping in order to inspect and verify their cargoes and destinations, and calls upon all States to cooperate with ECOWAS in this regard'. The Council did comply with its obligation to impose a reporting requirement on the entity exercising delegated Chapter VII powers when it 'Requests ECOWAS to report every 30 days to the Committee established under paragraph 10 below on all activities undertaken pursuant to paragraph 8 above'. It is unclear, however, whether ECOWAS complied

3. A delegation of powers to enforce a Council declared no-fly zone: the case of Bosnia

By its resolution 781 the Council expressly established a ban on all military flights, fixed or rotary-wing aircraft, in the airspace over Bosnia–Herzegovina to ensure the safety of humanitarian flights and to assist in the cessation of hostilities. The ban was to be implemented by a monitoring system operated by UNPROFOR. The Secretary-General subsequently submitted various reports in which he detailed violations of this ban on military flights in the airspace of the Republic of Bosnia and Herzegovina.[77] Accordingly, the Security Council in resolution 786 warned of the possibility of 'further measures necessary to enforce the ban' in the case of additional evidence of violations. It was in resolution 816 that the Council decided to extend the ban to cover 'flights by all fixed-wing and rotary-wing aircraft in the airspace of the Republic of Bosnia and Herzegovina, this ban not to apply to flights authorized by UNPROFOR'. Moreover, the Council provided the means to enforce this ban when, '*[a]cting* under Chapter VII of the Charter of the United Nations', it,

Authorizes Member States, seven days after the adoption of this resolution, acting nationally or through regional organizations or arrangements, to take, under the authority of the Security Council and subject to close coordination with the Secretary-General and UNPROFOR, all necessary measures in the airspace of the Republic of Bosnia and Herzegovina, in the event of further violations, to ensure compliance with the ban on flights referred to in paragraph 1 above, and proportionate to the specific circumstances and the nature of the flights.

with this requirement, since in the four reports of the Secretary-General concerning the implementation of Council resolution 1132 there is no mention of ECOWAS having submitted any reports as required by the resolution. (Reports of the Secretary-General on the situation in Sierra Leone: S/1997/811, S/1997/958, S/1998/103, and S/1998/249.) The Fourth Report does note, however, that the ECOWAS force in Sierra Leone, ECOMOG (ECOWAS Monitoring Group), 'responding to an attack by junta forces . . . launched a military attack on the junta, which culminated approximately one week later in the collapse of the junta and its expulsion by force from Freetown after heavy fighting.' (S/1998/249, para. 6.) This action brought the rule of the military junta in Sierra Leone to an end, and the democratically-elected President of Sierra Leone returned to the country on 10 Mar. 1998. In response, the Security Council on 16 Mar. 1998 in resolution 1156 terminated the prohibitions on the sale or supply to Sierra Leone of petroleum and petroleum products. Despite the desirability of this outcome it must, however, be noted that the legality of the military action cannot be based on an argument that the Council had delegated Chapter VII powers to ECOWAS. Resolution 1132 is clear in its terms when it limits the delegation of power for the enforcement of economic sanctions by means of a naval interdiction. Accordingly, the legal basis for a more general use of force by ECOWAS must be sought elsewhere: an enquiry which is beyond the scope of this present study. Cf., however, the case of Haiti where the Council did delegate Chapter VII powers in order to restore a democratically-elected government: see *supra* Section V(1) in Chapter 5.

[77] At the date of adoption of resolution 816 the Secretary-General had submitted the following reports to the Security Council: S/24783, S/24810, S/24840, S/24870, S/24900 and Add.1.

Accordingly, the Council delegated to all Member States, subject to certain conditions, the power to use force if necessary to enforce the ban on flights within the airspace of Bosnia and Herzegovina. The North Atlantic Council approved the means for the enforcement of the ban of 8 April 1993 and notified the UN of its willingness to undertake the exercize of delegated Chapter VII powers.[78] UN Member States acting through NATO subsequently conducted, in coordination with the UN Secretary-General, the monitoring and enforcement of the no-fly zone pursuant to the Council's authorization in resolution 816: an operation code-named 'Deny Flight'.[79] Operation Deny Flight began on 12 April 1993 with aircraft from France, the US, and The Netherlands participating.[80] The operation was largely successful in achieving its objective. As the UN Secretary-General stated in a report dated 16 March 1994:

Since the adoption of resolution 816 (1993) on 31 March 1993, it is clear that the procedures agreed with NATO and executed under Operation Deny Flight have been almost entirely successful in stopping flights by combat aircraft in Bosnia and Herzegovina. There have been only two verified exceptions. The first occurred in July 1993: the aircraft was not engaged as it heeded the warning to land immediately. The second resulted in the shooting-down of four combat aircraft on 28 February 1994.[81]

There are three pertinent observations to be made about the delegation of powers in resolution 816. First, Member States that decide to take up the delegation of powers may decide to do so on a unilateral basis or decide to focus their efforts through a regional arrangement. *In casu*, NATO was the regional arrangement which became the focus of Member States' efforts to monitor and enforce the no-fly zone. In fact it was only Member States that were part of NATO that decided to take part in this operation. However, according to the nature of the Council's authorization, UN Members that were not Members of NATO could have participated, it was just that they chose not to do so. Accordingly, there was not a specific delegation of powers as such to NATO but a general delegation of powers to UN Member States.[82]

Second, a condition of the delegation is that any measures taken are expressly stated to be under the authority and control of the Council and are to be taken in close co-operation with the Secretary-General and UNPROFOR. We recall from Chapter 1 that any exercize of delegated

---

[78] As noted in S/25567.
[79] A NATO Factsheet of 20 Dec. 1995 notes that there had to this date been 23, 021 sorties flown over Bosnia–Herzegovina.
[80] As noted in S/25567.
[81] S/1994/300, p. 8. See also S/1994/444; NATO Basic Factsheet, Oct. 1994, No. 4; and White, N., 'The Legitimacy of NATO action in Bosnia', *New Law Journal*, 144 (1994), p. 649 at p. 650.
[82] On this distinction between a specific delegation and a general delegation of powers, see *supra* note 44 and corresponding text *et sequentia* in Chapter 1.

Chapter VII powers is always under the overall authority and control of the Council. However, for the Council to expressly reiterate this and provide for practical expression of this authority by requiring measures to be in co-operation with the Secretary-General is helpful.[83] With this clear expression of intention, there can be no ambiguity that Member States, acting through NATO, are monitoring and enforcing the no-fly zone in Bosnia with the sole aim of achieving the objectives specified by the Security Council. In order to ensure its authority and control over the operation, the Council has stipulated certain procedural conditions to be observed by Member States when exercizing the delegated powers. Resolution 816 provides:

5. [The Security Council] *[r]equests* the Member States concerned, the Secretary-General and UNPROFOR to coordinate closely on the measures they are taking to implement paragraph 4 above, including the rules of engagement, and on the starting date of its implementation, which should be no later than seven days from the date when the authority conferred by paragraph 4 above takes effect, and to report the starting date to the Council through the Secretary-General; . . .
7. *Also requests* the Member States concerned to inform the Secretary-General immediately of any actions they take in exercize of the authority conferred by paragraph 4 above;
8. *Requests further* the Secretary-General to report regularly to the Council on the matter and to inform it immediately of any actions taken by the Member States concerned in exercize of the authority conferred by paragraph 4 above; . . .

The stipulation of these conditions enables the Council, through the Secretary-General, to exercize in an effective fashion its overall authority and control over the operation.[84] The imposition of a reporting requirement on the Secretary-General and not the Member States exercizing the delegated powers is appropriate, since the resolution envisages the Secretary-General also performing a key role in terms of the exercize of

---

[83] Kofi Annan, UN Under-Secretary-General for Peacekeeping Operations, as he then was, stated the following in respect of command and control issues involving NATO: 'Of course, command and control becomes an issue when two organizations with their own established lines of political and military decision-making are to co-operate. There can be no doubt that the Security Council is the ultimate legal and political authority in deciding on a United Nations operation. The Council uses this authority guardedly and generally insists on retaining control over the operations to maintain international peace and security which it has mandated. In most cases, the Council entrusts the SG with the responsibility of overseeing the faithful implementation of its resolutions. . . . Understandably, for NATO, it is critical to determine at what level of its own political and military hierarchy command and control should be submitted to the authority of the Security Council through the SG of the United Nations. Obviously, member states of NATO have an interest in retaining control over their troops; that may not be difficult to reconcile with the interest of the United Nations in staying on top of an operation mandated by the Security Council.' (Annan, K., 'UN Peace-Keeping Operations and Co-operation with NATO', *NATO Review*, 41 (Oct. 1993), p. 3.)

[84] This authority and control of the Council over the operation was expressly recognized by a Final Communiqué of a Ministerial Meeting of the North Atlantic Council. (NATO Basic Factsheet, Oct. 1994, No. 4.)

delegated powers. As we have just seen, a condition of the delegation of powers is that Member States exercize the powers in co-operation with the Secretary-General: that is, with his consent. This approach is further reiterated by the Secretary-General who states that the aircraft of Member States implementing resolution 816 have flown in the airspace of Bosnia and Herzegovina at his request.[85] This is important since it illustrates the control the Secretary-General maintains, as required by resolution 816, over the exercize of the delegated powers. This authority and control of the Council, being exercized through the Secretary-General, is important also in terms of the legality of a subsequent interpretation made by Member States of their delegated mandate. UN Member States carrying out Operation Deny Flight have interpreted their mandate in resolution 816 to justify anticipatory self-defence measures taken against Serbian anti-aircraft missile systems in Bosnia. This is an appropriate interpretation considering that NATO aircraft have, pursuant to resolution 816 and the request of the Secretary-General, a legitimate reason to be in the airspace of Bosnia and Herzegovina and thus, if there is the threat of an attack, they have the right to use force in self-defence so long as the requirements for a lawful exercize of self-defence are fulfilled. In accordance with this right of self-defence, a NATO Press Release states 'NATO aircraft, in response to yesterday's SA-2 attacks on NATO aircraft and on request of UNPROFOR, today . . . fired . . . missiles into surface-to-air (SAM) missile sites in the areas of Busovaksa Krupa, Otoka and Dvor. The action was taken after a threat was detected against NATO reconnaissance aircraft flying in the area as part of Operation Deny Flight, in support of UNPROFOR forces in the area.'[86] It would seem that, in the circumstances, the NATO aircraft did lawfully exercize their right to self-defence, since the need for the response was immediate and necessary, and the response made was proportionate. There was an element of immediacy and necessity, since a Serb missile site had locked onto a NATO reconnaissance aircraft. Moreover, the proportionality element was satisfied, since the response was directed only at those missile sites with surface-to-air capability.

The third noteworthy element of the delegation is the stipulation by the Council that any use of force by Member States to ensure compliance with the ban must be 'proportionate to the specific circumstances and the nature of the flights'. This proportionality requirement did operate as a limitation on the exercize of delegated enforcement powers. Non-military aircraft operating in the no-fly zone were not shot down by NATO aircraft.[87]

[85] S/1994/300, and S/1994/444.

[86] NATO Press Release (94) 111, 23 Nov. 1994.

[87] The Secretary-General states: '. . . The procedures have not prevented many violations of the "no-fly zone" by non-combat aircraft . . . the overwhelming majority of these have been helicopters transporting individuals . . . of little military significance. Although such aircraft

4. A delegation of powers to ensure implementation by parties of an agreement which the Council has deemed necessary for the maintenance or restoration of peace: the case of the Dayton Peace Agreement for Bosnia

The signing of the General Framework Agreement for Peace in Bosnia and Herzegovina and the Annexes thereto (the 'Dayton Agreement') by representatives of the Republic of Bosnia and Herzegovina, the Republic of Croatia, and the Federal Republic of Yugoslavia on 14 December 1995 at the Paris Peace Conference marked a major development in efforts to restore peace to the region of the former Yugoslavia. The State Parties to the Agreement recognized the important role that external entities have to play in the process of restoring peace to the region, and accordingly, in Annex 1-A (the Agreement on Military Aspects of the Peace Settlement) of the Dayton Agreement, they invite the Security Council

to adopt a resolution by which it will authorize Member States or regional organizations and arrangements to establish a multinational military Implementation Force (hereinafter 'IFOR'). The Parties understand and agree that this Implementation Force may be composed of ground, air and maritime units from NATO and non-NATO nations, deployed to Bosnia and Herzegovina to help ensure compliance with the provisions of this Agreement (hereinafter 'Annex'). The Parties understand and agree that the IFOR will begin the implementation of the military aspects of this Annex upon the transfer of authority from the UNPROFOR Commander to the IFOR Commander . . . [88]

Moreover, the Annex provides that the Parties understand and agree that NATO may establish such a force, 'which will operate under the authority and subject to the direction and political control of the North Atlantic Council . . . through the NATO chain of command'.[89] The Annex to the

are routinely intercepted and warned, the nature and specific circumstances of the flights have not so far justified shooting them down.' (S/1994/300, pp. 8–9.)

[88] Article 1(1)(a) of the Agreement on the Military Aspects of the Peace Settlement (Annex 1-A to the Peace Agreement). For the details of the transfer of authority from UNPROFOR, the peacekeeping force, to IFOR, the peace-implementation force which possessed the authority to use enforcement measures to ensure implementation of the Dayton Agreement, see the report of the Secretary-General dated 13 Dec. 1995: S/1995/1031, para. 10. The Secretary-General in a letter to the Council, reported that the transfer of authority from UNPROFOR to IFOR took place on 20 Dec. 1995. (S/1995/1050.) The Secretary-General noted that the effect of this, as stated in Council resolution 1031, was 'the authority to take measures conferred upon States by resolutions 770 (1992), 781 (1992), 816 (1993), 836 (1993), 844 (1993) and 958 (1994) shall be terminated, and that the provisions of resolution 824 (1993) and subsequent resolutions regarding safe areas shall also be terminated from the same date'. (S/1995/1050.) On that day, all NATO and non-NATO forces participating in the operation came under the command and control of the IFOR Commander. (NATO Factsheet on 'NATO's Role in the Implementation of the Bosnian Peace Agreement', Jan. 1996, No. 11.)

[89] The Secretary-General notes that the modalities of the participation of non-NATO States in IFOR are to be agreed between those States and NATO. (S/1995/1031, 13 Dec. 1995, para. 7.)

General Agreement goes on to note that the purpose of the obligations set out in the Annex are to establish a durable cessation of hostilities; provide for the 'support and authorization of the IFOR and in particular to authorize the IFOR to take such actions as required, including the use of necessary force, to ensure compliance with this Annex, and to ensure its own protection'; and to establish lasting security and arms control measures as outlined in Annex 1-B to the General Framework Agreement.[90] Accordingly, the Parties to the Agreement requested the Council to ensure, by use of force if necessary, that they comply with their obligations under the Agreement.[91]

The Council accepted the invitation of the Parties to establish a force to ensure implementation of the Agreement when, in resolution 1031, the Council, acting under Chapter VII of the Charter, decided to authorize 'the Member States acting through or in cooperation with the organization referred to in Annex 1-A of the Peace Agreement [NATO] to establish a multinational implementation force (IFOR) under unified command and control in order to fulfil the role specified in Annex 1-A and Annex 2 of the Peace Agreement'. The resolution then stated that the Council '[a]uthorizes the Member States acting under paragraph 14 above to take all necessary measures to effect the implementation of and to ensure compliance with Annex 1-A of the Peace Agreement, stresses that the parties shall be held equally responsible for compliance with that Annex, and shall be equally subject to such enforcement action by IFOR as may be necessary to ensure implementation of that Annex and the protection of IFOR, and takes note that the parties have consented to IFOR's taking such measures'. The Council thus delegated its Chapter VII military enforcement powers to Member States on the condition that they act 'through or in cooperation with' NATO to ensure the implementation of the Dayton Agreement.[92]

Although the Council did not expressly state that command and control was to be exercized by NATO, this is a reasonable interpretation of the Council's delegation of powers, especially having regard to the provision in Annex 1-A of the Dayton Agreement which states that the IFOR 'will

---

[90] Article 1 of Annex 1-A of the General Framework Agreement.

[91] For example, a later article of Annex 1-A, Article IV (3), provides that all Parties understand and agree that they shall be subject to military action by IFOR, including the use of necessary force to ensure compliance, for, *inter alia*, the failure to remove all their Forces and unauthorized weapons from the four kilometre Agreed Cease-Fire Zone of Separation within 30 days after the date of the Transfer of Authority.

[92] Moreover, Council resolution 1031 '[a]uthorizes the Member States to take all necessary measures, at the request of IFOR, either in defence of IFOR or to assist the force in carrying out its mission, and recognizes the right of the force to take all necessary measures to defend itself from attack or threat or attack'. IFOR is composed of troops from Fifteen of the sixteen NATO countries as well as forces from non-NATO countries. (Letter dated 23 Jan. 1996 addressed to the President of the Security Council transmitting the second report on the operations of the IFOR, S/1996/49.)

operate under the authority and subject to the political control of the North Atlantic Council . . . through the NATO chain of command'.[93] It is thus clear that the forces contributed by non-NATO countries are in general subject to command and control by the IFOR Commander.[94] Moreover, this legal position is of importance to clarifying the relationship between NATO and States that wish to contribute forces to the IFOR. The issue which arises here is whether the NATO command could refuse to accept troop contributions from a State. It would seem from the terms of the delegation of powers to Member States that since a condition of the delegation of Chapter VII powers, as explained above, is that States act through or in cooperation with NATO, then in the absence of such agreement by NATO a Member State would have no right to participate in the action.[95] In this way the Council has, in effect, delegated to NATO its power under Article 48(1) of the Charter to determine the composition of a force carrying out military enforcement action.[96] This is not unprecedented. We recall from above in Chapter 3 that the Security Council delegated the power to

[93] Accordingly, a NATO Factsheet notes that: 'The Implementation Force has a unified command and is NATO-led, under the political direction and control of the Alliance's North Atlantic Council, as stipulated by the Peace Agreement.' (NATO Factsheet on 'NATO's Role in the Implementation of the Bosnian Peace Agreement', Jan. 1996, No. 11.) The Factsheet notes that: 'Overall military authority is in the hands of NATO's Supreme Allied Commander Europe, General Joulwan, who has designated another NATO Commander, Admiral Smith, as Commander in Theatre of IFOR.' (*Ibidem.*)

[94] Accordingly, the Third Report to the United Nations Security Council on IFOR operations by NATO, notes that Sweden, Austria, the Czech Republic, Finland, Hungary, Lithuania, Malaysia, Poland, and the Ukraine, (all non-NATO countries) have transferred their forces, formerly in UNPROFOR, to being under IFOR command and control, and that a Russian force has been deployed under separate command arrangements. (S/1996/131.) Importantly, the NATO Commander has stated that there is a process whereby regular political consultations take place between non-NATO IFOR contributors and the NATO Command. (Letter dated 23 Jan. 1996 addressed to the President of the Security Council transmitting the second report on the operations of the IFOR, S/1996/49.) We recall in this regard from Chapter 1 that States whose forces are to be used in enforcement action must be consulted in respect of the use of their troops in such action: see *supra* note 136 and corresponding text in Chapter 1.

[95] Accordingly, the Secretary-General notes in respect of IFOR that 'NATO may establish such a force, which will operate under the authority and subject to the direction and political control of the North Atlantic Council through the NATO chain of command. The modalities of the participation of non-NATO States in IFOR are to be agreed between those States and NATO'. (S/1994/1031, para. 7.) Cf. the view of the representative of Malaysia who stated in the Council: 'The Council would also have to be involved in the implementation of the international force to be led by the North Atlantic Treaty Organization (NATO). The Council has also to decide formally on the future of the United Nations Protection Force (UNPROFOR). In the consideration of the relationship between IFOR and the Security Council, it will be necessary to clarify all aspects of the issue, both military and non-military, political and humanitarian alike. Malaysia has conveyed to NATO its intention to participate in the international force. We expect specific details pertaining to the involvement of non-NATO forces to be resolved expeditiously. . . . For those not part of NATO, we especially look to the United Nations to define its role as an overall authority for overseeing the full implementation of the Framework Agreement.' (S/PV. 3595, pp. 29–30.)

[96] Accordingly, the following statement by the representative of Malaysia (*ibidem*), although possibly of political importance, is not of legal significance: 'this is a force [IFOR] that

determine the composition of a force carrying out military enforcement action to the unified command, a UN subsidiary organ, in the case of Korea.[97]

However, this operational command and control by NATO over IFOR does not detract from the overall authority and control which the Council exercizes over IFOR in any action it may take to enforce the provisions of the Agreement. It is clear that NATO considers that IFOR operations are under the authority of the UN Security Council when it noted in its official Fact Sheet that '[u]nder the authority of UN Security Council Resolution 1031 of 15 December 1995, NATO is undertaking the implementation of the military aspects of the Bosnian Peace Agreement, signed by all Parties to the conflict'.[98]

An important element of this overall authority and control of the Council is that the States exercizing these powers report back to the Council on the conduct of their operations.[99] Accordingly, the Security Council imposed an obligation on Member States exercizing the powers delegated by resolution 1031 to 'report to the Council, through the appropriate channels and at least at monthly intervals, the first such report [to] be made not later than 10 days following the adoption of this resolution'. The necessity for the imposition of such an obligation is reiterated, in addition to our discussion in Chapter 4, by the importance that several Members of the Security Council placed on this provision.[100] In accordance with this obligation, NATO has regularly submitted reports to the Council on the conduct of IFOR operations.[101]

---

acts on behalf of the international community. Proceeding from this, it is important that all geographical regions and all the groups concerned should be represented in the composition of the force.' (S/PV. 3607, p. 33.)

[97] See *supra* note 128 and corresponding text in Chapter 3.

[98] NATO Factsheet on 'NATO's Role in the Implementation of the Bosnian Peace Agreement', Jan. 1996, No. 11.

[99] As the French representative to the Council states: 'the resolution [1031] is the expression of the authority of the Security Council. The resolution that has been adopted determines the imminent deployment of the multinational force. Reports on the activity of this Force will be regularly submitted to the Security Council. It will thus be able to follow the conduct of the operation. Lastly, it is important for the Security Council to take a further decision on the mandate which it has today delivered and to decide whether the extension of that mandate is necessary.' (S/PV.3607, p. 22.) See also the statement by the Russian representative in the Council: S/PV.3607, p. 25.

[100] As the Brazilian representative stated: 'In the resolution [1031] ... States ... are requested to report to the Security Council on a monthly basis. As the implementation force takes up its position in a terrain that is still fraught with uncertainties, it is essential that the organ responsible for safeguarding international peace and security [the Security Council] be given the necessary tools to enable it to exercize the role ascribed to it by the Charter. ... The creation of multinational forces at the behest of the Security Council has ceased to be an unusual feature. If these forces are to be perceived by the international community as legitimate and credible, however, the necessary accountability towards the Security Council must be strictly observed.' (S/PV.3607, p. 27.) See also the statements by the Chinese (S/PV.3607, p. 14) and Ukrainian (S/PV.3607, p. 29) representatives in the Council.

[101] See, for example, the following: S/1996/49, and S/1996/131.

The overall authority and control which the Security Council exercizes over its delegated power to take military enforcement action is of considerable importance to the legality of the operation.[102] Accordingly, the Russian representative stated that the Security Council and no other council, an implicit reference to the NATO Council, must specifically take a decision regarding the need to extend the duration of the military aspect of the operation at the end of the year; a measure that would ensure reliable control on the part of the Security Council.[103] The Russian representative emphasized that there should in no way be a replacement of the United Nations responsibility in that area by any regional arrangement.[104] However, the Russian representative to the Council emphasized what he considered to be the most important feature of the resolution: that the Member States were authorized to do only what the Bosnian sides agreed to and that this happened to include the use of force in the operation. The point made by the Russian representative about authority and control being exercized by the Council is well taken and, as already explained, is required in such a case. Nevertheless, it is important to emphasize that the Council in delegating its powers is not restrained 'to do only what the Bosnian sides agreed to', since the authority of the Council does not in these cases derive from the Agreements concluded by the parties but from its powers under Chapter VII of the Charter. The Russian representative may not have been suggesting the converse, but the issue is of such importance that it requires clarification. In fact, the decision by the Council under Chapter VII gives IFOR the right to achieve the objectives specified in resolution 1031 regardless of the consent or otherwise of the Parties to the Dayton Agreement.

---

[102] See also statement in the Council by the representative of France: S/PV.3607, p. 21. Accordingly, the expression of concern by the Nigerian representative to the Council at the delegation of these military enforcement powers to Member States can be dismissed. The Nigerian representative stated that his Government would have preferred a United Nations operation under the political control of the Security Council and the managerial supervision of the Secretary-General: the Security Council 'should not contract out what would normally be a United Nations responsibility to a group of powerful States'. (S/PV.3607, p. 15.)

[103] S/PV.3607, p. 25. This decision was taken by the Security Council in resolution 1088 which '[a]uthorizes the Member States acting through or in cooperation with the organization referred to in Annex 1-A of the Peace Agreement [NATO] to establish for a planned period of 18 months a multinational stabilization force (SFOR) as the legal successor to IFOR under unified command and control in order to fulfil the role specified in Annex 1-A and Annex 2 of the Peace Agreement'. With the spectre of the expiration of SFOR's current mandate in June 1998, there were on 20 Feb. 1998 consultations between the North Atlantic Council and the non-NATO countries contributing to SFOR with a subsequent agreement 'that, subject to the necessary mandate from the Security Council, NATO is prepared to organize and lead a multinational force in Bosnia and Herzegovina following the end of SFOR's current mandate in June 1998.' ('Fourteenth monthly report to the United Nations Security Council on Stabilization Force operation', S/1998/238, Annex, para. 21.)

[104] S/PV.3607, p. 25.

The IFOR Commander is given the power of authoritative interpretation over the terms of the Annex by Article 12, dealing with 'Final Authority to Interpret', which states: 'the IFOR Commander is the final authority in theatre regarding interpretation of this agreement on the military aspects of the peace settlement'.[105] This provision is of considerable importance, since it gives to the IFOR Commander for all practical purposes an unreviewable power of discretion in deciding whether one or more of the Parties to the Agreement is in violation of their obligations and, thus should be, subject to enforcement action by the IFOR in order to ensure their compliance with the terms of the Agreement, *as required by and to the satisfaction of the IFOR Commander.* In effect, the Parties to the Agreement have sought to delegate to the IFOR Commander the power to decide when enforcement action should be taken against one of them. This intention of the Parties to the Agreement could not, however, be given effect to without the express consent of the Security Council. The Parties do not themselves possess the competence to delegate such a power to States acting without the sanction of the Security Council. This would otherwise represent a violation, by the States seeking to exercize such a delegated power, of the prohibition on the use of force by States against the territorial integrity of another State as contained in Article 2(4) of the Charter. The only right to use force that States possess which they can entrust to other States is their right of self-defence.[106] However, it seems clear that the IFOR carrying out military enforcement action against one of the parties for failure to comply with some of the obligations under Annex 1-A of the Dayton Agreement can in no way be said to be an exercize of a right of collective self-defence. For example, the enforcement of a no-fly zone against civilian aircraft in the absence of an anticipated or actual armed attack would not seem to be justifiable under the law of self-defence;[107] nor would the dismantling of

---

[105] On the more general powers of authoritative interpretation given to the IFOR Commander and the High Representative under the agreements, see Gaeta, P., 'The Dayton Agreements and International Law', *EJIL*, 7 (1996), p. 147 at pp. 156–8.

[106] For the notion of collective self-defence under international law, see Brownlie, I., *International Law and the Use of Force by States* (1963); Bowett, *Self-Defence Under International Law* (1958); and Dinstein, *supra* note 5.

[107] Among the extensive powers granted by Annex 1-A of the General Framework Agreement to the IFOR Commander is the power to ensure compliance with the Security Council declared no-fly zones and to decide when exceptions to the general prohibition of the use of aircraft are allowed. The relevant part of Article 6 of Annex 1-A states: 'The Parties understand and agree there shall be no military air traffic, or non-military aircraft performing military missions, including reconnaissance or logistics without the express permission of the IFOR Commander. The only military aircraft that may be authorized to fly in Bosnia and Herzegovina are those being flown in support of the IFOR, except with the express permission of the IFOR. Any flight activities by military fixed-wing or helicopter aircraft within Bosnia and Herzegovina without the express permission of the IFOR Commander are subject to military action by the IFOR, including the use of necessary force to ensure compliance.' Accordingly, resolution 1031 '[a]uthorizes the Member States acting under paragraph 14 above, in accordance with Annex 1-A of the Peace Agreement, to take all necessary measures

unauthorized road checkpoints be either.[108] Accordingly, it is the Council which has decided to delegate to NATO and Member States co-operating with the regional arrangement the power to take military enforcement action.

A question which is of considerable importance is whether the powers delegated to IFOR require the Force to arrest and detain persons indicted by the UN International Criminal Tribunal for the former Yugoslavia (ICTY). Security Council resolution 1031 mentions the War Crimes Tribunal in operative paragraphs 4 and 5 which provide:

[The Council] Reaffirms . . . also that all States shall cooperate fully with the International Tribunal for the Former Yugoslavia and its organs in accordance with the provisions of resolution 827 (1993) of 25 May 1993 and the Statute of the International Tribunal, and shall comply with requests for assistance or orders issued by a Trial Chamber under article 29 of the Statute . . . Recognizes that the parties shall cooperate fully with all entities involved in implementation of the peace settlement, as described in the Peace Agreement, or which are otherwise authorized by the Security Council, including the International Tribunal for the Former Yugoslavia, and that the parties have in particular authorized the multinational force referred to in paragraph 14 below to take such actions as required, including the use of necessary force, to ensure compliance with Annex 1-A of the Peace Agreement; . . .

Moreover, Members of the Council have placed considerable emphasis on the importance of the work of the War Crimes Tribunal in contributing to the restoration and maintenance of international peace and security in the former Yugoslavia.[109] Thus the US representative to the Security Council stated:

Let me emphasise that Annex 1-A of the Dayton Agreement obligates the parties to cooperate fully with the International Tribunal. The North Atlantic Council can now underscore this obligation by explicitly authorising IFOR to transfer indicted

to ensure compliance with the rules and procedures, to be established by the commander of IFOR, governing command and control of airspace over Bosnia and Herzegovina with respect to all civilian and military air traffic'. Accordingly, the Secretary-General recommended 'that UNPROFOR's responsibilities concerning the monitoring of the ban on military flights in the airspace of Bosnia and Herzegovina pursuant to Security Council resolution 786 (1992) be discontinued and that the airfield monitors engaged in this task be repatriated. For the same reason, and in view of the handover of UNPROFOR's military responsibilities to IFOR, I recommended that responsibility of UNPROFOR for operating Sarajevo airport pursuant to Security Council resolution 761 (1991), as well as Tuzla airport and other airfields, be transferred to IFOR.' (S/1995/1031, para. 42.)

[108] This was done routinely by SFOR: see, for example, 'Twelfth monthly report to the United Nations Security Council on Stabilization Force operations', S/1998/39, Annex, para. 8; and 'Fifteenth monthly report to the United Nations Security Council on Stabilization Force operations', S/1998/310, Annex, para. 14.

[109] See, for example, the statements in the Security Council by the representatives of the United Kingdom (S/PV.3595, p. 4); and Czechoslovakia (S/PV. 3595, p. 9).

persons it comes across to the Tribunal and to detain such persons for that purpose.[110]

Even if, however, an implicit connection can be made between the delegation of Chapter VII powers to IFOR and the work of the Tribunal, so that IFOR can use its coercive powers to assist the Tribunal in its work,[111] the position still remains, as established in Chapter 4 above, that a delegation of powers is permissive and not mandatory. Accordingly, *in casu*, it is up to NATO to decide whether to utilize the Chapter VII powers delegated by the Council to assist the Tribunal in its work: in particular, to arrest, detain, and transfer to The Hague those persons indicted as War Criminals by the War Crimes Tribunal for the former Yugoslavia. The Council did not, nor could it, impose on the IFOR an obligation to carry out such measures. Thus, the representative of the UK stated:

... *should it be decided that*, in the execution of its assigned tasks, the Implementation Force should detain and transfer to the appropriate authorities any persons indicted by the Tribunal who come into contact with it in Bosnia, then the authority to do so is provided by the draft resolution before us, read together with the provisions of the Peace Agreement.[112]

The NATO command in charge of IFOR has interpreted its delegated power in a narrow fashion so that it will arrest and detain those persons indicted by the Tribunal only if the IFOR comes across these persons in the execution of the tasks it has chosen to carry out. Accordingly, at a News Conference of the NATO Secretary-General and the NATO Supreme Allied Commander, the Commander stated that if IFOR comes into contact with indicted war criminals in their 'normal activities' they will detain them and turn them over to the proper authorities: that is, the Tribunal.[113] It was thus clear that IFOR would not, as distinct from its successor the Stabilization Force (SFOR),[114] go out of its way to arrest those persons indicted as war criminals by the Hague Tribunal. However, in resolution 1037 the Security Council '[r]eaffirms that all States shall cooperate fully with the International Tribunal for the former Yugoslavia and its organs in accordance with the provisions of resolution 827 ... and the Statute of the

---

[110] S/PV.3607, p. 20.

[111] See Akhavan, P., 'The Yugoslav Tribunal at a crossroads: The Dayton Peace Agreement and beyond', *Human Rights Quarterly*, 18 (1996), p. 259.

[112] S/PV.3607, p. 8, emphasis added.

[113] NATO News Conference of NATO Secretary-General and SACEUR, 19 Jan. 1996. Moreover, NATO has consistently reaffirmed its support of the work of the ICTY: see, for example, S/1996/131, 26 Feb. 1996, para. 12. IFOR has assisted the Tribunal in its work by carrying out air reconnaissance of suspected mass grave sites and reporting all suspicious activities detected near such sites by IFOR patrols carrying out their duty. Moreover, IFOR responded positively to a Tribunal request to assist in the secure transfer of two individuals from Sarajevo to The Hague on 12 Feb. for further investigation by the Tribunal. (*Ibidem.*)

[114] See *infra* note 118 and corresponding text.

International Tribunal and shall comply with requests for assistance or orders issued by a Trial Chamber under article 29 of the Statute'. It is clear that this decision by the Council reaffirms the obligation on States to comply with such requests. The Secretary-General had earlier emphasized the nature of the obligation on States to comply with an order by a Trial Chamber when he stated: 'an order by a Trial Chamber . . . shall be considered to be the application of an enforcement measure under Chapter VII of the Charter of the United Nations'.[115] Accordingly, when the Trial Chamber makes an order for the arrest of an indicted war criminal there is a legally binding obligation on States under Article 25 of the Charter to carry out such action in a manner consistent with the UN Charter.[116] This does not mean that a State could, for example, invade the territory of Bosnia and Herzegovina in order to arrest indicted war criminals, since this would be contrary to the prohibition on the use of force under Article 2(4) of the Charter. However, we recall the earlier point that the legal basis for IFOR being in the territory of Bosnia and Herzegovina is not *per se* the Dayton Peace Agreement, but Security Council resolution 1031. Put differently, the legal basis for States that are taking part in the IFOR operation being stationed within the territory of Bosnia–Herzegovina was stimulated by, but does not rest on, the Dayton Peace Agreement. Accordingly, it may be contended that when a war criminal comes within an area under the control of a State, then the State is under an obligation to arrest the alleged criminal and transfer him to the custody of ICTY officers.[117] Article 25 of the Charter imposes an obligation on the State concerned to carry out such action, regardless of the terms of the Dayton Agreement. However, this obligation is distinct from the position of IFOR as a whole which, as explained earlier, has no such obligation imposed on it by the Council. This analysis applies *mutatis mutandis* to the case of SFOR with the same legal position being the result. Nonetheless, to the credit of the SFOR commanders, the Stabilization Force has rendered invaluable assistance to the Security Council by carrying out action to arrest persons indicted by the ICTY,[118] and by providing support for investigative work of the Office of the Prosecutor of the ICTY.[119]

---

[115] S/25704, para. 126.

[116] See also *supra* note 102 and corresponding text in Chapter 3.

[117] See also Figa-Talamanca, N., 'The Role of NATO in the Peace Agreement for Bosnia and Herzegovina', *European Journal of International Law* (1996), p. 164 at p. 173.

[118] See 'Seventh monthly report to the United Nations Security Council on Stabilization Force operations', S/1997/636, Annex, para. 4; 'Twelfth monthly report to the United Nations Security Council on Stabilization Force operations', S/1998/39, Annex, para. 3(d); and 'Fourteenth monthly report to the United Nations Security Council on Stabilization Force operations', S/1998/238, Annex, para. 4.

[119] See, for example, 'Eighth monthly report to the United Nations Security Council on Stabilization Force operations', S/1997/718, Annex, para. 17; and 'Twelfth monthly report to the United Nations Security Council on Stabilization Force operations', S/1998/39, Annex, para. 3(c).

In conclusion, the Dayton Peace Agreement represents a successful institutional innovation by States in their attempt to restore and maintain peace in Bosnia. Earlier practice has seen parties to other conflicts conclude agreements that were intended to provide for a peaceful resolution to the conflict, but without any mechanism in the agreement for enforcement action to be taken against a party that breaches its obligations under the agreement.[120] The case of the Dayton Agreement is thus innovative since the parties ask the Council from the beginning to constitute a military force with powers of military enforcement that can take action to ensure the parties comply with their obligations under the Agreement. This represents a positive step forward in the development of the institutional processes used to combat a threat to, or breach of, the peace. It combines the 'local legitimacy' of an Agreement concluded between the parties with the enforcement authority of the Council and the enforcement capability of Member States to ensure compliance with the provisions of the Agreement. The fact that the parties to the Agreement themselves requested that such a force be established and that they agreed to enforcement action being taken against any one of their number who violates their obligations under the Agreement lends an important element of legitimacy to any subsequent Security Council authorized enforcement action.[121] Moreover, such an arrangement reaffirms and provides practical expression to the role and authority of the Security Council in matters pertaining to international peace and security. The decentralized nature of international law allows individual States—in the case of the Dayton Agreement primarily the USA, to its credit—to engage in a political process that results in an agreement being concluded,[122] but which then sees the enforcement of this agreement being handed over to the Security Council as the organ of the international community; thus allowing for a truly collective response. This process is not inconsistent with the intention of the Framers of the Charter and may well constitute a model for emulation in the resolution of future conflicts.

III. THE POLICY OF DELEGATING CHAPTER VII POWERS TO REGIONAL ARRANGEMENTS

The delegation of Chapter VII powers to regional arrangements is a desirable process, since, as shown above, it can lead to military enforcement

---

[120] Consider, for example, the Governors Island Agreement in the case of Haiti: see *supra* Section V(1) in Chapter 5.

[121] Cf. the problems of local legitimacy that the UN faced in the case of Somalia, see *supra* Section I(3) in Chapter 5.

[122] See also Falk, R., 'The Complexities of Humanitarian Intervention: A New World Order Challenge', *Michigan Journal of International Law*, 17 (1996), p. 491 at p. 498.

action being taken on behalf of the Council to achieve the Council's stated objectives. Moreover, the former Secretary-General, Boutros-Ghali, stated in his *Agenda for Peace* that an important reason for the use of regional arrangements in such a role is that the process contributes to 'a deeper sense of participation, consensus and democratization in international affairs'.[123] However, as Higgins has observed: 'The involvement of UN regional arrangements has not had the effect of enlarging the sense of a broader participation . . .'.[124] An important reason for this is that very few regional arrangements have the capability[125] or international legitimacy[126] to carry out such military enforcement action. Consequently, it falls to a small number, in practice NATO, to shoulder the burden of responsibility. However, it may well be inappropriate for the Council to rely solely on NATO and its member states to carry out military enforcement action by exercizing delegated Chapter VII powers. The UN Charter system of collective security always envisaged potential universal participation in carrying out such action.[127] Reliance solely on NATO leads, moreover, to an additional issue which arises from the *dédoublement fonctionnel* of States in such cases: where States act as Members of the United Nations and as members of a regional arrangement. Three of the Permanent Members of the Security Council are also members of NATO, and as such the desirability of delegating Chapter VII powers to NATO alone may be questionable. It is true that a regional arrangement, such as NATO, may be better prepared and equipped to carry out a large-scale and co-ordinated military enforcement action rather than a coalition of Member States. However, reliance on NATO alone as some kind of police force may reinforce the view that the activation of the Charter system of collective security is dependent solely on a Permanent Member having a major interest in the resolution of a particular situation which constitutes a threat to interna-

---

[123] Boutros-Ghali, B., *An Agenda for Peace* (1992), para. 64.

[124] Higgins, R., 'The United Nations Role in Maintaining International Peace: the Lessons of the First Fifty Years', *New York Law School Journal of International and Comparative Law*, 16 (1996), p. 135 at p. 143. On the more general issue of democracy in international law, see Crawford, J., *Democracy in International Law* (1994).

[125] Higgins, *ibidem*, p. 143.

[126] In the case of Liberia, a regional arrangement, ECOWAS, did carry out military enforcement action: see *supra* note 4. This action has, however, been the subject of considerable criticism on the basis that ECOWAS lacks legitimacy to carry out enforcement action in order to establish democracy within a country when it is itself composed of States that are ruled by military dictatorships: see Ofuatey-Kodjoe, W., 'Regional organizations and the resolution of internal conflict: the ECOWAS intervention in Liberia', *International Peacekeeping*, 1 (1994), p. 261 at p. 295; and Adibe, C., 'The Liberian Conflict and the ECOWAS–UN Partnership', in *Beyond UN Subcontracting* (Weiss, T., ed.) (1998), p. 67 at p. 84.

[127] Article 43 of the Charter which contains the mechanism by which States were to supply forces to the Council for military enforcement action was directed at '(1) *All Members* of the United Nations'. (Emphasis added.)

tional peace and security.[128] The continual reinforcement of this view[129] may lead to a retrogression in international order so that States undertake heavy rearmament programmes and rely solely on strategic alliances for protection due to a perception that the Security Council and in particular the Permanent Members are either unable or unwilling to maintain international peace and thereby the security of individual States. Moreover, the perils of waiting for action by a regional arrangement were well illustrated in the case of Bosnia where the perception that the problem was a European one led the Security Council, and notably the United States, into waiting for action by European States, that was not forthcoming, to address the problem.[130] The responsibility for the maintenance and restoration of peace under the Charter rests with the Council. This responsibility cannot be delegated, but only the power to carry out action required to fulfil this responsibility. The responsibility of the Council in such a case is to ensure that a situation that may be deemed to be a regional one receives an international response, where the matter constitutes a threat to international peace and security.

Having regard to these considerations, it is suggested that the best approach is for the Council to delegate its powers to UN Member States with provision for the use of the established mechanisms of a regional arrangement, and to leave it up to those States to decide whether to use the mechanisms of a regional arrangement or to act individually.[131] The major

[128] It was, however, never intended by the Framers of the Charter that military enforcement action would be undertaken only when it was in the interests of one or more of the Permanent Members of the Council. As Higgins has stated: 'Collective security under the Charter was never meant to be predicated upon short-term national interest. It was the long-term interest in international peace and security that was to be the motivating factor. If the enforcement of peace is to be left to a decision by those with the capability as to whether an attacked state "matters" or not, the reality is that the UN has no real collective security capability at all.' (Higgins, R., 'The United Nations 50 Years On, Part III: Achievements and Failures', *European Journal of International Law*, Special Issue (1995), Chapter 6, p. 14, at pp. 17–18.) Moreover, President Franklin D. Roosevelt observed that the creation of the United Nations 'spells—and it ought to spell—the end of the system of unilateral action, exclusive alliances and spheres of influence, and balances of power, and all the other expedients which have been tried for centuries and have always failed'. (As quoted in Urquhart, B., 'The Role of the United Nations in Maintaining and Improving International Security', *Survival* (Sept.–Oct. 1986), at p. 388.)

[129] See the statements in the Security Council debates concerning the crisis in Bosnia and Herzegovina by the representatives of Albania (S/PV.3136, p. 54) and Pakistan (S/PV.3136, p. 35).

[130] See Higgins, *supra* note 128.

[131] In order for States to use a regional arrangement in such a way, the Security Council, in the resolution that delegates its powers, would have to make express mention of the arrangement. This is, as explained above, a substantive requirement that Article 53 requires to be satisfied before, in this case, UN Member States could use the mechanisms of a regional arrangement to carry out military enforcement action: see *supra* note 4 and corresponding text.

In such a case, it would be appropriate for the Security Council to require that a Member State who wishes to act individually must establish co-ordination mechanisms with the command structure of the regional arrangement in order to ensure co-ordinated action.

advantage of this approach is that it combines the legitimacy of a system where any State that wishes can participate in the enforcement action[132] together with the technical competence of an organization that has trained and developed procedures for a form of coalition action thereby increasing the effectiveness of any such action.

---

[132] This was illustrated by the case of Russian participation in NATO action in the former Yugoslavia where a Russian representative was stationed in NATO headquarters and was in constant contact and consultation with the NATO chain-of-command.

Concluding Remarks

The aim of any collective security system is to preserve, and ensure the observance of, certain community defined values. The determination of what are these community values in the case of the United Nations—what constitutes a threat to, or breach of, international peace—and what is the appropriate measure to maintain or restore peace has been left to the Security Council under Chapter VII of the Charter. This situation is justifiable since it was envisaged that the Security Council, acting within its designated institutional competence, would be acting as the 'delegate' of the international community of States. It was envisaged that in determining and enforcing community values the designated institutional competence of the Council would be such that any action taken would, in general terms, be directed primarily at the attainment of the interests of the international community and not that of individual State actors. The danger with the delegation of Chapter VII powers by the Security Council is that the interests of States—that take up a delegation of powers directly or which seek to influence a UN organ in the exercize of delegated power—may not converge with the most effective way to achieve the community defined values at best and at worst may even conflict with the attainment of such an objective. This is where application of the legal framework governing the process of delegation of Chapter VII powers is of primary importance. The role of law here is to prescribe the limits which regulate the delegation and exercize of these powers to ensure that the community defined goal is achieved. In particular, we recall the limitations pertaining to the UN Secretary-General, UN subsidiary organs, UN Member States, and regional arrangements. However, this does not mean *per se* that the legal framework governing such delegations is antithetical to the attainment by States of their self-interest. Indeed, the normative effect of the operation of this process may lead to the development of States' perception as to what constitutes their self-interest: so that States conceive of their interest, in part, as being the attainment of the interests of the whole. It is this evolution in perception by States of what constitutes their self-interest that may well prove to be the most effective guarantor of international peace and security. The practice of the Council delegating Chapter VII powers has allowed expression to be given to this notion, and may well be the greatest contribution of this process to the future maintenance of international peace and security.

However, a word of caution is required. In developing the possibilities under the Charter to the very limit, care should be taken as one day the political consensus that currently exists with regard to the way in which delegated Chapter VII powers are to be exercized may no longer exist. And then reliance on legal norms will matter. Accordingly, the limitations on the process of a delegation of Chapter VII powers must be constantly kept in view, even while acting with imagination in the new world order.

Bibliography

Abi-Saab, G., *The United Nations Operation in the Congo* (1978).

——'Membership and Voting in the United Nations', in *The Changing Constitution of the United Nations* (Fox, H., ed.) (1997), p. 19.

Acevedo, D., 'Disputes under consideration by the UN Security Council or Regional Bodies', in *The International Court of Justice at a Crossroads* (Fisler-Damrosch, L., ed.) (1987), p. 242.

Adibe, C., 'The Liberian Conflict and the ECOWAS–UN Partnership', in *Beyond UN Subcontracting* (Weiss, T., ed.) (1998), p. 67.

Akande, D., 'The International Court of Justice and the Security Council: Is There Room for Judicial Control of Decisions of the Political Organs of the United Nations?', *ICLQ*, 46 (1997), p. 309.

Akehurst, M., 'Enforcement Action by Regional Agencies with Special Reference to the Organization of American States', *BYIL*, 42 (1967), p. 175.

——*A Modern Introduction to International Law* (1982).

Akhavan, P., 'The Yugoslav Tribunal at a crossroads: The Dayton Peace Agreement and beyond', *Human Rights Quarterly* (March 1996), p. 259.

Alexandrowicz, C., 'The Secretary-General of the United Nations', *ICLQ*, 11 (1962), p. 1109.

Allott, P., *Eunomia: New Order for a New World* (1990).

Alston, P., 'The Security Council and Human Rights: lessons to be learned from the Iraq-Kuwait crisis and its aftermath', *Australian Year Book of International Law*, 13 (1992), p. 107.

——and Bustelo, M., eds., *Whose New World Order: What Role for the United Nations* (1991).

Alvarez, J., 'Judging the Security Council', *AJIL*, 90 (1996), p. 1.

——'What's the Security Council For?', *Michigan Journal of International Law*, 17 (1996), p. 221.

Amerasinghe, C., *The Law of the International Civil Service* (1994), p. 27.

Annan, K., 'UN Peace-Keeping Operations and Co-operation with NATO', *NATO Review*, 41 (October 1993), p. 3.

——'Peace-Keeping in Situations of Civil War', *New York University Journal of International Law & Politics*, 26 (1994), p. 623.

Arangio-Ruiz, G., 'The "Federal Analogy" and UN Charter Interpretation: A Crucial Issue', *EJIL*, 8 (1997), p. 1.

Augelli, E., and Murphy, C., 'Lessons of Somalia for Future Multilateral Humanitarian Assistance Operations', *Global Governance*, 1 (1995), p. 339.

Aust, A., 'The Procedure and Practice of the Security Council Today', in *Peace-Keeping and Peace-Building: The Development of the Role of the Security Council* (Dupuy, R-J.) (1993), p. 365.

Avakov, V., 'The Secretary-General in the Afghanistan Conflict, the Iran-Iraq War, and the Gulf Crisis', in *The Challenging Role of the UN Secretary-General* (Rivlin, B., and Gordenker, L., eds.) (1993), p. 152.

Bailey, S., *Voting in the Security Council* (1969).

——and Daws, S., *The Procedure of the Security Council* (1997).

Bedjaoui, M., *The New World Order and the Security Council: Testing the Legality of Its Acts* (1994).

Bekker, P., *The Legal Position of Intergovernmental Organizations: A Functional Necessity Analysis of Their Legal Status and Immunities* (1994).

Bentwich, N., and Martin, A., *A Commentary on the Charter of the United Nations* (1950).

Bethlehem, D., ed., *The Kuwait Crisis: Sanctions and their Economic Consequences* (1991).

Bindschedler, R., 'La Délimitation des Compétence des Nations Unies', *Hague Recueil des Cours*, 108 (1963-I), p. 312.

Black, C., and Falk, R., eds., *The Future of the International Legal Order*, v. 3 (1971).

Blokker, N., and Schermers, H., *International Institutional Law* (1995).

Blum, Y., *Eroding the United Nations Charter* (1993).

Bob, C., and Franck, T., 'The Return of Humpty-Dumpty: Foreign Relations Law After the Chadha Case', *AJIL*, 79 (1985), p. 912.

Borgen, C., 'The Theory and Practice of Regional Organization Intervention in Civil Wars', *New York University Journal of International Law & Politics*, 26 (1994), p. 797.

Borg-Olivier, A., 'The United Nations in a Changing World Order: Expectations and Realities', in *Peacemaking, Peacekeeping and Coalition Warfare: The Future Role of the United Nations* (1994), p. 19.

Bothe, M., 'Les limites des pouvoirs du Conseil de sécurité', in *Peace-Keeping and Peace-Building: The Development of the Role of the Security Council* (Dupuy, R-J., ed.) (1993), p. 67.

Boulden, J., 'The UN Charter, Article 43 and the Military Staff Committee: From San Francisco to the Collective Measures Committee', in *The Use of Force by the Security Council for Enforcement and Deterrent Purposes: A Conference Report* (Cox, D., ed.) (1990), p. 26.

Boutros-Ghali, B., *Contribution a' l'étude des ententes régionales* (1949).

——*An Agenda for Peace* (1992).

——*Supplement to An Agenda for Peace* (1995).

——*The United Nations and Somalia, 1992–1996* (UN Publications).

Bowett, D., *Self-Defence in International Law* (1958).

——*United Nations Forces* (1964).

——'Structure and Control of UN Forces', in *The Strategy of World Order: The United Nations* (vol. 3) (Falk, R., and Mendlovitz, S., eds.) (1966), p. 591.

——*The Law of International Institutions* (1982).

——'The Impact of Security Council Decisions on Dispute Settlement Procedures', *European Journal of International Law*, 5 (1994), p. 89.

——'Judicial and Political Functions of the Security Council and the International Court of Justice', in *The Changing Constitution of the United Nations* (Fox, H., ed.) (1997), p. 73.

Bradley, K. St C., 'Comitology and the Law: Through a Glass, Darkly', *Common Market Law Review*, 29 (1992), p. 693.

Brower, C., and Lillich, R., 'Opinion Regarding the Jurisdiction and Powers of the United Nations Compensation Commission', *Virginia Journal of International Law*, 38 (1997), p. 25.

Brownlie, I., 'The Use of Force in Self-Defence', *BYIL*, 37 (1962), p. 183.
——*International Law and the Use of Force by States* (1963).
——'The United Nations as a form of Government', *Harvard International Law Journal*, 13 (1972), p. 421.
——'Humanitarian Intervention', in *Law and Civil War in the Modern World* (Norton-Moore, J., ed.) (1974), p. 217.
——*Principles of Public International Law* (1990).
——'The Decisions of Political Organs of the United Nations and the Rule of Law', in *Essays in Honour of Wang Tieya* (R. St J. Macdonald, ed.) (1993), p. 91.
——'State Responsibility: The Problem of Delegation', in *Völkerrecht zwischen normativem anspruch und politischer Realität* (Ginther, K., Hafner, G., Lang, W., Neuhold, H., & Sucharipa-Behrmann, L., eds.) (1994), p. 299.
——'International Law at the Fiftieth Anniversary of the United Nations', *Hague Recueil des Cours*, 255 (1995), p. 9.
——'International law in the context of changing world order', in *Perspectives on International Law* (Jasentuliyana, N., ed.) (1995).
——*Basic Documents in International Law* (1995).
Bustelo, M., and Alston, P., eds., *Whose New World Order: What Role for the United Nations* (1991).
Cahier, G., 'La Nullité en droit international', *Revue Générale droit International Public*, 76 (1972), p. 645.
Campbell, I., 'The Limits of the Powers of International Organisations', *ICLQ*, 32 (1983), p. 523.
Caron, D., 'The Legitimacy of the Collective Authority of the Security Council', *AJIL*, 87 (1993), p. 552.
Cassesse, A., ed., *United Nations Peace-Keeping: Legal Essays* (1978).
——*International Law in a Divided World* (1994).
Chaumont, C., ed., *Hommage d'une Génération de Juristes au Président Basdevant* (1958).
Chayes, A., in '1991 Friedmann Conference on Collective Security', *Columbia Journal of Transnational Law*, 29 (1991), p. 510.
Cheng, B., *General Principles of Law as applied by International Courts and Tribunals* (1953).
Childers, E., 'Gulf Crisis Lessons for the United Nations', *Bulletin of Peace Proposals*, 23(2) (1992), p. 129.
——and Urquhart, B., *A World in Need of Leadership: Tomorrow's United Nations* (1996).
Chinkin, C., *Third Parties in International Law* (1993).
Chopra, J., and Weiss, T., 'Sovereignty is No Longer Sacrosanct: Codifying Humanitarian Intervention', in *At Issue: Politics in the World Arena* (Spiegel, S., and Pervin, D., eds.) (1994), p. 412.
Ciobanu, D., *Preliminary Objections to the Jurisdiction of the United Nations Political Organs* (1975).
——'The Power of the Security Council to Organize Peace-Keeping Operations', in *United Nations Peace-Keeping: Legal Essays* (Cassesse, A., ed.) (1978), p. 19.
Claude, I., 'Collective Legitimization as a Political Function of the United Nations', *International Organization*, 20 (Summer 1966), p. 367.
Colombo, C., *International Law of the Sea* (1967).

Condorelli, L., ed., *Les Nations Unies et le Droit International Humanitaire* (1996).

Conforti, B., *The Law and Practice of the United Nations* (1996).

Conlon, P., 'Lessons From Iraq: The Functions of the Iraq Sanctions Committee as a Source of Sanctions Implementation Authority and Practice', *Virginia Journal of International Law*, 35 (1995), p. 633.

Cot, J-P., and Pellet, A., eds., *La Charte des Nations Unies* (1991).

Cox, D., 'Enforcement, Deterrence, and the Role of the United Nations: Introduction and Summary', in *The Use of Force by the Security Council for Enforcement and Deterrent Purposes: A Conference Report* (Cox, D., ed.) (1990), p. 32.

Crawford, J., *The Creation of States in International Law* (1979).

——*Democracy in International Law* (1994).

——'The Charter of the United Nations as a Constitution', in *The Changing Constitution of the United Nations* (Fox, H., ed.) (1997), p. 3.

'Creation of a Standby United Nations Military Force', *The Record of the Association of the Bar of the City of New York*, 48 (1993), p. 981.

D'Amato, A., 'Peace vs. Accountability in Bosnia', *AJIL*, 88 (1994), p. 500.

David, R., ed., *The Legal Systems of the World Their Comparison and Unification, Sources of Law*, vol. 2, Chapter 3 (1984).

Davis, D., 'The Policy Implications of Command and Control in Multinational Peace Support Operations: A Report of a Round Table held at George Mason University', in *Peacemaking, Peacekeeping and Coalition Warfare: The Future Role of the United Nations*, Proceedings of a Conference Co-sponsored by National Defense University and Norwich University (Mokhtari, F., ed.) (1994), p. 95.

Davis, K., *Administrative Law Treatise* (1978).

de Smith, S., Woolf, H., and Jowell, J., *Judicial Review of Administrative Action* (1995).

Di Blase, A., 'The Role of the Host State's Consent With Regard to Non-Coercive Actions by the United Nations', in *United Nations Peace-Keeping* (Cassesse, A., ed.) (1978), p. 55.

Dinstein, Y., *War, Aggression and Self-Defence* (1994).

——'The Legal Lessons of the Gulf War', *Austrian Journal of Public and International Law*, 48 (1995), p. 1.

Dixon, M., 'Delegation, Agency and the Alter Ego Rule', *Sydney Law Review*, 11 (1987), p. 326.

Djiena Wembou, M-C., 'Réflexions sur la validité et la portée de la résolution 678 du Conseil de Sécurité', *African Journal of International & Comparative Law*, 5 (1993), p. 34.

——'Validité et portée de la résolution 794 (1992) du Conseil de Sécurité', *African Journal of Intenational & Comparative Law*, 5 (1993), p. 340.

Dodd, T., 'War and Peacekeeping in the Former Yugoslavia', *House of Commons Research Paper, 95/100*, 12 October 1995.

Draper, G., 'The Legal Limitations upon the Employment of Weapons by the United Nations Force in the Congo', *ICLQ*, 12 (1963), p. 387.

Drewry, G., and Oliver, D., *Public Service Reforms: Issues of Accountability and Public Law* (1996).

Dugard, J., *Recognition and the United Nations* (1987).

Duke, S., 'The State and Human Rights: Humanitarian Intervention Versus Sovereignty', in *Peacemaking, Peacekeeping and Coalition Warfare: The Future Role of the United Nations*, Proceedings of a Conference Co-sponsored by National Defense University and Norwich University (Mokhtari, F., ed.) (1994), p. 149.

Dupuy, P-M., 'The Constitutional Dimension of the Charter of the United Nations Revisited', *Max Planck Yearbook of United Nations Law*, 1 (1997), p. 1.

Dupuy, R-J., ed., *Manuel sur les organisations internationales* (1988).

——ed., *Peace-Keeping and Peace-Building: The Development of the Role of the Security Council* (1993).

Dutheil de la Rochere, J., 'Etude de la composition de certains organes subsidiaires récemment crées par l'Assemblée générale des Nations Unies dans le domaine économique', *Annuaire français de droit international* (1967), p. 307.

Eagleton, C., *The Responsibility of States in International Law* (1928).

——*International Government* (1957).

Elaraby, N., 'United Nations Peacekeeping by Consent: A Case Study of the Withdrawal of the United Nations Emergency Force', *New York University Journal of International Law & Politics*, 1 (1968), p. 149.

——'The Office of the Secretary-General and the Maintenance of International Peace and Security', *Revue Egyptienne du Droit International*, 42 (1986), p. 1.

Falk, R., 'The Complexities of Humanitarian Intervention: A New World Order Challenge', *Michigan Journal of International Law*, 17 (1996), p. 491.

——and Black, C., eds., *The Future of the International Legal Order*, vol. 3 (1971).

——and Mendlovitz, S., eds., *Regional Politics and World Order* (1973).

Farber, D., and Frickey, P., *Law and Public Choice* (1991).

Fawcett, J., 'Intervention in International Law', *Hague Recueil des Cours*, 103 (1961-II), p. 351.

——'Security Council Resolutions on Rhodesia', *BYIL*, 41 (1965–6), p. 103.

Fenrick, W., 'Legal limits on the use of force by Canadian warships engaged in law enforcement', *The Canadian Yearbook of International Law* (1980), p. 113.

——'Some International Law Problems Related to Prosecutions before the International Criminal Tribunal for the Former Yugoslavia', *Duke Journal of Comparative & International Law*, 6 (1995), p. 103.

Ferencz, B., *Global Survival: Security through the United Nations* (1994).

Fidler, D., 'Caught Between Traditions: The Security Council in Philosophical Conundrum', *Michigan Journal of International Law*, 17 (1996), p. 411.

Fielding, L., 'Maritime Interception: Centrepiece of Economic Sanctions in the New World Order', *Louisiana Law Review*, 53 (1993), p. 1191.

Figa-Talamanca, N., 'The Role of NATO in the Peace Agreement for Bosnia and Herzegovina', *European Journal of International Law*, 7 (1996), p. 147.

Finer, S., Bogdanor, V., and Rudden, B., *Comparing Constitutions* (1995).

Firmage, E., and Wormuth, F., *To Chain the Dog of War* (1989).

Fisler-Damrosch, L., ed., *The International Court of Justice at a Crossroads* (1987).

——and Scheffer, D., eds., *Law and Force in the New International Order* (1991).

Fitzmaurice, M., and Lowe, V., eds., *The International Court of Justice After 50 Years: essays in honour of Sir Robert Jennings* (1996).

Fox, H., ed., *The Changing Constitution of the United Nations* (1997).
—— and Wickremasinghe, C., 'UK Implementation of UN Economic Sanctions', *ICLQ*, 42 (1993), p. 945.
Franck, T., *Comparative Constitutional Process: Cases and Materials, Fundamental Rights in the Common Law Nations* (1968).
—— 'Finding a Voice: How the Secretary-General Makes Himself Heard in the Councils of the United Nations', in *Essays in Honour of Judge Manfred Lachs* (Makarczyck, J., ed.) (1984), p. 481.
—— 'Legitimacy in the International System', *AJIL*, 82 (1988), p. 705.
—— 'The "Powers of Appreciation": Who is the Ultimate Guardian of UN Legality?', *AJIL*, 86 (1992), p. 519.
—— 'Fairness in the International Legal and Institutional System', *Hague Recueil des Cours*, 240 (1993-III), p. 9.
—— 'The United Nations as Guarantor of International Peace and Security', in *The United Nations at Age Fifty: A Legal Perspective* (1995), p. 25.
—— 'Community Based on Autonomy', *Columbia Journal of Transnational Law*, 36 (1997), p. 41.
—— and Bob, C., 'The Return of Humpty-Dumpty: Foreign Relations Law After the Chadha Case', *AJIL*, 79 (1985), p. 912.
—— and Patel, F., 'UN Police Action in Lieu of War: "The Old Order Changeth"', *AJIL*, 85 (1991), p. 66.
Freedland, M., 'The rule against delegation and the *Carltona* doctrine in an agency context', *Public Law* (1996), p. 19.
Freedman, J., 'Delegation of Power and Institutional Competence', *University of Chicago Law Review*, 43 (1976), p. 307.
Freedman, L., and Karsh, E., *The Gulf Conflict 1990–1991* (1993).
Freudenschuß, H., 'Between Unilateralism and Collective Security: Authorizations of the Use of Force by the UN Security Council', *European Journal of International Law*, 5 (1994), p. 492.
Frowein, J., 'Collective Enforcement of International Obligations', *ZaöRV*, 47 (1987), p. 67.
Gaeta, P., 'The Dayton Agreements and International Law', *European Journal of International Law*, 7 (1996), p. 147.
Gaga, G., 'Use of Force Made or Authorized by the United Nations', in *The United Nations at Age Fifty: A Legal Perspective* (Tomuschat, C., ed.) (1995), p. 39.
Gardam, J., 'Proportionality and Force in International Law', *AJIL*, 87 (1993), p. 391.
—— 'Legal Restraints on Security Council Military Enforcement Action', *Michigan Journal of International Law*, 17 (1996), p. 285.
Garvey, J., 'United Nations Peacekeeping and Host State Consent', *AJIL*, 64 (1970), p. 241.
Gendron, M., 'The Legal and Strategic Paradigms of the United Nations' Intervention in Somalia', in *Peacemaking, Peacekeeping and Coalition Warfare: The Future Role of the United Nations*, Proceedings of a Conference Co-sponsored by National Defense University and Norwich University (Mokhtari, F., ed.) (1994), p. 71.

Gill, T., 'Legal and Some Political Limitations on the Power of the UN Security Council to Exercise its Enforcement Powers under Chapter VII of the Charter', *Netherlands Yearbook of International Law*, 26 (1995), p. 33.

Glennon, M., and Hayward, A., 'Collective Security and the Constitution: Can the Commander in Chief Power Be Delegated to the United Nations?', *The Georgetown Law Journal*, 82 (1994), p. 1573.

Gomula, J., 'The International Court of Justice and Administrative Tribunals of International Organizations', *Michigan Journal of International Law*, 13 (1991), p. 83.

Goodrich, L., *Korea: A Study of US Policy in the United Nations* (1956).

——and Hambro, E., *The Charter of the United Nations* (1949).

——and Simons, A-P., *The United Nations and the Maintenance of International Peace and Security* (1955).

——Hambro, E., and Simons, A-P., *Charter of the United Nations: Commentary and Documents* (1969).

Gordon, E., 'Legal Disputes under Article 36(2) of the Statute', in *The International Court of Justice at a Crossroads* (Fisler-Damrosch, L., ed.) (1987), p. 183.

Gordon, R., 'Humanitarian Intervention by the United Nations: Iraq, Somalia, and Haiti', *Texas International Law Journal*, 31 (1996), p. 43.

Gordon, W., *The United Nations at the Crossroads of Reform* (1994).

Gowlland-Debbas, V., *Collective Responses to Illegal Acts under International Law: United Nations Action in the Case of Southern Rhodesia* (1990).

——'The Relationship between the International Court of Justice and the Security Council in the Light of the *Lockerbie* case', *AJIL*, 88 (1994), p. 643.

——'Security Council Enforcement Action and Issues of State Responsibility', *ICLQ*, 43 (1994), p. 55.

Graefrath, B., 'Leave to the Court What Belongs to the Court: The Libyan Case', *European Journal of International Law*, 4 (1993), p. 184.

——'Iraqi Reparations and the Security Council', *ZaöRV*, 55 (1995), p. 1.

Gray, C., 'After the Ceasefire: Iraq, The Security Council and the Use of Force', *BYIL*, 65 (1994), p. 135.

——'Regional Arrangements and the United Nations Collective Security System', in *The Changing Constitution of the United Nations* (Fox, H., ed.) (1997), p. 91.

Green, L. (statement made during ILA Meeting), 'Report of the 49th International Law Association Conference held at Hamburg', *ILA Reports* (1960), p. 115.

——'Iraq, the UN and the Law', *Alberta Law Review*, 29 (1991), p. 560.

Greenwood, C., 'The relationship between ius ad bellum and ius in bello', *Review of International Studies*, 9 (1983), p. 221.

——'New World Order or Old? The Invasion of Kuwait and the Rule of Law', 55(2) *The Modern Law Review* (1992), p. 153.

——'The International Tribunal for Former Yugoslavia', *International Affairs*, 69 (1993), p. 641.

——'The United Nations as Guarantor of International Peace and Security: Past, Present and Future—A United Kingdom View', in *The United Nations at Age Fifty: A Legal Perspective* (Tomuschat, C., ed.) (1995), p. 69.

Greenwood, C., 'International Humanitarian Law and the *Tadic* case', *European Journal of International Law*, 7 (1996), p. 265.

Greig, D., 'Self-Defence and the Security Council: What Does Article 51 Require?', *ICLQ*, 40 (1991), p. 366.

Gross, L., 'States as Organs of International Law and the Problem of Autointerpretation', in *Law and Politics in the World Community* (Lipsky, G., ed.) (1953), p. 63.

——'Voting in the Security Council: Abstention in the Post-1965 Amendment Phase and its Impact on Article 25 of the Charter', *AJIL*, 62 (1968), p. 315.

Halberstam, M., 'The Right to Self-Defense Once the Security Council Takes Action', *Michigan Journal of International Law*, 17 (1996), p. 229.

Halderman, J., *The United Nations and the Rule of Law* (1966).

Hall, W., *International Law* (1909).

Hamilton, M., 'Power, Responsibility, and Republican Democracy', a review of *Power Without Responsibility* (Schoenbrod, D.), in *Michigan Law Review*, 93 (1995), p. 1539.

Hammarskjold, D., 'The International Civil Servant in Law and in Fact', *Press Release, Secretary-General/1035*, 29 May 1961.

Hampson, F., 'States' Military Operations Authorized by the United Nations and International Humanitarian Law', in *Les Nations Unies et le Droit International Humanitaire* (Condorelli, L., ed.) (1996), p. 371.

Harper, K., 'Does the United Nations Security Council Have the Competence to Act as Court and Legislature?', *New York University Journal of International Law & Politics,* 27 (1994), p. 103.

Hartley, T., *The Foundations of European Community Law* (1994).

Hayward, A., and Glennon, M., 'Collective Security and the Constitution: Can the Commander in Chief Power Be Delegated to the United Nations?', *The Georgetown Law Journal*, 82 (1994), p. 1573.

Herdegen, M., 'The "Constitutionalization" of the UN Security System', *Vanderbilt Journal of Transnational Law*, 27 (1994), p. 135.

Herndl, K., 'Reflections on the Role, Functions and Procedures of the Security Council', *Hague Recueil des Cours*, 206 (1987-VI), p. 297.

Higgins, R., 'The Legal Limits to the Use of Force by Sovereign States: United Nations Practice', *BYIL*, 37 (1962), p. 269.

——*The Development of International Law Through the Political Organs of the United Nations* (1963).

——'International law, Rhodesia, and the UN', *The World Today*, 23 (1967), p. 94.

——'Policy Considerations and the International Judicial Process', *ICLQ*, 17 (1968), p. 58.

——*United Nations Peacekeeping*, vol. 1 (1969).

——*United Nations Peacekeeping*, vol. 2 (1970).

——'The Place of International Law in the Settlement of Disputes by the Security Council', *AJIL*, 64 (1970), p. 1.

——'The Advisory Opinion on Namibia: Which UN Resolutions are Binding under Article 25 of the Charter?', *ICLQ*, 21 (1972), p. 270.

——'A General Assessment of UN Peace-Keeping', in *UN Peace-Keeping* (Cassese, A., ed.) (1978), p. 1.

Higgins, R., *United Nations Peacekeeping*, vol. 3 (1980).

——'International Law and the Avoidance, Containment and Resolution of Disputes', *Hague Recueil des Cours*, 230 (1991-V), p. 9.

——'The New United Nations and Former Yugoslavia', *Foreign Affairs*, 69 (1993), p. 465.

——*Problems and Process: International Law and How We Use It* (1994).

——'Final Report of the Legal Consequences for Member States of the Non-Fulfilment by International Organizations of their Obligations Towards Third Parties', *Report of the Institut de droit International*, 66-I *AIDI* (1995), p. 251.

——'The United Nations 50 Years On, Part III: Achievements and Failures', *European Journal of International Law*, Special Issue (1995), Chapter 6, p. 14.

——'The United Nations Role in Maintaining International Peace: The Lessons of the First Fifty Years', *New York Law School Journal of International and Comparative Law*, 16 (1996), p. 135.

——'The UN Security Council and the Individual State', in *The Changing Constitution of the United Nations* (Fox, H., ed.) (1997), p. 43.

Hirsch, M., *The Responsibility of International Organizations Toward Third Parties: Some Basic Principles* (1995).

Hirsh, J., and Oakley, R., *Somalia and Operation Restore Hope: Reflections on Peacemaking and Peacekeeping* (1995).

House of Lords, Select Committee on the European Communities, *Delegation of Powers to the Commission (Final Report)*, 3rd Report, Session 1986–7.

Hulton, S., and Mendelson, M., 'La Revendication par l'Iraq de la Souveraineté sur le Koweït', *Annuaire français de droit international*, 36 (1990), p. 195.

—— and —— 'Les Décisions de la Commission Nations Unies sur la démarcation de la frontière entre l'Iraq et le Koweït', *Annuaire français de droit international*, 39 (1993), p. 178.

—— and —— 'The Iraq-Kuwait Boundary', *BYIL*, 64 (1993), p. 135.

Hume, C., 'The Secretary-General's Representatives', *SAIS Review* (1995).

Hutchinson, M., 'Restoring Hope: UN Security Council Resolutions for Somalia and an Expanded Doctrine of Humanitarian Intervention', *Harvard International Law Journal*, 34 (1993), p. 624.

Jennings, R., 'Nullity and Effectiveness in International Law', in *Cambridge Essays in International Law* (1965), p. 64.

——'Gerald Gray Fitzmaurice', *BYIL*, 55 (1984), p. 18.

Johnstone, I., *Aftermath of the Gulf War: An Assessment of UN Action*, International Peace Academy, Occasional Paper Series (1994).

Jones, T., 'The International Law of Maritime Blockade—A Measure of Naval Economic Interdiction', *Howard Law Journal*, 26 (1983), p. 761.

Joseph, H., 'Humanitarian Assistance Operations Challenges: The Centcom Perspective on Somalia', *Joint Forces Quarterly*, 1 (November 1993).

Jowell, J., 'Restraining the State: Politics, Principle and Judicial Review', *Current Legal Problems*, 50 (1997), p. 189.

Joyner, C., and Schachter, O., eds., *United Nations Legal Order*, vol. 1 (1995).

Kaikobad, K., 'Self-Defence, Enforcement and the Gulf Wars, 1980–88 and 1990–91', *BYIL*, 63 (1992), p. 300.

Karsh, E., and Freedman, L., *The Gulf Conflict 1990–1991* (1993).

Kelsen, H., *General Theory of Law and State* (1945).

——'Collective Security and Collective Self-Defence under the Charter of the United Nations', *AJIL*, 42 (1948), p. 783.

——*The Law of the United Nations* (1951).

——'Is the North Atlantic Treaty a Regional Arrangement?', *AJIL*, 45 (1951), p. 162.

Kennedy, D., *International Legal Structures* (1987).

Keyes, J., 'From *Delegatus* to the Duty to Make Law', *McGill Law Journal*, 33 (1987), p. 49.

Kirgis, F., 'The Security Council's First Fifty Years', *AJIL*, 89 (1995), p. 506.

Kirk, G., 'The Enforcement of Security', *Yale Law Journal*, 55 (1946), p. 1081.

Kischel, U., 'Delegation of Legislative Power to Agencies: A Comparative Analysis of United States and German Law', *Administrative Law Review*, 46 (1994), p. 213.

Kissinger, H., 'Balance of Power Sustained,' in *Rethinking America's Security* (1992), p. 238.

——*Diplomacy* (1994).

Klabbers, J., 'No More Shifting Lines? The Report of the Iraq-Kuwait Boundary Demarcation Commission', *ICLQ*, 43 (1994), p. 904.

Klepacki, Z., *The Organs of International Organizations* (1973).

Knapp, V., ed., *International Encyclopedia of Comparative Law, National Reports*, vol. 1.

Koskenniemi, M., 'The Police in the Temple. Order, Justice and the UN: A Dialectical View', *EJIL*, 6 (1995), p. 325.

——'The Place of Law in Collective Security', *Michigan Journal of International Law*, 17 (1996), p. 455.

Krent, H., 'Fragmenting the Unitary Executive: Congressional Delegations of Administrative Authority Outside the Federal Government', *Northwestern University Law Review*, 85 (1990), p. 62.

——'Delegation and its Discontents', book review of *Power Without Responsibility* (Schoenbrod, D.), *Columbia Law Review*, 94 (1994), p. 710.

Kufuor, K., 'The Legality of the Intervention in the Liberian Civil War by the Economic Community of West African States', *African Journal of International & Comparative Law*, 5 (1993), p. 525.

Kunz, J., 'The Legal Position of the Secretary-General of the United Nations', *AJIL*, 40 (1946), p. 786.

Lanham, D., 'Delegation and the Alter Ego Principle', *Law Quarterly Review*, 100 (1984), p. 587.

——'Delegation of Governmental Power to Private Parties', *Otago Law Review*, 6 (1985), p. 50.

La Pergola, A., and Del Duca, P., 'Community Law, International Law and the Italian Constitution', *AJIL*, 79 (1985), p. 598.

Lash, J., 'Dag Hammarskjold's Conception of his Office', *International Organization*, 16 (1962), p. 551.

Lasswell, H., and Kaplan, A., *Power and Society: A Framework for Political Inquiry* (1952).

Lauterpacht, E., 'The Legal Effect of Illegal Acts of International Organizations', in *Cambridge Essays in International Law* (1965), p. 88.
——*Aspects of the Administration of International Justice* (1991).
——Greenwood, C., Weller, M., and Bethlehem, D., eds., *The Kuwait Crisis: Basic Documents* (1991), p. 248.
Lauterpacht, H., *Private Law Sources and Analogies of International Law* (1927).
——'The Groatian Tradition in International Law', *BYIL*, 23 (1946), p. 1.
——ed., *Oppenheim's International Law: A Treatise* (7th edn., 1948).
Lauwaars, R., 'The Interrelationship between United Nations Law and the Law of other International Organizations', *Michigan Law Review*, 82 (1984), p. 1604.
Lavalle, R., 'The Law of the United Nations and the Use of Force, Under the Relevant Security Council Resolutions of 1990 and 1991, to Resolve the Persian Gulf Crisis', *Netherlands Yearbook of International Law*, 23 (1992), p. 3.
Lawrence, D., 'Private Exercise of Governmental Power', *Indiana Law Journal*, 61 (1986), p. 647.
Lee, R., 'The Rwanda Tribunal', *Leiden Journal of International Law*, 9 (1996), p. 37.
Lenaerts, K., 'Regulating the regulatory process: "delegation of powers" in the European Community', *European Law Review*, 18 (1993), p. 23.
Leurdijk, D., *The United Nations and NATO in Former Yugoslavia: Partners in International Cooperation* (1994).
Lie, T., *In the Cause of Peace* (1954).
Lillich, R., and Brower, C., 'Opinion Regarding the Jurisdiction and Powers of the United Nations Compensation Commission', *Virginia Journal of International Law*, 38 (1997), p. 25.
Linde, H., 'Due Process of Lawmaking', *Nebraska Law Review*, 55 (1976), p. 197.
Lorenz, F., 'Rules of Engagement in Somalia: Were They Effective?', *Naval Law Review*, 42 (1995), p. 62.
Lowe, V., and Fitzmaurice, M., eds., *Fifty Years of the International Court of Justice: essays in honour of Sir Robert Jennings* (1996).
——and Warbrick, C., 'Current Developments: Public International Law', *ICLQ*, 40 (1991), p. 965.
McCain, J., 'The Proper United States Role in Peacemaking', in *Peace Support Operations and the US Military* (Quinn, D., ed.) (1994), p. 85.
McCausland, J., 'Coalition in the Desert', in *Peacemaking, Peacekeeping and Coalition Warfare: The Future Role of the United Nations*, Proceedings of a Conference Co-sponsored by National Defense University and Norwich University (Mokhtari, F., ed.) (1994), p. 4.
McDougal, M., and Gardner, R., 'The Veto and the Charter: An Interpretation for Survival', *Yale Law Journal*, 60 (1951), p. 209.
MacDougall, M., 'United Nations Operations: Who Should be in Charge?', *Revue de droit militaire et de la guerre* (1994), p. 21.
McMahon, E., '*Chadha* and the Nondelegation Doctrine: Defining a Restricted Legislative Veto', *Yale Law Journal*, 94 (1985), p. 1493.
McWhinney, E., 'The International Court as Emerging Constitutional Court and the Co-ordinate UN Institutions (Especially the Security Council): Implications

of the Aerial Incident at Lockerbie', *Canadian Yearbook of International Law* (1992), p. 261.

Malanczuk, P., 'The Kurdish Crisis and Allied Intervention in the Aftermath of the Second Gulf War', *European Journal of International Law*, 2 (1991), p. 114.

Malcolm, D., 'The Limitations, if Any, on the Powers of Parliament to Delegate the Power to Legislate', *Australian Law Journal*, 66 (1992), p. 247.

Mashaw, J., 'Prodelegation: Why Administrators Should Make Political Decisions', *Journal of Law, Economics and Organization*, 1 (1985), p. 81.

Membership of the European Community: Report on Renegotiation, Presented to Parliament by the Prime Minister by Command of Her Majesty, March 1975, Cmnd. 6003.

Mendelson, M., 'Diminutive States in the United Nations', *ICLQ*, 21 (1972), p. 609.

——and Hulton, S., 'La Revendication par l'Iraq de la Souveraineté sur le Koweït', *Annuaire français de droit international*, 36 (1990), p. 195.

——and—— 'Les Décisions de la Commission Nations Unies sur la démarcation de la frontière entre l'Iraq et le Koweït', *Annuaire français de droit international*, 39 (1993), p. 178.

——and—— 'The Iraq-Kuwait Boundary', *BYIL*, 64 (1993), p. 135.

Mendlovitz, S., and Falk, R., eds., *Regional Politics and World Order* (1973).

Meron, T., 'Status and Independence of the International Civil Service', *Hague Recueil des Cours*, 167 (1980-II), p. 285.

——'In re Rosescu and the Independence of the International Civil Service', *AJIL*, 75 (1981), p. 910.

Meyer, J., 'Collective Self-Defense and Regional Security: Necessary Exceptions to a Globalist Doctrine', *Boston University International Law Journal*, 11 (1993), p. 391.

Miller, A., 'Universal Soldiers: UN Standing Armies and the Legal Alternatives', *Georgetown Law Journal*, 81 (1993), p. 773.

Miller, E., 'Legal Aspects of the United Nations Action in the Congo', *AJIL*, 55 (1961), p. 1.

Miller, L., 'The Prospects for Order through Regional Security', in *Regional Politics and World Order* (Falk, R., and Mendlovitz, S., eds.) (1973), p. 51.

Mokhtari, F., ed., *Peacemaking, Peacekeeping and Coalition Warfare: The Future Role of the United Nations*, Proceedings of a Conference Co-sponsored by National Defense University and Norwich University (1994).

Morgenstern, F., 'Legality in International Organizations', *BYIL*, 48 (1976–7), p. 24.

——*Legal Problems of International Organizations* (1986).

Morriss, D., 'From War to Peace: A Study of Cease-Fire Agreements and the Evolving Role of the United Nations', *Virginia Journal of International Law*, 36 (1996), p. 801.

Mubiala, M., 'La Mission des Nations Unies pour l'assistance au Rwanda (1993–1996)', *African Journal of International & Comparative Law*, 8 (1996), p. 393.

Murphy, C., and Augelli, E., 'Lessons of Somalia for Future Multilateral Humanitarian Assistance Operations', *Global Governance*, 1 (1995), p. 339.

Murphy, J., 'Force and Arms', in *United Nations Legal Order* (Schachter, O., and Joyner, C., eds.), vol. 1 (1995), p. 272.

Murphy, S., 'The Security Council, Legitimacy, and the Concept of Collective Security After the Cold War', *Columbia Journal of Transnational Law*, 32 (1994), p. 201.

Nkala, J., *The United Nations, international law, and the Rhodesian independence crisis* (1985).

Nolte, G., 'Restoring Peace by Regional Action: International Legal Aspects of the Liberian Conflict', *ZaöRV*, 53 (1993), p. 602.

Norton-Moore, J., 'The Role of Regional Arrangements in the Maintenance of World Order', in *The Future of the International Legal Order*, v. 3, (Falk, R., and Black, C., eds.) (1971), p. 122.

——ed., *Law and Civil War in the Modern World* (1974).

——'Toward a New Paradigm: Enhanced Effectiveness in United Nations Peacekeeping, Collective Security, and War Avoidance', *Virginia Journal of International Law*, 37 (1997), p. 811.

Obadina, D., 'The New Face of Ultra Vires and Related Agency Doctrines', *African Journal of International & Comparative Law*, 8 (1996), p. 309.

O'Brien, J., 'The International Tribunal for Violations of International Humanitarian Law in the Former Yugoslavia', *AJIL*, 87 (1993), p. 638.

O'Connell, D., *The International Law of the Sea* (Shearer, I., ed.), vol. 2 (1984).

O'Connell, M., 'Enforcing the Prohibition on the Use of Force: The UN's Response to Iraq's Invasion of Kuwait', *Southern Illinois University Law Journal*, 15 (1990–1), p. 453.

Ofuatey-Kodjoe, W., 'Regional organizations and the resolution of internal conflict: the ECOWAS intervention in Liberia', *International Peacekeeping*, 1 (1994), p. 261.

Oliver, D., and Drewry, G., *Public Service Reforms: Issues of Accountability and Public Law* (1996).

Orford, A., 'The Politics of Collective Security', *Michigan Journal of International Law*, 17 (1996), p. 373.

Osieke, E., 'Ultra-Vires Acts in International Organizations', *BYIL*, 48 (1976–7), p. 259.

——'The Legal Validity of Ultra Vires Decisions of International Organizations', *AJIL*, 77 (1983), p. 239.

Paenson, I., *Manual of the Terminology of Public International Law (Law of Peace) and International Organizations* (1983).

Parsons, A., 'The Security Council An Uncertain Future', *The David Davies Memorial Institute of International Studies, Occasional Paper No. 8* (1994).

Patel, F., and Franck, T., 'UN Police Action in Lieu of War: "The Old Order Changeth"', *AJIL*, 85 (1991), p. 66.

Peck, J., 'The UN and the Laws of War: How Can the World's Peacekeepers be held accountable?', *Syracuse Journal of International Law & Commerce*, 21 (1995), p. 283.

Pellet, A., 'The Road to Hell is Paved with Good Intentions: The United Nations as Guarantor of International Peace and Security', in *The United Nations at Age Fifty: A Legal Perspective* (Tomuschat, C., ed.) (1995), p. 113.

——and Cot, J-P., eds., *La Charte des Nations Unies* (1991).

Penna, D., 'The Right to Self-Defense in the Post-Cold War Era: The Role of the United Nations', *Denver Journal of International Law & Policy*, 20 (1991), p. 41.

Pervin, D., and Spiegel, S., eds., *At Issue: Politics in the World Arena* (1994).

Politakis, G., 'UN Mandated Naval Operations and the Notion of Pacific Blockade: Comments on Some Recent Developments', *African Journal of International & Comparative Law*, 6 (1994), p. 173.

Post, H., 'Adjudication as a mode of acquisition of territory?', in *Fifty Years of the International Court of Justice* (Lowe, V., and Fitzmaurice, M., eds.) (1996), p. 237.

Prins, G., *The Applicability of the 'NATO Model' to United Nations Peace Support Operations under the Security Council*, A Paper of the UNA–USA International Dialogue on the Enforcement of Security Council Resolutions (1996).

Pyrich, A., 'United Nations: Authorizations of Use of Force', *Harvard International Law Journal*, 32 (1991), p. 265.

Quigley, J., 'The "Privatization" of Security Council Enforcement Action: A Threat to Multilateralism', *Michigan Journal of International Law*, 17 (1996), p. 249.

Ramcharan, B., 'Lacunae in the Law of International Organizations: The Relations between Subsidiary and Parent Organs with Particular Reference to the Commission and Sub-Commission on Human Rights', in *Festchrift Ermacora* (Nowak, M., et al., eds.) (1988), p. 37.

—— 'The Office of the United Nations Secretary-General', *Dalhousie Law Journal*, 13 (1990), p. 742.

Ratner, S., 'The Cambodia Settlement Agreements', *AJIL*, 87 (1993), p. 1.

Reisman, M., 'Allocating Competences to Use Coercion in the Post-Cold War World: Practices, Conditions, and Prospects', in *Law and Force in the New International Order* (Fisler-Damrosch, L., and Scheffer, D., eds.) (1991), p. 26.

—— 'Peacemaking', *Yale Journal of International Law*, 18 (1993), p. 415.

—— 'The Constitutional Crisis in the United Nations', *AJIL*, 87 (1993), p. 83.

—— and Stevick, D., 'The Applicability of International Law Standards to United Nations Economic Sanctions Programmes', *European Journal of International Law*, 9 (1998), p. 86.

Reuter, P., 'Les Organes Subsidiaires des Organisations Internationales', in *Hommage d'une Génération de Juristes au Président Basdevant* (Chaumont, C., ed.) (1958), pp. 415–30.

Reynolds, F., ed., *Bowstead on Agency* (1985).

Rivlin, B., 'Regional Arrangements and the UN System for Collective Security and Conflict Resolution: A New Road Ahead?', *Foreign Relations*, 11 (1992), p. 95.

Rosenne, S., *Developments in the Law of Treaties* (1994).

—— *The World Court: What it is and how it works* (1995).

Rosner, G., *The United Nations Emergency Force* (1964).

Rostow, E., 'Until What? Enforcement Action or Collective Self-Defense?', *AJIL*, 85 (1991), p. 506.

Rostow, N., 'The International Use of Force after the Cold War', *Harvard International Law Journal*, 32 (1991), p. 411.

Rudden, B., *A Source-Book on French Law: Public Law: Constitutional and Administrative Law, Private Law: Structure, Contract* (1991).

Russett, B., and Sutterlin, J., 'The Utilization of Force by the Security Council in Interstate Conflict', in *The Use of Force by the Security Council for Enforcement and Deterrent Purposes: A Conference Report* (Cox, D., ed.) (1990), p. 31.

——and—— 'The UN in a New World Order', *Foreign Affairs* (1991), p. 69.

Sands, J., 'Blue Hulls: A Maritime Agenda For Peace', in *Peacemaking, Peacekeeping and Coalition Warfare: The Future Role of the United Nations*, Proceedings of a Conference Co-sponsored by National Defense University and Norwich University (Mokhtari, F., ed.) (1994).

Sargentich, T., 'The Delegation Debate and Competing Ideals of the Administrative Process', *American University Law Review*, 36 (1987), p. 419.

Sarooshi, D., 'Humanitarian Intervention and International Humanitarian Assistance: Law and Practice', *Wilton Park Papers*, 86 (1994).

—— 'The Legal Framework Governing United Nations Subsidiary Organs', *BYIL*, 67 (1996), p. 413.

—— 'The Powers of the United Nations International Criminal Tribunals', *Max Planck Yearbook of United Nations Law*, 2 (1998), p. 141.

Schachter, O., 'The Quasi-Judicial Role of the Security Council and the General Assembly', *AJIL*, 58 (1964), p. 960.

—— 'Authorized Uses of Force by the United Nations and Regional Organizations', in *Law and Force in the New International Order* (Fisler-Damrosch, L., and Scheffer, D., eds.) (1991), p. 65.

—— 'United Nations Law in the Gulf', *AJIL*, 85 (1991), p. 452.

—— *International Law in Theory and Practice* (1994).

Scheffer, D., 'Commentary on Collective Security', in *Law and Force in the New International Order* (Fisler-Damrosch, L., and Scheffer, D., eds.) (1991), p. 100.

——and Fisler-Damrosch, L., eds., *Law and Force in the New International Order* (1991).

Schermers, H., and Blokker, N., *International Institutional Law* (1995).

Schoenbrod, D., 'The Delegation Doctrine: Could the Court Give it Substance?', *Michigan Law Review*, 83 (1985), p. 1223.

—— *Power Without Responsibility: How Congress Abuses the People through Delegation* (1993).

Schreur, C., 'Regionalism v. Universalism', *EJIL*, 6 (1995), p. 477.

Schwarzenberger, G., 'Hegemonial Intervention', *Year Book of World Affairs* (1959).

Schwebel, S., *The Secretary-General of the United Nations* (1952).

—— 'The Origins and Development of Article 99 of the Charter', in *Justice In International Law: Selected Writings of Judge Stephen M. Schwebel* (1994), p. 233.

Sereni, A., 'Agency in International Law', *AJIL*, 34 (1940), p. 638.

Sewall, S., 'Peace Enforcement and the United Nations', in *Peace Support Operations and the US Military* (Quinn, D., ed.) (1994), p. 101.

Seyersted, F., 'Can the United Nations Establish Military Forces and perform other acts without specific basis in the Charter?', *Österreichische Zeitschrift für öffentliches Recht*, 12 (1962), p. 188.

—— *Objective International Personality of Intergovernmental Organisations* (1963).

—— *United Nations Forces* (1966).

Sharples, R., *World Under Management? Details, delegation and divine providence, 400 B.C.–A.D. 1200.* (1995), An Inaugural Lecture delivered at, and published by, University College London.

Shearer, I., ed., *O'Connell's International Law of the Sea*, vol. 2 (1984).

—— 'International Law and the Gulf War', in *Whose New World Order: What Role for the United Nations?* (Alston, P., and Bustelo, M., eds.) (1991), p. 73.

Shraga, D., and Zacklin, R., 'International Criminal Tribunal for the Former Yugoslavia', *European Journal of International Law*, 5 (1994), p. 360.

Siekmann, R., *National Contingents in United Nations Peace-Keeping Forces* (1991).

Simma, B., ed., *The Charter of the United Nations: A Commentary* (1994).

—— 'From Bilateralism to Community Interest in International Law', *Hague Recueil des Cours*, 250 (1994-VI), p. 9.

Simons, A-P., and Goodrich, L., *The United Nations and the Maintenance of International Peace and Security* (1955).

—— Goodrich, L., and Hambro, E., *Charter of the United Nations: Commentary and Documents* (1969).

Skubiszewski, K., 'The International Court of Justice and the Security Council', in *Fifty Years of the International Court* (Lowe, V., and Fitzmaurice, M., eds.) (1996), p. 606.

Smith, N., 'Restoration of Congressional Authority and Responsibility over the Regulatory Process', *Harvard Journal on Legislation*, 33 (1996), p. 323.

Société Française pour le Droit International Colloque de Bordeaux, *Régionalisme et Universalisme dans le Droit International Contemporain* (1977).

Sohn, L., 'The Authority of the United Nations to Establish and Maintain a Permanent United Nations Force', *AJIL*, 52 (1958), p. 229.

Spiegel, S., and Pervin, D., eds., *At Issue: Politics in the World Arena* (1994).

Spielman, J., 'The Middle East and the Persian Gulf', in *A Global Agenda: Issues Before the 48th General Assembly of the United Nations* (Tessitore, J., and Woolfson, S., eds.) (1993), p. 43.

Stern, B., ed., *Les aspects juridiques de la crise et de la guerre du Golfe* (1991).

Stevick, D., and Reisman, M., 'The Applicability of International Law Standards to United Nations Economic Sanctions Programmes', *European Journal of International Law*, 9 (1998), p. 86.

Stewart, R., 'Beyond Delegation Doctrine', *American University Law Review*, 36 (1987), p. 323.

Stoelting, D., 'The Challenge of UN-Monitored Elections in Independent Nations', *Stanford Journal of International Law*, 28 (1992), p. 371.

Stone, J., *Legal Controls of International Conflict* (1959).

Stowell, E., *Intervention in International Law* (1921).

Sur, S., 'Security Council resolution 687 of 3 April 1991 in the Gulf Affair: Problems of Restoring and Safeguarding Peace', *UNIDIR Research Paper No. 12* (1992).

Sutterlin, J., *The United Nations and the Maintenance of International Security: A Challenge To Be Met* (1995).

—— and Russett, B., 'The Utilization of Force by the Security Council in Interstate Conflict', in *The Use of Force by the Security Council for Enforcement and Deterrent Purposes: A Conference Report* (Cox, D., ed.) (1990), p. 31.

——and—— 'The UN in a New World Order', *Foreign Affairs* (1991), p. 69.

Suy, E., 'Some Legal Questions Concerning the Security Council', in *Festschrift Schlochauer* (von Muench, I., ed.) (1981), p. 676.

—— 'The Role of the United Nations General Assembly', in *The Changing Constitution of the United Nations* (Fox, H., ed.) (1997), p. 55.

'Symposium on the Prospective Role of the United Nations in Dealing with the International Use of Force in the Post-Cold War Period: An Analysis in Light of the Persian Gulf Crisis', *Georgia Journal of International & Comparative Law*, 22 (1992), p. 33.

Szasz, P., 'The Role of the UN Secretary-General: Some Legal Aspects', *New York University Journal of International Law & Politics*, 24 (1991–2), p. 161.

—— 'The Proposed War Crimes Tribunal for Ex-Yugoslavia', *New York University Journal of International Law & Politics*, 25 (1993), p. 405.

—— 'Centralized and Decentralized Law Enforcement: The Security Council and the General Assembly acting under Chapters VII and VIII', in *Allocation of Law Enforcement Authority in the International System, Proceedings of an International Symposium of the Kiel Institute of International Law* (Delbruck, J., ed.) (1995), p. 31.

Tangney, P., 'The New Internationalism: The Cession of Sovereign Competences to Supranational Organizations and Constitutional Change in the United States and Germany', *Yale Journal of International Law*, 21 (1996), p. 395.

Taubenfeld, H., 'International armed forces and the rules of war', *AJIL*, 45 (1951), p. 671.

Taylor, C., 'The Fourth Branch: Reviving the Nondelegation Doctrine', *Brigham Young University Law Review* (1984), p. 619.

Teson, F., *Humanitarian Intervention: An Inquiry into Law and Morality* (1988).

—— 'Collective Humanitarian Intervention', *Michigan Journal of International Law*, 17 (1996), p. 323.

Thakur, R., 'From Peace-Keeping to Peace-Enforcement: the UN Operation in Somalia', *The Journal of Modern African Studies*, 32 (1994), p. 387.

Tomuschat, C., ed., *The United Nations at Age Fifty: A Legal Perspective* (1995).

Torres Bernardez, S., 'Subsidiary Organs', in *Manuel sur les organisations internationales* (Dupuy, R-J., ed.) (1988), p. 109.

Tribe, L., 'Structural Due Process', *Harv. CR-CLL Rev.*, 10 (1975), p. 269.

Tyagi, Y., 'The Concept of Humanitarian Intervention Revisited', *Michigan Journal of International Law*, 16 (1995), p. 883.

UN Department of Public Information, *The United Nations and the Situation in Somalia*, Reference Paper, DP1/1321/Rev.3, 1 May 1994.

United Nations Publication, *The Blue Helmets: A Review of United Nations Peace-keeping* (1990).

Universal House of Justice, *The Promise of World Peace* (1985).

Urquhart, B., 'The United Nations and International Law', *The Rede Lecture* (Cambridge University Press, 1985).

—— 'The Role of the United Nations in Maintaining and Improving International Security', *Survival*, Sept.–Oct. 1986, p. 388.

—— 'Learning from the Gulf', in *Whose New World Order: What Role for the United Nations?* (Alston, P., and Bustelo, M., eds.) (1991).

——and Childers, E., *A World in Need of Leadership: Tomorrow's United Nations* (1996).

Vellas, P., *Le Régionalisme International et l'Organisation des Nations Unies* (1948).

Verhoeven, J., 'Etats allies ou Nations Unies? L'O.N.U. face au conflit entre l'Irak et le Koweït', *Annuaire Français Droit Internationale*, 36 (1990), p. 167.

Virally, M., *L'Organisation Mondiale* (1972).

von Clausewitz, C., *On War* (edited and translated by Howard, M., and Paret, P.) (1976).

Wade, W., and Forsyth, C., *Administrative Law* (1994).

Walter, C., 'Security Council Control over Regional Action', *Max Planck Yearbook of United Nations Law*, 1 (1997), p. 129.

Warbrick, C., 'The Invasion of Kuwait by Iraq,' *ICLQ*, 40 (1991), p. 965.

——and Lowe, V., 'Current Developments: Public International Law', *ICLQ*, 40 (1991), p. 965.

Watson, G., 'Constitutionalism, Judicial Review, and the World Court', *Harvard International Law Journal*, 34 (1993), p. 1.

Weiss, T., 'Overcoming the Somalia Syndrome—"Operation Rekindle Hope?"', *Global Governance*, 1 (1995), p. 171.

——ed., *Beyond UN Subcontracting* (1998).

——and Chopra, J., 'Sovereignty is No Longer Sacrosanct: Codifying Humanitarian Intervention' in *At Issue: Politics in the World Arena* (Spiegel, S., and Pervin, D., eds.) (1994), p. 412.

Weller, M., 'The Kuwait Crisis: A Survey of Some Legal Issues', *African Journal of International & Comparative Law*, 3 (1991, March), p. 1.

——ed., *Iraq and Kuwait: The Hostilities and their Aftermath* (1993).

——'Peace-Keeping and Peace-Enforcement in the Republic of Bosnia and Herzegovina', *ZaöRV*, 56 (1996), p. 71.

Weston, B., 'Security Council Resolution 678 and Persian Gulf Decision Making: Precarious Legitimacy', *AJIL*, 85 (1991), p. 516.

White, N., *Keeping the Peace: The United Nations and the maintenance of international peace and security* (1993).

——'The Legitimacy of NATO action in Bosnia', *New Law Journal*, 144 (1994), p. 649.

Wickremasinghe, C., and Fox, H., 'UK Implementation of UN Economic Sanctions', *ICLQ*, 42 (1993), p. 945.

Willis, J., 'Delegatus Non Potest Delegare', *The Canadian Bar Review*, 21 (1943), p. 257.

Wolfrum, R., ed., *United Nations: Law, Policies and Practice*, Vol. 2 (1995).

——'The Protection of Regional or Other Interests as Structural Element of the Decision-Making Process of International Organizations', *Max Planck Yearbook of United Nations Law*, 1 (1997), p. 259.

Wood, M., 'Security Council Working Methods and Procedure: Recent Developments', *ICLQ*, 45 (1996), p. 150.

Wormuth, F., and Firmage, E., *To Chain the Dog of War* (1989).

Yassky, D., 'A Two-Tiered Theory of Consolidation and Separation of Powers', *Yale Law Journal*, 99 (1989), p. 431.

Zacklin, R., 'Les Nations Unies et la crise du Golfe', in *Les aspects juridiques de la crise et de la guerre du Golfe* (Stern, B., ed.) (1991), p. 67.

——and Shraga, D., 'International Criminal Tribunal for the former Yugoslavia', *EJIL*, 5 (1994), p. 360.

Zöckler, M., 'Germany in Collective Security Systems—Anything Goes?', *EJIL*, 6 (1995), p. 274.

Zourek, J., 'La Notion de Légitime Défense en Droit International', *AIDI*, 56 (1975), p. 1.

Index